Also by Noel Fitzpatrick

Listening to the Animals: Becoming the Supervet

Noolx

NOEL FITZPATRICK

Being the Supervet

How
Animals
Saved
my Life

First published in Great Britain in 2020 by Trapeze,
an imprint of The Orion Publishing Group Ltd
Carmelite House, 50 Victoria Embankment,
London EC4Y 0DZ

An Hachette UK company

1 3 5 7 9 10 8 6 4 2

Copyright © Fitz All Media Limited 2020

A CIP catalogue record for this book is
available from the British Library.

ISBN (Hardback) 978 1 4091 8379 2
ISBN (Export Trade Paperback) 978 1 4091 8380 8
ISBN (eBook) 978 1 4091 8382 2

Typeset by Input Data Services Ltd, Somerset

Printed and bound in Great Britain by Clays Ltd, Elcograf S.p.A.

www.orionbooks.co.uk

To Keira and Ricochet
My best friends

CONTENTS

The End

The two things I miss most about being a country vet in Ireland are the effervescent hue of green, which burns your eyes with joy, and the taste of the rain, which makes you drunk with pleasure. Somehow the rain in the west of Ireland tastes different, as if you were parched and God had poured it straight from heaven and into your mouth.

In West Cork the rain came hurling in from the Atlantic with such strength that if I drove my beat-up, rusty Mazda at a certain speed, the rain would kind of flow off the windscreen, so I could see where I was going in spite of the broken windscreen wipers. I would wind down all the car windows to let out the condensation and permanently keep a large pile of newspaper on the passenger seat in order to wipe a little patch in the mist on the glass.

That morning, the clouds tumbled as giant balls of sodden cotton wool, bandaging the raw green of trees and grass down the mountainside, punctuated by streams and tarns. The radio signal was intermittent out on those coastal mountain roads, but I had a cassette player which was blaring out 'Crazy' by the brilliant vocalist Seal: '*In a world full of people only some want to fly*' – indeed, I mused to myself as I rounded one of the myriad corners on the winding mountain road. I can't sing or dance, but sitting in my ragged-edged driver's seat with its broken springs I was doing both. The rain lashed down, the mist rose up, the dripping hedgerows tickled the rusted yellow sides of the Mazda as it splashed through the potholes. With my arm resting on the open window, it felt as if I could actually touch the blanket of cloud hugging the morning in its billowy embrace. Then, as if some celestial magician had waved his wand, the fog cleared, the rain stopped, the sun came out and the valley opened up like a glistening trinket box. I marvelled at the rainbow that followed and slowed down a bit to take it all in.

Then I saw him – a young lad, no more than ten years of age, sitting under a tree on a grassy bank by the side of the road, tears streaming down his face. I pulled over and asked if he was OK and then saw that he was cradling a small brown rabbit. He just rocked gently back and forth with the creature in his arms and said nothing. I got out and sat down beside him. I asked him again if he was all right. Again he said nothing. For the longest time, I just sat there looking at him, wanting to reach out and touch the rabbit, wanting to reach out and hug him, but I did neither. It was clear to me that the rabbit was dying.

Finally the small boy looked up at me with painfully sad big eyes and said, 'You're the veterany, aren't ya?' I nodded. 'Can you save him?' I shook my head. Again he said nothing, but just crouched forlornly over his stricken friend and cried without a sound.

We sat there together in silence, gentle drops of rain falling from the leaves on the tree above, and not for the first time nor the last I marvelled at the magnificence of creation all around me – and the fleetingness of our tenure in its midst. I looked up. It was a chestnut tree. When I was his age, I had often climbed such a tree in the garden of my childhood home. There I had dreamed up the adventures of my very own superhero whom I called Vetman, and launched him on his missions to save all the stricken animals of the world. I was suddenly overwhelmed by an intense sadness – a reali-sation of my profound limitations because I knew I couldn't save that boy's rabbit.

I had grown up on a farm, where a pragmatic attitude to animals was the norm – we lived among them, we did our best to look after them, we killed them and then we ate them. Rabbits were a pest to most farmers, eating valuable crops and of no consequence. But to that boy, the small creature in his arms meant the world. I knew from my own experience – taking care of mice or kittens, or sitting huddled in a dark, musty cattle shed talking to my beloved farm dog Pirate – that he and I were like alien beings in both our worlds. Souls like him and me related to the life and death, health and sickness and the love of animals as sentient creatures – crea-tures who feel, need and want, just as humans do. And here we were, sitting together, burying our pain as deep as we could inside us in an unspoken shared sorrow.

I had flashbacks to that night way back in 1978 when I was ten years old and had lost my first ever patient in a moonlit frosty field on our farm in Ballyfin in County Laois – a lamb that I couldn't save. I had felt worthless and pathetic. That morning, fourteen years later, sitting with the boy and his dying rabbit in the spitting wind, those same feelings washed over me once again. I had locked myself away for a decade to

3

study to become a veterinary surgeon, I had taken my oath to look after the welfare of all animals, and now the kindest thing to do was to allow the poor rabbit to escape his pain by putting him to sleep. Again I wished, as I had done way back then, that I might be clever enough to rescue life from the jaws of death and bring hope to that little boy. I wasn't. Even if I had been, it wasn't the right thing to do and, as would often prove the case in my early career, there was nothing I could do.

After a long silence, the boy looked up at me and asked, 'What happens next, Mister?' I paused, reached out and put my hand on his shoulder and said, 'Well, I think we maybe should help him on his way now, don't you?' He nodded, but then again asked, 'But, what happens next, Mister?' I hesitated at first, but finally leaned forward and whispered, 'You mean, what happens after he's gone?' He nodded. Wow. *What happens next?* Here I was, sitting under a chestnut tree on the side of a hill in West Cork, and a small boy was asking me the meaning of life itself.

They certainly hadn't prepared me for that in vet school.

What does it all mean? What is it all about? What is it all for? Maybe he was only asking me what would happen to the body of the poor rabbit after I had euthanised him, but all these 'Big Questions' came flooding into my head. Lost in these impenetrable reflections, I had a sudden sense of my profound responsibility – what I said next could shape how this lad might feel about life and death for the rest of his days.

I had no idea how I should answer. I looked out on the beautiful valley with its rivers and lakes and trees to the mountain beyond. The sun glistened on the rising mist blanketing the serene and idyllic beauty of the morning. I looked to the mountaintop, at the very edge of the horizon, and then a thought descended upon me, as if from the rain that I can still taste today. 'Do you see the top of that mountain over there?' He looked at the valley, then the mountain, and then the very top as far as he could see, then he looked back at me and nodded. 'Well,' I said, 'even though you can't see the other side, you still know there's something great over there, don't you?'

He paused for a long moment, both of us looking at the edge of heaven as if for the very first time. I was suddenly quite pleased with myself and my metaphor, hoping that I could inspire a young mind to think beyond this worldly existence to a more eternal and ethereal realm, over the rain-bow bridge – quite forgetting that most ten-year-olds have no grasp of metaphor. At that age, I grappled even with the existence of the literal. The boy stared at the mountain for what seemed like an eternity, then he looked up at me and said, 'Of course there is, Mister – sure that's Dunmanway!' And so, Dunmanway in County Cork will forever be a kind of heaven in my eyes.

As a surgeon, I would spend every day of the rest of my life walking the path between life and death at the top of that mountain – and trying to offer some kind of peace, and a measure of hope at the end of it all. I have put countless animals to sleep and, although my words of compassion, empathy and sympathy vary depending on the circumstance, the sequence of events in the aftermath is always the same – human lives unravel in front of my eyes. At the moment of passing of a deeply loved animal friend, the facade that we put up to friends, family and society comes crashing down. What's left is the raw core of our inner selves that we have shared with that animal – and, possibly, with no other human being ever. All the things we thought so important fade to insignificance and the things we didn't realise about ourselves suddenly come into sharp focus.

To some people, an animal may be only a rabbit, or a dog, or a cat, but to me and to the family in my consulting room, the essence of that animal and why we care for it is the very lifeblood of what makes us most 'human'. In that moment, the entire fabric of *who* and *what* we are comes undone – a divorce, the joys and tragedies of children, a lover held then lost, the job we wish we had or the one we wish we'd never found, the horrible boss, the partner we take for granted, our mortality and our very reason for existence – all unfolding in front of us as we hold a paw while life ebbs away. And for this: unconditional love – a kind of love rarely seen among humankind. It's a kind of love that makes us the very best we can ever be, and prevents us from being the worst we can be – a love that saves us from ourselves. This is the kind of love and sense of belonging in 'oneness' with animals that I have devoted my life to – and one that has saved my life many times over.

In the course of writing this book, a realisation of this 'oneness' came into sharp focus. I nearly died myself; through the guidance of an animal's paw I travelled many journeys of enlightenment; a bit too late, I had the greatest awakening of my life; and the world realised what it was to slow down, to hit the pause button and stop completely. The enormity of every challenge we have ever faced was suddenly thrown into stark relief by the threat posed to mankind by the tiniest microbe – coronavirus (Covid-19).

Talking to the boy all those years ago under the chestnut

tree by the side of the road, he told me he had adopted the rabbit as a baby from the wild when the rabbit's family had been killed by a farm machine, and he kept it in a makeshift hutch hidden on the farm. His father didn't really understand his love for a rabbit; he was much like my own father, I expect. The boy and I came from working farming stock and there was no time to indulge in such 'childish' feelings. But as I have grown older, and long after I became a vet and undertook further studies to become a specialist and a professor, the more I have realised that while it's necessary to have scientific knowledge and professional acumen, none of the letters after my name really matter by comparison with the motivation behind Vetman, my imaginary hero who wanted to help all the animals and show mankind that together, as one, our planet and *all creation* can be so much better.

The more one learns, the more arrogant one can become if one invests in ego above compassion – and the further I too could have strayed from the childish notion that love and common sense will prevail. All knowledge in books is only there because someone wrote it once who believed it to be true. A year ago if I had written that a pandemic would stop the world, people would have believed it to be science fiction, and yet in a lecture on 'One Medicine' in October 2019 I said exactly that. That 'science fiction' has become our reality and as this pandemic pursues its deadly path across the globe, the truth is being rewritten day by day.

It may seem like impossible 'science fiction' now, but I have always believed that it is only in looking after animals that we will look after ourselves and that the medical professions, both veterinary and human, must unite in the guise of One Medicine. In my view, we must rewrite our perception of 'the truth' in medicine. To fail to do so, we risk our own annihilation through our arrogant neglect of the diseases, ecosystems and habitats that affect our animal friends on whom we depend. We claim superiority in sentience, in our ability to solve problems, in our trillions spent in the pursuit of new planets while we continue to destroy our own, and yet it requires only the tiny microbial spike of coronavirus to burst our overinflated balloon. It's no coincidence that 'corona' refers to the 'crown' of spikes on this virus, because this minute pathogen has become the cruel master of our planet for a while. We will only ever reclaim any authority over disease if we work together, studying disease in man and animal and finding cures side by side in One Medicine.

I often wonder how many of the people governing the countries of our planet we actually trust to do the right thing. Animals don't judge us, they accept us and allow us to be truly ourselves, and they trust us to do the right thing. I believe we can learn and grow from this special kind of simple, unconditional love – and that it can save us from ourselves. Each and every one of us can be a happier person, a more effective manager, better in business, a more deter-mined leader, a more caring partner, more patient, more positive, more passionate and compassionate, less irritable, less worried and less consumed with the material world we have built around us.

I believe that my love of the patients I treat, and for my dearest companions Keira, my Border terrier dog, and Ricochet, my Maine Coon cat, has rescued me from the ego-tistical self-serving indulgence of being 'the Supervet'. In my everyday working life, time and again animals have shown me that they can help us to be whomever or whatever we want to be – if only we *listen*.

The boy's rabbit was dying from myxomatosis, which

was endemic where I grew up in rural Ireland. It is a deadly disease caused by a virus that jumped from Brazilian cottontail tapeti rabbits, which have adapted to live with the virus, to European rabbits for whom it is frequently fatal. Myxomatosis is transmitted to rabbits by an intermediate host like a mosquito, flea, mite or louse and brings about a horrible death, which I have seen many times. Our corona pandemic also causes horrible death, also likely originated in an animal host such as a bat, and may have been transferred to us via an intermediate carrier of the virus. At the time of writing, we don't know for sure. All I do know is that the future of medicine and the salvation of the planet will be built on the pillars of the four E's – ethics, evidence, efficacy and education.

We need to *educate* veterinary and human medicine that a 'joined-up' approach provides greater *evidence* of *efficacy* for any investigation or treatment, and that this is the only truly *ethical* approach. I know with absolute certainty that in the next generation the human race will pay the price of disregarding naturally occurring disease in animals – be it infection, cancer or any other ailment – and snubbing the lessons that a collaboration between human and veterinary doctors could yield through One Medicine. The stakes are too high for us to continue to ignore the obvious evidence that nature is screaming out at us. We have to listen to the animals because they could save our lives – and those of our children after us.

There is only one reason for me to write this book, and it's the same reason that I take time to hold a hand in a consultation, hold a scalpel blade in surgery, hold a paw in recovery, hold a pen to write a scientific paper or lecture, or hold One Medicine as the central goal of my lifetime's work.

It is to help one person or one animal to have a better life or to be a better 'being'. I believe that all animals and humans are 'beings', connected by oneness which is greater than any of us; greater than a moniker like 'the Supervet'; and greater than anything I can achieve in my lifetime. But if this book helps one person or one animal, that will be enough for me.

The small boy put the limp and quietly gasping rabbit in my arms and in the back of my car I administered the necessary injection – straight into the heart, which is the quickest way in such circumstances; horrible and necessary and peaceful all at the same time. I showed him the body and he nodded, his tears drying in salty rivulets down his cheeks.

'He's at peace,' I said. 'Shall I take him?' He nodded.

'You OK?' I asked. He just looked at me, eyes wide with fear of the unknown. I put my hand on his shoulder for a brief second and whispered, 'It'll be all right.' As I was getting into the car to drive off, he gently nudged me and said, almost in an embarrassed whisper, 'Thank you for taking time, Mister. Thank you for the time.' Then he turned and started up the lane to the farmhouse. I laid the little body on the window-wiping newspaper on the passenger seat, and drove off into the azure light of a new day.

I don't know what happened to that boy, or if anything I said or did that morning actually mattered, but it changed forever what I felt about birth, death and the blink of an eye in the middle which we call life. It's all time and time is all we have – but what will we do with ours?

Thank you for allowing me to share with you how animals saved me from wasting my time and from profound darkness when I couldn't see the light. Thank you for even beginning

to consider the inevitable truth that we are all on this journey side by side – you, me, human, animal.

I can only hope that the crisis we face together in Covid-
19 brings unity in the wake of our isolation, compassion from
our implosion, solidarity from our insularity, and oneness
from our numbness. We are all in this together. We are truly
one, both in the beginning and in the end – always one.

CHAPTER ONE

Internalisation

*'We need to internalize this idea of excellence.
Not many folks spend a lot of time trying to be
excellent.'*

Barack Obama

Internalisation of an ideal, a belief or a set of values makes them integral to your attitude and way of thinking. The internalised quality becomes central to who you are, how you act and how you live your life. Indeed, if I spent half the time internalising the love and success I have enjoyed as I do the pain and failure, I would be twice the person.

For me, however, the single greatest quality I could aspire to internalise is integrity. Integrity to me means being honest and having strong moral principles. Integrity is taking responsibility for my actions, personal and professional, and looking in the mirror without lying to myself. It's the ability to question objectively my *raison d'être*: why am I here at all? If I'm lying to myself, then no matter how I dress it up to assuage my moral (or immoral) conscience, I am lying to myself and to everyone else too.

When it comes to the welfare of the animal that I'm treating and my responsibility to their guardians, my moral compass has invariably guided me and I genuinely feel that my integrity has always been 100 per cent intact. With equal honesty I can also acknowledge that I've fallen short more than once in my own life because I have on occasion lacked that same focus and compass that has served me so well as a vet.

I have learned too that the solution to my challenges with love, trust, intimacy and respect in relationships has been staring me in the face these last thirty years. Now I aspire to learn from the masters – the animals I have been trusted enough to treat, and my own two animal friends, Keira and Ricochet, who teach me lessons about care and integrity every day. With her barley-straw hair and massive 'sticky-out' eyebrows, now slightly greying (just like her dad), Keira has been my trusty companion and comfort blanket for the past thirteen years. She has been at my side through the most challenging years of my career, with the building of my practice, Fitzpatrick Referrals. My new best buddy Ricochet, meanwhile, is a giant black fluff-ball of feline gloriousness, with gorgeous big, bright-yellow eyes, who has reached his big panda paws inside my heart and claimed a huge part of it. From morning nose nuzzles to calming night-time chin cuddles, he's a whirlwind of love, buoying me up in his vortex. I am desperately in love with both of them.

If I wasn't honest with them for one second, I would not be getting a lick on the face or a wet nuzzle in the eye socket. They would sniff out my hypocrisy of promising a walk, or setting up a routine for feeding, and then not delivering, or of being too irritable to receive love – and they would tell me in no uncertain terms to stop being a moron. Being the guardian of a dog or cat demands a commitment to do the thing you promised to do, long after the mood in which you made that promise has left you. For me, commitment is 'internalised' integrity.

As a surgeon holding life and death in my hands each day, if I lose my integrity for one second, I have lost everything. If I have internalised integrity I will always have the courage to care about and do the right thing, whatever the personal consequences. You will too, and animals can teach us that.

My head was exploding, my heart racing and eating up my chest, my gut felt like a bucket of churning nails and I couldn't breathe as my throat clamped shut. My security guard, Tony, closed the door. I looked around at the room: a stark, bare, white-walled space. Everything was gleaming, neat and angular – the table, the chair, the sofa, the toilet, the shower, even the curtain. Small spots of light around the room oozed a dim, rippling glow – no doubt intended to be a comforting cocoon of solace in preparation for what lay ahead, but to me in that moment it represented an ominous twilight. I turned off all the lights, lay down on the sofa and stared at the ceiling, terrified.

My thoughts raced back to a world long ago, where there were no angles, just soft blurry edges of my childhood in Ballyfin, in my small white rickety bed that squeaked like a lonely mouse every time I turned over. Here in this room the blackness was different to the darkness that I had felt that night in Ireland when I had gone back to bed after I lost the lamb and my life changed forever. There was still a hazy glow now as I closed my eyes and I didn't know whether it came from outside or inside my head. I just lay there motionless, waves of helplessness washing over me. Almost forty years later, on 25 November 2018, again I felt I wasn't good enough, strong enough or brave enough.

That night, as a boy, I had looked up at the millions of lights puncturing the heavens – at the enormity of creation – and felt like a worthless speck of dust. I had looked for the brightest star that I could find and had wished on it with all my heart that I might one day be strong enough, brave enough and clever enough to pluck that star from the firmament and hold its light inside me.

Soon afterwards, Vetman took shape in my childish imagination:

*One day he was searching in the jungle for more
medicines to make,
And he found a giant crater near a lake
A huge bright star had crashed to Earth
And in the magic stardust that had fallen from above
Vetman found the actual molecules that make up love
Love is in the Stars!
Vetman called it 'magic bionic dust'
And from it he made a love-filled glue
To fix up all of the waifs and strays – shiny and new.
His 'magic bionic dust' healed up all of their wounds
And maybe if we could just believe in love
It might just heal us too.*

In real life, in two hours I was due onstage in front of several thousand people at The O2 Arena in London for the last date of the 'Supervet Live' tour, when I would attempt to pluck the giant star from the screen behind me and hand a little light to everyone in the audience to take with them out into the world. But I couldn't speak. I had completely lost my voice; I couldn't even whisper. I'd been performing live in large arenas every weekend for the previous two months, yet I hadn't felt utterly petrified until now. Perhaps it was because I'd seen so many wonderful acts in this magnificent arena; perhaps it was because I'd prepared all my life for this moment, and now I didn't know how I could perform; perhaps it was that I was letting down the child who dreamed that Vetman could fly and save the world. Or perhaps it was just that I was exhausted: the tour had been building up to this climax over twenty previous arena performances – I'd done three shows in Peterborough and Brighton in the previous thirty-six hours alone – and I'd blown the gaskets. I didn't know, but shaking with unspoken fear and feelings of profound unworthiness about being there at all, I just curled up in the darkened room like my ten-year-old self on that fateful night in County Laois and lay thinking of the star as all of my dreams came crashing down around me.

I couldn't go onstage – we would have to cancel the show. I'd just had that very conversation, so various members of the crew were scurrying around, but it was too late – people were already piling into the arena. I tried over and over to voice just one phrase: 'Peggy Babcock's knapsack strap snapped and her animal manimal made maximal fun of the nun when the seashells she sells were shining night starlight of volitional unconditional love.' Ridiculous nonsense, I know – an amalgamated tongue-twister I had devised as a pre-show warm-up. The star from my childhood had become my talisman while I was writing the show and simultaneously working my normal day as a surgeon. I needed something to remind me why I was doing this at all, but now I couldn't even say it.

There was a knock on the door. The voice doctor had arrived. She'd helped innumerable stricken performers in the final gasps before a cancelled performance, and as I bent over and she jabbed vitamin B12 into my right butt cheek, she told me that everything would be fine. She prescribed 60mg of the steroid prednisolone and I downed it like it was my last supper, feeling very melodramatic indeed. And she was gone as quickly as she had arrived – some kind of miraculous angel sent to those in need of one last hurrah before they inevitably collapsed in a heap of their own making. I have it on pretty good authority that you can't be doing this kind of thing too often or you really mess yourself up – but for one final jig from the Leprechaun of Love, it was worth it.

I lay back down on the sofa, where no doubt countless numbers of my rock and pop heroes had rested their own butt cheeks, injected or not, and closed my eyes. I wondered whether they ever thought about the fragility of existence amid all our endeavours – how much we take for granted until it's gone. How *did* all those artists cope with performing in front of thousands of people night after night? What power of belief had *they* internalised that allowed them to do that? While they had done that for a living since they were teenagers, I'd just been endlessly studying, plying my trade with a scalpel blade rather than a musical instrument. But as a surgeon, I did understand the knife-edge of hope and desolation.

I thought of my own mortality, even if going onstage wasn't life or death. What if the drugs didn't work? What if I was dumbstruck with fright when I stepped onto The O2 stage?

I felt none of the anticipated euphoria of that grand finale of the tour. I knew this would likely be the biggest public event of my life, but I just felt numb and not only because of the local anaesthetic I'd sprayed on my throat. I was paralysed with fear that I was going to let everyone down. I had no idea what would happen next.

Then a miracle happened. I had administered one-shot, high-dose steroids loads of times to animals in crises, but before that night I'd had no personal experience of them myself. Although I hope never to need them again, wow, it felt good. About an hour after swallowing the dose, the vice-like grip on my larynx released. I started to enunciate Peggy Babcock and friends, then after another thirty minutes I could project. Within two hours I was walking onto the stage. Sound, lights, action. The crowd erupted in applause. It all passed in a whirlwind.

In the show, I explored my life story with the hope that I might inspire folks who were going through tough times, or were wishing on a star as I had many years before. I wanted to convey to the audience the power of internalising positive thought, to believe that their dreams were possible, no matter how many bullies might have told them otherwise, and to find hope and some kind of redemption through the bond of unconditional love we share with animals. I told them about growing up on a farm in Ireland, feeling alienated and being bullied at school; how I befriended our farm dog Pirate and invented Vetman who would save all of the animals and save me in the process. What it was like going through vet school and all of the exams, and the funny times too along the way, like when I was a knitwear model, or went to Philadelphia to study because I thought that's where Rocky lived. I laughed with the crowd as I recounted my foray into acting and my appearances on *Casualty*, *The Bill* and *Heartbeat*, and in the 'less-than-epic' movie *Ghost Rig*.

We journeyed together through my days as a large animal vet in rural Ireland, when I performed my first orthopaedic procedure on the kitchen table in the cottage of a farmer named Larry. Larry had left me a very important legacy with the immortal observation that, 'Everything is impossible until it happens' – an aphorism I still internalise today for inspiration and guidance. I also recalled the night when a cow had shat on my head while I was paring her hooves by the lights of a tractor, and how I had decided that farm-animal practice probably wasn't my destiny as I wiped the excrement out of my ears.

I talked about my struggles to find my way up the rungs of the profession when for whatever reason I wasn't deemed clever enough to get an internship or a residency. I explained how frustration with the status quo leads to innovation and progress, but how with that comes a great burden of ethical responsibility and the pain of failure. I discussed bionic artificial limb implants in a dog and a cat and what that would have meant for my Uncle Paul, an amputee with a horrible, crusty raw stump caused by chafing from his primitive wooden leg. This story led to the birth of *The Supervet* TV show which began in 2014 on Channel 4 and which has forever changed my life in so many ways throughout the 110-plus episodes we've now filmed.

Finally, I talked about how man and animal were studied side by side in the very first *Theatrum Anatomicum* (anatomical teaching theatre) in Italy in 1637, and then how human and veterinary medicine went their separate ways, never to join up again. I talked about success and failure in surgery for both animals and humans and how a reunification of medicine, One Medicine, could be beneficial for all patients. I suggested that this approach might be a better and kinder way forward for the planet, especially as we continue to exploit animals without giving them a fair deal, forcing species after species towards extinction. I talked about my faith in a more compassionate and respectful world and how I hoped I was making a difference. I wanted everyone to take home a little of the love in Vetman's stardust; to internalise its power and potential to make dreams come true.

Keira made a special appearance at the end and, as usual, stole the show – she was the real star and once again she received a standing ovation. I bowed on Keira's behalf to the refrain of 'One More Light' by Linkin Park, a song in honour of their singer Chester Bennington, who had been overwhelmed by addiction, depression and darkness and taken his own life.

I have internalised all kinds of pain in my life, some of which I can now talk about, some of which remains buried in the recesses of time. Many of us pretend to be able to 'deal with stuff' – ostensibly we move on and carry on with a semblance of sanity in our lives, so perhaps no one would ever guess at our trauma. But for most of us, somewhere inside, the demons continue to lurk. For some, those demons are so close to the surface that even an apparently innocuous trigger can make us irritable, in the same way that a horse who was once scared by a man in a long coat will shy away from all men in long coats forever. For others, the scars of childhood trauma are repressed, buried deep inside, because that was the only way we could deal with it.

When we experience a cataclysmic event in our lives, old wounds can be exposed, and we relive the emotional pain with all the dreadful repercussions that entails. When that happens, we have a choice. We can choose to let the light in and seek help to heal, or we can decide to run like hell and keep running, kicking dirt behind us like a cat trying to cover its shit, and never to return because it stinks. From my own experience I know that the former choice is the most difficult – letting the light in forces us to confront our hidden horror.

Some deeply internalised childhood traumas with the deepest scars can bleed the worst if they are reopened by some body blow of circumstance later in life. There is no doubt that both of my parents were superheroes and no fault lies with them; they were doing their best for me, my four sisters and my brother, in the context of a rural Catholic Irish farming community in County Laois in central Ireland, where work, unshakable faith in God and the integrity of the family were sacrosanct. I internalised these values. Mammy walked miles for buckets of water from a well, or milk from a local farm while carrying a baby and with two other small children walking along beside her, while Daddy worked any and every hour that God sent looking after the animals and the land. In a relatively insular farming environment, I stood up and took things 'like a man', I did not show weakness, and it was God's will to suffer things that should not be spoken of – even if the hurt ran deep.

Yogic philosophy tells us we are born with a karmic inheritance of mental and emotional patterns, known as *samskaras* (from the Sanskrit: *sam* meaning 'complete', and *kara*, 'action'), through which we cycle over and over again during our lives. In that sense, I have inherited the scars of my father and have scratched the scabs off these for years, yearning for some kind of approval that is never going to happen. I am a surgeon and it's my job to resolve physical in-juries, but I have found that the impact of emotional damage can be much harder to cope with. In my case, this has caused damage which can't simply be cut out and I've sublimated and covered it up with study and work for forty years.

Sensory input comes into a part of the brain called the thalamus and is then sent to the neocortex, which is the thinking or rational brain, and also to a small almond-shaped mass of grey matter between the cerebral hemispheres called the amygdala. The amygdala is the 'fight or flight' centre where emotions and moods – fear, anger, aggression and sadness – are experienced and then shunted and stored in the hippocampus, a seahorse-shaped structure behind the amygdala. The hippocampus collates the outputs from the amygdala and is responsible for processing emotional responses and long-term memory, so that one can recognise similar triggers and possibly avoid them in the future. This can be a good or a bad thing. If the emotional record in the hippocampus recognises the stimulus as potentially painful, it feeds back to the amygdala to trigger fight, flight or freeze. This can provoke a sudden powerful emotional response, which is entirely spontaneous and urgent, over-riding rational thought in the neocortex – and may be regretted later. In his 1996 book *Emotional Intelligence: Why It Can Matter More Than IQ,* Daniel Goleman coined the phrase 'amygdala hijack' to describe this overwhelming emotional response, which can be completely disproportionate to the inciting cause.

I suspect that most medical professionals have to suppress their 'fight, flight or freeze' responses every single day of their lives or no surgeon would ever be able to pick up a scalpel blade.

I have internalised a lot of pain in my amygdala down through the years, as I think many of us have, and when the scars are inflamed, we sometimes react with emotion, rather than reason, as the brain explodes with noise, confusion, depression, fear and self-destructive behaviour. It's been my 'trauma centre' since childhood, absorbing all the slings and arrows life has thrown at me, and although I wasn't to know it at the time, a bullet was about to strike right to its heart and 'hijack' was imminent.

I didn't ever travel far from home as a child except for the annual trip to the seaside in Tramore. I served at Mass on Sundays and went to a small local Catholic primary school, where the curriculum wasn't what it could have been and nobody noticed, or if they did, they didn't say. When I moved to secondary school in 1985, aged eleven, I found myself ill-equipped both academically and emotionally to deal with the onslaught of an all-boys school surrounded by lads from the far corners of Ireland, who were far better educated than me and had all experienced life. I rapidly realised I was different.

The other boys saw it too and it didn't take long before the bullying started. Some of my fellow pupils took great pleasure in bashing my bike and my bag of books, and then they'd throw me into a nearby disused quarry, hurling my books down on top of me where I lay in a slurry of mud and stinking silage effluent. Eventually the physical violence didn't register at all, and they found that it was only by de-stroying the copybooks in which I had invested all of myself that they could really hurt me. As their torture continued, I became more and more withdrawn and buried myself away to study for hours, hoping they'd all have gone somewhere else when I finally emerged to cycle home. This was a trauma I'd been running from all my adult life – now thirty years later I had begun to shine a little healing light on those wounds, by writing about my experience in my memoir *Listening to the Animals* and speaking the truth on the tour. Yet still the emotional scars remained and would soon be laid bare and bleeding.

The 'Supervet Live' tour had been truly amazing. I had met so many people on the road across the UK and Ireland who were hugely gracious and genuinely humbling. There were too many to mention – a little girl who had endured cancer, watching episodes of *The Supervet* to keep her company during a year of chemotherapy; an elderly man who had saved up for six months to attend the show and who had given me a hug and thanked me, saying that he could die happy; a small boy in a wheelchair with mental and physical disabilities who had knitted me a scarf, and when he'd met me after the show had uttered the exact same words as the young lad on the hillside in Cork way back: 'Thank you for taking the time.'

Time is indeed all we have. I wish I had wasted less of those precious moments worrying about things that might never happen – I wish we all could. When we forget our true purpose, we waste so much time lying to ourselves about what is and is not important. I thought I had found my true purpose, but at that moment I had no idea that very soon, everything I ever believed in would come crashing down.

Being 'the Supervet' was about to become an ocean of pain.

Driving home that night from The O2 Arena, slumped on the back seat exhausted, taking one final journey with Tony, who had been driver, security guardian, morning alarm clock and friend on the tour, I reflected on how lucky I was to have had this magnificent journey. I was really honoured to have such an amazing opportunity to directly communicate with so many people about what I feel is a fundamental truth for humanity – that the salvation of mankind lies in our respect for animals and for each other.

Each night on the tour, I felt really fortunate to be a vet and to experience unconditional love and hope through the integrity of the human–animal bond on a daily basis. I thought about how hard I'd had to work to arrive at this moment: the endless studying and exams; the regular sixteen-hour days, seven days a week; the stress over money worries and bank loans to build the practice; the pain of failure in surgery; the often exasperating responsibility of managing more than 250 work colleagues; and the personal life sacrifices – but it was all my very willing choice – and as I looked back in my mind from the back of the tour van, I wouldn't have had it any other way. I was living my dream to give animals a fair deal through medical advancement and more collaboration with human medicine for the greater good, and it was a wonderful way to spend a life, I thought. Exhausted and voiceless though I was, I felt that I had been blessed and I never wanted to give it up.

The next morning, I went back to the day job and Fitzpatrick Referrals. The nurses were joking about my touring 'holiday', delighted that I had completely lost my voice, but I wasn't really in the mood for their teasing. I knew it was going to be a tough day, because later that morning I would be putting to sleep a beautiful two-year-old yellow Labrador called Monty – the antithesis of my tour experience, from elation to deflation from the outset.

Monty had failed to respond to multiple medical and surgical interventions for severe elbow osteoarthritis affecting both front legs; I had tried my best, but it wasn't enough.

Now he was suffering and the family and I had decided that it wasn't right to put him through any more. During my show at The O2 Arena, my failure to save Monty had been on my mind. As I was delivering my message of hope, I had been heartbroken inside. I had known Monty for a long time. He was my friend and it was my duty to carry out the euthanasia myself – to be there to hold his paw and his family's hands while they said goodbye.

As I walked into my office I knew this sad task awaited, so when my practice manager Brian knocked on the door I thought it was to offer some words of support, to welcome me back after the final leg of the tour, or possibly to join in the joke about me being quiet, for once. One look at his face told me otherwise. His normally vibrant Scottish eyes looked grave and his usual upbeat demeanour was replaced with an ominously stooped sluggishness. I knew instantly that I was about to get bad news, but I didn't know just how bad. Brian took the chair opposite my desk; he looked at me sadly, took a deep breath and handed me a thick white envelope with the letters RCVS printed in bold blue ink. Nobody in the veterinary profession likes getting a big thick white envelope with RCVS on it. That can only mean very bad news indeed.

The RCVS, the Royal College of Veterinary Surgeons, is the governing body of the veterinary profession in the UK. I have the utmost respect for the RCVS and am deeply grateful to practise the vocation that I love, and to be able to serve the companion animals of the UK and those who love them. I'm proud to be an ambassador for its values, and to do everything in my power to uphold its moral code, its good name and the good reputation of veterinary professionals in society. However, at that moment, my heart hit the floor. I looked at Brian dumbfounded. Even if I had been physically able to speak, I would not have known what to say. He simply said, 'I'm sorry to be the bearer of bad news.'

He had received the letter along with a bundle of paperwork from the RCVS a few days earlier, but knowing that I would be profoundly affected and not wishing to upset me when I was on tour, he had kept it from me until that morning. Four fellow veterinarians, none of whom I knew personally or had ever met, had accused me of malpractice, not acting in the best interests of an animal who, in their view, should have been euthanised. They made claims of 'overtreating' that animal to the point of 'experimentation', and suggested that I was doing this for egotistical reasons – that in filming this segment for Channel 4's *The Supervet* I had put self-promotion above my commitment to the health and welfare of my patient. In their eyes, I was therefore drawing the veterinary profession into disrepute. They requested a full disciplinary hearing. Depending on the outcome, I could face a suspension or even be struck off, meaning I would no longer be allowed to practise veterinary medicine, which had been the central purpose of my life for as long as I could remember.

My head exploded and my world imploded. My amygdala spontaneously erupted with fire. Having opened the envelope, I glanced through its reams of contents – four separate but related depositions asserting that I was guilty of gross professional misconduct and bringing my beloved profession into disrepute. I had just spent two months of weekends travelling across the nation to spread the good word about the veterinary establishment and the guardianship of unconditional love embodied by vets everywhere. I had interrupted the tour for two weekends to lecture in Phoenix, USA, as a keynote speaker at the American College of Veterinary Surgeons (ACVS) Surgery Summit, which had been a lifetime ambition for me, and at the European Society of Veterinary Orthopaedics and Traumatology (ESVOT) Congress in Barcelona, Spain. My lectures were on the theme of 'Just because we can do something, does not make it the right thing to do', and one of my talks was titled 'Revolution or evolution? Ethics and engineering of bionic biology'. In it I spoke about the ethical implications of advanced veterinary surgery and the pressing need for a robust framework for the entire profession within which to discuss and disseminate the aforementioned four E's: ethics, evidence, efficacy and education.

Every single day of the preceding twenty-eight years I had devoted all my energy to every single animal that was entrusted to my care, to every single person who loved or cared for that animal, and to all of the veterinary colleagues I knew and loved, especially those in my 'Fitz-Family'. I had plunged into endless financial debt to build my practice up from a derelict farm, I had blown several personal relationships because of my vocation, and I had many struggles with mental distress. In fact, it would have been physically impossible for me to spend any more hours doing exactly what the complainants said I wasn't doing – trying to uphold my oath to do everything in my power to alleviate pain and suffering for animals, and this is now what it boiled down to. Was I really that much of a charlatan and hypocrite? I couldn't come to terms with any of it. It was anathema to me – the direct opposite of everything I stood for, had striven for and fought for.

Brian gave me a hug and left. I stumbled from my desk onto my bed, which is about six feet beyond a doorway from my office/bedroom where I had mostly lived for a decade – day and night. I fell onto the mattress, buried my head in the pillow and cried my eyes out. The pillow was drenched with tears, I couldn't think straight and in that moment I wanted to run out of the practice and never come back. I banged my head on the pillow over and over. Why was this happening? How could this happen? What did it mean? Maybe what I had thought was my crystal-clear life's purpose was in fact a myth, because others felt that I was disingenuous and that I had both internalised and externalised a lie.

This was the price of being 'the Supervet'.

The focus of the complaint to the RCVS was the case of a Hermann's tortoise called Hermes, so-called because in 2016 he had been found abandoned in a cardboard box of the delivery company of the same name. The story of Hermes and what happened after he came into Fitzpatrick Referrals had been filmed and first broadcast in Episode 4, Series 12 of *The Supervet* on 4 October 2018. His lovely mum Helen, a human critical care nurse and one of the most compassionate people I have ever met, had rescued and looked after him. Hermes was only five years old and could expect to live to the age of forty-five or more. However, during hibernation, three of his legs had been eaten off by rats. Hermes' wonderful primary care vet exclusively treated and held a certificate qualification in the care of exotic species. She had been dressing the wounds on his stumps and treating infection for quite some time when she referred him to me to see if I could help.

Two front limbs had been removed at the bottom of the arm bone (humerus) just above the elbows, and one back leg had been severed at the bottom of the thigh bone (femur) just above the knee. With only one functional limb, Hermes couldn't move around. Helen recognised that his quality of life was obviously impaired, but she knew him well, and in the weeks before I saw him he was still interacting with her daily with a positive spirit – he hadn't given up. And because he could potentially have such a long life, she didn't want to give up on him either.

There are always emotions involved. I see this all of the time in my clinical practice, and it's always really tough. It is inevitable that guardians will internalise the pain and suffering of their animals and feel terrible when they are disabled and hurting. The job of a veterinary surgeon is to be the advocate for the animal, regardless of the feelings of the guardian, while at the same time being empathetic and acknowledging their emotional and psychological trauma.

The fact is, however, that you can't help every animal and there are some animals that you shouldn't help. It's not enough to be able to do something, it must always be in the animal's best interests. Therein lies the professional ethical dilemma. As more techniques become available, as possibilities open up, this creates a different and more challenging landscape for decision-making – if there are only two chocolates in the box, the choice is easier than if you have ten different flavours. Sadly, though, veterinary medicine is struggling to come to terms with this dilemma, and there is a paucity of crystal-clear guidance in such matters.

When I met Hermes, I had been performing limb amputation prosthesis surgeries for more than a decade, and so at this point I think it's fair to say that I had more experience than any other veterinarian in the world about the pros and cons of this procedure. I had seen these prostheses perform both well and poorly in humans and animals, and we had learned a lot. To my knowledge, the procedure had never before been performed on a tortoise, but Hermes' other options were not looking good. Stump socket prostheses, where one makes a silicone-lined cup into which a stump can fit and to which is attached an artificial limb, have been around for hundreds of years. This wasn't possible for Hermes because they wouldn't stay on, and because when he retracted his limbs into his shell, they wouldn't fit. I had put wheels on a tortoise before. Small multi-directional wheels stuck to the underside of his shell might have worked fine if he had two legs left, but with only one, that was also a non-starter. It was possible to keep him alive as he was, but without the ability to move, neither Helen nor I, nor her primary care clinician, felt that this was either ethical or sustainable. We were left therefore with two stark options: try to give Hermes bionic limbs which were anchored to the remaining bone stumps, or allow him to pass away peacefully.

Of course, with Hermes there were challenges and risks associated with implanting limb amputation prostheses, as there would be with any surgery. His stumps had been treated for infection, and since healing in tortoises takes longer, there had been a delay before coming to see me and there would be further delay before surgery was possible. There was the concern, therefore, that this time frame was too long and quality of life during this period too poor to justify continuing, and also the risk that infection could come back. Furthermore, even if it were scientifically possible to make implants small enough to fit his tiny bones, as far as we knew nobody had ever done it before, and so it would be challenging and there could be mechanical failure. In addition, the bone and skin may have difficulty growing around the implants.

All of the same potential complications existed as they did for a human or a dog or a cat, but these were amplified by the timescale for healing, the tiny bones and other factors of the unknown. If Helen decided to proceed, Hermes' surgery and aftercare would involve a team effort, including many veterinary professionals, my intern team and nurses, as well as the clinical team at her primary care hospital, in particular Hermes' primary care vet whose clinical practice was exclusively for exotic species, so she was accustomed to all aspects of tortoise care from feeding to blood sampling. And so, taking all of this into consideration, the fundamental dilemma remained: was it morally the right thing to do to proceed with surgery?

When faced with such a decision, people often ask me, 'What would you do?' I used to answer readily, saying what I would do if it were my animal friend. Nowadays I say that I can't say what I would do, for fear that my 'guidance' or 'opinion' might be deemed 'coercion' of the animal guardian. Many people have come to see me because they have already seen multiple other veterinarians who have done their best, but it hasn't worked out or not been possible to effect a resolution of the problem. Some veterinarians might disagree with me offering any solution, hope or comfort for the animal or the guardian. All I can do is clearly and objectively explain *all of the options* to the legal guardian and advise on welfare and ethical considerations.

In the case of Hermes, Helen and I discussed his situation and whether euthanasia might be the most appropriate ethical choice many times, and on several different occasions. Ultimately the decision to proceed or not at the time of surgery was taken by Helen; the primary care clinician and I could of course decline to treat and we could recommend euthanasia, but we could not force Helen to put Hermes to sleep.

Helen decided on surgery.

The operation was performed in November 2017. Myself, a team of intern vets, several nurses and an external consultant with specialist training and an additional degree in exotic species, with whom I had consulted throughout Hermes' treatment, operated and placed three limb amputation prosthesis implants in Hermes' legs. We planned the procedure carefully in every way – both from a design and engineering perspective and from a clinical management perspective. We built a special heated and lighted enclosure in one of the wards for him. It was delicate surgery with tiny implants, each of which had a little peg and two little plates attached to the humerus and femur bones with 1.5mm screws, a platform upon which the bones could sit, and onto which the skin could grow, and a spigot peg sticking out onto which we could attach artificial feet. The internal implant is an 'endoprosthesis' and the external foot attachment is an 'exoprosthesis'. We had used similar implants in many dogs and cats before and the surgery went very much according to plan. After the surgery we nursed Hermes, his wounds continued to heal well and he went home. Within a week he was making valiant attempts to get around on his pegs, even before we could fit his new feet.

Very sadly, however, at home two months later he developed suspected internal organ failure and died during the night. In the absence of postmortem studies, we'll never know the cause and Helen, myself and the team were absolutely crushed. We had all loved him so much – especially Helen – but we all took solace in the fact that he had been recovering in the most supportive environment imaginable and none of us had any regrets. We knew that we had done the right thing for our little friend; had he not died of an unforeseen and seemingly unrelated condition, Hermes might have long outlived me. The TV cameras had captured the whole journey, and we told it as it was on *The Supervet*, as we always do, with a little RIP card for him at the end of the show.

Obviously, the four veterinarians who had filed the complaint with the RCVS had seen me treat Hermes on *The Supervet*. They could not have known about the case otherwise, since Helen and the primary care veterinarian who had referred the case to me were happy with the service and care afforded to Hermes. Collectively we had all acted in the patient's best interests, and I had consulted with another senior specialist about the case and had observed all due diligence.

The complainants, however, felt very differently about the treatment. They alleged that, because I had explained on *The Supervet* that to our knowledge it was the first time this would be attempted in a tortoise and the outcome was unknown, this was de facto an 'experiment'. Their opinion was that I was operating with an untested procedure because I had a vested interest in doing so, because it was being filmed for *The Supervet*. They further alleged that, because I had told Helen that the chances were fifty–fifty, I was misleading her and therefore guilty of unprofessional conduct. They felt that I personally did not consider the whole animal welfare and that making the surgical procedure front and central to the animal journey on the programme was cruel, unprofessional, unethical and unjustified. The complainants argued that Helen could not possibly have known what was in Hermes' best interests because she was too emotionally invested, and in their view, as advocates for the welfare of the animal, they felt that euthanasia would have been the preferred 'treatment' to alleviate pain and suffering. They argued that euthanasia was a 'professional privilege', which vets have and human doctors do not, and it was therefore my moral obligation as a veterinary surgeon to counsel euthanasia as the only option.

Furthermore, they alleged that I was drawing the veterinary profession into disrepute through this action and through showing the provision of advanced procedures generally on the Channel 4 show, which they contended was contrary to the public interest. They declared that because I was on television, I actually had *more* responsibility for animal welfare than an average vet, though we all take the same oath. The public therefore needed to be protected from me, not just in the UK, but in every country in which the programme is shown. One of the complainants stated that *The Supervet* made her ashamed of our profession, because of the disregard for quality of life and blatant 'overtreatment'. She further added that if veterinarians continued to tolerate the television show then there was a risk of undermining public confidence in all vets.

To my mind, I had been doing my best for a wonderful animal friend. I had gone through my normal consultation process for advanced procedures at the time. I had worked closely with the primary care clinician who exclusively dealt with exotic species and I had consulted with another veterinary specialist in exotic species to help look after Hermes' medical needs, to plan anaesthesia and perioperative management protocols if we were to operate. If I had felt that anything more was required, or had been given professional guidance that I needed to seek written approval from a centralised ethical body before even considering helping Hermes, then, clearly, I would have done so – I would have done whatever was needed to avoid the pain that I would now endure in fighting this allegation. It would be the job of the RCVS to decide who was right or wrong – and the only person who would pay any price for this decision would be me.

It is complicated, because the case with Hermes was unprecedented and there were no rules for the application of bionic limbs to tortoises, but I'll do my best to put my position into some kind of perspective, as follows. In proceeding on Helen's wishes with the effort to provide Hermes with limb prostheses, both the referring vet and I deemed that it was an act of recognised veterinary practice (RVP) because it had been successfully performed on other animals many times before, and because many surgeries have been performed by surgeons in the UK either for the first time ever or where the outcome is necessarily unknown. Indeed, it is not uncommon for a vet to rate the chances of successful treatment at fifty–fifty, or even less for many operations in primary care and specialist practice. And again, it is not uncommon for a guardian to decide to proceed with surgery in that knowledge.

The complainants argued that I should have *insisted* on euthanasia 'by recommendation', even though Helen knew all the options and the risks of surgery and resolutely did not want that outcome. This begs the question: does a group of veterinary surgeons, or any veterinary surgeon, in fact know better in a holistic sense of overall welfare adjudication than the guardian of the animal? If so, then I feel it would be best to have clear, unequivocal guidance for future cases in this regard from the highest levels of my profession, because if a vet can't 'actively recommend' a treatment, but can 'actively recommend' euthanasia, as the depositions seemed to suggest, is that helpful for the client's decision-making? And will clients be happy with the profession not being able to give the options, but rather having the power to enforce euthanasia?

There have certainly been cases in my career where I have advised euthanasia against the wishes of a family or guardian, because I felt that they were too emotionally invested, and the kindest thing would be to let their friend pass peacefully away. I have, in fact, had vitriolic communications in this circumstance too from both clients and vets telling me what a bad person I am. One cannot insist on euthanasia, since the guardian has a right to as many opinions as they wish, and from a legal perspective euthanasia ultimately has to be their decision. The complainants disagreed, and in their eyes the decision for euthanasia should have been definitively recommended and treatment declined. Of course, the RSPCA will on occasion remove an animal from the care of its guardian and either treat or euthanise with or without prosecution. A vet does not have that power but can report the guardian to authorities in extreme circumstances. None of the vets involved with Hermes and Helen felt that this was such a circumstance, and all felt that she, and they, were acting in the best interests of the patient.

One never operates on any animal because either you or the guardian of that animal 'wants to'. When we sign up to be veterinary surgeons we instantly become the advocates for the animal. They cannot talk to us and each of them processes pain differently: some suffer quietly and others vehemently protest with the least provocation. So what parameters does one use to measure pain in a dog or a cat – or in this case a tortoise? There are scientifically validated pain assessment scales which are ubiquitously used, but it's challenging when dealing with reptile species of the family Testudinidae of the order Testudines. For any animal could a scientific pain scale be the best gauge? Or does the guardian know best the level of pain their pet is enduring? Does the vet know best? Do two or three vets together know best? Does it depend on the experience of the vet? Does an ethics panel with veterinary and lay representation know better than the guardian?

These are all questions that should guide medical and surgical intervention, as well as the decision for euthanasia, in veterinary practices across the world. At the time I operated on Hermes, there wasn't any formal guidance from the RCVS suggesting that an ethics committee judgement might be required for such a case. If there had been, I would of course have complied. There is still currently no definitive centralised RCVS-governed and approved ethical adjudication platform for individual patients that can be readily accessed on a daily basis by people, with any level of experience, performing advanced surgery in clinical veterinary practice. I have requested this guidance on a number of occasions, but so far without conclusive action. If such a panel existed, then I would use it regularly for advice on my cases, so that issues like the Hermes complaint just wouldn't arise. Central approval could be sought ahead of time, and, if denied, I could pass on the adjudication to the client, thus avoiding personal criticism for either denying or providing said treatment. The current legal framework, therefore, is that in all but extreme circumstances it remains the job of the individual veterinary surgeon to consult with the guardian and colleagues, and make a subjective clinical judgement about what best to do in any given situation.

A key issue for the complainants and the RCVS was the length of time that Hermes had waited before surgery in order for his stumps to heal and his infection to clear up. They felt he had suffered beyond hope of recovery; Helen and the primary care clinician had monitored Hermes throughout this time and had felt quite differently. Hermes was at my practice in total for eighteen days during the several months of his recovery – nine days after cleaning up his amputation stumps, and nine days after implanting his prostheses. Yet, the complainants held me personally responsible from an ethical perspective for the entire period of his care, even when I was not present.

Helen had many years of experience in caring for tortoises and had wanted me to try my very best for Hermes. Helen's primary care clinician, who was well accustomed to judging the welfare of tortoises, believed, as I did, that Helen had not been overly emotionally biased when she asked me to perform the surgery and that she did have Hermes' best interests at heart. As a critical care nurse herself, Helen understood that there was a line in the sand and if Hermes was deemed to be suffering beyond reasonable hope, or if further complications occurred, then she would absolutely have agreed on euthanasia. This had been established from the outset.

When I had consulted with Helen regarding Hermes, the TV cameras had been rolling – as they often are for months at a time. We see whatever cases come in, and it is what it is, as they say. Many of my euthanasia cases don't appear on the programme at the families' request, which is entirely understandable. Despite what the show's critics may think, with regard to *The Supervet* not presenting a 'balanced view' of veterinary practice, firstly the programme isn't set in a primary care practice with a mixed caseload, but rather in a referral centre where my caseload is highly specialised. Cases that just need medication generally don't get referred to see me and if I do see a patient where I feel surgery isn't in their best interests, and simply prescribe some medicine, sending the family on their way, such a case wouldn't appear in the programme since it's a single consultation and each 'story' needs to have some kind of narrative arc for the viewer. Secondly, the production company and the broadcaster have a job to do – and that is to deliver a mainstream television programme that people actually want to watch, while also observing the rules of their regulatory body, Ofcom, in doing so. Whether more screen time is given to surgery or to a cat in a swimming pool will be dependent on the editor and director of that particular show. In short, I do the same job anyway, day in, day out – whether the camera is recording or not.

The Supervet isn't a programme about science, it's about unconditional love. Nor is it a topical 'this is what things cost' show – that's a different audience entirely. I would actually be very interested to see such a topical show – where prices are transparently compared like-for-like between referral centres and primary care practices of various brands across the land – and would gladly take part. I expect people might be surprised at the findings. The minority may criticise, but the majority of viewers ultimately determine the relative weighting of content from the production broadcast perspective. As I've said, my ambition has always been to challenge the status quo for the betterment of animals. To help make that happen, I had set out to build as big a platform as possible. I'd tried with scientific publications, lectures and more and more degrees, none of which had made the slightest difference. That's where television and the subsequent media interest, the book and arena tour came in – I created the footage with my good friend, director and cameraman Jim Incledon, which went on to become the first *Supervet* TV series, because I knew that I would need a global platform to pursue One Medicine and get a fair deal for animals in my lifetime. Everything that I have tried to do is nothing more than the foundation to bring about 'the change I would like to see in the world' by living that change myself, as Mahatma Gandhi once said.

Given the format of *The Supervet*, it's not possible to show the process behind every nuanced decision or intervention with all cases all of the time. Yet this particular episode featuring Hermes was the only evidence presented in the case brought before the RCVS by the four complainants. If one was to apply the principles of scientific evidence as a foundation for any investigation, which both myself and the complainants strongly advocate (as one would with a scientific paper, for example), as well as the many years of academic training and problem-solving which my four veterinary colleagues undoubtedly had, why rely on abbreviated TV footage rather than simply coming to the practice and talking to me about their concerns over anything that I was trying to do for my patients or for veterinary medicine? To me this doesn't make rational sense from the perspective of scientific determination. In the deposition the reason for not doing so was described as 'perceived futility'. Allegedly, even if they had tried, I wouldn't have listened. Wow. Internalising criticism happens to be one of the things I can truly say I have practised religiously all my life, both personal and professional, so they probably should have given it a shot! The perception was that I was too arrogant and egocentric to listen to anyone's concerns. One definitely needs an ego to be a surgeon, to go on television, to do a live stage show – but if one's ego comes before one's moral principles as a surgeon, well, all is surely lost.

The lead complainant had given a lecture to vets a few weeks earlier, specifically naming *The Supervet* and showing an image of the treatment of Hermes, which she stated had been a 'clear-cut case of overtreatment' and a neglect of ethical protocols. Her lecture was followed by a standing ovation, which the complainants cited as good evidence of professional support for censure of my professional activities. Coincidentally, at around the same time I had delivered my Phoenix and Barcelona lectures on the same subject asserting, like she did, that ethics should be rigorously enforced and audited across all of veterinary medicine so that animal welfare is firmly protected. We were talking about exactly the same challenges, but from polar opposite perspectives.

My mammy Rita always said that 'pride will take a fall', and so I don't talk about pride in my own personal acumen or achievements, as I am only as good as my next surgery. However, I am intensely proud of my profession and what it stands for, and honoured to have been able to play a part in the creation of the veterinary school at the University of Surrey. I have worked with countless veterinary students, interns, residents and nurses and tried to help them as best I could. I'm proud too of *The Supervet* and the team who take great care and effort to create it. I think it's fair to say that generally the programme has been well received and folks can see that I'm trying to do my best for the animals and those who love them. Over the years I have had thousands of conversations and email exchanges with members of the public about the television show and more recently the live arena show, and I've read hundreds of fan letters from children telling me that it has inspired them to become vets, nurses, doctors or carers for animals or humans.

Now, faced with an accusation of drawing my profession into disrepute, I was beyond devastated, curled up on my bed like the scared boy I had been nearly forty years earlier back in my bedroom in Ballyfin. All I could think about was the pain of rejection, misunderstanding, alienation and fear.

It was hard for me to understand the point of view of the complainants. I knew they were doing what they felt was the right thing to do – to stand up for the animal as best they knew how – even if, in my opinion, it was not the best way to go about it. The RCVS had a statutory duty to investigate nonetheless.

I would spend many hours over Christmas 2018 and the New Year, and many more throughout 2019, putting together my defence of the case for my legal team. I was supported in this by Hermes' mum Helen, along with the primary care vet, my intern, nursing and specialist vet colleagues, who were all of the view that we had done our utmost in difficult circumstances. When I wasn't actually preparing my legal defence, I was worrying, losing sleep and slowly going out of my mind. There were times when I began to feel like I didn't want to be a vet any more at all, and that tore me apart. Looking back, the irony is not lost on me. Only months earlier I had been out on the road, sharing the story of Vetman's brightest star in the hope that audiences would internalise its light. I couldn't even do that myself any more – I could see only darkness ahead.

That November morning in 2018, after the tears had dried, I lay paralysed in shock, still clutching the RCVS letter, among the cold sweat of my bedsheets. I didn't have the mental or physical will to go on, but I had to get up. I had to pull myself out of it somehow. Monty's family was waiting in reception for me and I was supposed to go to my consulting room and put Monty to sleep. The only light in the sadness was that I could be there for his mum and dad, who are wonderful, gracious, kind, loving people. They had been through some really tough times and Monty had been there for their family through it all. He had been their constant support and now they were giving him the greatest gift of kindness by allowing him to die with dignity.

The phone on my office desk rang over and over, but I just lay here. I knew it was reception calling me; Monty and his family were ready. I was going to bring them death, but I knew too that it was my moral responsibility to be there for them and reassure them that they were doing the right thing with integrity. I also knew with all of my heart that I had acted with integrity when I had operated on Hermes.

From the bottom of the quarry, covered in bruises, I did what I have done all of my life in such circumstances. I reached deep inside and thought of Vetman who always had the strength to do the right thing, because his heart was made from the stardust of unconditional love. Finally, I found him. He'd been there all the time. I got up, washed my face, pulled on my scrubs and went downstairs.

I kissed Monty on the forehead. Mum and Dad held his head as I held his paw and injected the pentobarbital. Life ebbed quietly away with a single breath. They hugged me tightly and thanked me for all that I had done and for the peace they felt in knowing that they had done the best they could for their beloved friend. I still couldn't speak. I went back to my bedroom, lay down on the bed and sobbed my heart out again.

CHAPTER TWO

Nowness

'There is no need to go elsewhere for the truth.
Just go more deeply into what you already have in
the moment of now.'

Eckhart Tolle

The only thing that really matters is *now* and those who live in the absolute present, live in eternity, because the moment of *now* is the moment of *forever* – it is all there is and all there ever will be. There is no point in living in the past nor in existing only for the future – you can accept the past and influence the future, but if you carry the past into the future then you will always do what you've always done and you will always get what you've always got.

By default, or by design, however, my mind often refuses to stay in the 'moment of now'. Outside of the operating theatre, as a surgeon I am perpetually thinking of what I've done in the past or what might happen in the future regarding the animals in my care, and that spills over into my personal life too, so that I have really battled to keep my mind in the present. I've tried meditation, yoga, breathing exercises, psychological intervention techniques. I have read books, watched self-help videos, listened to CDs and podcasts on mindfulness and anchoring, all with varying degrees of success and mainly failure. For some reason I have lacked the patience, the willpower or the mental calm to cope with being in my own mind-space for more than a few seconds and, while my body may be all too present with its aches and pains, my mind is most often in another place and time. Of course, I perfectly understand what I should be doing – I should still my mind, observe my thoughts and anxieties like passing clouds, accept them without judgement simply as uninvited guests that I don't wish to feed with my energy – and let them go. But until recently, I got so distracted by the effort to let go that I couldn't *actually let go*. And so, for all of my life until very recently, nowness has eluded me.

I first came across the general idea of trying to be in the 'present moment' as a student in Dublin in the late eighties. I was studying in a park one day and noticed a Buddhist sitting nearby on a rug. Anyone in robes stood out in a Dublin park, so he drew my eye – and he seemed so peaceful, while I was a mess of anxiety about exams and study. I guess he saw the angst that was crushing my body and asked me what I was studying. We struck up a conversation and he was a very gentle, calming presence, so I found myself listening intently as he explained about 'sati', which is the mindfulness or awareness that is integral to Buddhist practice, and the first of the seven factors of enlightenment. He also talked about 'dharma', which roughly translates as a kind of path of rightness that makes life and the universe possible. In Buddhism, 'samadhi' is a kind of complete 'oneness' with meditation, and is the last of the eight elements of the Noble Eightfold Path. Of course, back then, I knew absolutely nothing about such a path, nor about dharma, samadhi or sati. The man encouraged me to think about whether I was on the right path in my life and suggested that if I knew for sure that I was and brought that feeling into the present, rather than the constant anxiety, it might put my struggles in context. I was quite sure of my path: I thought of Vetman and all I wanted to achieve as a vet, and indeed the waves of fear caused less nausea in my belly and my brain. Soon, he packed up his rug and headed off, saying as he went, 'Enjoy life *now* – because it's all you have.'

I was quite baffled, but like many other thoughts which were well worth the pondering, I promptly forgot about them and carried on. It wasn't until years later when I came across the work of writer and spiritual teacher Eckhart Tolle that any awareness of sati, samadhi or enlightenment was rekindled. Tolle had suffered from anxiety and episodes of acute suicidal depression for most of his life, when suddenly at the age of twenty-nine he had a profound personal epiphany that afforded him a life-changing insight. In that transformative moment, Tolle found the sense of 'me' that is always enough, at peace in and enthralled by the magic of now. In doing so, he learned to put aside his conscious self and fully inhabit his unconscious self. Tolle went on to write about his experience in his bestselling book, *The Power of Now*. 'I heard the words "resist nothing" as if spoken inside my chest,' he wrote. 'The next morning, I woke up and everything was so peaceful. The peace was there because there was no self. Just a sense of presence or "beingness", just observing and watching.' I yearned to have this kind of awakening to the *present*.

Being in the present is, of course, intrinsic to the work of a surgeon. When I'm at the operating table I am 100 per cent in the moment, utterly absorbed by the process – incising skin, retracting fascia, separating muscles, preserving nerves and blood vessels, cutting bone and teasing fragments into position, coaxing screws and implants into place. Almost unconsciously, I simultaneously hold many alternatives on standby in my head at all times; a surgeon must always consider failure and what might be done to avert it. In fact, when I'm in surgery my usual nagging worries don't even enter my mind, because that's my domain and where I feel most in control, regardless of the odds stacked against me. The world could collapse and I'd still be trying to navigate the anatomy of my patient. I'm also totally present when I'm in a consultation listening to families and what the animal itself can tell me, which is often volumes. As I listen to the guardians, I observe the patient – every subtle movement, twitch of an ear, grimace of the mouth, lick of the lips, tremble of a foot, reticence to move or be touched, pattern of the gait, subtle lameness, a toe out of place, a tail slung lower than it should be, a head held slightly to the side, a look in the eyes that may suggest pain or apprehension.

Beyond the practice, however, in my personal realm it is a very different story. Here I can relate to Eckhart Tolle's depression, but until more recently not to his sudden awakening to a transcendent light. Much as I've tried over the years to adopt Tolle's mindset, I have really struggled with accepting myself and being at ease with simply being alone with *me* in the present – I struggle to mute my conscious self and embrace my unconscious. After all, as a veterinary surgeon my entire decision-making process is based on rational cohesive thought, sandwiched between empathy and compassion. Indeed, I could make endless clinical diagnoses of all the issues in my life and doubtless proceed towards the most excellent and effective treatments – if only I could keep my mind in the present. I would imagine that for most of my emotional challenges I might not even need drastic 'surgical intervention' – a good dose of 'now' medicine would probably do the trick.

But saying and doing are two very different things. Usually this is because I'm worrying about something I've done or should have done, or about something I have to, might, could, should or possibly shouldn't do in the future. I'm sure I'm not unusual in that regard. In my worry and distraction 'now' becomes consumed in a fog of yesterday and tomorrow, obliterating the beauty of what is right in front of me here, now, right this second – and then it's gone. It's like I'm in a constant state of readiness, like a cat watching the ever-moving mouse of my thoughts, waiting to pounce on the next invention, the next solution to a problem, my next grand idea to change the world – instead of devoting a few minutes to saving myself.

Being in the present is not something that comes naturally to anyone in our modern age of constant distraction, where everything is immediately available to us on demand – social media, the newsfeed on our phone, newspapers, radio, television, music and movies. We have instant food, instant dating, instant gratification and instant fame – and yet all of this distracts us from the potential wonderment of *being fully in the present*. With our phones constantly in hand, calling and distracting us with the ping of yet another tweet or similar, no wonder we find it hard to simply savour 'now'. The tendency to ruminate on the past or fret about the future, which can be both a symptom and cause of poor mental health, can also feel like a powerful magnetic field, pulling one out of the present. In that regard, I wish we *could* bottle some kind of medicine to keep us mindfully present, because it could ward off so many of my mental health crises, which are often born of feelings of inadequacy and low self-esteem, feelings that sadly can be exacerbated by social media and the commentary of others.

I think we can all remember days that seemed to go on forever in our childhood, when the hours seemed endless and carefree, when we sat on a seashore or climbed a tall tree and life was one long, limitless expanse of time. I remember what it felt like as a child climbing the Slieve Bloom Mountains which I could see from my bedroom window: noticing everything, the sensation of my feet on the ground, the rain or sun on my face, the wind in my hair – or climbing the chestnut tree in our garden to the very top, and sending Vetman off on his missions in my head. Yet as we grow older, life rushes past and we forget to smell the daisies. Time, and with it the very essence of who we are, seems to stream away down a bottomless plughole leaving us parched, scrounging around for the drops left on the sides of the sink.

In my experience, by contrast, dogs and cats smell the daisies all of the time. Animals seem always to be in the now, wringing every last drop of joy from the novelty of the present. It's through listening to and caring for animals over the years that I have become aware of my own version of Eckhart Tolle's being fully in 'the moment of now'. For me, being with animals is a direct pathway to peacefulness, which I like to think of as 'Nowness'.

When I have experienced *nowness* – in the half-wakefulness of a few minutes with an animal coming around from anaesthesia; or when I am really at one with biology in an operation; or in the silent presence of Keira or Ricochet – the awareness goes beyond acquiescence or rising above

51

rumination on past or future; it requires no effort at all. Somehow in these moments, the animals give me access to a calming of my brain that happens automatically, just like breathing. It's as if my heart beats with the animal's without conscious thought at all. In those moments I fleetingly forget my worries and am truly 'present'. I had, I realised, experienced glimpses of nowness all through my life, but amid the distraction of everyday worries I had taken no notice of the potential epiphany within my grasp – if only I'd stayed in the moment long enough to take it in.

I have come to realise recently that if I can stay in this 'oneness' with animals, it allows me access more consistently to a restful and contented place inside myself. For me, all searching for meaning, peace, belonging and being 'present' in pure consciousness is to be had through this kind of nowness. I have found the ubiquitous rubric of 'mindfulness' somewhat nebulous. I haven't been able to let go of thoughts and feelings about the past and accept them without judgement. I know that various forms of mindfulness and meditation have worked very well for others in every form – from breathing exercises to states of meditative consciousness. But I have constantly become ensnared in any effort of *trying* to be mindful. The effort thwarted the intent.

Recently, I have become interested in the Vedic tradition that speaks of a much more fundamental connection to a oneness and universal consciousness. In particular I have become drawn to the insights of Maharishi Mahesh Yogi and Moojibaba. The concept of one universal consciousness makes sense to me because I see it as a reflection of a greater oneness in the universe: a oneness with nature, animals and ultimately the stuff we are all made of. I have only recently stood still long enough to notice that the nowness that I have tapped into through my bond with animals is an effortless connection to a kind of eternity. In this regard, nowness seems to me more akin to the samadhi meditative state of eternal consciousness written in the Sanskrit of Buddhist and yogic traditions, which the monk had told me about many years earlier. Of course, these cultures had immense respect for animals as part of the 'oneness' of creation.

I've become increasingly interested in all of this because of recent life events – of which more later – and I have also realised through this exploration of how to be present that I carry many scars of past trauma with me that disrupt any effort for peace in my mind. As I referred to earlier, in Vedic tradition these scars are *samskaras*, or psychological imprints. These imprint scars within me affect what I think of myself and what I actually do every day. It's as though my default position is constant vigilance, ready to defend myself. I find it very difficult to be at rest, and I have been guilty of never giving my mind space or time to heal, regenerate and maybe think wiser rather than faster. Looking back to my own childhood, as I've also noted before, I can see that much of my anxiety and inability to be in the present – like many of the other conditioned responses I have in my life – is inherited from my daddy Sean. As a farmer, the air he breathed was that of the animals, the grass and the soil, and he was a workaholic. He rested a bit on a Sunday to please Heaven, insofar as it was needed, but if the silage, barley harvest, broken sheep fencing or cattle feeding needed doing, then Heaven would understand. I therefore grew up with an innate sense of never wasting a single second because the next task was soon at hand. I was always supposed to be weeding turnips, herding sheep, feeding cattle or cleaning out their yards and sheds, and there was no time to waste on what Daddy Sean called 'idle hands', for which he felt the Devil would find ready work!

I have only lately realised that the work ethic I inherited from my father is a double-edged sword. On the one hand, it's got me where I am today; on the other, it has made me a workaholic just like him, who feels guilty for enjoying any downtime. I remember vividly the day he found me asleep in a field of turnips that I was supposed to be weeding. I was lost in the nowness of dreams. He told me I was useless and that 'lying down on the job' was a sin like 'lying to myself'. I never forgot that, and it has shaped me both good and bad. Little did Daddy know what I have learned since – that my search for some kind of meaning – which many of us call God – is present everywhere, especially in the stillness. For him it was present in the church and the rosary and it served him well.

I didn't have regular playmates as a child since there were no friends in the vicinity when living on a farm, and only a handful of children in my primary school class. Some boys from my class came around on my birthday, but a once-a-year indulgence in sweets and biscuits didn't consistently teach me what it might feel like to be in the moment. My mammy and daddy did their best, though, for sure. When I started secondary school, I realised that I was so far behind my classmates I would have to study my arse off for the rest of my life to catch up, so there wasn't a moment to waste there either. We had school *six* days a week, and I did school-work every night until after 1 a.m. – including Sundays even during the holidays. I never stopped worrying about the next essay or exam. Of course, to some extent I could lose myself in the nowness of the biology lesson with Mr Murray or the physics experiment with Brother Maurice, but that was in a rather cerebral, actively conscious kind of way, and all the while I would be preoccupied by concerns about not being good enough in that moment of study or endeavour. Brother Maurice has recently passed away. I shall really miss my friend and mentor. He believed in me and encouraged me to be the best I could in the moment. I managed to see and speak to him for a short while through the window of the care home where he spent his final weeks when I visited Ireland briefly after coronavirus lockdown restrictions were lifted. As I stood there in the yard, in my mask, observing the strict social distancing rules, he finally reached out his hand toward the window to say goodbye. I knew in my heart it was the final farewell, and so did he. He said, 'Thank you for caring, Noel, and thanks for coming to see me now. Sure, you're a tonic – and you've always done your best, Noel. I'm very grateful for that.' I thank him for caring about me and for doing his best for me, for which I shall be eternally grateful. Even when I failed in a physics experiment in his lab, he would just smile and say, 'Thank you, Noel, that's good enough – for now! Better luck next time.' 'Now' was always enough for Brother Maurice – and I will always try to be better next time.

However, throughout my studies and career, I've found failure really hard and I have taken it deeply personally, and not much has changed to this day. Being a surgeon does imbue a keen sense of perspective and humility, but though I'm always grateful when things go well, I spend hardly any time at all rejoicing in the successes I have had. I have lately realised that I spend quite a bit of my time in a negative state of mind and I can never let myself forget for even one moment that I'm only as good as my next failure. Another recent realisation is that I have a profound and deep-seated need to be in control, which I can be as a surgeon, regardless of the odds stacked against me, but in real life that doesn't work – and that's probably one of the biggest reasons why I haven't done so well in my life outside of work, where control of circumstance is often not possible. One might think I'd have realised this earlier, but alas not.

I have also only recently recognised another legacy of my father: like him I welcome the company of animals more than humans. I chose to be a vet, rather than a human doctor, because I couldn't be bothered with people complaining all the time, but also because I felt a deep connection with animals. My father thought I chose to go to veterinary school because I grew up on a farm and hoped I'd become a farm vet, which I did for a while, but it went way deeper than that. My bond with animals was more compassionate, empathetic and intuitive than with any human – including my relationship with myself. I'm not sure that I can honestly say that I've experienced the same sense of being fully present nor felt a comparable pure uncomplicated, unconditional love for another human as I have for a dog, cat or other animal friend. Like my father, my commitment to animals has come, however, at the expense of my relationships. The people I love have struggled to understand why I find it difficult to be fully present with them, and so over the course of my adult life, the demise of my romantic relationships has been mostly my fault. I'm trying hard now – it's a work in progress.

But here's the thing – I am perhaps not uniquely awful in this regard. I suspect that many of us are probably guilty of the same inattentiveness at least some of the time. How often, for example, with your lover, your mother or your child is that feeling of being totally in the present replicated each and every day of your lives? For sure we may have been so in love with someone that we were totally present in that moment as we kissed under the street lamp. We have been totally present with our mother, father, brother, sister for moments shared which could reach beyond eternity. We have been present at the birth of a child and been awed in the magnificence of nowness – and for those who are parents, there are no doubt many such moments in the life of a child. I haven't experienced that yet, and I hope to. And yet, I'll bet there has been an occasion in most of our lives when the love has faltered, or somehow lost its intensity. Have you ever found yourself in the company of someone wishing you were somewhere else, as they sat opposite scrolling social media on their phone? There have been times when my parent(s) and/or sibling(s) have driven me crazy. And I doubt if any child brings its parents only an uninterrupted flow of joyful moments.

In extreme circumstances a lover, parent, sibling or child can deal pain, break your heart in a million pieces, and leave you bereft and profoundly empty. On the other hand, how often has your dog or your cat left you wishing you were not sharing that moment with them? Not often, I'll bet. In my experience, a cat or a dog only breaks your heart when they are sick, injured or in pain, and when they die. For the most part, the daily interactions of a dog or cat with their family and their guardians offer pure golden molecules of unadulterated nowness.

Every day in my consulting room I comfort families for whom life has unravelled because the dog or cat they love is suffering, or they are saying a last goodbye to their friend. Increasingly over the years, I have been involved with more and more complex surgeries, such that nowadays I only very rarely perform simpler routine surgeries at all. Every day, people ask me to beckon the future by evolving solutions which don't exist right now. This does add a whole new level of focus on the here and now for the 'human parents', and it's especially true if families have already visited several previous veterinarians and have come to see me with the perception that I'm their last hope. It's in circumstances like these that one's heart is truly laid bare by an animal friend. The family members are totally *present* with their best friend, as if the last gasp of their own lives depended on it and thoughts of everyday worries seem inconsequential by comparison. It's in those moments that I have been witness to the most intense nowness with fellow human beings.

All of my life, I've found it easier to relate to animals. Remarkably, thinking about it, I have only very rarely been nervous in the presence of an aggressive animal, since animals mostly bring me peace and calm in the moment, while I am frequently nervous around humans. It takes me a long time to trust someone enough to spend any significant time with them. I am wary of humans. I found it difficult as a child to be around people. I stayed on my own or with the animals on the farm as much as I could. In later life, I didn't have a girlfriend until I was twenty-one years old. I still find it difficult in small groups of people now, but I'm mostly fine in larger, less personal crowds. In my relationship with fellow human beings, it has been art, theatre, film and music that have been my saviour, and allowed me access to infinite nowness, both with and without other people along for the ride.

Looking back, in truth, I think my soul has always been most present in the arts – not science. Any rare moments of nowness in my childhood outside of my companionship with animals were inextricably linked to superheroes, literature, drama or music. I always enjoyed the immersive experience of watching grainy black-and-white films and *The Six Million Dollar Man*, or on one memorable occasion *Rocky*, on our wind-up coin-box television; reading my *Wolverine* comic books; my adventures with Vetman in my made-up world – or getting lost in a book by Oscar Wilde. This perhaps explains my tendency to be a 'creative' scientist rather than a straight-line thinker. I have never seen a dividing line between art and science.

In later life, my drive to attend drama school was in large part a hunger to understand how language becomes life, but perhaps, unknowingly, it also satisfied my longing to exist most purely in the moment – and gave me a better handle on understanding human relationships. I didn't have access to the theatre in my childhood, but under normal circumstances – before Covid-19 and the world's theatres went dark – I try to go as often as I can. I can be totally lost in the artistic magnificence of a carefully crafted set as a story is brought to life by the performers. In one way or another, the drama theatre has made me a better surgeon in the operating theatre, because it opened my mind to possibility. Of course, the epiphanies of science require one to be in the now – but art sometimes allows a more effortless route for fresh thinking. Perhaps science through art might just be the key: to ultimate nowness, a realisation that we are part of everything – of all creation – and totally unique in the enormity of it all. How great is that? Only you can be in the *moment* of *you*, and that's an artistic and a scientific fact!

Drama gave me the confidence to grow to be someone I dreamed of becoming, and I'm still dreaming. Surgery isn't performed in a 'theatre' by default or mistake. In an operating theatre, magic is moulded from broken biology through the miracle of medicine. Back in the seventeenth century, the spectacle of anatomic dissection of man or animal in the *Theatrum Anatomicum* was an actual live performance for the students and spectators who crowded into the stalls on either side. In terms of how I actually think, theatre, drama and the movies, especially superhero movies, had as much to do with me gaining the confidence to perform complicated innovative surgery as any science book ever did. But of all the creative arts, music was truly my salvation, and throughout all of my life, the most direct route to nowness for me.

I live in my own head so much of the time, focused on my patients, that without my regular live music fix every couple of weeks I would probably have turned to drugs or alcohol, or some other '-aholism' to add to my chronic workaholism. Practising veterinary surgery requires one to be as much an emotional guidance counsellor as a skilled wielder of a scalpel blade. If one internalises all the pain of failure, the pain of one's clients and one's patients, not to mention the many shared insecurities, frailties, fears and desperation, it's possible to go quite mad – and I've been close.

When I listen to music, I can always be totally in the moment – instantly engrossed in the ethereal sea of sound. As a child I found an old Sony radio on a scrapheap, made an aerial out of an old coat hanger and that's how I heard Led Zeppelin on Radio Luxembourg for the first time. There was no looking back. All of a sudden, this entire 'secret' world of the airwaves became mine. Alone in my bedroom with the radio playing I could escape the insularity of feeling like an alien, stuck in Esker in the middle of nowhere; through music I could conjure any thought, feeling or image I chose; I could escape all the hurt in my life and find healing in that tide of nowness. In my early teens, I didn't have friends to talk to so I often sought refuge in all kinds of comforting magical melodies, to patch up the holes in my fraying mind.

From the rock of Queen, Simple Minds, AC/DC, Iron Maiden and Def Leppard, to the poetry of Genesis, The Police, David Bowie, The Cure and Dire Straits, to the pop pleasure of Madonna, Duran Duran, Spandau Ballet, Wham! and Rick Astley, the genius of The Rolling Stones, Depeche Mode, Bruce Springsteen, Michael Jackson and Prince, and of course the greatest rock 'n' roll band of all time – U2. Every Saturday night I listened over and over to their album *The Unforgettable Fire* on an old black record player with its worn-out stylus in my study room of the farmhouse as I wrote my essays, drew science diagrams and studied into the night, with all the magnificent hiss, crackle and fizz of a scratchy needle on vinyl.

U2's song from this album, 'Pride (In The Name Of Love)', summed up my relationship with time: 'One man come in the name of love, one man come and go'. I always knew that my time on earth was transient – I was just passing through. And yet I spent my childhood wishing time away: I consciously detached from the present when I was being bullied. Sometimes the moment was just too unbearable to live in, so I became accustomed to being somewhere else. Asked about the inspiration for the song, Bono told *NME* magazine that he remembered a wise old man who said to him, 'Don't try and fight darkness with light, just make the light shine brighter.' He explained it had made him reflect on how Martin Luther King had tried to do just that and bring people together in spite of all of the differences that had driven them apart. The song is about the pride of a man whose actions are motivated by an awareness of the dignity of all human life.

For me, that awareness extended to all animal life too as the very source of salvation for myself and for mankind. This song became my anthem as I grew into adulthood and I resolved to try to be an advocate for the animals *in the name of love* – because if we don't appreciate our commonalities and our shared planet, and if we don't look after animals now, we won't have the world we know and love to look forward to in the future.

Very soon, coronavirus, which had evolved to transfer from an animal to a human, would remind all of us of the intimacy between the human and animal worlds and there would be a growing realisation that the fate of the animals is inextricably linked to our own. Global challenges generally seem so far from the moment of now that we sublimate their importance until they actually come crashing right into our every waking present. We might take little notice of conservation of animals and their habitats until a virus destroys our lives and livelihoods because we have destroyed theirs. Then we take notice *right now*. We might take little notice of the bushfires due to global warming which burn thousand-year-old forests and kill millions of animals until they also burn down our houses and fill our towns with smoke. Then we take notice *right now*. The things that we have pushed out of our minds to focus on current concerns have become our current concerns. The coronavirus pandemic has made us think about our interaction with the planet and looking after both animals and humans *in the name of love*. And to further echo Bono's words it has also brought 'people together in spite of all of the differences that had driven them apart'.

I have had an acute sensitivity for our interdependence

with the animal kingdom since childhood. In a very real sense, my companionship with animals on the farm, and especially with Pirate, was a great comfort to me then, and in later life, my patients have brought me tremendous solace too. But it is my relationships with Keira and Ricochet that have really defined me. They have comforted me when I have succumbed to despair, depression and very challenging feelings of inadequacy and profound pain. They have anchored me in nowness and in no small way have quite literally saved my life.

I can always rely on Keira for a stress-busting dose of 'nowness remedy'. When faced with any threat to the lightness of the moment, she will study my mood for a few seconds and then roll over to see if this worrisome thing will tickle her tummy. Failing that, she scoots her bottom along the ground and twists her head just enough so her ears do that 'cute thing' to try to charm whatever challenge I face into submission. Next comes a sniffing at my head and a lick on my face, as if to determine what the bad feelings are made of, and then if all else fails, she just runs around in circles. With her carefully choreographed routine, she brings me back to the present, no matter how upset or depressed I am, and saves me from the indulgence of wasting yet another second of potential joy in her presence.

And then in early February 2020 as I started to write this book, Ricochet arrived. I had always wanted a Maine Coon cat, but in truth, given my workload, I was afraid of responsibility for another living creature as well as Keira and worried that I would not be able to give him or her enough love and attention.

Then the decision was made for me. I may be a professor of orthopaedic surgery and as good as I can be at this point in time at what I do as a surgeon, but I'm also a workaholic, quite insular and emotionally 'challenging'. I find it difficult to deal with issues of the heart, so I haven't always been honest with myself and others in this regard. I'm not the easiest person to be with – and I'd just had one of the worst years of my life. Luckily for me, then, that my lovely girlfriend, Michaela, knew just the remedy. She found a gorgeous five-month-old black-smoke Maine Coon kitten with a bent front leg, an ear infection, cross eyes and a 'quirky' personality who needed a home with someone who would love him as he was and help him when he needed it. 'They're perfect souls for each other,' she thought the first time she laid eyes on him, and she was right. It was love at first sight. A big hairy bundle of bouncy magnificent Maine Coon nowness with a puffed-out, giant, feathery russet ruff under his chin, I named him Ricochet after the cat that teamed up with Vetman in one of his early adventures of my childhood dreams. And also because his Irish name would be 'Rick O'Shea'.

In retrospect, it almost feels as though Ricochet was sent to save *me* – and when he found me, I needed rescuing badly indeed. The RCVS complaints procedure which had devastated me had been going on for over a year, and had taken a profound toll on me psychologically. Even if one has done nothing wrong, the pressure of just enduring the case cast a shadow over literally everything in my life. This ongoing stress, on top of the gradual attrition of long nights, chronic physical issues and emotional challenges, had taken its toll. I had reached rock bottom psychologically, and no therapy or advice worked even a small percentage point compared to the comfort of having my new friend Ricochet by my side.

Yet there were even tougher times ahead of me, and for Ricochet too. His original guardians had absolutely done their very best for him, but ever since he had turned up as a kitten, I'd had nagging concerns about his health and sensed that the ear infection he'd come with wasn't something routine. He had been on antibiotics for a while before but the infection persisted, such that his ear needed to be cleaned every day – a procedure he did not enjoy. He also had crossed eyes which, while it only added to how adorable he was in his perfect/imperfect state, made me wonder as to whether there was something affecting both his eye and ear. On top of that, there was his turned out left front leg, which was caused by external rotation of his front paw and meant that he walked with a ballet-style turn-out. This wasn't necessarily a problem, he was happy and raced around the house with no care that his foot was at an angle, but I wanted to make sure.

After cleaning out the wax and infection discharge, it was clear that there was a big red lump growing up inside his ear canal and also into the back of his nose. A horrified shock echoed through my body – it was as if history was repeating itself: in 2013 I had discovered a lump in my nose which turned out to be a rare form of soft tissue tumour. There's nothing quite like cancer to focus one's mind on the moment of now. Your entire past life flashes before your eyes because all of a sudden there might be no future.

In Ricochet's case, I knew right away that the lump had ruptured through his eardrum and was growing from inside his skull. A CT scan confirmed my fears – there was a growth inside his tympanic bulla, which is an eggshell-shaped bulb on both sides under the skull. The pressure inside Ricochet's bulla was so great that the wall had abnormally thickened about tenfold and the normally empty shell was full of tissue. Sadly, this growth would have been causing significant pain and discomfort and was clearly very aggressive, so we suspected that it hadn't just grown from inside the ear out through the ear canal, but also likely up inside his skull to the back of his nose too. I knew that given his age and breed, the mass was much more likely to be benign than malignant – but it was an absolute mess. We had all known of Ricochet's 'special needs' – but none of us could have guessed at the full extent of his issues. Surgery would be needed if Ricochet was to survive, and the sooner the better.

I was not the best man for the job and so I immediately called the supremely skilled Gerard McLauchlan and Laurent Findji at our soft tissue surgery and cancer hospital. Gerard is an interventional radiologist who looks inside the body using scopes and image guidance to facilitate diagnosis and surgery, and Laurent is a soft tissue and cancer surgeon. Their examination found that Ricochet's tympanic bulla was bunged up by a growth called a feline inflammatory polyp (FIP), causing a massive build-up of pressure inside his skull. The cause of such a polyp which originates in the lining of the bulla is unknown – it could be congenital, i.e. he was born with it, or a response to an inflammatory process from a chronic viral or bacterial infection. Sadly, nobody could have known.

When sound waves go down through the ear canal, or outer ear, and hit the eardrum (tympanic membrane), they vibrate the three tiny bones (auditory ossicles) – the hammer, anvil and stirrup – amplifying the sound which vibrates in the middle ear (bulla), and above that the semi-circular canals and inner ear (cochlea) convert sound waves into nerve impulses via the auditory nerve. The middle ear is connected to the back of where the nose and mouth join in the throat (the nasopharynx) by the auditory or Eustachian tube which allows air from the pharynx to pass in and out of the middle ear to normalise pressure. This tube accounts for your ears 'popping' when pressure on either side changes rapidly. Ricochet's polyp was entirely filling up the bulla and aggressively expanding like some kind of molten alien with long tenacious tentacles, pushing everything out of its way, exploding through the eardrum externally into the ear canal and forcefully pushing up into the back of the nasopharynx through the auditory tube. Using Gerard's scope, it was clearly visible, rearing its ugly head both outside and inside the skull. Poor Ricochet.

As the team prepared Ricochet for surgery, I instantly turned into a paranoid doting daddy getting in everyone's way. I had often been bemused by people who bemoaned the amount of hair I clipped off their dog or cat when I performed surgery, but now I was the one getting inordinately upset when the beautiful Maine Coon ruff on Ricochet's chin was all shaved off. Laurent and I scrubbed for surgery, just like we both do daily, but this time we were operating on my beloved friend, and it was a whole different ball game. Normally I'm the lead surgeon and what the lead surgeon says goes, but that day I was Laurent's 'assistant', and only too glad to bow to his knowledge and expertise in treating my boy. Laurent cut through the skin and muscle down onto the tympanic bulla, then drilled a large hole through the dramatically thickened bone which was as hard as rock, and thicker than most he had seen before. The inside of the bulla of a cat differs from a dog or a human in that it has a septum that divides it into two compartments which communicate through a fissure. Part of this septum needed to be removed in order to achieve access to the tissue growing inside both compartments. Laurent had to carefully scrape and tug away the abnormal tissue while preserving tiny threadlike nerves on the walls of the bulla: too much damage to these little nerves could cause permanent side effects. If, on the other hand, one is too timid and doesn't scrape away enough of those abnormal cells, then there is a risk of regrowth. This requires a balancing act between scraping and tugging the tissue which requires real finesse. Any functional surgeon can drill bone and any surgeon can tug tissue, but not every surgeon has the dexterity and judgement of a specialist like Laurent.

Laurent tugged and gently scraped and finally removed an octopus of abnormal tissue from Ricochet's ear. It had a body which was in the main part of the bulla, a tentacle into the smaller compartment of the bulla, another tentacle up the auditory tube and another through the eardrum into the ear canal. It was a tremendous relief to see it lying innocuously on the operating table rather than growing in my poor boy's skull. When we looked at the tissue under a microscope, it was an ulcerated fibrovascular tissue covered by a stratified squamous and columnar epithelium with inflammatory cells, primarily lymphocytes, plasma cells and macrophages, within its stroma – lots of fancy words, but the bottom line was that it wasn't malignant. Yay, Ricochet would hopefully now share a full lifetime of joyful days. I was hugely grateful to my colleagues and, even without a scalpel blade in my own hands, I have rarely been so *present* as when Laurent was wielding his and I prayed that my boy would be OK, or later when I was so relieved as he woke up in my arms back in the wards.

I knew that any damage to the tiny nerves could result in temporary or permanent vestibular syndrome, facial paralysis or Horner's syndrome, or that chronic infection could ensue. As soon as Ricochet woke up it was apparent that he indeed had Horner's. This is where the sympathetic nerve pathway which powers parts of eye function without any volitional action has been affected by damage, causing Ricochet to have a small pupil, droopy upper eyelid, slightly recessed eyeball and, most strikingly, the white curtain of his third eyelid had crept in to cover half of his eyeball. Within a couple of days, he was out of pain and raring to go, but was seeing the world like a pirate with an eye patch. It didn't bother him at all. What did bother him, however, was having to wear a neck collar after his castration. He absolutely hated it and I couldn't help feeling sorry for him. Little did I know that only too soon I would be in exactly the same boat with an uncomfortable neck collar of my own.

At this same time, the world was at last beginning to wake up to the very real threat posed by a mysterious new virus, Covid-19. Quite suddenly all of humanity was forced more than ever before to consider nowness with unprecedented urgency, as the impact of coronavirus sent shockwaves across the globe. Then just before the entire country went into lockdown I myself came very close to death – not from the virus, but by breaking my neck. From an early age I always understood my life was transient, but I hadn't anticipated it being over quite so soon. It was a close shave and I suffered a serious injury, so you can imagine my gratitude and relief that on the scale of things I'm still around to tell the tale, of which more later, but I was literally locked down in a neck brace as a result. Two bits of good news, though: unlike Ricochet, I still had all my bits, and because my neck was in a brace, I could only look forward – and that's exactly what both Ricochet and I needed to do.

At first, I was in terrible pain, bed-bound and unable to work and so I was in self-enforced isolation. But within just a few weeks most of the UK population, barring key workers, were asked to stay at home, to no longer travel to work or study, and to make only the briefest essential trips outside. With schools, universities and all 'non-essential' shops and venues closed for business, the world slowed down, then more or less ground to a complete halt. Veterinary clinics needed to practise social distancing like everyone else and at Fitzpatrick Referrals we worked in small rotating teams treating emergencies only and seeing clients from the mandatory two-metre distance in the car park. At the start of lockdown I was at home anyway, recovering from the trauma of my accident, but later when I was well enough, there were days when for the first time in my professional life I couldn't be at work consulting and operating – even if I'd been able to. At this point in our 'hectic' evolution, this overnight change in our lives pressed a giant pause button, allowing a window for reflection for everyone, me included.

For many of us, we endured this strange state of limbo in communal grief and fear, not only because of the scale of death and suffering, but also for the loss of normal life as we knew it. In the absence of certainty, we were forced to exist in the moment, and to spend time with ourselves, our *real* selves, not the work persona or the made-up person we present on social media – but the real you and me. I think this kind of personal evolution will have repercussions that last well beyond the virus.

In my case, those days yielded this book, forcing me into the painful presence of myself, which I have found a disconcerting place to be and way more challenging than I would have imagined. Outside of work, I used to think that I was fine with my own company, but of course I was never really on my own. I was always at work in my head and in constant contact with the practice. I had pushed into the inner recesses of my mind all of the things that happened in my childhood and afterwards, some of which I would prefer to leave where they are in the past, but I discovered that they, more than anything else, have determined my relationship with the present moment. I'm a worrier and outside of my vocation and the surgery practice I am at odds with myself: saving someone else's life is a lot easier than saving my own.

Ricochet was a massive silver lining in the wake of my accident and during the subsequent months of lockdown. Housebound, he and I had the entire writing of this book to fall in love and forge our unbreakable bond, for which I shall be eternally grateful. My mental health was not in a good place and Ricochet kept me from looking backwards or indulging in the kind of self-withdrawal and navel-gazing that I had been guilty of when I'd had psychological issues before. We both tried desperately to look forward together. He jumped up on my knee and I cuddled him and kissed his forehead, breathing in all of his whiskered love as he peered at me through his squinty eye long after his collar had come off. But I remained in a physical and indeed emotional prison of my own making. I knew that to heal I needed to develop a grasp on nowness in a non-self-conscious, intuitive and non-defensive way. And yet, although I could not have had a more perfect opportunity to practise being mindfully present, I found it impossible to still my anxious mind. I have seen the hard way that what resists persists, and the harder I tried to resist the thoughts in my mind, the harder they banged on the door. My vision was impaired by an invisible shroud of anxiety from the past and worry about the future, and I was absolutely unable to be *present*.

A month after the surgery I had resigned myself to the

fact that Ricochet's vision would be permanently impaired and he'd be 'Pirate Ricochet' for life. After what seemed like an eternity, but was only a few weeks, I noticed over the space of two days that the third eyelid curtain was a little less prominent. Then suddenly, as if by some miracle, he jumped up on my bed one morning to nuzzle me awake, and as I groggily opened my eyes, there were two huge, glorious yellow irises staring down at me. I was blown away by this vision, and in my state of half-awake/half-asleep, as the sun peered through my window and reflected on the extraordinary iridescence of Ricochet's eyes, I held the intense glow inside me for a moment. The warmth filled me up in a dreamlike state – and then an astonishing thing happened. Quite suddenly, in that moment, everything changed. It was as if the dark blanket that had weighed down on me for most of my life was suddenly lifted along with Ricochet's third eyelid. I literally and spiritually awakened to a new dawn. I was completely and absolutely *present*, without another thought in my head except wonderment, gratitude and elation in nowness. I felt unbelievably happy and serenely peaceful. For a moment, everything was enough; everything was perfect. I'd had a little glimpse of Eckhart Tolle's revelation all those years ago – a transformative epiphany allowing me to realise that maybe there was a sense of 'me' that might just be enough. As Eckhart put it – 'the peace was there because there was no self. Just a sense of presence or beingness.'

Ricochet lay the full length of his considerable body along my chest and tucked his chin right up next to mine, purring and breathing gently in unison with me. It was as if our hearts were beating in synchrony. I put my arm around him, closed my eyes, opened my heart completely to him and breathed in the light streaming through my window, and now streaming into my heart. My ever-buzzing mind had quietened. Ricochet had given me the present of peace in the present. *This*, I thought, is *nowness*.

The animals we have in our lives teach us more about ourselves than we will ever care to admit. They share our elation and our despondency, they travel the journey in all of its ups and downs, and they enlighten us with wisdom that will only come to us if we stay in the moment and listen, see, feel, smell and taste – but not with our regular senses. If we can let go of ourselves and allow the moment to reveal itself, then there's another sense that I have experienced – a kind of liberation from time and space that feels like eternity. This can and will only happen when we let everything else go – none of it really matters anyway.

We take ourselves so seriously, and we think that 'this' is all there is. We forget that we've been around for thousands of years, we don't know what the future holds, and present tense is all we have. I used to think that my thoughts were who I am; that my thinking made me – but animals have taught me that, in fact, it is only by letting go of my conscious thoughts that I can touch pure consciousness and be *present* – if I can let the thoughts in and out without becoming anchored to them then I am free to float in a kind of peace and happiness that transcends thought, because it just *is*. Animals always just *are* – without agenda, without constantly feeling the need to feed their thoughts with attention, consumed with *who* and *what* they are, and so they have led me to an understanding of letting go of myself and of what others think of me, good or bad – so that I can be in nowness. In fact, it turns out that *I am not* my thoughts at all, but rather only really *me*, when I let all of my thoughts disappear.

In all of our infinite complexity, we need to realise that we are the masters of our own consciousness and we make our own present. Personally, I also need to realise that I have the wherewithal in my cellular make-up to forge new neuro-cellular pathways of love or hate, confusion and distrust or harmony and trust. Only I can make that choice – no one can do it for me. Transformation is not some distant goal, but rather is within me *right now*. I know that I am lucky in so many ways and I don't for one second forget that someone else's circumstance may be far more challenging than mine – held back by social or economic disadvantage, relationship or family circumstances, a mental or physical disability, or living in a geographical location where it's impossible to re-alise what they see as their true state of self. Yet, I strongly believe that no matter one's situation, if one were to expe-rience the love of a dog or cat right now in this moment, then a small light would come on in your soul – and if we all resonated with that light, then the world would be a much better place, or to quote Bono, together we could 'make the light shine brighter'.

Keira, Ricochet and all the other animals in my world have given me the key to unlock the door inside me which frees me from pain, guilt, worry, fear, anxiety and judgement of the past or future and allows me to be reborn in every single moment of nowness, escaping the endless noise of my mind. Ricochet and Keira are my shining beacons of light. This kind of nowness that I have discovered requires us to open our hearts, close our eyes, hug the animals we love and breathe in their light. Through this love, the light of the *present* can and will revolutionise your life. Animals want to save us, if only we will let them. Having spent thirty years trying to be a proper vet, maybe I'm starting to evolve as a proper human. I feel like I'm just beginning to understand how to be OK in the company of humans too – and even how to be less scared of intimate love. I understand now that there isn't a wrong time or a right time for love – there's just a right here, right now time.

Keira and I are old friends, and we know each other's foibles. She's more or less deaf now and developing cataracts, so she sits at my bare feet as I type at my desk, soothing me with a hairy blanket of nowness. Ricochet, by contrast, is vastly independent and, like cats do, he will tell me when he's ready for affection and when he's not. When I'm working at my desk, I hear 'Buurrrph' when he's approaching – which is the sound signalling an incoming Ricochet love missile – and he demands attention *right now*: no excuses are acceptable. He puts his paws up on my leg, another 'Buurrrph' and up he jumps on my knee, pushes himself up with his back legs and throws his giant paws up on my neck to pull my head away from the computer screen. I am immediately summoned to submit to wet-nose-rubbing, furry-cheeked kisses in that very moment. He grabs me into sudden nowness no matter what I'm doing. He pushes his big nose against mine, looks deep into my eyes – and forces me in the moment to stare into my own soul. He is my guardian angel and the confidant for all my problems who has pulled me back from the brink of madness time and time again. I now walk around my house with six legs everywhere I go, or with ten legs, if Keira gets up from her snooze to follow.

Happily, Keira accepted Ricochet like a brother, and because she's a bit hard of hearing she doesn't even mind him tearing up newspaper or bashing his jingly-jangly ball around. She even helped me and Michaela to train him on a lead. They absolutely love getting out for an adventure every day, rain or shine, which gets me out too. It's quite extraordinary that I had forgotten how to smell the daisies until Ricochet stopped every ten feet to do just that. Nowadays I am making a conscious effort to leave my phone and headphones behind, and embrace the sounds, sights and smells of nowness on our walks. The world we have created is so fast and so all-consuming that we too easily miss all those interesting nooks and crannies right under our nose – we walk straight past them, our thoughts elsewhere. But Ricochet and Keira are never *not* in the moment and every moment spent in their presence is filled with joy and discovery. The raucous rush of life seems a world away on our walks. It's been forty-plus years since I felt that nowness. Even more than Keira, Ricochet is endlessly fascinated by the magnificence of nature. Every flower, every rustling variegated leaf of a tree dripping rain into a lake, every piece of moss or crawling insect, every butterfly and moth, and especially every bird or floating piece of paper, is an endless enchantment in his eyes, and in that moment also in mine. Meanwhile Keira sniffs the bird poo, and we're all enraptured together in nowness.

Coronavirus lockdown has just possibly, after all, brought with it some other silver linings in its intrinsic nowness. Families have been forced to live together in close proximity 24/7, and while undoubtedly this has brought problems and tensions to the fore, it has also shown us just how much family and love really matter to us. When many of us couldn't go to work, go on a shopping trip or holiday, go to the gym or social club, eat out at a restaurant or go to the pub, we have, I think, been forced to think of a simpler time. Perhaps we have been forced to think for the first time in our lives about how we really interact with each other, with animals and with our planet. We have looked out for our neighbours and colleagues, but it's also been important to rejoice in the innate bond of love we have shared with our animal companions – which I think makes us more human, more kind, compassionate and empathetic, and maybe even more content being in nowness with them. We need to remember this connectedness, because we do indeed share one planet, and when all this is over, I really hope we don't forget that profound interdependency in the hubbub of everyday life.

In joy and in sadness, in good times and bad, animals can teach us so much about being completely and totally *present*. When you come home after a long hard day and your cat scurries around your legs or your dog licks your face, you and you alone are their only focus at that moment. So, next time, stop – put aside thoughts of what's in the fridge, or that email you forgot to send, or who has been horrible to you today – and take a moment to just fully experience the pleasure and awakening of being fully *there* with your eager four-legged friend in the beautiful and boundless nowness. It is there for you every single day of your life, right inside you all along, if only you can stop for a moment and dive straight in – with a paw ready, willing and able to hold your hand on a magnificent journey of discovery.

CHAPTER THREE

Truth and Trust

'Politicians should trust people with the truth.
Very often, we don't do that.'

Leo Varadkar

Truth and trust are the fundamental pillars upon which all
meaningful friendships and relationships are built. Truth is
the lifeblood in the body of trust: without blood there is no
life, without body there is no action. Without truth and trust,
no life or action will ever be worthwhile.

In a world of fake truths, alternative truths, half-truths
and outright lies, we often lose faith in public figures whom
we should trust the most. We've become almost immune to
people in positions of power moulding the truth to suit their
purpose – thereby negating trust, while sowing coercion and
fear. The pursuit of power and money has become the foundation stone of everything from politics to gang culture: in
a society where prejudice and bigotry have trumped honesty
and tolerance, our politicians prey on the insecurities and
isolationist paranoia of the few and ignore the greater good
of the many. Gang culture, meanwhile, is often the default

resort of young people yearning vainly for meaning, leadership and some sort of misguided validation. Hatred and violence have replaced love and integration as knife crime, drugs, prostitution and human trafficking become a currency for 'trust among thieves'.

In my profession as a surgeon, the bond of trust with my patient and client is the most sacred currency I possess. In my life outside of my vocation, on the other hand, I have sometimes fallen short. Hand on heart, I can't say that I have always been absolutely truthful with myself or others in the past. Trust of my own judgement as well as trust in people has always been difficult for me. In this regard, I doubt I am alone, but I am trying to learn and be better.

It's not surprising that being bullied at school and having some challenging childhood experiences left me wary of the motivations of others. As a result, I lost all trust in human nature and seemingly the truth didn't matter, because even when I reported the bullying to the Patrician Brothers, it just got worse. For me, therefore, school became a prison. The joy of learning and discovery was overshadowed by unremitting emotional and sometimes physical pain. My heart would collapse as I walked through the gates each morning. I knew I just had to respectfully serve my time and hope for better days when I could fly free in some other sky, in some other place and time. Unfortunately even when I left home for university, I continued to struggle with forming trusting friendships. While my fellow students enjoyed the social scene, I still lived a fairly lonely, insular life by choice. For the first couple of years of veterinary school, all I did was cycle to and from the campus, practise karate and study. Not the most promising start for someone with the dream of changing the world and standing up for all of the animals on earth.

In confronting my challenges with trust, I look once more to Keira and Ricochet, because I believe that animals can teach us how to be honest with ourselves and others and how to trust again, even when we have been badly let down – or we have let ourselves down. As far as I can tell, a normal domestic cat or dog doesn't lie about how they are feeling. Keira and Ricochet tell the truth all of the time and they trust me implicitly, as if their life depended on it – because it does – as do the lives of every animal I have ever operated on. 'Daddy, I'm hungry, I look to you for food; Daddy, I'm feeling vulnerable, please cuddle me; Daddy, it's rainy and I don't want to go for a walk, let's sit on the sofa instead; Daddy, I peed on the carpet and I look at you for tolerance; Daddy, I prefer this big sparkly ball of foil to you right now – deal with it!'

Unless conditioned by our behaviour to distrust us, in my experience dogs and cats usually trust us implicitly as their guardians. Conversely, for a dog who has been brutally beaten and slept in its own faeces for two years, it will be really hard and possibly take many years to relearn a different truth and regain trust for humans. For us, too, if we have been let down, it can be really hard to trust again. The pain of betrayal can be so unbearable that our whole world closes. I have been on both sides of this equation in the past – I have been let down and I have let down. My relationships with humans have been a million times more difficult than those with animals, no matter how much patience and understanding that animal needed. But most difficult of all has been my relationship of truth and trust with myself, which is something that remains very much a work in progress.

The dogs and cats that I have met in my practice have only ever been truthful with me about how they feel. They may be timid, affectionate or angry – but they always tell the truth, and usually their emotional responses are legacies of their previous conditioning. Every single animal patient that has ever looked at me before being anaesthetised has had to place their absolute trust in my actions as a surgeon, and I have learned from their example that their trust demands honesty. Some may say I'm crazy for even thinking that – but I believe that the dogs and cats I operate on have feelings and thoughts and are sentient. I recognise that their guardians have made a choice to trust me in signing the consent form, as for paediatric human patients – but I believe that if a vet or vet nurse is empathetic and receptive to sentience, then a bond of intuitive rather than cognitive trust can be formed with the animals themselves.

In the space of a single week in 2019, in my professional capacity, I met a politician on the election trail; a social worker dealing with knife crime and drug culture in London; and a prisoner who was feeding chickens in HMP Guys Marsh in Dorset – an intriguing snapshot of varying personal approaches to trust and truth. I felt that the politician was pulling a curtain over the truth to garner my trust – because of his charitable work with animals, I think he assumed that he would have my loyalty, that I would consider him honest and that I would respect him. He didn't have my loyalty; I didn't respect him, nor did I consider him honest; I suspected he had been using the ostensibly charitable endeavour to further his own agenda and he had clearly learned nothing at all from the animals he had purportedly been helping. That's the first thing about respect and trust – they can't be bought by influence and favours; they can only be earned with time and effort. Baboons know this instinctively in the wild, and our companion animals from hamster to horse know it too.

I empathised with the social worker who was trying to win the trust of teenage boys to explain the truth that gang violence and drug dealing are unlikely to make for long-term happiness. I had hoped that there might be some way to teach these boys a different kind of trust and truth by talking to them about what I had learned from my relationship with dogs, which I hoped could become their experience too – one born of loyalty, respect and honesty. It was these three qualities that the social worker and I would most have wanted these young men to aspire to, but their circumstances were really tough. They were from broken homes and living in poverty, often in an environment with heavy drug use where crime and corruption were the norm. We wanted them to be loyal to themselves and be honest about their futures, and it would take courage and self-respect for them to venture outside of the approval that they craved from their loyalty to their gangs. That's easier said than done, however, when truth and trust are conditioned so adversely by your environment and peer group.

I was making *Animal Rescue Live* for Channel 4 when I visited Guys Marsh, a Category C men's prison in Shaftesbury. The heavy industrial gates on giant hydraulic arms, the high concrete walls and reinforced-steel barriers that blocked out the light, all topped with a daunting two metres of vicious razor wire – it was an ominous setting for altruistic endeavour. I had never been inside a prison before, and as I passed through several security checks I looked up at the tiny patch of sky still visible between the cell blocks and didn't want to imagine what it might be like to be locked up inside. I was meeting three prisoners whose job was to look after the chickens. They were the lucky ones – they got to see the clouds, breathe fresh air and care for fellow living creatures.

The chickens had been rehomed from factory farms and the eggs they laid were used in the prison kitchens. As I chatted to these young lads, I couldn't help but smile at their obvious genuine affection for the chickens and I realised that they were ordinary men, just like me. They weren't heinous villains or abhorrent humans, but they had all made a series of really bad decisions and committed crimes which had led to this catastrophe. They had betrayed trust and truth in themselves and those around them, and had paid the price with their freedom.

I empathised here too, because truth and trust with yourself above all else is what matters. I have in the past hit a brick wall when I wasn't honest with myself and lost my self-respect and loyalty to my personal principles, and so although I've never done anything illegal, I have certainly crashed and burned. I have learned that if I can't trust myself to do the right thing with decisions in my own life, then I can't expect truth in life generally. Truth and trust don't exist in a vacuum – I have to tend them every minute of every day. Like for the chickens, wholesome eggs don't appear by chance, but rather because of careful husbandry.

Later, I received a letter from David, one of the prisoners I had talked to during the day. He had just been released and wrote that the day I had visited was the best day of his prison life, because I treated him with kindness and respect. I'd like to think that that's how I treat everyone, and so thought nothing of it at the time. He wrote that the chickens had brought him joy and peace and a chance to feel some normality; these animals had depended on him and it had helped him regain his self-respect. Looking after them had also allowed him and the other prisoners to break free from the frustration of confinement, but it had also been a welcome release from the prison of themselves. David also thanked me for *The Supervet*, which he said served him well 'behind the door'. That's all I could have hoped for being 'the Supervet' – that it could shine a light in even the darkest of circumstances.

The wonderful actor Tom Hardy, whom I first saw in a play in London in 2003 with my dear friend and mentor Malcolm Drury, once said, 'I look both ways before crossing a one-way street. That's how much faith I have left in humanity.' I concur. And perhaps even more so today – with the kind of exposure that comes with being on television, I remain sceptical about people's motivations. Television puts you in the spotlight. People are suddenly curious about your personal life, your sexuality, your partner, how much money you make, and what kind of underpants you wear. It's all madness. No wonder then that I seek refuge in the company of animals – after all, my patients couldn't care less if I am gay or straight, whom I kissed before or after them, whether I'm prince or pauper – they sense the truth of who I really am, and quickly learn to trust me or not.

It seems that it's human nature to want something from others, whether or not it is offered or they are ready to give it willingly. People who give of themselves with their time and their attention through pure altruism are rare. 'What's in it for me?' is the more common attitude. Apathy and distrust make us guarded and selfish – that's alarming I think. Cats and dogs on the other hand give out unconditional love and trust readily, unless we give them a reason not to. I believe that most animals and humans are not born bad; rather our character traits are innately giving and truthful, and shaped for good or for bad at a very early age by our interactions in the world.

I have loved the veterinary profession all my life, since I first saw Mr McInerney, the local vet, ministering to the animals on the farm where I grew up. I believe that we are extraordinarily lucky to be the guardian angels of unconditional love in companion animal practice, and I have done and will do all that I can to uphold our good name in society, which is why the RCVS case hit me so hard. If they adjudicated that I was not acting in the best interests of my patient, the ultimate price of trying to help Hermes would be losing my licence to help any animal at all. It was a deeply personal attack and it was painful to realise that people wanted to destroy the very thing that was my lifeblood, coursing through my arteries and veins, just as the soil had been the lifeblood for my farmer father. The complainants' perceived truth was directly opposed to mine and there was no trust in what I, Hermes' mum Helen and the primary care vet passionately held to be true – in following this truth, in the midst of this accusation, I had consequently lost all trust in my own profession.

My own scientific and surgical truth has certainly changed as I have continued to learn and gain more experience. When I make a diagnosis, I take a careful clinical history and I examine every patient as a holistic whole. If the guardian says that he/she thinks it's, say, Freddie the Labrador's back left foot that's the problem, and Freddie is holding his trembling back foot off the ground – should I jump straight in and say, 'Ah yes, Mrs Smith, I can see you are right; perhaps there is some toe arthritis or a nail-bed infection.' No. I examine all of the facts to find my own truth. Because of experience, I have a Rolodex of possibilities in my head and a toe problem isn't highest on my list; in fact, Freddie might have an ankle cartilage problem, a knee problem such as a rupture of the cranial cruciate ligament, hip dysplasia or perhaps even a degenerate disc protrusion in his lower back impinging on a nerve root. Appropriately channelled experience changes truth for the better and strengthens trust. For me, making a diagnosis is all about trusting in experience, knowing that I'm sufficiently skilled at what I do and always doing the right thing for the patient, and for society, according to my oath.

Truth isn't only the very essence of surgical decision-making – it's fundamental to scientific endeavour. In my experience, it's not only ethics, but also evidence and efficacy which are not spoken about often enough in veterinary consultations. If Keira or Ricochet were to be operated on, I'd want to know all the options, how many such procedures the clinician had performed, their success rate and level of general or specialist training, and details of the aftercare provision – and I'd also expect total transparency with regard to costs, whether the intended surgical practice is owned by the same group as the primary care practice (an internal referral) or a different group (an external referral), and if there's any incentive to refer to one place or another. That's truthful and that's trustworthy, but in my experience it doesn't always happen.

Nowadays, I perform many revision surgeries following lots of different treatments that have not gone according to plan. Failure can happen in any surgery, but I feel strongly that if we talk about ethics and morals, the conversation needs to go beyond advanced procedures and look at all procedures, including some considered routine. I might question the decision-making, for example, in cases where I have placed custom knee replacements because a specialist surgeon or primary care clinician has operated several times with suboptimal technique and implants for the rupture of a cranial cruciate ligament. We need to consider all such situations from the point of view of all animals, and sit at the table with RCVS, with mutual loyalty, respect and honesty, and be fully truthful with each other, safe in the trust that all veterinarians absolutely have the best interests of their patients at heart and are not motivated by being on television, by money, by 'trying something new', or by any other incentive that I or others could be accused of. Let's get it all out in the open, because that's what the animals we are dedicated to serving would expect us to do, in my opinion.

Perceived truth is only as good as the trust you have in the person offering it. How many of us believe everything that is written in newspapers or on the internet? Only we can decide who or what to believe in – but the most important person to believe in is ourselves. In our personal lives, most of us try to surround ourselves with people we trust who are telling the truth. Sometimes people surround themselves with 'yes people', or people who encourage us on a path incongruent with our core values, which is a recipe for delusion and disaster. What if the truth changes? If one finds out that the people one thought were 'true' actually had an agenda, and weren't who or what they purported to be? I have seen this happen for friends who are prominently in the public eye and it's happened in my own life, too, both before but especially after I came into the public eye.

Herein lies the crux of the dilemma of trust in medicine too. In medicine and science, what we hold true today could be disproved tomorrow. Likewise, the truth of what might be considered the best treatment in a given circumstance may change over time. The inevitable evolution of medical practice today gives rise to new truths through evidence of

87

efficacy and ethical adjudication at an often astonishing rate. There are many in the veterinary profession who see what I do as too much, too soon; but I predict that, over time, the techniques shown on *The Supervet* will gain acceptance anyway regardless of the critics and the 'old truths', because the animals and those who love them need solutions for their medical challenges – solutions we can provide today. After all, in terms of medicine generally, who exactly determines the 'truth' and how much trust we place in it? Is it the scientific publications on evidence and efficacy? The truth as politicians or lobbying groups ascertain it? Is it the guardians or family members of a child or loved one, or of a dog or cat? Or the human and veterinary medical professions, regardless of what the guardians and society think?

This is an ever-moving target since evidence is being updated constantly as other newly discovered facts come into play. Nowhere has this been more evident than in the rapidly evolving knowledge regarding the coronavirus pandemic. As the global crisis unfolded, we listened as the experts expounded new theories on this novel disease, only for them to be debunked week by week. When different medical specialists, epidemiologists, vaccine and treatment manufacturers and politicians all have their own perspectives or unspoken agendas, it is extremely difficult to know whose truth to trust.

The body of knowledge we have today surpasses that of ten months or ten years ago and 'the truth' has been transformed. When I founded Fitzpatrick Referrals my dream was to build the greatest veterinary hospital that had ever existed for the care of animals, where we would offer all of the options to all families all of the time. This wasn't about buildings of bricks and mortar built with a bank loan, stress and a sleep disorder – this was about people with honest minds and hearts. I modelled my endeavour on that of Dr William Worrall Mayo and his sons Charles and William James Mayo when they founded the Mayo Clinic in 1914, a world-renowned American centre for treatment and re-search in human medical care. They were among the first to recognise the value of 'super-specialists', because no one person can know everything or do everything well, which is why Laurent operated on Ricochet and not me.

Charlie Mayo wrote: 'Probably the most interesting period of medicine has been that of the last few decades. So rapid has been this advance, as new knowledge developed, that the truth of each year was necessarily modified by new evidence, making the truth an ever-changing factor.' The truth was 'ever-changing' in 1910, so I feel it's reasonable to infer that it is still changing 110 years later. As his brother Will Mayo wrote, 'We think of truths as ponderables capable of being measured and weighed, but introduce a new fact or a new thought and a new truth is developed.' But perhaps it is their father Dr William Worrall Mayo who should have the last word: 'The sum-total of medical knowledge is now so great and wide-spreading that it would be futile for one man to attempt to acquire, or for any one man to assume that he has, even a good working knowledge of any large part of the whole [. . .] The best interest of the patient is the only interest to be considered, and in order that the sick may have the benefit of advancing knowledge, union of forces is necessary.'

I concur with Dr William Snr that union of forces is neces-sary, and the most favoured union in my eyes would be that of human and veterinary medical cooperation through One Medicine, where we trust each other to do the right thing for each other and the greater good, for that can give rise to more rapid evolution of many truths concerning the causes and effects of disease.

I don't suppose that anyone who has had life-saving cardiac bypass surgery, limb-saving knee replacement, stem cell treatment, cancer drugs or a new spinal disc bemoans the advance of human medicine, or thinks very much about all of the animals who gave their lives in experiments to give us these advancements. That's an unpalatable truth of progress. An even more unpalatable truth is that no progress can happen in clinical veterinary practice unless someone is Patient Number One. My life's purpose is to give animals a fair deal in return for all they have given to us. As such, I have long been an advocate of studying everything that has ever been discovered in experimental animals and the humans they have helped, and giving domestic animals in real need with real disease the benefit of these same medical advances. In 1946 dogs were given shoulder replacement surgery as an experiment to help humans, but didn't get shoulder replacements to help their disease until I carried out the procedure on a dog called Suzie in 2010. Of course it wasn't the first one, though it's listed in *Guinness World Records* as such, and I got praised by some and criticised by others for giving a dog that option for her debilitating shoulder arthritis.

Everyone's truth is ultimately down to interpretation of the 'facts' and your trust in the source. In treating naturally occurring cancer, infection or arthritis, for example, using the best techniques so far developed and incrementally improving them, veterinary clinicians can learn more and can share this information with other veterinary and human patients affected by those same diseases, so that in the fullness of time, we may reduce, refine and replace many of the experimental models of today with a self-informed clinical

cycle of information. This is the very essence of One Medicine, by which both animal and human patients win. If we
use technology developed over many years, and 'tweak' it for
the next patient, this is an act of 'recognised veterinary practice' (RVP), and not an experiment – rather it is an evolution
in treatment for that particular disease and, as we learn, all
patients win. Nevertheless, I get equal criticism and praise
for this approach: criticism for what is deemed by some to be
'experimenting' on clinical patients, and praise from others
for trying to find a solution for animals in pain or dying. This
is what real life is like being 'the Supervet'.

My own perception is that everyone's 'truth' in such a
scenario is different and is shaped by their belief structure –
and all I can do is live according to my own truth and invite
any of the critics to come and observe me in consultations or
in theatre for a few hours to see if their 'truth' can perhaps
be revised with more information. Of course nobody would
want their child to have an implant or a drug that wasn't
deemed safe, so for many years the paradigm has been that
treatments for humans depend on testing on animals to
prove efficacy and potential toxicity. Modern technology now
allows us to look inside an animal using high-resolution CT
scans and blood tests to determine outcomes that before now
required the death of an animal. It may therefore be possible
to interrogate the treatment of naturally occurring disease
in animals as a model for human disease without having to
give that disease to an otherwise healthy animal and then
kill the animal. However, herein lies the misconception – if
human medicine does learn from experience in veterinary
medicine, that does not make the procedure performed on
the animal in veterinary practice an experiment.

I have discussed the challenges associated with the ethical

governance of both routine and advanced surgeries in veterinary medicine with many colleagues, most notably Professor
Matthew Allen from the University of Cambridge. He and I
strongly feel that the use of an implant that is an evolution
of previous thought, designed with an expectation that it is
superior to previous implants because it overcomes or avoids
their limitations, should not be considered experimental as
long as the procedure has undergone ethics review and is performed by an appropriately skilled surgeon with the informed
consent of the family. The consent process should involve a
detailed explanation of alternative treatment options, the
potential risks of the procedure and the qualifications of
the surgeon performing the surgery. This transparent and
comprehensive approach is the best possible way to leverage
lessons learned in both veterinary and human patients, and
to apply that knowledge and expertise to the care of the next
patient, animal or human.

Veterinary implants do not currently need to undergo
the sort of detailed regulatory review that is required by
mandate for human implants and as a result new commer-
cial implants are introduced into the veterinary market all
the time without robust data on the performance of that
implant, or stringent oversight of the credentials of the
surgeons implanting the new device. While most surgeons
are absolutely diligent about weighing up the risks before
using a new implant, it is our opinion that the use of any
new implant should be subject to ethical approval and
appropriate certification of the surgeon performing the procedure. The clinical outcomes from these early cases should
be documented and reported on an ongoing basis to confirm
safety and effectiveness. Only then can we really know if
the new implant is living up to expectations and only then

is it fair to all surgeons, all implants and all patients.

It is not an experiment to undertake the first procedures with a new implant – this would only apply to radically new surgical techniques or materials. In those situations, a more comprehensive legal and ethical framework should be adopted, similar to that used to evaluate new pharmaceuticals such as cancer drugs or arthritis medications. Such a new treatment should be part of a prospective clinical trial, as it would be in humans.

To date, human medicine has generally not allowed knowledge gleaned from the clinical treatment of a dog or cat affected by disease to act as an appropriate precedent for human patients. Human medicine largely ignores the model of naturally occurring disease in animals. For the last 200 years of human medical advance, it has been a legal requirement for drug or medical device manufacturers to carry out most safety and efficacy testing through experimentation in research animals. The results of these experiments are often not shared in full with the veterinary profession, or converted into treatments for veterinary patients, because it is more lucrative for a company to sell the intellectual property and know-how to human medicine than giving access for veterinary use from the outset. It is conceivable that veterinary and human medicine could progress as One Medicine, with less requirement for animal experimentation; however, the governing bodies would need to agree a legally tenable pathway to protect safety and efficacy for human patients, and the implant and drug companies and their shareholders would need to be convinced that doing so would be equally, or more, profitable. In addition, human life is valued higher than animal life overall, and therefore most money is spent developing implants and drugs for humans, not for animals.

93

However, I feel that the tide is changing and with increasing acknowledgement of the value of dogs and cats in our lives, society will demand the highest level of medical care for animals as intrinsic family members. And for me, the best chance to advance veterinary medicine is through a general acceptance of One Medicine – an honest two-way street of information exchange between human and animal medicine that truly benefits the animals too.

I first met Denise and Peanut the kitten in April 2015, both of whom had challenges with trust and truth. Peanut's mother was feral and had given birth in a hole in a disused shed. She had left the scene and Peanut was trapped in the bottom of the hole, unable to climb out because his front legs were affected by a severe growth deformity. His cries attracted a passer-by who took him to a rescue centre. The local vet understandably and justifiably advised euthanasia because the truth was that Peanut's limbs were unsalvageable. The rescue centre, however, did not wish to euthanise him.

Denise had been treated for cancer and had had multiple surgeries, including to remove disease in her lung. There had been many complications and the chemotherapy had been horrendous. She was broken, directionless, robbed of her independence, dreams and passion for life. She'd had to give up work and, unable to deal with her incapacitation and their fractured relationship, her husband had taken a job abroad. Before his departure he had flippantly told Denise that she should rescue some kittens, one suspects because he felt they might help her fill a void. Denise did just that and it turns out that it was the best thing she ever did.

Five kittens arrived from the rescue centre in one basket and in another was four-week-old Peanut, and Denise was asked if she could look after him too. Peanut was a little black-and-white mischief machine, and having been born with a deformity that meant he didn't have functional wrists (carpi) on either of his front legs. Both front feet curved and collapsed inwards, held only by residual sinews of what should have been his tendons and ligaments, so he was shaped like a peanut and he dragged his floppy paws along the ground as he gamely tried to scurry along on his forearms, the paper-thin skin getting thinner and weaker with every scuffle. That didn't stop him trying, though: he was up for all kinds of adventure and had the heart of a lion, but now his limbs were completely messed up: there was no muscle over the ends of the pressure points where his stumps rubbed on the ground, so he was beginning to develop pressure sores.

Denise was well equipped to take in the most challenging, dysfunctional and debilitated animals because she had been a nurse and was blessed with a giant heart made of solid gold. She convinced herself that all six tiny furry creatures would take her mind off herself and fulfil her need to nurture, when of course she needed rescuing every bit as much as the kittens.

Two days after Peanut arrived, Denise was smitten and took him to the local vet who said that Peanut had only two options – euthanasia or a miraculous surgical intervention – and since the latter did not exist, he recommended the former. Denise was wary that she was already too emotionally invested, and yet she couldn't bring herself to put him down. She was also aware that Peanut's survival had somehow become inextricably linked to her own. This, of course, is never a good reason to keep an animal alive in spite of their suffering, and Denise knew that too. She might have lost her heart to little Peanut, but she was also rational and determined. Very determined.

Denise took him to see another veterinary team and they together constructed splint bandages to try to protect his delicate skin, but also allow him the freedom that he demanded. Even though he was grounded, he ran full pelt up and down the stairs, on and off furniture and used the spiral staircase as his personal climbing frame. Even with the splints his feet were becoming scarified and bloody and it became apparent to Denise that he could not feel either front foot. The nerves had not developed properly. When she tried to crate him, he wasn't having any of it, sticking his poor legs out of the crate and banging furiously at the door in a real strop. He did not have his own best interests in mind – he craved freedom and as much mischief as possible. Once out of the crate, he quickly realised that if he stuck close enough to one of the other kittens, or one of Denise's other four cats, he could escape, free to explore the great outdoors – which in his case was a forest and a nearby quarry. Heaven for a growing, inquisitive kitten; hell for his deformed front feet.

Peanut was very affectionate and allowed Denise to persist with daily splint changes, but before long he developed an infection, which the vet tried to treat, using a baby grow to protect his limbs. No matter what Denise did, Peanut still managed to escape like a feline Houdini and the pressure sores on his carpi worsened. The prognosis looked hopeless, Denise was desolate, and her vet suggested that she bring Peanut to see me. She started a fundraising page on social media for possible surgery even before her arrival at our referral centre.

We have strict rules on fundraising because we don't ever want to spend people's money without utmost caution and it's important our practice isn't mentioned, so that every animal across the UK is treated with equal opportunity.

Further, it's important that people don't use the name of any vet, including me, to raise such money.

It was clear when I examined him that Peanut's paws could not be saved. Stump-socket prosthetics which are put on and taken off were not a good option because of his thin infected skin and his outdoors lifestyle. Limb amputation prostheses which were anchored to his skeleton were the only realistic option. To my knowledge, we remain the only practice in the UK performing limb amputation prostheses, in spite of us having carried out our first surgery more than a dozen years ago and having published a scientific paper on the results of the first-generation implant. Considerable improvements have been made since then which are constantly subject to scientific review and ethical governance, and progress has certainly been made. I suspect there are many reasons why the technology isn't more widely used. It is still considered 'experimental' by many veterinarians and the public, which is understandable because not many vets globally have performed the surgery. Most cats and dogs can manage very well on three legs and even some large dogs can function well. But some don't, and certainly no quadruped will fare so well with only *two* legs.

Then, there's the financial aspect of such surgery. At every juncture of Peanut's treatment, Denise had to defend her intentions to her well-meaning friends. There's the perception that because a procedure like a limb amputation prosthesis is expensive, the vet must be 'rolling in it', but frankly, orthopaedic surgeons make more profit out of performing routine surgeries quickly than can ever be made out of complex limb replacement operations. Why spend so much on one animal when it could be used to save so many vulnerable animals or children at home and abroad? Why spend so much money when a kitchen extension costs less? I grew up in Ireland in a rural community similar to the one that Denise lived in, where £30–40 was a huge amount of money and it certainly would not have been spent on a cat. The local farmers, including my own father, would have thought it absolutely ludicrous. They were struggling to make a living and were unlikely to pay for operations that would cost more than the value of the animal in question. Even today, most clients are not prepared to spend what it actually costs to perform a limb amputation prosthesis procedure. The cost of designing and fabricating the implants alone is prohibitive for some. In some ways, thought processes around the value of an animal and the surgeries that society considers acceptable have changed very slowly, whereas nobody would baulk at similar more advanced procedures in a human.

Denise told me that all of her neighbours and friends had significant reservations about surgery, either from a practical, financial or ethical perspective, all of them well-meaning and ultimately looking out for Peanut's welfare. Their view was that the surgical technique was in its infancy, would likely fail, and there would be too much pain and discomfort during recovery. Even if all of the concerns were true, and indeed any surgery could fail, Denise's friends and family did not know the actual facts, and had jumped to their own understandable conclusions. I'm not sitting in judgement here – we all do it, every day, about people we have never met or situations that we have never been in. Denise, however, remained undaunted – it was euthanasia or try her best for Peanut. She felt that he trusted her – and needed her – and she would have crossed the earth to repay that trust.

I am not for one second suggesting that I am a better or more talented or more knowledgeable vet than any of those who had seen Peanut before me or offered an opinion. The key difference, though, is that I do have experience with limb amputation prostheses and if I was going to have an operation on my wrist, I wouldn't be seeking out a specialist in gastroenterology. Different horses for different courses.

Denise discussed the possibility of a 'miraculous surgical intervention' with many vets and people concerned with animals in her rural community – equine, farm animal, small animal, farriers and rescue centres. Many were totally against any new 'unproven' techniques. Hip replacement was once unproven for cats but has now been shown to have excellent outcomes, even if some vets still disapprove, alleging that just removing the femoral head yields similar results, which has also been disproved, incidentally. Some pointed out that vets are obligated to 'do no harm' and argued that because prosthetic implants are currently unregulated and unproven, they therefore carry a huge risk and would subject Peanut to unnecessary pain and discomfort, even death, and would ultimately fail. That all may well have turned out to be true, but the fact is that unlike in human medicine, no veterinary implant in spinal or orthopaedic surgery is 'regulated' at present – any vet can use any implant at any time with or without a training course as long as he or she is providing the level of care that would be expected of another vet at that same level of expertise. Indeed, I have many times witnessed the consequences of surgeries performed badly after a one-day training course and have seen failure, unnecessary pain and discomfort, amputation and even death. There's no question that all vets have to learn, but the animal-loving public have a right to demand trust that we are telling the truth about what we are doing, why we are doing it and how often we have done it before. Then decisions can be made with integrity and transparency.

In the face of her well-meaning but sceptical confidants, Denise's argument was to query whether their objections to Peanut's limb surgery could also apply to her own invasive cancer treatment. Should Denise not have had a life-saving thoracotomy to excise tumour spread due to the risks involved and the extensive list of potential complications, not least the resultant pain and discomfort and the threat to life, especially given that she would die without the operation and may die even with the operation? She told me afterwards that the general attitude was that because she was human and Peanut was a cat, this anthropomorphic argument didn't apply and their 'perceived truth' remained unchanged.

Denise's neighbour, Stewart, for example, was a retired vet from the Department for Environment, Food and Rural Affairs (DEFRA), who trained in the early seventies. I have huge respect for vets like Stewart because like many of my mentors in rural Ireland, his generation were truly marvellous clinicians. I owe people like Stewart a great deal of gratitude for teaching me to look at the patient carefully and perform a thorough clinical examination using all of the senses, rather than just reaching for the next blood test or scan. Stewart had grown up in the era just when antibiotics were becoming available, and, in fact, at that time in the seventies in his part of the world, no vets dedicated their practice to small animals; they worked primarily with large farm animals, attending the occasional smaller animal alongside. Plates and screws and rods inside bones were relatively new technology for dogs and cats back then, and Stewart was very concerned that the potential 'new' technique proposed for Peanut would ultimately cause harm, because it was metal sticking out through bone and skin and therefore prone to infection. He is of course correct, and forty years after his career in veterinary medicine was beginning, that is exactly the challenge that remains today, a problem myself and others have fervently sought to conquer. On this basis, therefore, he did not feel that the technique was justified. That was his truth, and I respect that.

Another friend of Denise's, a vet student, felt that the procedure was unethical because Peanut might experience undue pain and suffering like animals experimented on with implants who are promptly euthanised. To my mind, this was the more disturbing view, since veterinary undergraduates are the future, and yet I have heard this from them again and again: i.e. it's fine for an otherwise healthy animal to undergo 'controlled' pain in an experimental procedure testing an implant or drug in a trial, then be euthanised, so that it can be of benefit to humans, but it's not all right to perform what they see as 'untested' surgery because an animal might suffer. The irony is that vets supervise animals in both scenarios. And none of the undergraduates who have expressed this opinion to me have ever actually seen a skeletally anchored limb amputation prosthesis.

How, then, can the veterinary profession make advances in treatment? Should we test implants on experimental animals with induced disease so that those who really have the condition can then be treated? Or simply not move forward as a profession and watch while human medicine advances? Of course we need an ethical framework – no rational person would ever argue otherwise – but were these opinions valid enough for Denise to decide against Peanut's operation? If Peanut was going to die anyway, should we have put him to sleep right away or try to save him using a tried-and-tested technique of which I had ample surgical experience? Would we deny this choice to a human patient? No. Therefore, what if human and animal medicine worked in tandem and advanced hand in hand – one informing the other so that we could have ever better implants?

The veterinary profession has some big decisions to make about access to and regulation of new technologies. Transparency is needed on the manufacture and standard of the implants, the standard of training required by the treating clinician, and also on which patients can have access to which implants. For example: whether it's more 'ethical' to fully amputate the leg of any dog or cat, regardless of size, or should the guardians have the choice of a limb amputation prosthesis? Should there be different guidance for animals with slower healing like tortoises, where it can be perceived that they may 'suffer' for too long during recovery?

In other areas of orthopaedics, after taking a short course should non-specialists be allowed to perform advanced surgery? How is 'advanced' defined – is it the physical nature of the implant or technique, or even a simple implant relative to the less advanced skill of the surgeon? Is there a difference between the skill level of non-specialists with hundreds of hours of hands-on clinical experience and newly graduated specialists? (I myself was performing advanced surgery as a non-specialist until I took my specialist examinations in 2013.) Trust is generally based on evidence and evidence generally based on best perceived truth at that moment in time. What is deemed 'ethical' or 'unethical' by an expert regulatory board would necessarily become the perceived truth and society would need to be able to trust that truth. But, as I have explained, to my knowledge such an expert regulatory board hasn't yet been formed for companion animal veterinary medicine anywhere in the world. I for one would most welcome it.

At that point for Peanut, in the absence of an ethical guidance or adjudication panel, however, the stark reality was that if a solution to his situation could not be found, he would soon die, and so I proceeded to discuss all practical and ethical aspects with Denise and gave her some time to make her final decision and also a while longer for Peanut's infant bones to grow.

The dilemmas we face in veterinary medicine regarding truth and trust are not dissimilar to those in society at large and in our personal lives. Whom can we trust and are we ourselves worthy of others' trust? These are questions I ask myself daily. Ask yourself, are you prepared to change your mind about yourself or anyone you know if further evidence became available, and would you be willing to look at that evidence?

Everyone's truth is different – it all depends on perspective – but many never choose to reconsider the facts and change their beliefs either because they are blinkered or biased anyway, or because they feel that their firm opinion will not be changed. Nevertheless, it is my belief that anyone can and should be prepared to do so. Even though I truly believe that I always act in the best interests of my patients, and would be hard pushed to give up some of my most strongly held beliefs about a fair deal for all animals, I am still prepared to listen to rational and impartial arguments as to why I might be wrong.

They say a leopard doesn't change its spots – which is a physiological fact – but we are not leopards, and we *do not need to be* our thoughts. We create our own thoughts and beliefs which then prompt us to do and say things that ostensibly make us who we are. But we can choose to take control, change our thought process and change our truth – even change who we think we are, and who others think we are too. Think about what you'd like to change, and trust yourself to make your own new truth. No matter how painful change is, you need to constantly remind yourself whether the pain of not changing is worse. *You* are all that you've got and *you* can make that change. If being or doing something makes you unhappy, if you regret not doing something, if you are constantly criticised or taken for granted by your friends and it hurts you, then you and you alone have the ability to make a 'miraculous personal intervention'. Find a plan and a purpose that work for you, and keep focusing on a realistic goal that motivates you to do whatever it is you really want in your heart. Be 100 per cent honest with yourself, take personal responsibility for your thoughts and your actions. Change your truth. Exercise more and eat a healthy diet, take up that sport you might be good at, learn to play guitar whether you'll be good or not, register for a part-time course and work towards a degree that really makes you feel worthwhile, or cherish being allowed to travel again post-coronavirus and see all of the places you have ever wanted to see. Be who you really want to be, not who others see or who you try to become to please them. Find the child full of endless possibility inside you. Learn to dream again. Force yourself to find new friends and only surround yourself with positive people. Change your truth. Today if possible.

When I was trying to change my truth about myself, in the midst of a significant emotional crisis, I sat up in bed one night at work and read David's letter again. By his own admission, he had lost trust in himself and lacked truth which had led him to commit a crime that had landed him in jail. Soon after his release from HMP Guys Marsh, he had faced coronavirus lockdown with the rest of the world. He wrote that he was very grateful for the world we live in and even for lockdown and rejoiced in his freedom to look at the sky from his garden, to be able to see over the fence. He said he was making plans to climb Mount Everest. He felt that every dream he'd ever had was now possible, because when he was behind bars in the dark despair of self-pity, he had realised that he had to seek inside himself to figure out his core values, rather than look to others for some kind of affirmation. In confinement, he'd had to face the truth of his actions and of what he had become – and in so doing he'd arrived at a new truth. He knew what he had to do to become a better person for his victims, his family, and ultimately in order to trust himself again.

I learned a lot from David. Facing up to the truth is really hard, but if I can't be truthful to myself, then how can I expect others to trust me and what I perceive as my truth? Every worthwhile dream becomes possible through trust that change for the better is achievable and absolute truthfulness with ourselves about our core values.

Michaela gifted me two large goldfish for the pond at the back of my house which, barring occasional sightings of Noel the Newt, had been uninhabited for the past twenty years. I named my fish 'Truth' and 'Trust'. Just knowing that truth and trust are real, and that I'm looking after them, helps me to cope in the prison of my own head too. I'm happy to report that they are thriving – all they need is a few crumbs of goodness from me every day for them to flourish.

CHAPTER FOUR

Empathy

'If you judge people, you have no time to love them.'

Mother Teresa

Animals don't care about our race, colour, religion, sexuality or political leaning, or even if we smell. In fact they may prefer it if we do smell a little. I believe that dogs and cats have the ability to feel what we are feeling and that they tap into our inner core – what really makes us tick – in a way that many humans find impossible. Humans on the other hand find empathy a challenge, and yet I believe it is the key to an ethical life.

Empathy is the ability to walk in another's shoes – the capacity to imagine and understand what another creature, animal or human, might be experiencing. It seems to me that in the world we have created, empathy for our fellow man is in short supply – and even less in evidence from us for any species other than our own, *Homo sapiens*.

Homo sapiens is Latin for 'wise man', and was first used to name the human species in 1758 by Carl Linnaeus, the father of species taxonomy. In fact, 'archaic' *Homo sapiens* is the term for Neanderthal man and we have somewhat arrogantly termed ourselves *Homo sapiens sapiens*, or very wise men, although perhaps it would be more apt to recategorise us *Homo stultus* (foolish man), *Homo pravus* (immoral man) or *Homo egoisticus* (which needs no translation!).

Whenever something doesn't suit our self-centred agenda, our morals go out of the window. Lack of empathy fuels hatred, prejudice, injustice and man's inhumanity to man and animal. I believe that we should look to our animal friends, from whom we would see and learn a greater degree of fairness and compassion for each other and the world around us. Natural habitats have an inherent equilibrium, which we disrupt through our pursuit of domination and financial gain, and our blind affiliation to the ubiquitous aphorism that 'more is better' – more land, more produce, more consumption, more wealth – so we continue to decimate and degrade rainforests, pollute our waterways, fan wildfires and shrink the polar ice caps. Worse still – in the eternal pursuit of more for ourselves, we end up with less for our children, and much less for the animals whom we drive to extinction as we edge our shared planet ever closer to meltdown.

We only have to look at social media platforms generally to see lack of empathy made manifest. I often wonder if the social media trolls would be so thoughtless if they ever met their victims face to face, but that's precisely the problem with the medium. In that disembodied, strangely impersonal world, the troll can say bad things or insult someone with impunity. In the moment of firing off some text, there may be lack of empathy towards the personal feelings of the human being at the receiving end of their cruelty or criticism. However, I catch myself and wonder what must be going on in the lives of these people to prompt such thoughts and I try to take a moment to empathise with their circumstances, conditioning and perceptions, regardless of how differently I may see the world.

I think if we all had a pause button on our phones and computers that was bigger than the send button, and if it froze the screen for just a few seconds before we fired something off which we might regret later, that would be a good thing. I know that I have in the past sent reactionary emails which I subsequently regretted. I now try really hard to walk away from the screen, to 'put myself in their shoes' for just a moment, and then respond in a more coherent and respectful way. Recently I walked away from my computer to the bathroom to take a pause mid-email – which was, let's just say, 'quite stern'. While I was gone, Ricochet must have walked on my keyboard and pressed the 'x' key for a very long time. Having contemplated my message for a minute in the toilet, I came back, unwittingly lifted Ricochet off my desk, where he often roams or reclines, and being happy that my sentiment was appropriate, I just pressed send. About five minutes later, I got an email back to say the recipient was sad that I didn't agree with him, but happy that I still loved him – Ricochet had put a hundred kisses at the end! His big paws had inadvertently pointed me towards empathy in the most emphatic way.

Of course, I'm a realist – and this is the real world of 2020 – so if one wants a social media presence at all, which is in fact necessary for business and life for most of us nowadays, then all one can do is join in the zeitgeist and hope to create some positive noise amid the dull humming and the superficial world of naysayers. Of course, in the greater context, social media bullying is but a blip on the scale of our global challenges with empathy. Around the world, people are persecuted, tortured and killed because of differences over culture, religion, sexuality and race, and it has always been thus. Despite every country in the world signing up to a commitment to the Responsibility to Protect (R2P) at a UN summit in 2005, obliging states to protect all populations from genocide and ethnic cleansing, day after day in Myanmar, Rohingya Muslims are being killed in huge numbers, their women are raped and their villages burned to the ground. Kurds are decimated in northern Syria and ethnic cleansing continues in South Sudan. On our own coastline here in the UK, refugees from all over the world come in dinghies to seek asylum, clinging to their last vestiges of hope and humanity, broken and exploited, trying to make a better life for themselves and their families. They are human beings just like us; they could be our sister or our brother; they may have been doctors, teachers, lawyers or mechanics; they may speak multiple languages; or they may have been a world-class football player in Iran, or a brilliant pianist in Afghanistan. We don't know because few of us stop to think about the lives these people might have led in their home country. These faceless woes are not going away anytime soon – and for better or worse I do think about these things often. I frequently check myself before I say I'm 'having a bad day', when in fact, I have nothing at all to complain about by comparison with many people the world over. I'd like, if I can, to try to disseminate some kind of empathy for our fellow man through the only currency I know – which is the love of animals. I'm not sure how I might do that yet, but writing it down here is my first step.

In my vocation I try to quell the battles waged by my patients' biology, to bring peace and harmony where there is anarchy and discord. I see each and every day in my consulting room that animals teach us humility and under-standing; in being kind to our canine or feline friends we somehow become kinder to each other. I have never met a truly bad and evil person who really loved a dog or a cat un-conditionally and received that love back. Animals can teach us humility, understanding and empathy for them and for our fellow man. I often find myself wishing that we could learn from the compassion we feel for animals and apply the same high standard in our relationship to our fellow humans. If I could translate the loving kindness I see in my consulting room every day into a common global language, there would be no bigotry, prejudice or hatred – only empathy.

The horrifying footage of the unlawful killing of the American George Floyd sent shockwaves across the globe. Millions saw for themselves the true optics of racism – a black man forced to the ground, a white police officer's knee on his neck, other officers watching on, and all ignoring his repeated and vain appeals of 'I can't breathe'. George Floyd's killing didn't just grab our attention, it captured our emotion and resonated profoundly with our own sense of well-being. And in case anyone is in any doubt as to whether this could happen here in Britain, we should remember the deaths of Sean Rigg, Wayne Douglas, Christopher Alder and Ibrahima Sey, all of whom were killed while in police custody, and all in our own backyard. I count some police officers among my friends and feel really fortunate to live in a society where I truly believe that most police officers, like vets, want the very best for those entrusted to their care, and do their best to look after all of us. However, there's no denying that this is our world, a world that we intimately relate to, where in-stitutional racism remains real and tangible in many walks of life. Whatever any of these men may or may not have done, bad or good, they were human beings with red blood coursing through their veins. These were real lives and this is all happening during our lifetime. 'What can I do? I'm only a vet,' I might say. 'What can I do, I'm only a shopworker,' someone else might say. If we all say that then we have learned precisely nothing about empathy from our past.

Parallels can be drawn between how we treat each other and how we treat animals. We are a nation of animal lovers and I think we could become a nation of human lovers too, with social policies that make a real and tangible difference to racial, religious and sexual prejudice for all our brothers and sisters. I consider Ricochet and Keira my brother and sister. When Ricochet jumps up on my knee and pushes his nose in my chin for a kiss, I tell him I love him and I shall look after him forever. When Keira licks my face, I tell her I love her and always will. When was the last time you or I told a human whom we deemed 'different' to us that we love them? I hear the phrase 'it's only a dog' or 'it's only a cat' all the time, while it seems to me that across the world there's an unspoken prejudice against humans of other 'types' and we may as well say, 'It's only a human.' Surely when one of us is hurt, we are all hurt? When one can't breathe, none of us can breathe?

My fellow countryman, the statesman and philosopher Edmund Burke, said that, 'The only thing necessary for the triumph of evil is for good men to do nothing.' Like many Irishmen before me, Edmund Burke included, I chose to make my home and pursue my endeavour in the UK. I feel deeply fortunate to live and work with colleagues of all nationalities in a country where the majority of people are doing the best they can most of the time. I am deeply grateful for being allowed to build my dream and to work with so many good people with strong ethics and unwavering empathy for the animals and the families we serve. I sincerely believe that my small band of brothers and sisters can and do make a difference by changing things for the better for thousands of animals and their families, and, through *our* TV show, we have positively influenced the lives of animals and humans alike through a common currency of empathy.

Empathy itself falls into four categories: cognitive, affective, emotional and somatic. Cognitive empathy is the ability to understand another's point of view and place yourself in their shoes. Affective empathy is the ability to understand how another person might be feeling and respond appropriately. With emotional empathy, on the other hand, you not only understand how the other person feels, but you feel the same emotion – you feel distress at someone's pain, or happiness at their joy, for example. Somatic empathy, meanwhile, means that you can actually physically feel what another may be experiencing, someone else's pain, or their blushing embarrassment, say. I know of people who in different geographical locations have simultaneously experienced similar physical pain or tears when a sibling, child, parent or friend has been hurt or injured in some way. This physical reaction is probably based on mirror neuron responses in the somatic nervous system. I have also seen innumerable people cry in my consulting room, and often not tears of distress or even of self-pity, but rather tears of empathy for a much-loved animal friend in pain. This is a good thing – it makes us more human.

I have experienced somatic synergy with all creatures since I was a child. When Ricochet had ear pain, extraordinary as it may seem, I felt I had ear pain too. That's a completely mad thought, I know, and it was certainly my imagination, but it seemed real enough to me at the time. I remember the first time that I felt an acute empathy for animals. Growing up on the farm, the role of animals was functional: Pirate's job was to round up sheep, cats were there for rodent control, cattle were milked and eaten, our sheep were bred or were eaten, and horses were ridden. Daddy would often scold me for being 'too soft', saying I needed to 'harden up'. When I found some kittens nestled deep in the hay shed, I empathised so strongly with their crying that I secretly sneaked in to feed them every morning and night with fresh milk from the cow that Daddy milked for our table. My father hadn't found out until they were frolicking around the barn and it was too late for him to do anything about it. I remember too, however, crying my heart out after I heard the plaintive cries of puppies in a sack being drowned by a man whom I choose to forget because I can't find any part of me that can empathise with him. I guess there are times when cruelty, malice and evil of our fellow man is of such magnitude that one can't possibly relate to it understand and empathy proves impossible.

I have never been able to bear the perceived maltreatment of any animal. My daddy was kind to the animals, he wanted the best for them and he loved them. I saw him comfort a stricken calf with a broken leg, bottle-feed a lamb for months and hold another hypothermic lamb in the open kitchen oven and rub the sides of her chest gently to warm her up. But he was a farmer, and I grew up surrounded by the 'functionality of farming'. On one occasion, for example, when I asked Daddy why we had to beat the cattle with sticks and pitchforks to get them into the lorry, he simply replied, 'Sure, they're not going to go to the factory themselves, are they?' Later during vet school I spent compulsory time 'on the line' in a meat factory, and it must be said that for the first several years of my career I made my living as a vet primarily from farm animals, which in itself was a noble calling. But I was still 'soft'. I have always felt the pain of animals – and of humans – at a deeply visceral level.

I am always worried about my patients and the more complex the surgery, the more I worry. Every animal and every person who loves that animal is intensely vulnerable in the moment of the decision on whether to proceed with a difficult surgical intervention or to amputate or euthanise. A clinician must seek first to understand before they are understood, and when presenting the options to the guardian, as rationally as possible, they should always take a moment to express that they care wholeheartedly, and are acting with sincerity and commitment. With the kinds of surgery I perform, which can be 'last chance', the option for euthanasia is sadly often included in this conversation. In fact the greater the empathy in a given situation, the more significant and far-reaching the interaction. If empathy and ethical decision-making could be internalised at every level of society, becoming ordinary everyday values . . . well, what a world that would be.

When Denise brought Peanut back to my consultation room for possible surgery, it was not an ordinary day and Peanut was not an ordinary patient. It would not be an ordinary consultation. When I had first examined him in April 2015, he had been seven months old and so his bones were not developed enough for surgery. Denise had done her best in the interim and dressed his wounds for four long months. Now at eleven months, the radius and ulna bones in Peanut's forearms were fully grown and the growth plates had closed, but his stumps were in a really bad way. He scuffled around my consulting room on them, with his little crumpled paws folding inwards, covered in sores, bleeding and oozing pus due to infection.

Denise was close to tears and I could see her pain, fear, anxiety and love pour out to her little helpless friend. She was in a deep state of somatic empathy with Peanut. She was in bits and he was in bits. I was also in bits as I put my arm around her shoulders to comfort her. I sensed Peanut's frustration with his disability and his absolute commitment to carry on. He was full of life, seizing every moment as an opportunity for mischievous fun, albeit while struggling with, and dramatically mutilating, his crippled paws in the process. He was a gutsy fighter – a survivor if ever I'd seen one.

The challenge for any clinician in such circumstances is to try to be rational and compassionate. One empathises with the emotional predicament of the guardian, but one's moral and ethical responsibility rests always with the patient. Would surgery or euthanasia be the best option, especially given that bilateral application of a skeletally anchored amputation prosthesis was not an established technique? Which choice is most ethical? How would any technique become 'tried and tested' without Patient Number One? As Will Mayo said, 'The best interest of the patient is the only interest to be considered.'

Did I have the moral right to rob Peanut of his ostensible desire to battle on when the technology existed that might provide an excellent quality of life after a period of recovery? Conversely, was it my moral duty to put him to sleep, as the complainants said I should have done in Hermes' case? The inherent risk of surgery notwithstanding, would recovery be any more prolonged, challenging or painful for Peanut than if he had a more tried-and-tested procedure like a total hip replacement, for example? One of the challenges in Peanut's case was that I couldn't give Denise a percentage chance of success, since I had never performed such surgery on two front legs before, and, to my knowledge, nobody else had either. In addition, the proposed implants that were to be used were next-generation, designed to be even better than the earlier version, but still unproven. Seven years previously I had performed the surgery on two back legs in a cat called Oscar. But that was entirely different because Oscar still had use of the ankles (tibiotarsal joints) of his hind legs, so his implants at that time were simple rods inside the main ankle bone (calcaneus), called an Intraosseous Transcutaneous Amputation Prosthesis (ITAP). Amputation prosthesis implant technology had progressed considerably since then, and so the implants we proposed for Peanut were entirely different. Rather than a rod inside the bone, myself and my team had developed an implant called a Percutaneous Fixation To the Skeleton (PerFiTS) that is anchored to bone using plates and screws in addition to a rod inside the bone. This next-generation implant was designed to avoid problems encountered with earlier iterations. This wasn't a revolution or an experiment; this was iterative incremental improvement, the way medicine has always progressed.

It was impossible to compare Oscar's operation with that planned for Peanut. Technological improvements are driven by past experience, both good and bad, and sometimes this includes clinical failures. Oscar had enjoyed normal mobility for four years after surgery, until one of his ITAP implants had become infected and failed. We subsequently replaced this implant with a PerFiTS in his shin bone (tibia). Seven years after the original surgery, the second original ITAP implant broke. A full decade later he is still running around on the PerFiTS implant in one back leg. Without Oscar being Cat Number One to receive PerFiTS, the huge strides made in understanding the design, fabrication and implementation of the implants in order to best mitigate against failure would not have been possible. Now Peanut would become Cat Number Two for double amputation prostheses, but the first to have this performed in the front legs. It has always been thus in any medicine, human or animal – we do our best, we operate with full disclosure, honesty and ethics consideration, we learn and we do better next time. How has progress ever been otherwise? Denise knew very well that the implications and consequences of not trying would be that Peanut would die. Our veterinary oath is 'do no harm' but would we do more harm by leaving him as he was to suffer, by putting him to sleep, or by attempting surgery using all knowledge available to date? Denise was very clear that if he was suffering at any time after surgery without reasonable hope of recovery in an acceptable time frame, he would be put to sleep. If Peanut were to be operated on, he would rise on Oscar's shoulders and the shoulders of all the other animals in the previous decade that had been operated on with earlier iterations of technology. I had succeeded and I had failed – and I was honest.

To the average person, a bionic leg is a bionic leg. Or as one young boy called Flynn said to me recently when I told him some people didn't approve, 'I don't know what all the fuss is about, Noel; it's only a bionic leg in a cat.' To him and his generation this is obvious. However, not all bionic legs are the same and the technology has improved considerably since the early exoprosthesis models that simply fit like a sock on a stump on the outside, and which aren't anchored to the skeleton at all.

I explained to Denise that the endoprosthesis implant designed for Peanut would need to have two plates – one anchored to each of the radius and ulna bones of the forearms. There would be an abutment region, which was a platform on which the paired bones would sit. Under this would be a hemispherical dome of specially coated porous metal mesh – the dermal integration module (DIM) – onto which the skin would be attached and should permanently grow. The pore size and architecture of this mesh are vital and since cat skin is thinner than dog or human skin, the shape and pores must vary accordingly. Extending out through the skin would be the spigot or rod, onto which an exoprosthesis would be attached. Together the endo- and exoprostheses constituted a next-generation bionic leg. The endoprosthesis was intended as a permanent implant, while the exoprosthesis could be removed and replaced as the bearing surface wore out, rather like new brake pads.

Denise needed to decide if she could trust my ethics and capabilities as a surgeon and if I had empathy as a human being. She later confided that she had met another of my clients with her dog in my waiting room. The client was acutely dissatisfied and was complaining loudly that my treatment had not met her expectations: the 'last chance' operation I had performed on her dog had failed and she cautioned Denise against entrusting Peanut to my care. Sadly, as I have said, any surgery can fail, however ordinary or extraordinary: for most of the advanced procedures that I perform, the complication rate is no higher than for that in my more routine surgeries. However, expectations seem somehow heightened when one attempts extraordinary interventions, and the sense of disappointment also tends to be intensified – another reason why many surgeons choose not to perform such procedures. One has an easier life and more sleep-filled nights if one avoids the learning curve for complex surgery, which takes many years. I read not long ago about a human doctor being vilified in the newspapers because his mortality rate for heart surgery in babies was among the highest in the UK. What the papers omitted to mention was that he was one of only a handful of surgeons prepared to operate on babies for whom this potentially life-saving intervention was sadly their only chance of life. They didn't praise him for all of the babies he had saved. Not very empathetic – but such is the world we live in.

I am pretty open with people about how disappointed and upset I get when I have done my very best for an animal, yet I fail. I am most certainly not infallible and I continue to try to learn all I can every day from both my successes and failures so that I can do my best for my patients and impart this knowledge to future generations. The biggest lesson I can teach trainees is to have humility – because biology will most certainly humble them too. Denise has always been very frank with me since we first met and has variously described me as 'grumpy, curt, exhausted, disillusioned, charming, buoyant, ebullient, thoughtful, pensive and kind or a mixture of all the above'. In my defence, though, apparently I was 'always professional and focused on the task in hand as a life's purpose with ridiculously long hours', and 'compassionate and sensitive, yet robust and driven, albeit slightly bonkers!' Phew – I'm glad she got to that bit.

Denise left Peanut with us that day for tests to determine if surgery was possible. Later that evening, I called her to discuss the results of CT scans and also electrodiagnostic tests to assess nerve function in the lower and upper parts of the limb. The CT scan told us his paws were dramatically deformed: some of his wrist (carpal) bones had not developed at all from birth. The electrodiagnostics revealed that he had no sensation in any part of his forearms below his elbows. His front paws were therefore unsalvageable. He could move his elbows using the muscles higher up, but the lack of nerve function in the lower limbs meant that he couldn't even feel how much damage he was doing to his stumps as he tried to scurry about outside. Implantation of limb amputation prostheses appeared to be medically possible and offered Peanut a realistic chance of regaining functional use of his front legs.

I have often heard mentors of both veterinary and human medical students admonish them for becoming emotionally invested in their patients' well-being and outcome. In my opinion, to a reasonable extent that's how it should be. I don't believe in 'detached medicine', a scientifically sterile medicine based only on rational thought; instead I believe that animal and human patients benefit not only psychologically but also physiologically from emotional care alongside physical care. One should empathise with the patient and hold their hand or their paw when comfort or reassurance is needed. In other words, an empathetic interpretation of circumstances can invariably help inform the path to recovery.

Everybody who has trained to become a veterinarian or a doctor has paid a huge price in time diverted away from living a 'normal' social life. For my own part, I often wonder what might have happened had I chosen a different career. I would likely have children and be financially better off had I not taken the route I have, which has exacted a considerable physical and emotional toll, not to mention the significant ongoing financial worries (quite contrary to popular perception).

I have received generous praise for success and profound criticism and threatened lawsuits for failure, while all the time caring desperately and trying to do the right thing. Sadly, being 'the Supervet' isn't so much about sipping pina coladas as it is about filling in paperwork and, when necessary, defending myself from accusers, detractors and critics. As medical professionals we are expected to be empathetic to our clients' needs, but in my experience it's very rare for a guardian (or in the case of a human doctor, their patient) to ask about our needs. Having a few letters after one's name doesn't make one immune to feeling disappointed, frustrated, angry, inadequate and sick to the core. We are human and we have emotions too. Perhaps this is a contributory factor in the high depression and suicide rate among medical professionals and especially vets. That's the reality.

Thankfully I am now joined by a team of colleagues with whom I can share the work, and my hope is that, over time, I'll make myself redundant as my physical ability declines because everything in my head and heart will be in theirs. I know that I'm not the most patient surgeon with myself or with my mentees and I need to work on that, but I sincerely hope they will be patient with me and empathetic enough to stick around until that day comes. I also have realised that to pass on what is in my head requires more than just telling and showing – I need to demonstrate more empathy and try to see things from the mentee's perspective. Surgery cannot be learned from a book – hand skills and surgical judgement take time to develop, so patience is needed on the part of both teacher and student. I need to get better at delegating, standing back and observing, rather than always stepping forward and doing. This is easier said than done, though, when clients decline treatment by a pair of hands other than my own. Sadly, however, my hands will not keep going forever and a degree of acceptance for both prospective client and surgeon will hopefully become apparent over time.

The next generation who choose the path of advanced surgery will need to deal with the same challenges I have, and will in turn also need to take on board that empathy is not always a two-way street between client and medical practitioner: sometimes the pain of failure can go hand in hand with the pain of client grief or, at worst, of threatened legal action. I also sincerely hope that transparent discussion of these challenges will help future generations of vets to innovate without fear of professional jeopardy. A better balance must be struck between the need for clinical documentation and the need for clinical innovation. Expectations and protocols for clinical audit and ethical review should become more uniform and streamlined so that they can be more broadly accepted by both surgeons and the families of animals. It would be a real shame if fewer animals were able to get access to cutting-edge treatments that could significantly improve their lives simply because of overwhelming bureaucracy. It's tempting to lead a less stressful life operating routine high-revenue cases with limited follow-up, to not have difficult conversations with clients, not publish evidence for efficacy, not advance techniques, and not worry about what other people think, but that doesn't move veterinary medicine forward.

These are ongoing challenges for me, for my team, for my colleagues in the profession, and for future generations. I strongly believe that we need to embrace and regulate innovation, because that's what I believe the guardians of animals want. I am prepared to bet all of my professional credentials and all of my effort to date on one simple truth: people don't care *what you know* until they know *that you care*.

In my experience, empathy is by far the characteristic of a medical professional that people value most highly. I have known of the most underqualified medical professionals who people love and recommend to all of their friends because of their 'bedside manner', and I have known of the most talented surgeons who are technically brilliant, but nobody trusts them and nobody likes them because they have a 'God complex', and their ego is often perceived to be more important than the patient's well-being. In their view, emotions don't cure anything – it's all down to them! Not to take this too far, clearly a hip doesn't replace itself through love, nor does a displaced fracture heal itself through karma, but I've seen lots of instances in human medicine where positive mental attitude has helped people to get through cancer, cope with bowel disease or calm down a skin problem. Of course, where mental dysfunction comes into play, emotional comfort can really have a huge impact.

For dogs and cats recovering from a physical ailment, it's very important that they don't feel isolated and suffer from social symptoms such as separation anxiety or suppressed hyperactivity which may manifest later as a behavioural problem. Frequently I've seen an inpatient develop a particular liking for an intern, nurse or ward auxiliary and they will only eat or go for walks when that person is there. Their environment and compassionate care during recovery absolutely has a bearing on their outcome. When I designed the practice, it was to my knowledge the first time a referral hospital in the UK was built without any cages – instead we installed compartments in the wards with Perspex doors, underfloor heating, radio and even television, so that the surroundings would be as much a home away from home as possible – all with a view to enhancing healing. As I often say, 'Hugging is half of healing.'

In our everyday life, empathy may not come easily. It may be impossible for you to immediately empathise with where a friend, co-worker or even sports team colleague is coming from when he, she or they behave in some way that's unacceptable or unpalatable to you. It may be difficult when your partner is bad-tempered or seemingly hurtful. Empathy is not easy. How can we possibly see things from the perspective of another if we haven't stood in their shoes? I concede that here too I am still a work in progress; in fact, initially I found it impossible to empathise with the people who accused me of malpractice in treating Hermes the tortoise. I simply couldn't see where they were coming from at first, but then I read some of the publications that the complainants had written in their careers and one of my clinical colleagues, with my blessing, invited one of them to come and give a lecture on their perception of ethics and what was deemed 'overtreatment' to myself and my entire team. I have always been willing to listen to anyone's perspective and still am, as are all of my clinical colleagues, many of whom were present. Consultant surgeons Professor Nick Bacon, Dr Jonathan Bray and Padraig Egan discussed their experiences openly with the complainant and encouraged active dialogue in the context of the broad range of surgical treatments available for companion animals throughout the UK, many of which were unknown to the complainant, who was no longer working at the coalface of clinical practice. Opinions were sharply divided in the sense that I and my colleagues remained open-minded to the advancement of twenty-first-century veterinary surgery, even if the complainant disagreed in this particular case, and, while the complaint remained deeply hurtful to me, I could at least try to open my mind to their truth. The empathetic perspective of the complainant towards Hermes led them to the conclusion that euthanasia was the only appropriate route forward. Their mind could not be swayed on this, and my colleagues and I did our best. We didn't agree, but we could at least try to empathise.

Over many months, since the bombshell regarding the RCVS investigation, I have made a daily effort to practise empathy with everyone I interact with, from client to work colleague, to cameraman for the TV show, to business associate – and it's surprised me how calming this has been, even if I'm the first to admit that I haven't achieved perfect equilibrium in all cases despite my efforts. I think at some point probably all of us have held ill feeling towards what others have said or done; for how they have treated you or others; for their meanness and lack of generosity; or for their evil, self-centred, greedy, arrogant, aggressive, violent, or abusive behaviour. Or maybe it's just a sibling or friend who has taken you for granted once too often, or frequently sought favours and then not been there for you on the rare occasion that you needed something from them. What I've found useful is to try to let go of all preconceptions and reel back time to when I didn't know that person. I try to imagine meeting them for the very first time and focus with all of my heart and mind on that moment. I let whatever sounds, thoughts, feelings and smells that arise just flow through me and I try not to linger on them. Even if this moment only lasts a few seconds, I try hard to imagine what that feels like. And then as soon as I can, I hug Keira or Ricochet and channel that feeling of all the love, compassion, joy and hope into meeting that person for the first time. This may not work for you, but I've found it helpful.

Then I try to imagine that the person I'm thinking of could change their ethical map. Perhaps they feel some remorse for their behaviour? Usually I've never asked them. Maybe I haven't spoken to them in years? Maybe the molecules of affection I once had for them are still in the air somewhere and could be recaptured if only I could find a box in which to contain the pain and the hurt that's happened since. Maybe I could try to see it from their perspective, no matter how painful that may be, for even one or two seconds. Maybe they are fundamentally good and they were led astray by money, lust, power, greed, conceit, anger, jealousy, malice, or were just misguided. To heal and allow myself or yourself to move on, perhaps you or me simply need to create a tiny space in our souls where empathy and forgiveness might be possible, and let go of the anger and hurt. Maybe you or I never speak to them again, and maybe they will never change – but in trying to empathise at least what I've found is that it makes my world better, and that can only be a good thing. Perhaps trying a similar approach might make your world better too.

Denise and I had consulted many times in person and by phone over several months while Peanut attained skeletal maturity and we got his infection under control. I empathised with her perspective regarding wanting to try her best for Peanut amid all of her own health struggles, but like all vets, I am the advocate for the animal and we only proceed with surgery when it's in the patient's best interests, as I've said before. Peanut's fate was still in the balance as Denise and I discussed again the potential implications of proceeding with his limb amputation prosthesis surgery and his uncertain long-term prognosis, should Denise decide to go ahead. I could only do my best, but it *was* possible.

By coincidence, surgery was undertaken on Denise's birthday, 20 January 2016. I never tell people the time of surgery because it puts too much psychological pressure on the guardian waiting for the phone call, but also on me. Denise told me that she had a very strange feeling at twenty past four in the afternoon. I picked up the scalpel at around that time, a form of somatic empathy perhaps. I removed Peanut's front feet and wrists, and inserted the plates of the endoprosthesis implants up along the radius and ulna, screwing them to both bones. I stitched the muscle and tendons down to the abutment, and then prepared the skin, which was pulled down like a cuff over the DIM and then repeated the process for the other leg. These endoprostheses would later be coupled to exoprostheses (his prosthetic feet, which were like rubber bungs on the bottom of pogo sticks). The endo- and exoprostheses together were his new bionic limbs. Worryingly, though, there was very little muscle on the right forearm, and so the metal would be directly under the skin, but I did the best I could.

When I called Denise later that night, she told me that everyone involved with the fundraising for Peanut's operation had been waiting with bated breath. I learned later that about 1,800 of the group – people from across the British Isles, Australia, Germany, the Netherlands, Spain, France, Tunisia, Canada and nineteen states of America – had lit candles, prayed and sent their love and support to her that night. Someone commented that the astronauts on the space station might have been able to see the constellation of candles burning for Peanut that night on Earth.

Peanut recovered at the practice and I changed his

bandages every day, until I was confident that the skin had healed adequately and risk of infection was minimal. He didn't appear to be in any discomfort at all after a couple of days since surgery, and already he was so sprightly that he wanted to jump and run. I was a little concerned that the skin would always be tightly adhered to his bone and metal on the right forearm, but those were intrinsic anatomical constraints, and I could only work with what I had. When Denise arrived, he immediately tried to jump up onto the table to his cat carrier. I issued strict instructions as I always do – no running, no jumping, no slipping, no sliding, and crate rest at all times.

Peanut was thrilled to be home but abhorred his jailed status and rebelled, stamping his new 'paws' in a belligerent staccato and sticking his legs out through the bars of his crate. Denise was understandably worried that he would damage his skin further, so she ordered a polyfibre-fronted crate and slept on the floor with him until it was delivered. Even when it arrived and he could no longer stick his feet out, there was no respite because Peanut now had his very own polyfibre drum kit which he bashed incessantly with his rubber-bung feet, simultaneously caterwauling like a singer in a very bad rock band. I took pity on poor Denise and allowed her to take him out for periods on a lead, first indoors and finally outdoors. This idea of 'controlled' exercise was laughable to Peanut – he was literally bouncing off the walls with his new pogo sticks. He had tasted life without pain and with functional legs. Freedom beckoned and he was raring to go.

As soon as Denise let him off the lead, he was out of the door, and shortly thereafter I received a miraculous video of Peanut frolicking among the jagged outcrops and shrubs of the quarry, bouncing like a pogo-cat from mossy rock to leafy ledge. He was a Peanutter! I say miraculous because it truly was awe-inspiring, but also terrifying – because I'd never had a patient on two bionic front legs before – and given that it would take about twelve weeks for the bone to grow onto the endoprosthesis, he was testing the implant to the max. Peanut was not exactly the most compliant patient, but I had considerable empathy with him – so Denise and I by mutual consent I let him get on with his life.

As with all scientific progress, we can do all we like with computer modelling, finite element analysis, kinematic gait predictions based on body weight, CT scan predictions of the likely bone implant interface loading strains – but when you see a cat ricochet around a quarry, that's a whole new level of testing! The proof of the prosthesis was in Peanut's pogo-ing! I hasten to add, however, that not all patients recover as quickly as Peanut, and some don't recover at all.

Sadly, more heartache was yet to come. About nine weeks postoperatively, Peanut stayed sleeping in his basket which was most unusual. Normally he was up and at the day as quickly as he could. Denise felt his right leg and it was hot to the touch. She instantly knew that the infection had returned and embarked on the long drive back to the practice. I was operating on another case when she arrived, so she dropped Peanut off with us and I called her later. Bad news. The original thin skin and pressure sores had healed but because there was no muscle or tendon between the skin and metal on the right forearm, when he lay down or scuffed the skin over the metal on the underside of the implant running through the rocks and trees, gradually the skin had perforated and the metal was exposed. Nature had taken its course and in spite of best planning and best intentions, sometimes bad things happen. I would need to reoperate to have any chance of saving the limb. Once again Peanut's life was in the balance.

One of the many challenges with advanced surgical procedures is that many people are not prepared to tolerate the costs of potential complications. Some argue that all operations should come with a guarantee, but then why would anyone endeavour to perform any sort of advanced surgery? With that model, most practices would be bankrupt if they did. I had done my best to keep the costs for Peanut as low as I could within the limits imposed by the finances of Fitzpatrick Referrals. Long before I pick up a scalpel blade to operate a case involving custom implants, I have to figure out a way to cover the costs of design engineering time and the efforts of my long-time collaborator, amazing engineer and friend Jay Meswania, without whom none of my advanced surgeries would ever happen. And then there's the cost of Fitzbionics, the manufacturing facility I set up some years ago, with magnificent machinists John McBarron and Dennis Jervis, who toil away at crafting the designs in metal and plastic. All team members are integral to giving Peanut the chance of a quality of life.

All in all, from sedation and CT scan through implant manufacture, surgery and ward aftercare, about forty of my colleagues are employed, from design engineers and factory machinists to nurses, theatre and ward auxiliaries, all of whom need to put bread on their table. The drugs, drapes, stitches, surgical gowns, scrubbing brushes, floor disinfectant, lighting, heating blankets and other invisible costs right down to the protective clothing that ward auxiliaries wear when dealing with infected cases have to be paid for. I was distraught when the skin over Peanut's implant broke down and I felt my failure keenly – perhaps I should have more empathy for myself.

Denise, however, was unerringly gracious. She empathised with my distress, but I have been in identical situations before where people were not so understanding. The biggest variables are not the biology, the implant, my surgical technique or the aftercare, but rather the biological response of the body and the emotional response of the guardian. One's professional reputation is only as good as the one case that goes wrong and which someone complains about – especially if one is in the public eye. It's easy for people to focus on failure and ignore hundreds of successes. Sadly, within myself I do the same – as I've often observed, I remember all of my failures and rarely rejoice in my successes.

We operated on Peanut one final time. I took another sample for bacterial culture and gently filed away some of the metal to make the abutment region of the implant thinner than we had originally planned. I flushed the area and moved skin across the hole over the metal from an area of the leg that had no metal beneath the skin using a skin-sliding technique. The hole thus created over the raw bleeding tissue would hopefully grow in with a scar by using appropriate dressing, whereas skin directly over metal has no blood supply from beneath and can't spontaneously heal.

The bacterial sample had cultured a bad bug, *Staphylococcus aureus*, and I was terrified that 'biofilm' may have formed on the implant. This is where the bacteria communicate in groups rather than acting as individual bugs, a phenomenon known as 'quorum sensing', which allows the bacteria to form an army to create a slimy shield to fend off any antibiotic. I was also worried, given that previous antibiotics had been used, whether the bacteria could have grown into resistant 'superbugs'.

After this second operation, thankfully the skin did heal and the bacteria were conquered. Soon he was back running in the quarry again, grabbing every golden nugget of time with his two bionic paws. Denise is aware to this day that there is only a sliver of skin to protect him from a new infection. Having recently been through another round of intense treatment for recurrence of her cancer, she knows only too well the fragility of life. Nevertheless, almost five years on from his surgery, the clumping of Peanut's feet as he strides into the house after his adventures and jumps up on her bed to rest on her chest continues to bring her hope and redemption. Denise has told me more than once that Peanut gives her the will to fight on; even when her cancer treatment is almost impossible to bear, and she feels like giving up, Peanut repays her faith just as she had faith in him. Their empathy for each other has truly saved their lives.

After Peanut featured in an episode of the *Supervet Revisited* on 9 July 2020, he received an outpouring of love on social media – many commented that he was a beacon of hope for the world in the dark times of Covid-19. It had been a long and arduous journey to ensure Peanut's ongoing zest for life, and I was absolutely delighted to receive a note from Denise's vet friend Stewart. He marvelled at how Peanut was now running around with his own inimitable 'swagger' and congratulated me on 'a job well done'. I gained such an immense feeling of peace from this one small expression of empathy. I am profoundly grateful to him for judging me by my actions over time rather than a perception forged in a moment.

As I've mentioned earlier, over this past year or so I've had cause to take a good long hard look in the mirror. I repeatedly ask myself if I have judged harshly and whether I would be willing to look at new evidence that might make me happier and someone else happier. Maybe you've had a similar experience? Is the basis on which you or I have made a decision about someone that is making us unhappy truly sound? Perhaps it is, perhaps it's not. If it is and they are truly bad people then we need to do ourselves a favour: empathise with the universe, forgive and let it go. If there is even a glimmer of hope that that person could in fact have acted out of character, maybe we should consider empathising with their feelings for a little while and try to make peace. I've done this more than once this past year and it's really brought me some inner peace and understanding, which I badly needed. For it is only by finding peace that we become peace, and it is only by finding love that we become love.

The love between Denise and Peanut has brought peace, redemption, happiness and ultimately salvation for them both. That is the power of empathy. I believe that hope, faith, love and belief are at the very core of empathy and that we can learn all of these things from our animal friends. It might just be that all the crazy animal lovers aren't the crazy ones after all, and that the salvation of man's inhumanity to man might come from a most unlikely source – man's humanity to animals.

CHAPTER FIVE

Genuineness

'Knock, And He'll open the door. Vanish,
And He'll make you shine like the sun.
Fall, And He'll raise you to the heavens.
Become nothing, And He'll turn you into everything.'

Jalal ad-Din Rumi

Greatness without genuineness is like rain without water. It doesn't exist. To be genuine is to be authentic, the real deal, without hiding your true motivations or feelings behind a facade. It is being yourself without pretence, being truthful and sincere in your dealings with others. A genuine friend is the one who is there for you in good times, and in bad. In the same way, you don't see a dog or a cat being nice to you if they don't want to be. If a dog or a cat doesn't like you, you know it – and the friendship work is all down to you. Dogs or cats are incapable of pretence. Their love is true.

However, I wonder how many of us, if we are really honest, feel we are surrounded by genuine people most of the time? Or can look in our own hearts and truly say we have been mostly genuine ourselves? But what if we could always be ourselves? Wouldn't it be fantastic if we could say to the world, 'This is who I am. This is me – take it or leave it'? That's what you get with a dog or cat and I wouldn't have it any other way. Having Keira and Ricochet in my life is a privilege. They remind me every day and in every single way of genuineness. They do not judge me for working late or being in a bad mood, nor do they judge me because of how I am dressed, or what colour, race, creed or gender I am. They are authentic with me and I with them; they accept me for who and what I am completely. We share an ineffable bond of genuineness.

In my professional life I have to be genuine, because X-ray pictures do not lie. There's no room for sticking my head in the sand, because it's plain to see whether you have done a good job or not. Everyday life, however, is rarely so black and white.

Humankind, sadly, is not one body of equality, and some-what of an oxymoron in that sometimes we are not 'kind' at all. Prejudice and disingenuousness are all around us. If you are wearing a turban or hijab; have a shaved head, tattoos or a ring through your nose; if you are perceived as 'gender-strange'; wear a hoodie on an urban street; or if you are black in a predominantly white environment – everyone will have their own preconceptions about you. I've found sometimes that people might not be genuine towards me or allow me to be genuine myself without reverting to the stereotypes in their heads.

Why is it that as a collective we cannot look in each other's eyes and see beyond an agenda or a negative association with sexuality, gender, colour, religion or some other prejudice or bias that continues to be fostered by Western culture, populist media and social media? Instead, we fill our vision with mist and our ears with white noise. As far as we know, dogs can see colour, though with less of a spectrum than humans, and cats see different colours to us, and may in fact see colours humans cannot see. So, it's not that dogs and cats can't see colour – it's just that they don't discriminate against colour. It's not that they can't hear nonsense – they just know when you're telling them rubbish. They see right through your pathetic excuses for inaction or action. When I am not genuine with Keira or Ricochet, I am rumbled straight away and rightly shunned. In the extreme, when someone is cruel to an animal, they lock down and will never be your friend until you put in some serious work in rebuilding their trust. Maybe it isn't so much that animals can't talk, but rather that we don't listen. If mankind were more *animalkind*, we might live in a more genuine world.

There has always been hypocrisy and pretence, of course, but I think it's fair to say that, generally, even a generation ago, before the age of ubiquitous television and social media, people were more genuine. Perhaps the flip side of this is that there is the same proportion of genuine people as there always was, but it's more difficult to express oneself in a truthful way for fear of offending someone in our uber-sensitive world.

Sometimes, we all see the same information but we each filter it through our own foggy lens of prejudice and indifference. Through our complacent acceptance of a constant flow of half-truths and whole lies, we rarely even question whether what we are ingesting is genuine. I can empathise with this tendency, but it seems that the more sophisticated our communication devices, the less discerning the human brain has become and the more our herd mentality drifts further from any clarity over right, wrong and any genuine integrity.

What motivates people to be fake, it seems, is to appear more appealing to other people, from whom they want something in some way. Dogs or cats occasionally do this too, especially when there's a tasty treat on offer – but it's pretty obvious and harmless flirting.

Human disingenuousness is much more subtle, hypocritical and sometimes even malevolent. People might be all smiles to your face at social gatherings, then bitch about you the minute your back is turned, and we now live in a world of fake news and deep-fake videos where people alter their social media photos to look more attractive, post about their wonderful life full of glitz and glam, and even sell videos with celebrity heads on other people's bodies. To my mind this is a very strange world indeed, and if one spends too much time in this arena of fakery we can begin to feel less worthy, less successful, less attractive and less confident. It's no wonder then that among young people rates of depression, social anxiety and feelings of inadequacy are at an all-time high. I see this playing out every day; I work with more than a hundred amazing, bright and talented young men and women, and I see them comparing themselves to others and sometimes being unhappy in their own skin.

Ironically, when we try to make ourselves more appealing by being fake, people are actually less attracted to us in the longer term. Those who do their own thing, regardless of the opinions of others, are ultimately the ones who win genuine affection. We trust genuineness because people who are true to themselves are also likely to be more honest. We respect genuineness because being true to yourself requires emotional resilience, confidence and tenacity. Also, genuine people often exude individuality, and uniqueness is a deeply attractive quality.

As long as you're not hurting anyone, you have the right to be who you are. I battle with this, nevertheless, and have to remind myself all the time that I should always try to show my authentic self to others, whatever they may think. If people can't accept the genuine me, I don't really want them in my life anyway. In fact, I do realise that if I can't accept the genuine me, I am only fooling myself – and I will never be happy. Being genuine, even if you're a genuine human being at your core, is still difficult.

Many of us find ourselves in social settings where we are so out of kilter with the situation that we can't be ourselves. When it comes to close gatherings of people, I'm a bit awkward. I can't 'do' meaningless mingling, facades or small talk, so I try to avoid being in such situations. I'm more comfortable with just one or two people, a handful of friends or in the company of animals than with groups of people I don't know. I'm fine communicating in a professional capacity with my veterinary colleagues at the practice, or speaking at a conference, because I feel that I can always just say it as I believe it to be, and I'm also fine in a large crowd attending a concert for example. But I do suffer social anxiety and am afraid of saying or doing something that might offend or upset someone. There's always that little pigeon on my shoulder about to blurt out the wrong thing. Ultimately, I just like to be as genuine and upfront as I possibly can all of the time and that isn't to everyone's taste.

People generally know I'm a vet and have all kinds of preconceptions about what that involves. When I was a farm animal vet folks would say things like, 'What's it like to have your hand up a cow's arse?' or, 'I hope you washed your hands before you came to dinner.' Nowadays it's more like, 'Oh, my cat's got a bit of a limp; maybe you could crank out a bionic leg while you're here.' This is, of course, not a reflection of anyone being disingenuous but rather that we all have preconceptions of others, me included. Mostly it's innocent banter and I expect that a plumber gets asked about jammed stopcocks or a carpenter about the best value in shelving units. However, since I have been on television in recent years, I have become more sensitive to the preconceptions of people I have never met, because everyone has an 'opinion', and it's frequently neither accurate nor genuine in my experience. I find this difficult.

I am what it says on the jar of Marmite, and it's certainly not to everyone's taste. For some, because I'm on television I must be putting on an act. Some say, 'His ego's so big now that he needs an arena to fit it in!' The invisible keypad warriors have said some fairly hurtful things. I have never met them, and they don't know me or I them; I'm just doing my best. It's strange to me that someone might say, 'I hate how he calls people "buddy", and gets all familiar. Why can't he be professional?' when I'm just giving someone a hug if I think it's the right thing to do. I'm not attached to any purely material or fame-seeking pursuit, but rather trying to build a platform to help animals and those who love them. I'm upfront about it and actively welcome anyone who has a genuine concern to come and talk to me in person. I am what I am.

I probably border on the extreme of frankness and tend to say what's on my mind. I find it hard to suppress my real feelings and this has got me into trouble on more than one occasion. I'm also quite introspective. I've studied and worked on my vocation to the point of neglecting what most people deem 'normal life' because I'm passionate about what I believe in. I guess my desire to achieve a fair deal for animals could be described as a devotion bordering on obsession. But I make no apologies for that. It's genuine. I was told by a psychiatrist once that I might be a bit mad because I am a 'zealot', but I can't think of a single musician, artist, actor, surgeon or scientist whom I admire that wasn't or isn't equally passionate about what they do. I'll wager that the three men in the world of music and film who I'm most inspired by are all passionate and genuine – Dave Grohl, Hugh Jackman and Bono.

Sometimes raw genuineness is a tricky path to tread. I am often told that I'm too blunt or too honest. Not everyone can deal with a heart worn on a sleeve. Animals are cool with that and I think they prefer it that way, but sometimes people find it somewhat disconcerting in the world at large. Inside my practice, though, I am very lucky to be surrounded by genuineness all day every day. It's a blessing I shall never take for granted because I know how exceptional and truly wonderful that is. I have performed surgery on animals for both princes and paupers, for rock stars and for people with emotional scars, for magicians and for many with very little magic in their lives at all. To animals we are all either 'nice' or 'not-so-nice' humans and they don't care what our social status is. Genuineness in everyday life can sometimes be hard to come by, and for those who live their lives in the glare of the public spotlight it can be an even more rare and precious commodity. I think that's why many people in the public eye really rejoice in and treasure their friendships with animals. Some in the public eye have come to see me personally with their animal friend and each and every one seemed genuine, generous and with a heart of gold as far as I could see. Indeed, as I often say, it's very rare in my experience to meet someone who truly loves an animal who isn't at heart a good human being who exudes authenticity.

The thing about being in the public eye is that sometimes people just see what they want to see and judge from afar. Every day in my practice the animals help me, all of my colleagues and all of the people who come to see us to stay 'real'. When you're surrounded by genuineness, if you aren't genuine for one second, you stick out like a sore thumb. Some cynics may feel that what they see on *The Supervet* is different to reality for me and my close working team. It isn't. We remain genuine and exactly the same when we are in consultations and when we are in theatre operating, whether the television cameras are there or not. In fact, the camera has become a little bit like a friend or confidant for me, to whom I turn every now and then to explain what I'm doing, because I genuinely want people to know, and to make things better for animals and for medicine generally.

To say that I'm grateful to the three hundred families who have contributed to more than one hundred episodes of *The Supervet* would be a massive understatement. These people have been so gracious that they have welcomed us into their homes to chronicle their painful emotions as well as their joy and happiness, their hearts and souls. Without them and the animals they love, I wouldn't be in the position to write this book or have the chance to change anything much at all in my lifetime.

There is only one person in the world, though, without whom I definitely would not have had the opportunities I've been lucky enough to have outside my day-to-day veterinary work and publications. Radio and TV presenter Chris Evans has been a genuine rock for me since I met him nearly twenty years ago.

As I recalled in my first book, *Listening to the Animals*, I first met Chris through the spinal injury of his German shepherd dog, Enzo, whom he loved like a brother. Chris gave me a chance to achieve the first step towards my aspirations when he sat and talked with me in the small kitchen at my practice in 2008. On many occasions since, Chris has been there for me when I have most needed a friend. He took the pitch for my very first TV show, *The Bionic Vet*, to then BBC commissioner Jay Hunt. Jay had believed in me then and did so again when, as head of Channel 4, she commissioned *The Supervet* in 2013. Jay is now European creative director of Apple TV and I'm very grateful for her help and advice.

Chris's honesty and generosity with his audience, associates, colleagues, friends, family – and most of all himself – has been a great example to me. His humility, his endeavour at all times to get better, and his commitment to treat each radio show as if it were his very first have been important lessons for me too. When going through the stress of my hearing with the RCVS, his advice was, as ever, invaluable, wise and refreshingly down to earth: 'Why are you letting these people tell you how to feel? Tell yourself how you feel, and get on with it!'

When Chris announced he was leaving the BBC to work at Virgin Radio in September 2018, I was sitting terrified in a hotel room about to run technical rehearsals for arena shows that I had only just written, did not have a final format and had never been rehearsed with any crew at all. Not only was I trying to prepare for the show, I was also battling to meet the print deadline for my book, so there I was handing over a computer memory stick with more desperate last-minute writing and refuelling every couple of hours with vats of coffee wheeled through the hotel-room door. I was feeling more disingenuous than I'd ever felt in my life before. There were readers waiting on a book due on shop shelves exactly one month later which hadn't even been printed yet, and people with tickets for a show due to be performed in Hull exactly ten days later which was far from finalised. And I had diarrhoea – I was quite literally 'shitting myself'.

Chris had been at the BBC for thirteen great years and now he was going to join Virgin Radio. Here was a man with eight to nine million listeners to his *Breakfast Show* every morning moving to a digital radio station, when digital hadn't become the currency yet. He was going to make it the currency. On air he had told his loyal audience, 'If you get to the top of your favourite mountain and you just stay there, then you become a mountain observer, and I need to keep climbing; I gotta keep climbing.' And so it was – a genuine statement of genuine intent. I took his advice and climbed. I delivered as best I could.

A few months later in early 2019 Chris reached out and said in his usual nonchalant fashion, 'Oh, we're doing the show on Sunday; why don't you come along?' I did and that's how I ended up on the first Sunday edition of his new Virgin Radio show and was subsequently welcomed on all of the next six weeks' broadcasts called 'The Ministry of Now'. In the studio alongside Chris for three hours every Sunday was a masterclass in how to communicate with sincerity for the greater good, from a man who absolutely loved and felt privileged to do what he was doing. Each week I read three books on wellness and it was from this opportunity that the idea for this book grew.

I remember vividly my last day on the last show. I arrived at the studio having stayed up most of the night writing what

I thought I was supposed to be doing, which was a summary of all we'd learned over the six weeks. Chris sat on the sofa outside the studio, typically Zen as he always is before a show. He took one look at what I was proposing and said, 'I don't get it, Buddy. I genuinely don't get it. I was at the BBC for thirteen years, and for that you did a good summary at my leaving do; it was nice. But you don't need to summarise six shows – radio is genuine and it's now. You'll lose them after five seconds, and when you've lost them, they're gone.' In an instant I realised that it's impossible to be really great at everything. In spite of my best intentions, I had failed. I got by when I was an actor; I got by when I presented a radio show myself, and I get by writing this book – but just as true greatness is not possible without genuineness, to be really great, like Chris is, you have to put in genuine and consistent effort over many years. That's what it takes to be good at anything worthwhile.

We went into the studio and, as he always did, Chris stood up and held the microphone like it was the most precious gemstone on planet Earth – and then he started talking to the listeners. We did our bit: Chris, his right-hand man Vassos and a little bit from me. While the first song was playing and we were off-air, he sat back on his chair, smiled and just looked over at me and said, 'Well, you wouldn't hand *me* a scalpel blade, would ya?' No I would not. Chris may well be a brilliant radio presenter, but he'd be a liability in the operating theatre.

A few weeks later, I was back on his weekday show to talk about my first book and he was typically generous, but I was distracted and not on particularly good form. He asked if I was OK. I said I was. I lied. He sensed something was up and in his own inimitable perceptive way, he simply said, 'Mate, just bring the best version of yourself to every situation.' Chris couldn't have known that I was heading back to the practice to put a ten-year-old Staffordshire bull terrier cross called Jen to sleep. Jen was gorgeous, with a brindle and white coat, perky ears and big 'cuddle me' brown eyes.

Three and a half years earlier, I had operated on her with a commercially available elbow replacement system, but it had ultimately failed. With huge dedication from her mum Sharron, Jen had coped better with the implant than before the surgery, but her bone hadn't integrated as well with the implant as had been hoped and her elbow collapsed over time. She also had bad osteoarthritis in five other joints on front and back limbs, so she couldn't walk more than a few yards. Poor Jen was hiding in bushes in the garden and suffering. It was time to let her pass peacefully away. Jen and I had a special bond, because I had seen her so many times, and when she had been at the practice I would always try to go and say goodnight before I went to bed. And so, from trying to sound upbeat about my book on Chris's show, I headed straight back to hold Jen's paw as I gave her a final injection.

Jen had been rescued from the life of a breeding dog confined to the corner of a cement yard in Ireland. Caring for Jen along with her other dog, Tye, had helped Sharron through the break-up of her marriage and a catastrophic mental breakdown. The joy of anticipation of each new day with Jen had helped Sharron to cope one day at a time, then she had lost her job and hit rock bottom again. But still, she had seen Jen through her surgery and rehabilitation, sleeping on the floor beside her crate, crying and talking to her through the night. Sharron had been so profoundly depressed that she didn't want to leave the house, but Jen's genuine enthusiasm for life, and the happiness she shared with Tye out on their rambles, got Sharron out of her worst moments of darkness and made her want to walk in the light again. Sadly, in spite of all our best efforts, Jen's life couldn't be saved.

Now as I prepared the fatal injection, Sharron lay by Jen's side and told me that she truly believed that the genuine unconditional love she and Jen had shared had saved her life, more than once. Then she whispered into Jen's ear, 'Thank you for giving me so much – I'll see you soon over the rainbow bridge.' Then it was over. Within two weeks, Tye seemed to have lost the will to live, as if he could not bear to be without Jen, and he too passed away.

Meghan Markel's dear friend Guy had also been a rescue dog like Jen, and also needed joint surgery. Guy is the sweetest, gentlest dog – a tan, black and white beagle cross with big floppy ears and huge, kind brown eyes. Meghan wanted to do all she could for Guy and, unlike many people in her position who might delegate the vet appointments and the aftercare following surgery, she brought him along to every appointment herself. The operation was involved and recovery was prolonged, but both Meghan and Harry were with him every step of the way. When they came to the practice, they sat on the floor beside Guy and comforted him, as any other dedicated, caring and sincere human beings who deeply love their animal friend would do.

It upsets me that much of what has been written about the couple in the newspapers is so completely disingenuous. It seems that as soon as anyone is in the public eye they become fair game, and the higher the profile, the harder time they get, because that's what sells newspapers. It seems that people become cynical and quick to put people down. It's almost as if the media world of today punishes sincerity:

anyone who does anything good must have some kind of ulterior motive. I empathised with Meghan in particular, because in my opinion she suffered unfair criticism on every level. I treat everyone the same and can only take people as I find them, and nothing I have read reflects the Meghan I got to know as a compassionate human and fellow animal lover.

The media love gossip, conflict, bad behaviour and bad news; less common are headlines about how altruistic, genuine, generous or kind people are, unless it's humorous or somehow catchy for social media. My two biggest hits on popular media were snaps of me dressed up in a suit for the royal wedding, and wrapping a wayward swan in my coat to rescue the poor creature from a road of busy traffic in Dublin, before turning up to the RTE news studios in a coat now covered in swan shit. That was definitely newsworthy.

Just at the beginning of the coronavirus pandemic, before any of us had any clue about what was about to happen and we went into lockdown, I gave a two-hour interview to a newspaper. The focus of the piece was my 'Animal People' podcast on which I interview people about the animals that have made their lives better and have some fun along the way. I talked at length about my vision for a better world with more respect for animals and each other. I explained the links and similarities between man and animal with regard to infection, cancer and other diseases and talked about my dream to see One Medicine become reality, studying cures for naturally occurring disease in man and animal side by side. I spoke about encouraging cooperation between vets and doctors in a new platform of One Medicine which would give animals a fair deal, reduce our reliance on animal experimentation over time, and expedite cures for cancer and infection in man and animal. This seems like total common sense, but it's not the accepted norm.

I also talked about some of the podcast guests – in particular Brian May, who is a staunch advocate for all animals and especially wildlife. Brian is a really genuine, sensitive and kind human being. I told the newspaper journalist about my podcast chat with Brian; how he has loved many animals in his life, especially cats; how, in fact, when he was a student at Imperial College, his companion in the astrophysics laboratory was a cat called Einstein; and about the fact that he didn't get the chance to complete his PhD thesis 'A Survey of Radial Velocities in the Zodiacal Dust Cloud' for thirty-seven years after graduating, because he became a little distracted by becoming a member of Queen – and one of the greatest guitar players who ever lived. One would have thought that this smorgasbord of chat would have been ample to fill the couple of pages, and so I was actually excited about seeing the article in print. I was happy with how the interview had gone and hoped it would make a difference to getting the message about fairness to animals and One Medicine out there. I'd also heard that the space in the newspaper had become available because a piece on Daniel Craig had been pulled because Bond 25, *No Time to Die*, wasn't going to be released due to coronavirus – my only ever chance to stand in for 007!

A couple of weeks later, I opened the newspaper to read the feature entitled: 'Why I walked out of Harry and Meghan's wedding!' I was devastated. I knew that the journalist would have handed in his article with good intentions and that a subeditor would probably have penned the headline, so it wasn't anyone's fault. Such was the way of the media world. I lay on my bed and looked at the ceiling. Was this misleading headline the price I had to pay in order to get attention for the message about One Medicine?

Nothing about that headline was genuine. When the journalist had asked me about the wedding, I told him I would make no comment about Harry and Meghan. Instead I said, 'I'll quickly tell you this – which will make you laugh,' and in two minutes I told him what had actually happened to me that afternoon, which had nothing whatsoever to do with their beautiful wedding. I felt honoured to be there and I certainly hadn't disrespectfully 'walked out'.

The headline was, however, factually accurate. That's the thing about misleading press coverage – I was just stupid and I should have known better than to say anything at all. For me this was a resonant example on a tiny scale of the machinations of media which 'massage' the truth and sometimes distort it. I did indeed have to leave the wedding mid-afternoon, which was a shame, but the reason why is even more embarrassing!

This is what actually happened. The night before the wedding, I stayed at a friend's house in the centre of Windsor, a very short walk from the wedding venue within the grounds of Windsor Castle. The next morning, in order to attend the wedding, I had to first go through a security screening. However, it transpired that because of a security lockdown no cars were allowed into the town, so I had to walk in the opposite direction and leave town in order to get a taxi to take me to the congregation point where my identity would be verified (yes, every guest went through the same hoops). And, of course, all mobile phones were to be left at home. Then everybody was taken in small buses to St George's Chapel at the castle. No exceptions. The intense focus on security was mandated by the Metropolitan Police at a time when there was significant concern for the safety of both the public and the guests regarding possible terror attacks. I say this because at the time there was much speculation in the media about the costs of security being an extravagance on behalf of the bride and groom, which would indeed be another misleading interpretation of what was happening in real life. I, for one, was more than happy and grateful to comply with the necessary arrangements. However – my feet were not so happy!

I had on a brand-new pair of shoes – with shiny soles – which I scuffed up and down the pavement a fair few times walking out of town to get the taxi, to try to stop them being so slippery. I was also wearing the first and only suit I have ever had made for me – from the finest fabric, at Ede & Ravenscroft, the oldest tailors in London!

I should have seen the signs of my impending doom earlier. By the time I reached the large roundabout about a mile out of town, which was as far as cars were allowed, I was already pouring sweat in the morning sun and had taken off my beautiful suit tails and waistcoat. My out-of-place sweaty white-shirted shuffle caught the eyes of many American tourists walking into town to join in the revelry, most of whom thankfully didn't recognise me as I looked down at my feet, which were already beginning to ache in my unforgiving new shoes. As I finally settled into the back seat of the taxi, which took ages to find due to the absence of a mobile phone, I slipped off my shoes and packed tissues down my back and in my armpits to stop the sweat ruining my shirt. As I closed my eyes and the cab took off, I thought to myself how much easier it was to walk for hours in wellington boots herding sheep from one bit of our farm to another. Still, nothing that couldn't be conquered by the indomitable willpower of a seasoned sheep-walker.

When I put the shoes back on and walked to the congregation point, a tragedy was acutely unfolding in my toes. In the church, I made my way wincingly to my pew. I was two rows behind Elton John and, as we all sat there waiting for the ceremony to begin, my feet were by now pulsating with pain. 'I bet Elton's wearing comfy butter-soft shoes,' I mused to myself.

After the wedding ceremony, funny, touching and genuine speeches from Prince Charles, Harry and Meghan, and a few tunes from Elton, in my head I was walking on clouds. I felt so very honoured to have been invited, but in real life I was walking on razor blades. I was rocking from one foot to the other in a grand gilded reception hall, surrounded by amazing paintings and chandeliers, as immaculate waiting staff offering trays of delicious canapés sashayed through the throng. My feet were killing me and I knew nobody to talk to, so I just very slowly nibbled on savoury snacks, smiling benignly. Unable to cope with communicating in crowds, all the while my head was throbbing anxiously, but my feet were throbbing more. Finally, I slowly and quietly asked one of the attendants which was the way to exit Windsor Castle.

Yet more foot-related trauma was about to ensue. I was shown out of a gateway, but it was on the opposite side of the castle walls to where I needed to be – or, at least, this directionless Irish leprechaun walked the opposite way to where I needed to walk. I couldn't get back into the castle grounds again because of security, and so I started to walk round the outside of the wall. Now, anyone who has ever walked round Windsor Castle will understand that it's a long way on a normal day – but in blistering heat, wearing a shirt, waistcoat and morning suit jacket, it's a whole new endurance test. The afternoon sun beat down on my sweltering brow and I began to experience what I have heard ladies describe forever – the 'near-death' experience of 'my feet are killing me!' Until that moment, I thought that it was an exaggeration, but by the time I'd walked a half-mile or so around the castle walls, I could see the oncoming lights of my imminent fatality.

To add insult to injury, quite a few people recognised me off the telly, and their interest was multiplied tenfold when I finally had to give up. My feet were absolutely, totally and utterly killing me. I've never felt foot pain like it. In that moment it seemed worse than the pain I'd experienced when the methadone wore off after my ankle surgery. I sat down on the side of a street and took off my shoes and socks. All around me was the joy and merriment of celebration, the streets crammed full of well-wishers joining in the mayhem and waving flags and banners. Some American tourists stopped and kindly asked if I was all right and if I wanted some water. I started walking again, but I was lost. I'd forgotten the name of the street where I was staying. All I remembered was that it was on a main road near a church. I couldn't remember anyone's phone number even if I could get access to a phone from a passer-by, and asking for directions to a church in Windsor was completely pointless – the town was full of them. I even tried asking for some help with my whereabouts from the crowd management staff in yellow jackets dotted throughout the town on this special day, but because of security they couldn't let me have a copy of one of their maps. Everywhere was pandemonium, I had no idea where I was, and I was wandering aimlessly along scorching concrete pavements barefoot, kicking litter with my blisters. Cheers and laughter filled the air, punctuated by muffled and not-so-muffled comments of 'Isn't that the bloke off the telly – the one who fixes all the animals?', or 'Hey, Mom, look – it's the Supervet!', or 'Oh my God, my mum loves you! Can I have a selfie?'

'Sure, absolutely, I'm totally in the mood for a selfie right now with my sweat-drenched shirt hanging out over my trousers, my tie hanging limp on my open collar, my beautiful tailcoat and waistcoat bundled up under my left arm, my sparkly new shoes in my right hand, and a sock dangling out of each pocket,' muttered the pigeon on my shoulder. I'm sure someone has pictures on their phone of this dishevelled wandering Irish bloke standing in butcher's, baker's, clothes and toy shops asking for directions. Finally, more by luck than design, I came across what looked like the main road I had originally walked down. At last, I saw the church. I tiptoed past its steps as if I had survived a trek through the Sahara on foot. Trembling, I placed the key in the door of my friend's house, crawled into the hallway and collapsed in a heap by the wall, hugging my knees to my chest to raise my swollen feet off the ground.

I gingerly made my way to where I had left my phone and I texted my friend Kristina: 'Do you have any salt? Do you have any plasters?' Like all ladies and no men that I know, she had that special soaking salt stuff which I could use to bathe my blistered and by now bleeding feet and she had a neighbour drop in some plasters. Now there's a genuine friend! And so, as the whoops and hollers of celebration echoed rapturously around the sun-glistened streets of Windsor on that glorious late afternoon, I sat in a basement, with my feet in a bidet full of salted water and hummed gently to myself, praying that the swelling would go down enough so I could put on any half-decent shoes at all to go back for the evening wedding reception. Luckily, I had a freshly laundered shirt and a new evening suit, and I managed to get my feet into a pair of evening shoes, or there would have been no wedding reception at all for me.

My shiny black wedding shoes might have looked splendorous enough to grace a royal wedding, but appearances can be deceptive, and in this case a glossy sheen really did hide genuine pain. Such was the torture they had inflicted, they have remained under my bed since. A couple of hours later, I sat in awe as I watched the genuine love of two genuine people lit up with fireworks across the sky. Initially I felt out of place, awkward and inadequate because I was in unfamiliar surroundings and didn't know anybody, but I met a lot of very genuine folks that evening, which was a real treat. I was very much sitting still, because my feet were so sore. There was no 'feet-on-fire' dancing for me. Instead I enjoyed conversations with lovely people from all kinds of backgrounds. I had no idea who most of them were and they had no idea who I was either; nobody needed or wanted anything; we were all at peace and being our most true selves. It was the most beautiful evening.

Through the years, my animal patients have shown me that accepting everyone for who they are and as they are, not being judgemental, admitting my own faults, accepting my own failure, speaking my mind and being true to myself, having self-esteem and forging ahead with resolute determination are the cornerstones of genuineness and indeed happiness. Dogs and cats don't often seem to suffer feelings of inadequacy; they don't micro-analyse everything and look for faults – and most importantly they're not cynical and looking for the 'headline' or what's in it for them. They are always what they appear to be, without a facade. They also accept me as I am, with all of my faults and inadequacies. In fact, what I may perceive as faults such as being insular, awkward in social circumstances, intense and obsessive, from their point of view might be considered virtues.

Animals have made me realise that genuine love does not have limitations – it's infinite. You can just *be* and let the world and those in it revolve – and be fine with whatever they choose to do, because that's up to them. My job is just to keep on being genuine in the midst of this infinite love that I'm lucky enough to have around me every day.

As a surgeon, my patients have taught me that I must look in the mirror and take responsibility for my own shortcomings and failings, and to take consistent action to hopefully become a better surgeon but also a better human being. The key to unlocking true potential, in my view, is being truly honest with yourself about what you stand for, who you are, what you want, and being resolute that this in itself is enough, because it's genuine.

Dogs and cats make me question my thoughts, beliefs and behaviours every day, and inspire me to alter them if they aren't compatible with the person I want to become. In all areas of life, failure is integral to learning and enlightenment. Those who are genuine try to discover their particular special and unique way of striving towards passions and purpose, even if it's a path that others think is so far off the beaten path that you're insane. It takes courage to explore and truly adhere to one's own beliefs and principles, even if others disagree. As long as one is genuine, respectful and not hurting anyone, man or animal, perhaps one is more sane and genuine than those who say otherwise. Cats and dogs don't exhaust themselves trying to convince others that they are right or genuine. They just 'are' genuine, and the rest will follow in time. As long as you are genuine, life is full of possibility and I believe that everyone is always ready for possibility, because all of this abundance is already within yourself. Look inside first and the outside will take care of itself.

Harry and Meghan's journey is, in my view, a true and genuine reflection of their unwavering principles, and they are consistently following the path most compatible with their own sense of integrity for themselves, and their beautiful son Archie. As Meghan said recently in the wake of George Floyd's death in a video broadcast to her alma mater, 'The only wrong thing to say is to say nothing' and, 'Always remember to put others' needs above your own fears.' I stand by her side in this sentiment.

My mammy Rita and daddy Sean brought me up well with the constant intent and action of genuineness. Without any prompting, knowing I was visiting my mother for Christmas, Meghan and Harry had sent a Christmas cake along with a beautiful letter to her expressing thanks, respect and appreciation. They wrote that I was a testament to her and the loving and supportive home I came from. They said other kind things too, which they did not need to, and it made Rita smile a lot, sitting in her chair in our living room wearing the hat that I'd got for her from the Queen's milliner, and eating a piece of the delicious cake. She could not have been happier – genuinely.

CHAPTER SIX

Rightness

'You are what you do, not what you say you'll do.'

Carl Gustav Jung

Rightness is not about being 'right' some of the time – it's about *doing* the right thing *all of the time*.

Doing the right thing, especially when nobody is watching, requires strength of character. It transcends acknowledgement from others about what the 'right thing' actually is. It's about having a definitive authentic purpose and it requires a moral compass, the poles of which are kindness, love, bravery and honesty encompassing the core values of rightness, fairness, accountability and conscientiousness.

If all politicians did the right thing all of the time, there would be no poverty, inequality or war; if all parents followed suit, there would be no child abuse; if we all did, there would be no violence or crime, and less alienation, despondency and despair. As human beings, we do some pretty senseless things, and I include myself in this. We are thoughtless, cruel, selfish, wrapped up in ourselves and we don't always manifest respect for others, or self-respect for ourselves. Even if deep down we know what is fair and right, we don't always do the right thing. Perhaps that's another reason why I have always found it much easier to relate to animals than humans. Dogs and cats are more tolerant, forgiving, kind, respectful, patient, genuine and authentic than many people I have met. They may be insular and bruised from a sad start in life, but they will learn to love again if humans do the right thing. They are what they are and they just want to be themselves, without any agenda but to be loved and share love. If you trip over them before you turn on the light they just shake it off, and as soon as the light comes on all is instantly forgiven. They don't wish that they thought or looked like another dog or a cat, or were more right or wrong than another cat or dog; they're fine in their own skin. They have an intrinsic sense of rightness.

Most of us strive to live a life that matters, or to leave something of intrinsic value after we are gone. Perhaps you have found a vocation that gives you purpose, have a child of whom you are immensely proud, a charity you contribute to, or maybe you campaign on behalf of a cause. Or perhaps you simply did the right thing and helped a friend when they needed it most. Maybe you haven't found your passion or mission in life, or haven't had the opportunity to do so because of circumstance, but again in that respect I've learned from animals too – for a cat or a dog it's never too late to do what they really want to do on any given day.

For all of us, each and every morning is a new opportunity to find purpose and do what's *right*. And of course, the right thing to do may change with the passing of time. Clearly some of us would not have made the same choices, had certain relationships or friendships, or even got married had we known what we know now.

We can all fall down from time to time and I know that I

have. Over time I've come to feel that a sense of rightness requires me to question my choices and motives. I think we all have to. Are we being truthful? Are we acting with good intent and integrity of purpose? Have we ever lied or stolen, cheated to get what we wanted, made a mistake then blamed someone else, been cruel or acted with contempt, humiliated someone out of spite, been so jealous that we did or said something out of character, been so full of rage that we hurt someone? Negative emotions can be overwhelming and sometimes consume our sense of rightness. Sometimes the bravest thing we can do is look in the mirror, acknowledge that we are helpless and ask for guidance. I have found in my life that if I have been wrong or been wronged, then I have to be open to allow rightness in, or history repeats itself. David, the inmate I met when I visited the prison, told me that asking for help was the most difficult thing he ever had to do – more difficult even than facing up to his crimes and the people he had hurt. It's been inordinately difficult for me too.

I've seen counsellors and therapists on and off over the years because of the stress of a life lived at a thousand miles an hour, and my tendency to internalise everybody else's woes – the animals' difficulties, the issues and challenges of my team – along with my own perceived problems. I say 'perceived', because of course most of the time it's all in my head. Are they insurmountable problems? Probably not. I am lucky. I'm not in a situation where my rights are being taken away by another person or people. I am deeply moved by the plight of people affected by war, injustice, poverty and disease, and about the damage we continue to wreak to the ecosystem of our planet, so that I frequently feel helpless and even close to despair. In my own life, however, I have free choice about right and wrong, yet I spend a lot of energy worrying about things beyond my control. 'It isn't true, and I don't understand why he or she thinks of me that way' are very common thoughts for me, but I can't change what another person may or may not think anyway. I should just accept that that's their prerogative, and I too have made mistakes along the way, but today I'm going to try to be as full of rightness as Ricochet and Keira are by just being themselves, each and every day. I should focus on how I want my world to be instead of constantly dwelling on my past failings, both personal and professional, to the extent that they are carried forward into the present. As my counsellor John said to me, 'What resists persists' – or, as The Beatles once said, I should just 'let it be'.

As far as we know, dogs and cats exist in the moment, conditioned by their past for sure, but many are open to a new start. This can be true for us too. There is some truth in the phrase that 'you can't teach an old dog new tricks', in that the older dogs get, and I suspect humans too, the harder it becomes to change the neural pathways we have laid down through repetition, but extensive research has shown that most dogs, especially up to the age of six or seven, can have negative behavioural characteristics completely changed if given a loving, patient, supportive and caring environment, around people with positive reinforcing moods and character traits. Likewise, we too can effectuate change for the good. Rightness *can* be learned. I liken human weakness to the dog who is normally perfectly behaved but one day he just can't help himself stealing that doughnut from the sideboard when nobody is watching. He thinks he's got away with it, but everyone can see that little bit of jam on his cheeks. It's obvious to everyone except himself that he needs to change his ways, and it's not that he won't ever be tempted by doughnuts again, it's just that to avoid losing his friends or being put in his crate, he needs to adopt more socially acceptable behaviour – and maybe he needs some help in doughnut-aversion therapy! Of course, the bigger moral in this canine fable is that stealing isn't right. The implications of cage-confinement for Fido are the superficial consequences – ultimately, it's about what such habitual bad behaviour can do to our souls. Doing the wrong thing is corrosive, and breeds badness, and the opposite is also the case – do the right thing and, in the end, usually the right thing will happen. The truth is that nearly everyone has fallen short in the rightness department at some point in their lives, but sometimes we simply can't face up to ourselves, can't look ourselves in the mirror and possibly can't admit our own failings.

This is true in any life, any job and any vocation, and I have seen it in my own vocation too. When I hire someone, I would take on any day the surgical intern or nurse who's prepared to be there no matter what, especially at 3 a.m. when a dog in recovery is in respiratory distress, I can't get an intravenous line in and I desperately need help, in preference to the one with all of the academic accolades who wouldn't put themselves out for anyone. I have seen trainees who are simply too busy trying to impress those who can advance their career, or writing the next academic paper, possibly even based on someone else's ideas, just to get the tick in the academic box. Yet, when they think I'm not watching, they are not going the extra mile of rightness – holding the paw of the patient, the hand of the client or having the backs of their colleagues.

Academically, we absolutely need scientific papers for evidence and progress, and we must all jump through the hoops of fire of examinations as there is no other way to assess competence. However, I worry that the need to pass exams and gain credentials has the potential to create clinical scientists and box-tickers because there's no exam for rightness or compassion. Given a choice, I would hire a hundred vets or nurses who have a big heart before I would hire a single one with loads of academic talent – but an ego to match.

The other thing that I worry about a lot is the increased focus over the past couple of decades on financial gain, which I am concerned has the potential to detract from the 'reasons of rightness' embraced by every aspiring vet when they signed up in the first place. To be frank, I really hope that because the majority of veterinary practices are now owned by corporate groups, who understandably have a need for optimised financial return, that rightness and a fair deal for animals does not get usurped by a drive for financial gain. This ship has already set sail, but I sincerely hope that the winds of rightness may prevail. It's simply the natural course of business in many healthcare sectors – human and animal – and may be for the best overall if investment is used wisely in the patient's interest. Should Fitzpatrick Referrals one day become part of a larger group, I would hope that it would be for all the right reasons and would do my best to ensure that it was with a group for whom the patient's interest is the core interest.

The whole structure of veterinary medicine has changed since I qualified and now Fitzpatrick Referrals is, to my knowledge, the last multi-disciplinary specialist referral centre of our size that remains independent. Most referral centres in the UK are operated by corporate groups, who may also own hundreds of primary care practices, which are understandably encouraged to refer patients within their own company for business reasons. My own personal opinion is that the right thing for all animals is to have all treatment options, and all guardians to have all specialist referral options available regardless of business associations. I believe in freedom of choice and of speech as reflections of rightness.

My business motto, as I've already mooted, has always been 'do the right thing, and the right thing will happen'. Our accessibility and prices are the same as any other referral centre in the UK and we offer some procedures that are currently unique. This creates a further challenge for me personally because sometimes the most difficult time to do the right thing is when I am confident that a limb or a life can be saved, but I can't perform the surgery because the family can't afford it. In medicine, finances should never be a motive for doing anything, but it is sadly often a motive for not doing anything.

Since I graduated, as for every vet, there have often been times when I've put an animal to sleep because the family couldn't afford treatment. Thankfully, with the advent of insurance, this is less so nowadays than it was when I started out and I have at all times in my career done my best for folks financially, within the limits allowed by my employer in the past or by my financing bank nowadays. I faced some of the same relative challenges twenty years ago as I do now. Back then, the buildings and facilities we have today were just dreams in my head. My operating theatre was a wooden hut in the shade of some trees at the back of a house. My orthopaedic drill at the time was a Makita DIY drill and my spinal drill was a Dremel wood drill, both covered with sterile sheaths. Yet the challenges about doing the right thing were the same.

On a miserably cold November afternoon in 2001, darkness

was closing in like a fog-gloved fist around that little building in the village of Ewhurst, Surrey. It was a small mixed practice and so I was still treating cows, sheep and horses, but had also started to take referrals in orthopaedics and neurosurgery after periods of training that I was lucky enough to have been allowed to participate in at various universities in the UK and USA, and attaining a couple of extra qualifications. It would take me more than another ten years to get enough credentials to be allowed to sit the examination for specialist status. For whatever reason, I just wasn't good enough in any interview process for anyone to give me an internship or a residency for structured surgical training.

That afternoon, an ashen-faced man stumbled over the stone doorstep of the practice, through the tiny waiting room and into my consulting room, carrying a dachshund who was clearly in distress and whimpering. It didn't take long to figure out that his back legs couldn't move. The poor little fellow couldn't stand and was dragging himself along using his front legs, his back legs flailing out behind him. When I pinched the toes of his back feet, he couldn't feel a thing. His back legs were paralysed. The poor man didn't know whether he should put him to sleep or put him through surgery, both from the financial perspective and also because he 'didn't want to put him through too much'.

Dachshunds are one of a number of breeds that are chondrodystrophic (literally, 'cartilage maldevelopment'), which means that they have disproportionately short limbs and other associated unique skeletal characteristics. Their little legs, long backs and characteristic pointy noses are very endearing traits to us, but sadly come hand in hand with the genetic propensity for the drying out of the intervertebral discs in the spine, which causes problems with great

164

frequency. By the early age of one year the discs often start drying out in this breed. A disc is like a jam doughnut, with a fibrous outer ring (the annulus fibrosus) and a pulpy inner centre (the nucleus pulposus). The discs undergo genetically predisposed change (chondroid and fibroid metamorphosis), losing their ability to stay spongy with high water content (hygroscopic tendency), and as the 'jam' in the nucleus dries out, the 'dough' of the annulus can tear, releasing the jam explosively, which is called a disc extrusion; or the dough may bulge, which is called a protrusion. Both are commonly referred to as a 'slipped disc', which isn't an appropriate term since the disc doesn't actually slip; it leaks or bulges. When disc material squashes the spinal cord it can quickly cause impact trauma (contusion) which may or may not be reversible, and also compression which is generally reversible with surgery. Some may recover, though often incompletely, without surgery.

Back in 2001 the diagnosis was always based on X-ray pictures with dye injected around the spinal cord, known as a myelogram. Myelography is still sometimes performed with CT scans (which are effectively 3D X-ray pictures) nowadays, but it's more or less been made obsolete with the advent of MRI scans (which are akin to 3D sequenced density maps of the body). Anyway, just from looking at the poor dog, it was clear that the options were limited. Most dachshunds who present like this are affected by a sudden disc extrusion as described above, but other possible diagnoses include: trauma causing a fracture; ANNPE (acute non-compressive nucleus pulposus extrusion) where a tiny shard of hydrated nucleus pulposus extrudes due to a sudden increase in intradiscal pressure and hits the cord like a bullet; FCE (fibrocartilaginous embolic myelopathy) where a tiny shard of nucleus comes out and blocks a small artery to the spinal cord, causing damage (ischaemic necrosis); or lastly, haemorrhage or inflammatory disease are also possible.

With any damage to the middle of the spinal cord (the thoracolumbar spine), the most common site of disc extrusions in dachshunds, there are grades of disease which can affect the hind legs (pelvic limbs). There are several grading systems, but the one we most commonly use has five levels of severity, as follows: Grade 1: pain only; Grade 2: wobbly with hind leg weakness (paraparesis); Grade 3: just about able to move back legs but unable to walk (non-ambulatory paraparesis); Grade 4: no voluntary hind leg movement, with or without urinary bladder control; Grade 5: complete absence of voluntary motion of hind legs, loss of sensation in the toes of their hind paws (loss of 'deep pain' and paraplegia) and inability to urinate. At each progressive stage, the prognosis for getting any patient back to normal, even with surgery, becomes more grave.

As I recall, this little fellow was only two years old, but he was Grade 5 – as bad as it got. If he had ANNPE (at that time called low volume high velocity disc extrusion), I knew he may not recover and I couldn't operate to save him. I hoped, therefore, that at worst he had a large volume disc extrusion that hadn't hit the cord too badly with contusion, and that when I removed the compressive material from under the spinal cord, he had a chance of getting better – but it was by no means certain.

When I explained the gravity of the situation and the guarded prognosis, the man became very upset. He looked like the kind of chap who would generally keep a stiff upper lip and even if he felt sad on the inside, I doubt that he showed it very often, but I could see some tears welling up. I went to put my hand on his shoulder to comfort him, as was my wont, but he pulled back. I said how sorry I was and that I would do all I could to help, and if we were lucky his little friend might pull through with surgery. The man nodded silently. I reiterated my sympathies and asked if the primary care vet who had sent him to me hadn't warned him about the grave outlook. He nodded again, and then said, 'The thing is that it's not just about the dog.' I was puzzled, immediately assuming there was some kind of undisclosed family tragedy or other complicating factor that I didn't know about. I already knew about his financial restrictions. It was only then that he told me that he was having the worst day of his life.

This man was among the commanding officers of the British Army and that very day he and his team had sent special forces to fight in Afghanistan alongside the Afghan Northern Alliance in the ground offensive against the Taliban and al-Qaeda. He next said something that affected me deeply and I shall never forget: 'I don't know for sure if we're doing the right thing today, but I know for sure that you will.'

Was it right to go to war after an aggressor committed a barbaric act by flying two aeroplanes straight into the Twin Towers in New York? We have always had wars and I expect we always will, but still I often feel overwhelmed by the scale of man's inhumanity to man. There are many days when I can't bear to read or listen to the news about atrocities happening all over the world. I feel so completely meaningless and helpless in the overall scheme of things and find it very difficult to discern rightness in the midst of such evil.

On one of the promotional trips for my last book, I appeared on a television chat show. Before going on air, I sat in the green room next to a woman who worked to help the victims of war in Darfur and another who appeared on a

167

reality TV show. Since the onset of conflict in Darfur in 2003, tens of thousands of women and girls have been raped as a despicable deliberate act of war, often multiple times and in front of their loved ones. The victim not only suffers the trauma of this violation and the risk of infectious disease, but also the stigma in such communities thereafter, and perhaps even unwanted pregnancy. In the face of these crimes against humanity, which to you and me are almost unimaginable, talking about what I do and about my book seemed suddenly so conceited. One of the runners looking after us was being appropriately respectful to the lady involved with the charities in Darfur, when the reality TV star interrupted to complain about how long it was taking for someone to come to do her hair.

I know it's all relative: we all live in different parts of the world and in different circumstances, with our own trials and tribulations and we all complain from time to time. We only have one life and can only do our best with what we have, but if we stop for a moment to think about the challenges people have in the wider world, it may help put some of our perceived crises into perspective. If I have a late night in the operating theatre I may feel exhausted, but I count myself lucky that I'm not doing a job I hate. I often remind my students of this when they ask why surgery doesn't always finish by 7 p.m. Gone are the days when I used to sometimes *start* one of my long list of elective surgeries even later than that because there weren't enough hours in the day, but nowadays we really do try to finish our non-emergency operations in normal working hours, because thankfully the team has grown such that I now operate a shorter list and we need to aim for less onerous working hours for my team in general. However, because my surgeries are often complex, the best laid plans don't always work out. Still, I am grateful daily for our practice where I'm always 100 per cent sure that rightness prevails and we always do the right thing for patient and guardian no matter what.

Doing the right thing requires all of us to dig deep and ask ourselves if we are really doing what we should be with our lives. Some people find fulfilment in working for a charity, some as doctors travelling to war zones, some as shopworkers, hairdressers or actors, some as a mother or as a teacher, some working in musical theatre, some being general practitioner vets and some being specialist vets. All of that is absolutely brilliant – whatever it is that makes you tick and brings you happiness. Whatever you do, the important thing is to do it for the right reasons and with the whole of your heart.

To do the right thing, however, demands commitment and is not without effort: if I truly want what I perceive as 'the right thing' to happen, then I need to *do* the right thing, *over and over again*. Dogs and cats learn quickly that doing the right thing earns them treats and ample cuddles as a reward. Conversely, they know that if they keep doing the same 'wrong' thing – pooing on the carpet, chewing your flip-flops, scratching the furniture – and expecting a different outcome, they're slightly bonkers, and yet we do this all the time. We work at exactly the same level of efficiency or productivity as we did last year, and expect a promotion; we treat our friends or our partner exactly the same as before and expect to be liked more; we study the same amount and get exactly the same grade as we do on every exam and feel we deserve more acknowledgement; we eat exactly the same crap every day and are surprised when we don't get slimmer; we do the same twenty minutes of exercise and wonder why we never get fitter. That's not how nature works. Use it or lose it. Make it happen by breaking the habit. If it's to be, *it's up to me.*

The term 'wellness' is widely used nowadays, encouraging us to look after ourselves. 'Doing the right thing for ourselves' is, I think, one of the most misunderstood statements ever. Doing the right thing for yourself isn't selfish, in fact it's the opposite – so long as it's not at the expense of anyone else's well-being. How can you help, look after, love or improve the lot of anyone else if you're not all right yourself? This is something I now understand, and is partly my inspiration for this book. When I founded VET Festival (VETFest), an educational, networking and social gathering for vets, wellness for my profession was a key foundation theme for the annual event. Alongside more conventional clinical education streams, invited speakers share their knowledge with us on all aspects of wellness of mind, body, spirit and team dynamics, so that as a profession we look after each other a bit better. I think as a vet in companion animal practice, it's hard to be loving and caring all day long for animals and those who love them, and take all of that on our shoulders if our body and spirit are so weak that we can't even hold our shoulders up. I'd like to help with that if I can for the greater good. The RCVS is also running a wonderful initiative on mental health problems among veterinary professionals called Mind Matters, which is helping to remove the stigma of talking about the issues arising from our stressful lives – 'mental health' remains a kind of taboo phrase, especially in the medical profession.

Meanwhile, however, as 2019 dragged on, so too did the wait to hear news of the process regarding the complaint made against me, and not once did any member of my profession, outside of very close friends, reach out to ask me how I was doing, even though many were aware of what was going on. This seemed strange to me in a profession of people who care passionately about the welfare of animals, but not so much about the welfare of their colleagues – not just from my own point of view, but for all vets and vet nurses generally. It just didn't seem right to me. I also wondered why it was taking so long to adjudicate on the complaint. I for one would have been happy to pay a lot more in annual dues to the RCVS if it meant that the staffing levels could increase and the complaints system operated more swiftly for the benefit of vets across the land.

I empathise with their dilemma. On the one hand they want to look after the mental health of practitioners and on the other hand, as noted before, they have a duty of care to the animals and to the public to thoroughly investigate serious claims of negligence or allegations of professional misconduct. All of this is absolutely necessary and as it should be. In the case of the RCVS complaint, everyone on both sides felt that they were right and had only ever acted in the patient's best interests. Rightness has a different hue depending on your perspective, but Hermes was to teach me more about right and wrong than any other animal of the many thousands that I have treated.

I fell into a profound depression during the ongoing complaints process, which cast a daily cloud over everything. I was having trouble sleeping and felt a kind of dull numbness in both my professional and personal life. No success brought me joy and any failure hit me harder than ever before. I was at rock bottom. It was my first thought every morning and my last every night; I felt the very essence of my existence was under attack. I sought psychological help from a few different quarters, but I felt like a charlatan as

I was acutely aware that there were people in the world suffering far greater trauma than me. I spent many hours preparing legal depositions, not to mention the many wasted hours of worrying, during which I suppose I could have been operating to save more lives, but I was fighting for my right to save lives at all.

I was very fortunate to have a wonderful adviser from our professional indemnity insurer who was a great comfort to me. Throughout that year, he woke up regularly to anguished emails sent by me at two or three o'clock in the morning. I'm quite sure he must have dreaded getting up and turning on his computer, only to see more of my written screams of despair, but he always got back to me – and held me up as I slipped further into darkness. He helped me to face a new day and to somehow pull myself together enough to go to my consulting room or operating theatre. He was inordinately patient and just kept telling me to focus on doing the right thing for other animals, and to 'Go and help the next one'. I owe both him and his legal team a great deal of gratitude for going above and beyond their professional duties and for being deeply compassionate human beings.

Just before St Patrick's Day in March 2019, about four months after the complaint had landed on my desk, I had more documentation to deal with and had been up most of the night before compiling notes and writing emails, so I'd been exhausted all day, when as evening descended an extra neurology case came in. The other neuro- and ortho-surgeons at the practice had worked a busy day too and were still dealing with cases, so I saw Olive, a beautiful eight-year-old dachshund carried in a large basket by her mum, Laura. Both patient and client were really lovely. I don't ask for a medal when I say that the right thing for me was to see the case, no matter how tired I was, because that's my job, that's my vocation and that's what I signed up for. And Olive is a brilliant example of when doing the right thing brings me more salvation than I bring to my patient. Indeed Olive, at that particular time, was like a little guardian angel sent from above – not just for me – but for many others too. Olive was the physical embodiment of rightness.

Olive had been rushed in because she was neurologic Grade 4 on her back legs. She could still just about feel her back legs, but was unable to move them and dragged them behind her. She couldn't urinate and I was very concerned that she could deteriorate to Grade 5 – and fast. We performed an MRI scan straight away to make an accurate diagnosis. It was a far cry from the myelogram for my dachshund friend way back in 2001, but, like him, Olive had a disc extrusion in the middle of her back which was squashing her spinal cord. Unlike 2001, I wasn't taking X-ray pictures and operating on my patient all in the same room, aka shed, but in the recently completed new operating theatre which, because of its design, airflow system and technology, was the most advanced ever built in veterinary medicine in the UK to our knowledge. I performed the same surgery as I had done in 2001: a procedure called a hemilaminectomy. This means opening a window in half of the lamina, which constitutes the vertebral roof over the spinal cord and the associated articular facet (the joint above the spinal cord between the vertebrae), in order to scoop out the material that had exploded from the disc and decompress the spinal cord. A window was then cut in the disc (fenestration) to prevent future leakage of the disc nucleus by removing the potential compressive material from that particular site.

It took a few weeks and dedicated hydrotherapy, but again,

like the 2001 case, Olive eventually recovered to the point of running around happily. I'd like to think that the recovery of his little friend brought some hope to the man from the military, and I know that for Laura, Olive's recovery brought more than just hope, since Olive helps Laura in her counselling and therapy practice.

Olive began her career as a therapy dog at just twelve weeks old and has worked with Laura every single day since then. She has met and helped innumerable people, young and old, with a range of physical and emotional issues, both in Laura's private practice and on visits to schools, hospitals and nursing homes. Olive is Laura's extra eyes and ears, often allowing access to a part of the patient's soul and mind that she can't reach without Olive in the room.

One of Olive's most amazing roles is accompanying Laura as a play therapist at a junior school for four- to twelve-year-old children. Laura explained that Olive is incredibly important in choosing the right therapeutic path for each child. First, she helps Laura to identify the best place to engage the child, outside walking or in the office, then, she greets them with warmth, happiness and positivity and leads them into Laura's room. This immediately distracts and disarms the child and opens up dialogue around Olive, creates a non-threatening environment and gives Laura a chance to find out about the child's issues. Further, Olive forms unique relationships with every child she meets and remembers them on their next visit, so this familiarity also helps the child to relax. They are not threatened by Olive who is so very engaging, due both to her size and how incredibly cute she is. She makes the child feel they are special to her and this immediately brings out the nurturing, loving, trusting and playful side of children.

Laura said that Olive shows awareness of different emotions and often instinctively goes to cuddle and comfort a distressed child. Having Olive to cuddle will often offer the security needed to help a child talk about more difficult issues and in turn help Laura to help them. The children confide their secrets in her, because they know that she will not gossip or talk about them behind their back; she accepts them as they are and doesn't judge or criticise. She teaches them that they are enough. In fact, Olive is often used by teachers as an example of how a good friend should behave.

The children also get to understand that how they behave has a direct impact on Olive – that she has feelings too and should be treated with respect and love. Laura talks to the children about what we can learn from animals which encourages good behaviours and doing the right thing. They learn empathy, recognising that animals have their place in our world as well as humans, and that they can help us to enjoy the moment we are in. This enables Laura to focus on mindfulness with the children, which also helps her to deal with their past experiences and encourage them not to yearn too much after the future, but rather to take responsibility for where they are in the present and do the right thing right now.

When Olive had needed surgery, nobody had known if she would recover or not. Laura had lost her right-hand woman in the therapy sessions and the children had made her cards and got her presents. As it turned out, Olive looked after me too. After completing her surgery, I went back up to my office to find more bad news by email from my legal support team about further delays in the complaint process. The complainants wanted to present more evidence from the TV show to back up their allegation that I was guilty of doing the wrong

thing and bringing the profession into disrepute. There
followed another very fraught and angst-ridden evening.
Having a much-needed cuddle with Olive in the wards was
the only thing that helped me that night to remember why I
did any of this at all.

When Olive was well on the road to recovery, I was still
going through endless restless nights, and then I received
a wonderful surprise in a large white envelope from the
school. The children from every year group had made a
beautiful giant album with loads of hand-drawn pictures
of their adventures with Olive, and a little note from each
of them about how much their dachshund friend meant to
them: 'Thank you for taking care of Olive. She takes care
of me.' 'When I am sad, Olive looks after me.' 'I think Olive
and Laura are the missing piece of my puzzle.' 'Thank you
for fixing Olive. We all love her. You had her back – and she
has ours.' 'Olive makes everyone's day better – thank you
for making her better.' Even after a devastating spinal surgery she'd shown the children that she didn't let this hold
her back, but remained enthusiastic and gulped down every
moment of the day.

Thinking of Olive and all of the children who loved her
brought me comfort. I kept the album by my bed along with
a hat knitted for me by an elderly lady who had presented
it to me after one of my live shows the previous year. She
had given me a big hug, said she hoped the hat would keep
my head warm, because I had 'a lot of thinking to do' and
thanked me for 'always doing the right thing'. As I attempted
to get to sleep again, I tried to hold on to this memory and to
the heart-warming messages about Olive from the children.
I indeed did have a lot of thinking to do!

It's never easy deciding what the right thing to do is for

an animal with spinal damage, given that no surgeon can tell for sure whether a dog with Olive's condition will recover or not. The operation itself is not rocket science – and is the same process every time: I just open a window and scoop stuff out. That's not the miracle. The miracle is whether the spinal cord is able to recover or not, and that all depends on how much damage was done by the nucleus when it exploded and hit the cord. Sometimes it is so significant that the cord never recovers. While between head and tail there are millions of cells in the epidermis, with a turnover rate of about twenty-eight days for us and twenty days for dogs, in the spinal cord of both dogs and humans the head of a single nerve cell (neuron) originates in the brain or brainstem, then projects as a single nerve fibre (axon) which extends all the way down to the lower back. In fact, you could imagine the spinal cord as like a large electrical cable made up of such axons all lined up side by side inside its casing, from brain down to tail. Inside the 'electrical cable' that is the spinal cord, each of the copper conducting wires, which are axons of the white matter, is covered in plastic insulation, and these wires in turn are covered in more plastic to group them together in a cable. (To be scientifically correct, there are also some uncoated axons in the grey matter of the cord as well.) These axons transmit information from the brain to everything that ever happens consciously or subconsciously in the body. Spinal cord injury is difficult to resolve, because there's limited capacity for regeneration – unlike cell renewal in the skin, spinal cord recovery requires complex cellular and molecular machinery for 'rewiring' the nerve signals. The miracle is in how healing happens at all.

When central nervous system nerves come out of the spinal cord and link (synapse) with peripheral nerves that supply muscles and all of the other body organs, those nerves are also composed of bundles, often with each individual wire similarly covered with plastic. That coating of the nerves, like the plastic around electrical wires, is called 'myelin', and it allows the electrical currents to pass unimpeded and at much greater velocity than without coating. That's how we move, eat, breathe and do anything at all. Myelin is formed of complex carbohydrate, fat and protein molecules layered concentrically around the nerve and, in fact, each layer is a tiny leaf of the lining (plasma membrane) of the very special cells that make it. In the spinal cord these cells are called 'oligodendrocytes', and in the peripheral nerves 'Schwann cells'. If myelin isn't made just right or gets damaged in diseases like multiple sclerosis, or in my dachshund friends by spinal cord injury, the electrical conduction is dramatically impaired. Of course, the disease of spinal cord injury is more complicated and complex than just losing myelin, with inflammation and a cascade of vascular, ionic and biochemical events associated with the insult to the nerves in the cord. What is clear is that the very existence of nerves that allow us to feel and move at all is about doing the right thing over and over again at a cellular level in biology, like coating a nerve with myelin and then the right things follow in our molecules.

Myelin increases nerve conduction velocities by some one hundred times and processing speed of information by three thousand times. Without it, we cannot function properly. When babies are first born, their movements are jerky, uncoordinated and awkward because the myelin covering many of their nerves has yet to mature. As myelin sheaths develop, movements become smoother, more purposeful and more coordinated, while language comprehension and speech also become possible. But it's more than just a physiological phenomenon, it's a philosophical phenomenon too. It has been shown in numerous studies that the more nerves are forced to fire by determination from the brain, the more this firing is sensed by the oligodendrocytes and Schwann cells and the more resilient the myelin and associated conduction becomes. The more we use our neurons to do anything at all, the more myelin gets laid down and the quicker our ability to perform that same action again. So, if you practise playing guitar or you are a surgeon every day, the more robust those neurons and that myelin becomes, controlling everything from your thought process to the dexterity of your fingers. Brian May and The Edge have tons of guitar-playing nerve myelin. I have none.

You can't directly action anything without the firing of neurons and it is the frequency of their firing that makes you who you are. The author Daniel Coyle describes in his book *The Talent Code* how many skill-acquisition experiments have been performed that demonstrate increased firing of well-myelinated nerves in direct association with effort in any field. In 2000 Torkel Klingberg demonstrated the same phenomenon with reading skills; in 2005 Fredrik Ullen with concert pianists; and in 2006 Jesus Pujol with vocabulary. We use it or we lose it. It's not just natural talent or propensity that define us – it's frequency and intensity of effort. This is part of neural conditioning and therefore, in a very real sense, you are who you think you are in terms of physical skills, but you can also make yourself who you want to be (within some naturally defined limits) – and you are your myelin. Likewise, therefore, if you repeatedly do the right thing, it's likely to become ingrained behaviour – and the converse is also likely to be true.

Cats and dogs teach us this all of the time. If they are allowed to get away with bad behaviour and if good behaviour isn't positively reinforced, then bad behaviour neural pathways become entrenched. And once those electrical cables of nerves and myelin are laid down, they're very difficult to unravel and rewire. Time and again we learn that for all animals with myelin, which includes all of us and cats and dogs, rightness is hard-wired into us from an early age and although it can be reprogrammed, it's challenging and requires consistent repeated effort. Myelin sheaths can dynamically change throughout life, but real hard-wired rightness requires proper effort.

For my own part, I am hard-wired to try to do the right thing for animals, and it isn't always plain sailing; sometimes the right thing to do is to put an animal to sleep. I have performed euthanasia probably more than one thousand times in my career, and it never gets easier. In fact, as I get older, it seems to hurt more. We have shown euthanasia being carried out several times on *The Supervet*, but most families understandably choose not to go through this intensely sorrowful event in public. For me too, when I have worked with a dog or cat and got to know them really well, it's an emotional, psychological and physical pain that's really difficult to cope with. I absolutely dread the day when I may have to put Keira or Ricochet to sleep, but of course will be equally distraught however their passing comes. No matter how much I know that's part of my moral responsibility in guardianship, I will be devastated, but I will do the right thing if it becomes necessary.

This dilemma was very much the same for a lady called Anne, who came to our practice around 9 p.m. one Friday night with her eight-year-old cavapoo Ruben in November

2019. Two days previously Ruben had yelped suddenly while out in the garden and had subsequently become progressively paralysed on his hind legs. Anne was absolutely devastated and, like many people in her situation, she didn't know what was the right thing to do – she worried about putting Ruben through too much if we tried to treat him, and she also worried about her restricted budget, much like the army man twenty years earlier. It turned out that she also had major health issues herself, and, all things considered, she wondered if she might have to let him pass away peacefully. He had been admitted by one of my colleagues, and by the time I examined him, Ruben was Grade 4. He was unable to urinate and, as with Olive, we feared he was heading towards Grade 5, where he wouldn't have been able to feel his legs at all. Time was of the essence because his loss of hind leg control had progressed so rapidly and we had already lost nearly two days since he first yelped painfully in Anne's garden.

The neuro-team were once again slammed with emergency referral cases and they couldn't deal with all of them that night. I was about to leave; I was tired after another relentless week and was looking forward to my bed at home rather than the one next to my office. Instead, I made the decision to stay and help out because it seemed like the right thing to do. I was well aware that Anne had a strict budget dictated by her insurance policy, and she had no financial resource outside of that. I agreed to the parameters – the ability to retain some control of decision-making, albeit within limits, is one of the reasons why Fitzpatrick Referrals currently remains independent, and would ideally remain so, if market forces allow.

When an animal like Ruben's life is on the line, once you have made the decision to do the right thing, the act itself imbues a kind of adrenaline surge that obviates all feelings of self-preservation and selfishness. I expect that the same is true for firefighters, policemen, doctors, paramedics, soldiers and all similar professions where people's lives are at stake. Sometimes rightness goes against all egotistical instincts and, if doing the right thing is important to you, you may even have to put your own physical well-being on the line for it. There are hundreds of thousands of key workers such as bus drivers, shop staff, council workers, medical professionals, care home staff, and members of the security forces and military across the globe who are making this personal sacrifice today and every day, but particularly during the time of Covid-19. The same is true in your life, no matter what it is that you do – if you are doing the right thing, you will find the energy and the will to do it from somewhere, and you will feel better for doing it.

There has never been a single time that I have regretted doing the right thing for an animal, regardless of the personal sacrifice willingly made, and as for human surgeons I expect, when you're actively involved with a case, your inbuilt surgeon hormones take over, and you are immune to tiredness or any other personal challenge until the operation is completed. With surgery, all one can do is weigh up the circumstances of the patient and the family at that moment, the risks versus the potential rewards, and the harm that can be done by doing nothing by comparison with undertaking surgery, and then proceed with the ethical welfare considerations of the patient at the heart of the decision-making. With spinal injury in particular, one can never know for sure whether one is doing the right thing because, as I've said, the recovery and outcome are uncertain.

As happened with Olive, we performed the MRI in about

twenty minutes and twenty minutes later Ruben was in theatre. Twenty minutes after that I had cut the window in the side of the vertebrae, scooped out a large volume of exploded disc material, cut a hole in the disc and taken out the rest of the nucleus, and within an hour and a half Ruben was in the recovery ward. All was well because we'd worked as a team and did what needed to be done. Rightness had prevailed. I went home and slept soundly.

Ruben improved well for two days and we were all optimistic. Anne had by then confided in me how much Ruben meant to her because she had gone through some tough times personally and was being treated for recurrent high-grade ovarian cancer. Ruben was her soulmate, companion, comfort and constant guardian in her times of need. Then the unthinkable happened. Ruben began to deteriorate again on day three. There was clearly something badly wrong. I hate making phone calls in the face of failure. I called Anne.

She was very upset as one might imagine, not just because Ruben had deteriorated, but because she lived alone and was weak after several cycles of chemotherapy so was unable to look after a paralysed dog. She felt guilty for putting him through surgery which so far hadn't worked out, she truly didn't know how long she was going to be around and she wondered how he would cope if she wasn't there any more – and last but not least, she had no more money available. Now another MRI scan was needed to see what was wrong, then potentially more surgery. Once again, she didn't know what was the right thing to do. I now also had a very difficult decision to make. Was the right thing to do to let Ruben pass away peacefully because we had tried and it didn't work; because his mum was in such anguish; because it may not be fair to put him through further surgery; or because there was no further money? Nobody would judge me, because I had 'tried my best'.

But had I really tried my best? This is the challenging question of ethical, practical and financial 'rightness'. If I rescanned Ruben and possibly operated again, would I be 'overtreating' him?

When I started out in veterinary medicine in Ireland in 1990, the surgery I had performed on Ruben might already have been considered 'too much', and he might have been put to sleep. Thirty years later, the definition of 'overtreatment' would be critical to an adjudication on the welfare of Hermes and whether it had been right to try to treat him. In thirty years' time, it will be for the graduates of tomorrow to decide where that line is drawn in the shifting sands of biological possibility and ethical adjudication. Anne now needed to decide whether to give Ruben another chance, and I needed to decide if I could achieve further treatment without any more budget. Was it fairer to give both Ruben and Anne hope or to have Anne cope with his loss at this point, rather than potentially prolong the emotional journey for her and the embarrassment of not having the financial wherewithal? Was I being fair to the bank that funds Fitzpatrick Referrals if I considered continuing to treat Ruben? This was an ocean of pain for a practice owner and an ocean of pain for the guardian of the animal.

Anne and I talked for a long time on the phone that day, and so I felt a profound sense of connection with her even though we had never met face to face. She confided that she felt an emotional burden on many different levels. Her ovarian cancer was sadly incurable and she had been given less than a year to live. She explained that she nevertheless maintained a positive outlook and commented that all life is uncertain and that we are all 'terminal', so all we can do is make the best of 'now'. She had three grown-up children and her maternal instinct for Ruben shone through. Ruben had been by her side during three years of cancer treatment – three years of pain, disappointment and loss. He got her out for walks and was a 'champion fox-poo-roller', 'prize-winning Frisbee catcher' and 'entertainer'. He had been a loving shaggy head on her lap, a furry rug by her feet, and he slept close by her bedroom door as if guarding her, so she felt safe. In an email she later sent me, she said Ruben was a 'non-judgemental, sentient being who has shared life's joys and sorrows and who is sensitive to my feelings and emotions when I have felt too fragile to communicate these to a fellow human being – an extraordinary connection of trust, understanding, joy and love'.

Anne said that Ruben had been hugely important to her after her diagnosis and throughout her treatment for cancer, especially when she had lost all hope. She told me how devastating it was to receive the news that her cancer was terminal, but also how much the manner in which a medical professional communicated that prognosis had been critical to her self-esteem and her ability to just get through that day. Even though she knew she was going to die, she said 'upfront facts delivered with sensitivity and compassion' had allowed her to maintain her dignity and feel that whatever happened would be the 'right thing'. It meant a lot to me that she thanked me for showing her the same respect and honesty when I talked to her about Ruben, and for treating them both with empathy and compassion.

In many ways Ruben became the physical embodiment of that rightness for her. If he had hope, she had hope. I explained that it would be morally wrong to give her false hope and our decision would only and could only be based on his welfare. She fully understood that, but asked me to explain the best and worst scenarios. I and the team felt that it was likely that a blood clot or, in spite of my best efforts, more leaking disc material had recompressed the spinal cord – a bit like putting your foot on a hosepipe. We felt that the spinal cord had shown real potential for recovery, and so we felt that it was ethically right to investigate and if necessary reoperate in the hope that we could take the foot off the pipe again. If on investigation we decided that we couldn't reoperate with a good chance of success, then he should be put to sleep. From a cost perspective there were no implants involved and we did not consider that, if it were necessary, cutting a bigger window and scooping out more stuff could be considered complex or as overtreatment.

Anne made the decision that I should try to help Ruben, so I did. The MRI scan did indeed reveal a large blood clot, which was unusual. I reoperated, decompressed the spinal cord and Ruben slowly recovered.

He spent just under a month with us at the hospital, because Anne couldn't cope with his initial recovery, and went home two days before my birthday in December 2019. I told Anne it was a wonderful birthday treat for me to reunite Ruben with her. Anne had become increasingly frail but a good friend brought her to visit Ruben during his stay, so we'd had lots of time to get to know each other better. I learned that she had suffered a physically and mentally abusive relationship with her alcoholic and controlling ex-husband. She felt that Ruben was the only male she could trust. When I had offered to help her, she told me that I had seemed like a kind man, the likes of whom she had rarely encountered in her recent life; someone helping her to shoulder some of the burden of life, which had given her comfort and peace in making what she felt had been the right decision. For my birthday she sent me an article about how doing the right thing earns us 'angel wings', with a note asking me to give my mother a hug from Ruben and saying that my mammy should be proud of inspiring me to do the right thing. I did indeed hug Mammy Rita on Ruben's behalf and passed on what Anne had also said: 'There can never be enough hugs in the world.'

The last conversation I had with Anne was in mid-January 2020, when she had come with Ruben for a check-up along with her friend Nicky, but wanted to have a quiet word with me on her own. We spoke for a long time about what most makes us 'human' – our vulnerability, sensitivity, compassion, empathy and sense of moral rightness. She said that she knew she was dying and that we may not meet again, so she wanted me to tell her and Ruben's story and, warts and all, since she had come to the conclusion that animals make us most human – and that if more of us experienced the love, hope and peace that Ruben had given to her, then all of life's challenges would be easier to deal with.

We spoke about doing the right thing, even when nobody's watching, and about empathy. She thanked me for giving Ruben hope, and for giving her the peace of knowing that she had done the right thing for him. She said that Nicky would look after Ruben after she had gone, for which she was very grateful, and that she could die happy knowing that he was safe. Anne especially wanted to tell me what solace it brought her to recall the first few magical nights with Ruben after he arrived as a frightened puppy nearly nine years previously, when they had formed an extraordinary bond of love and trust – 'a bond that will be as strong on those sleepless nights trying to tiptoe out of the room as when that bond is eventually broken when one of you is there no longer'. She often closed her eyes and remembered him then: now he would be looking after her and keeping her safe in her last months and weeks.

Anne passed away peacefully on 28 March 2020. I'm blessed to have had both her and Ruben in my life.

CHAPTER SEVEN

Innovation

'Innovation distinguishes between a leader and a follower.'

Steve Jobs

Being innovative means either: doing things that have never been done before; doing them in a way that hasn't been actioned before; or having such an entirely different approach to problem-solving to the extent that the innovator doesn't see challenges as anything other than an opportunity. Some people live their lives in a box, some think outside the box and some never even knew there was a box in the first place. *Possibility* is intrinsic to an innovator's DNA in a way which doesn't seem arrogant. How do they manage that? How do we become the best we can be, self-assured in our ability to innovate and create, in a modest and humble way, and carry others with us on our tidal wave of change?

Children are innovators from the moment they are born, because everything is possible and everything is a voyage of discovery. Then life takes over. Our contemporaries, our family or even our teachers and mentors tell us that dreams are impossible and we should limit our horizons. They tell us that we're not bright or 'gifted' enough; to give up our dream of becoming a Nobel Prize-winning scientist, or a professional football player, or a musician, or a famous writer because the chances of success are so slim. Maybe you yourself have had a fantastic idea for baking special cakes, or a gizmo for opening bottle caps, or a device that turns your garden gnome into a security system, only to see someone else go on to commercialise your brilliant innovation. That has happened to me on more than one occasion. Or perhaps you have just felt that you have no potential, or that nobody is ever going to listen to you, and your ideas don't matter because maybe they are not as good as everyone else's?

Of course these hurdles are difficult to overcome. Perhaps you'll never believe you're the best, maybe you can't see any way out of your situation, perhaps you don't imagine that you have it in you to be innovative. I think that everyone starts from that position. Down the years I have realised what I am and am not good at and, in all of my endeavours, I've learned to try to focus on my skills and gather people around me who have the skills that I lack. I am extremely fortunate to have wonderfully talented surgeons in the Fitzpatrick Referrals team who can perform surgeries for which I don't have the training and simply cannot do. Innovation thrives on diversity and delegation. I aim to provide for my colleagues a canvas on which they can paint their dreams. In so doing we all win, because we all innovate together for the greater good of our patients.

Looking back over the course of my career, there are many things I would have done differently and I have had hundreds of failures in my business, media and surgical career

– however, because I have failed I have succeeded, and in doing so I have learned these three key lessons from animals:

1. You have to equip yourself and believe yourself to be the very best at what you do with regard to what you can achieve at this moment in time. Or, if you know that you are not necessarily the best, then surround yourself with other people who are the best in their chosen field and create an environment in which together you have the tools and resources to challenge the status quo, push boundaries and grow. The alpha dog in any pack knows that he's not always the strongest or the smartest: his gift is to manage the expectations of all of those in his group so that they feel fulfilled and so that the team can win.

2. Animals are adept at spotting opportunities that we might miss. I learned this lesson a long time ago as a small child walking sheep from farm to farm along country roads with my daddy. I had been bemoaning the fact that I wasn't good enough at school and didn't see any opportunity a few hours before. Then, as we were walking the sheep, one of them spied a gap in a hedge I hadn't seen, and off through the gap the sheep went, with all of the rest of the flock following. Daddy sighed and told me I was an idiot for not seeing the gap, but afterwards when we had collected all of the sheep again, he just nudged me and said I should learn from a sheep, because 'they always see opportunity'. Of course I have seen cats escape into a nook or cranny in my consulting rooms down the years and had to build new cupboard defences, and I have seen dogs escape from where they should be all the time, sometimes coming a cropper and having an accident. But the one thing we can

be sure of is that dogs and cats, and sheep in this instance, see space, an endless possibility for escape from the confines that we dictate they must have.

3. Many times we don't see the opportunity for innovation because we do not leave our minds open to it. Our canine and feline friends reimagine a different game every time they play. A cat will turn a ball of fluff into the most exciting toy ever and a dog will create the greatest joy imaginable in his frolics with a grimy old sock. Moment by moment, every morning is infinitely full of possibility as each new sensation is an opportunity to rejoice in a fresh adventure. Wouldn't it be really great if we got out of bed every morning, let go of the impediments of the previous day and welcomed in a world of possibility?

I innovate only when I have to – when the existing techniques or implants are suboptimal or impracticable for a given application. Innovation is often the distillate of frustration, exasperation, deliberation and determination. Done well it brings elevation and clarity; done badly, however, it can bring endless problems and pain. The effort of innovation, though, doesn't always equal the equity of realised 'success' as society defines it. You may innovate in all kinds of ways that don't achieve tangible results, but I firmly believe that if you keep going, you will succeed. I also believe that we need to redefine what success looks like. Too often in the modern world it's through the prism of money or position in society. Sure, we need some money to survive, but how much money and at what cost to your soul? Furthermore, constantly striving for acknowledgement may counterintuitively stifle innovation, because we're so worried about criticism that we don't really want to 'rock the boat'. I've rocked a fair few boats in my life, and I have annoyed people who feel that I'm pushing things too far. I don't invite praise; I just want to make a difference to each of my patients. I don't invite criticism either, but that's very necessary because it's important to hold all innovators in medicine to account from an ethical perspective.

I've had some successes, but there is such a long way to go. We are very far away from a society where advances in veterinary medicine simultaneously inform human medicine, and vice versa. As I've illustrated before, at the moment animals' lives are sacrificed to develop drugs and implants used to cure humans, yet these innovative treatments rarely become quickly available for veterinary use, because the manufacturer needs to make back their investment from human medicine first. For example, if experimental animals are used to develop a new cancer drug or antibiotic, it most likely will not be available to treat disease in cats and dogs for many years. I'd like to change this unjust paradigm of innovation in my lifetime. There are, however, major challenges.

On the one hand, *The Supervet* TV programme raises awareness of progress, and on the other it has led to the RCVS complaint procedure regarding the treatment of Hermes featured on a show. Again, as discussed, my door remains open for anyone, including my critics, to come and spend some time with me and my team. It would certainly be easier to make a living performing less advanced surgery, without such scrutiny or criticism, but I have chosen to try to innovate for the benefit of my patients because I do not believe that maintaining the status quo is good enough. I also believe we owe it to the animals.

Currently any implant can be placed in a companion

animal by any vet in the UK without ethics approval, as long as the vet is considered to 'have appropriate evidence', that they explain what they consider to be the options to their client, and are doing as would be expected of any other vet of their skill level. However, for me specifically, because I am on TV, the suggestion is that I should have (1) an ethics adjudication panel, or (2) a Home Office licence for experimental animal work. Other vets in the UK can currently employ new implant designs if they wish without any of these. In my opinion veterinary governing bodies and academic journals need to clarify a detailed set of guidelines for all implants used by vets of every skill level with absolute accountability for the protection of animal welfare. This would lay down the rules within which any innovation at all can – or cannot – take place. Currently there isn't a clear definition of 'over-treatment' – for example, whether it's more likely to apply to a first-time custom implant in the hands of an experienced surgeon, or a widely used implant with a known high failure rate in the hands of an inexperienced surgeon. Unfortunately, it's not uncommon to see this latter scenario for revision surgery at our practice.

In human medicine, by law most drugs and implants require an animal study for efficacy and safety data to keep people safe, which is completely understandable. I am seeking to reduce, refine and replace this as new technologies and opportunities for fairness to animals evolve. On more than one occasion, people have suggested to me that it may be more appropriate if the implants I invent are put into a healthy research dog or cat sacrificed in a controlled laboratory experiment with the defined end point of death, as has been done in the past for some implants, before offering them to any 'client-owned' patients I may see in my practice.

There are three challenges with this as I see it: (1) Will veterinary medicine deny state-of-the-art technologies that are available now to dogs and cats who are suffering and offer only amputation, joint fusion or euthanasia? Even if I think I am more likely to succeed with an innovative implant than a commercially available one, I can use the latter without recrimination, but if I use the former I risk the accusation of 'experimentation'. If such innovation is not allowed, for my own part I cannot risk the livelihoods of more than 250 people at Fitzpatrick Referrals and my licence to practise. Additionally, much of the time I am revising other implants that have already failed anyway. (2) Will the veterinary profession and society prefer an experimental study on an otherwise healthy animal rather than helping an animal in need who is diseased? On some innovations I have five to seven years of follow-up evidence that I can publish if I am allowed to do so. All families absolutely knew that the implants were new and all other options were offered. Publishing this data will help save lives. However, some journals feel that custom implants need different governance to commercially available implants. Commercially available implants can be used, can fail and can be published without an experimental animal licence or ethics review. (3) Who would justify an experimental animal study that yields long-term follow-up of five to seven years when clinical studies already provide the evidence? As an example, since I put in my first total elbow replacement (TER) more than a decade ago, I have worked with three commercially available systems, but sadly over time experienced significant failure and pain for the animal and for myself with all of them.

After just such an elbow replacement had failed for Jen, Sharron's Staffie cross-breed rescue dog, I was determined to develop a TER system that would aim to resolve all of the problems I had seen with the existing systems. My ideas had been accumulating with each failed operation and for a couple of years I'd been actively working with Jay Meswania and his new colleague Verity Allum on a design that could work. We had made real progress with the development, but at some point one dog would need to become Patient Number One.

I first met seven-year-old Labrador Millie in spring 2019. It was a beautiful crisp morning and I could almost taste the freshness of the day as I walked her out into the yard to observe her gait with her guardians, Mike and Kim. Millie had been lame on her front legs since she was about eighteen months old. In fact, her developmental elbow disease had begun when she was a puppy, but it's often very difficult to notice when it affects both sides. Now she was crippled with horrendous osteoarthritis affecting both of her elbows. It was pitiful.

Mike and Kim had tried surgery and all kinds of pain medication and injections into the joints, but nothing was working any more. Every day was a struggle: sometimes she was yelping in extreme pain, but most often she was depressed and didn't want to go for a walk. When she did go out, she'd pull up after a few minutes and want to head home. She had lost all joy for life and was a shadow of her former self, so they had brought her to me to see if I could perform an elbow replacement and improve her quality of life.

Kim and Mike had almost not rescued Millie. Kim had first seen the eight-month-old puppy in the back of a stonemason's pickup truck at an animal shelter where she had gone to see if she could rehome an abandoned dog. The stonemason had found Millie abandoned in a lay-by on a main road with a broken leg, and Kim told the shelter that she'd adopt Millie if nobody claimed her. However, Millie was then transferred to another shelter and it took Kim and Mike three months to trace her through the dog warden before she was finally welcomed into their home and became best friends with everyone in the family. Mike loved her like a daughter. Kim was caring for her elderly parents: her father had had a stroke and had vascular dementia, while Kim's mum had a tumour the size of a melon on her leg, and Millie nursed them all, including Kim herself who would take Millie on a walk and scream at the hedgerows with frustration and exhaustion.

As I've said, it is often such moments of frustration, exasperation and screaming at hedges that breeds innovation. If the operation on Jen and other similar patients had gone really well, then I would not have felt the need to develop a new total elbow replacement. All of the previous TER designs had been implanted by multiple surgeons, as well as myself, without formal ethics approval or an experimental animal licence from the relevant regulatory bodies, since it wasn't deemed to be required. My design was simply an iterative development based on the reasons for failure I had experienced in my own previous patients, very much akin to other such developments that are applied widely in veterinary surgery also without formal regulatory approval. Millie potentially was Patient Number One for the custom elbow replacement system that Jay and I had worked on for years, but before I could contemplate surgery, given the ongoing RCVS complaint, I thought it best to seek written approval and hope for a prompt response so I could aim to operate as quickly as possible.

I had submitted several cases for formal ethics approval

by the RCVS in early 2019, one of which was an elbow replacement identical to Millie's. While I was waiting for approval, some of these patients and also Millie deteriorated and the families understandably asked me to act since all were suffering. I explained to Mike and Kim that the process was taking longer than I had hoped and they knew I could proceed either with the commercially available or the custom TER, and that both could fail. Kim and Mike were very much aware that Millie would be the first to have this particular custom TER.

Mike and Kim loved Millie. She was in extreme pain, all previous joint surgery, injections and medical intervention had failed, and they didn't want to put her to sleep, nor did they want to fuse her elbow solid (an arthrodesis) or amputate because she had arthritis on the opposite side too. Ethical panel adjudication was not a legal requirement and still isn't – for any surgeon – and, of course, the relief of pain and suffering is the ultimate aim of any veterinary surgeon. I felt I could get her out of pain in a reasonable time frame and so they elected to proceed with the custom design and I operated in June 2019.

The RCVS replied in July 2019 saying that the procedures I suggested, including custom TER, were recognised veterinary practice (RVP) and that they didn't wish to stifle veterinarian innovation, but that these were clinical decisions for each individual case and an ethics review shouldn't be seen as a 'rubber stamp' for a treatment. Furthermore, ideally these cases should undergo peer review before owner consent, but the RCVS response didn't advise on how that might be achievable on a daily basis. Their ethics review panel felt it was not within their scope to review individual clinical cases because these were not research applications;

they were considering setting up a pool of specialists to help and asked if I had further questions. I duly replied with a long list of queries regarding whether all implants and all surgeons should have similar peer review and if the paperwork I suggested for a peer review panel was appropriate. Exactly one year to the day I write this, and as yet I have had no response – so currently the issue of permission for innovation remains unresolved. I absolutely recognise that the RCVS is a very busy organisation; I have great respect for whatever they decide in the end regarding regulation of innovation and I will of course do whatever I'm instructed to do, as would any surgeon in this regard. However, I wonder whether vets or laypeople on a panel have the legal right to prohibit an operation that a client has chosen for their dog or cat? Is it fair if the ethics review process keeps an animal in pain for months longer than necessary? If a vet innovates, can other vets complain with no formal rules in place to protect that vet, the client and the patient?

I also asked for help from ethics review boards at universities; however, they responded that I should not transfer my own moral responsibility to them. I wasn't trying to 'pass the buck'. I was simply trying to do the right thing for my patients, arrive at a protocol that worked in real clinical practice, for example when a patient may have suffered for many months or years after previous failed operations. In such circumstances, ethics protocols designed for experimental animals with clearly defined end points simply do not work for these guardians who do not want to put their animal to sleep. I was also doing my best to protect myself and my colleagues from accusations of wrongdoing, while I honestly felt that a new implant would be a superior option to improve quality of life for my patient. Why would I use an implant that others still use, without ethics approval, but which I felt was likely to fail?

In the meantime, failing all else, I have set up an ethics review panel with my peers to evaluate patients as best I can. It's necessary, but I just wish it were easier and faster and that there was a central guidance panel, to which I'd be happy to contribute both financially and practically.

For Millie, the possible reward of surgery outweighed the risk. This is the general equation for all surgery, since all surgery carries risk. The difference here is that she would be Patient Number One. And yet, the same is true for a vet who has just taken a course, and for new implants launched by companies, which happens all the time without people knowing. I believe that in every case, full transparency is paramount. If there were fair, well-defined rules and jurisdiction for all vets across the nation, then the public could make up their own minds about what treatment they want for their animal friend. Then nobody can step out of line, and, importantly, I wouldn't need to put my career on the line in order to make progress.

The innovation process – from concepts in my head through design, fabrication and finishing – is as integral to resolving pain and providing quality of life as are my surgeries. Without the implants, there is no surgery, and without the surgery there is no innovation in clinical practice.

Millie's surgery was challenging, but no more or less so than with any previous TER system. Millie would stand on the shoulders of many failures like Jen before her – because, by definition, innovation requires failure. People think that being 'the Supervet' makes me the best opinion on all things veterinary, when nothing could be further from the truth. It's unlikely anyone would ask a cardiology consultant about their broken wrist, and yet they regularly expect veterinary 'surgeons' to be able to perform all kinds of surgery and a specialist surgeon like me to know about things that general practitioners are much better at than me. As the years go by, I know more and more about less and less. Super-specialism is necessary for optimal innovation. I know as much as I can after thirty years of effort about orthopaedics and neurosurgery, while I know hardly anything at all about skin, lung, liver or heart problems. In 2020 it is impossible for one person to be expert at everything, because the volume of knowledge, and more importantly practical hands-on experience, transcends the capacity of a single individual. I am quite sure that given the choice, a dog or a cat would want the best surgeon who could operate in the most efficient, effective and ethical fashion to always do the right thing, even if the right thing to do is not to operate.

I first set out to build Fitzpatrick Referrals as a hospital full of like-minded individuals who wanted to contribute new ideas of their own. We would break through the norm of veterinary hospitals and build three integrated but separate hubs, one for orthopaedics and neurology, one for cancer (oncology) and soft tissue surgery, and one for innovation in skeletal reconstruction and regenerative medicine. We would not try to be all things to all people, but we would endeavour to be the best in the world in our chosen fields and employ teams of people whose only job is to look after the dogs and cats in our wards, to try to provide as much of a home away from home as possible. I made many mistakes along the way and, as I've said, things have always been financially tough. I never paid much attention to the normal metrics of doing business; I just firmly believed that if we built the best possible practice, then people would bring their animals to see us

– we depend on the goodwill of clients who actively choose to take advantage of our services and of primary care clinicians who believe we shall do a good job for their patients.

Making *The Supervet* has, of course, brought with it both challenges and rewards. While we have shown people what is possible through innovation, because we aim to offer all of the options to all of the animals all of the time, some vets or potential clients may perceive wrongly that we are 'too advanced' and don't do 'normal' surgery. The thing about the television show, however, is that by its very nature, TV tends to focus on anything 'out of the ordinary'. On *The Supervet* the producers are more likely to feature a case in which osteoarthritis in a dog is treated with an innovative stem cell procedure, rather than one where I prescribe a routine course of tablets, or one in which we mend a fracture previously deemed impossible to repair, or perform a knee replacement with custom implants. But, in fact, as for any other company in the world that innovates, more than 90 per cent of what we do is normal service provision at an extraordinarily high standard and a competitive cost – or otherwise we'd never be able to afford to pay any wages or overheads and simply wouldn't survive.

Also, without this regular routine workflow, innovation wouldn't be possible. That's just an unavoidable fact – innovation can't exist in a financial vacuum, and contrary to popular opinion, as I've explained previously, advanced cases do not make more money than routine surgeries. Complex implant technologies require investment and time and for the foreseeable future will not make a similar profit margin to routine operations which can be performed more quickly and in larger numbers. I believe that this is one of the reasons for the lack of willingness to innovate in clinical veterinary practice, and I do worry about that from the perspective of all animals.

The Supervet has revealed that innovation and disruptive thinking in clinical veterinary practice is more problematic than it is in industry or business, because of the perception of 'overtreatment', when in fact it's just incremental baby steps forward. In the technical industries, for example, innovators are encouraged to push past conventional wisdom because they are aware that customers don't know what they want until they see it, whereas innovation in medicine is certainly not a straight-line process and being a surgeon means first 'doing no harm'. Innovation in medicine is a constant process of thought evolution that leads to iterative incremental progress over time. The families who come to see me for solutions when all else has failed, or for treatment that only we at Fitzpatrick Referrals provide at this point in time, applaud innovation, but as I've said, some in the veterinary profession are yet to be convinced. In veterinary medicine I think that innovation of thought and a deracination of cynicism will be as important for progress as any implant or drug innovation will ever be.

The future for innovation is a key question facing veterinary medicine right now. As I've touched on already, many university faculty members, older and younger vet professionals, new graduates and undergraduates I have spoken to actually do not want to do anything 'new' in clinical veterinary practice until someone else has 'tested' it out and there is evidence for efficacy so that the ethical implications do not have any direct ramifications for them personally. The obvious questions are who is going to 'test' new ideas, on what animals, in what environment and with what skill level?

Millie's innovative TER was an incremental improvement

that was born of failure with other devices. She is now one year out from surgery with her custom elbow replacement. Kim and Mike are delighted with her recovery to date and report that she's 'like a puppy again'. They have sent me videos of her enjoying herself running about with a spring in her step, and jumping in and out of streams. Of course, nobody knows how long this implant will continue to function, but based on similar metal and plastic – cobalt-chromium (CoCr) and polyether ether ketone (PEEK) – in other guises, we hope it will be until the end of her life. A high-resolution CT scan (with special software for removal of metal artefact) has shown the bone growing into the implant. This is a revolution; we can now actually look at the bone-implant interface – a kind of 'virtual' histology (the study of microanatomy with a microscope) – so now, unlike with an experimental animal, Millie's death was not necessary in order to prove that this implant incorporates well and works. In addition to this, Kim and Mike have told me that when she dies they would like to donate her body so that categorical and undeniable evidence of efficacy can then be published, without the need to take the life of another animal and still satisfy current FDA and MHRA standards of evidence-based medicine if such evidence were accepted, which it currently is not. Without belief in this kind of innovation by animal and human medicine, no progress of this kind can ever be possible. Technology has changed for the better, we must change our attitudes for the better too.

After her one-year check-up, Kim emailed me. She wrote, 'I can never thank you enough, Noel. You told the complete and honest truth: you gave us the worst-case scenario and you let us be the advocates for Millie. Our choice was either to let her continue in crippling pain, watching the spark in her life never return, or to act and take a chance so that she might enjoy the years she has left. This was a no-brainer as far as we were concerned. No matter how long this implant lasts with Millie, and no matter what the outcome had been, we will always know that we made the right decision. Thank you for caring, for giving us the choice and for giving Millie her life back.' She added some sage advice with, 'Please ignore the people who make judgements from armchairs, because they have no idea how committed you are to making a huge difference to this world. Thank you for making a huge difference to ours.'

The family of Bella also absolutely knew that there were no guarantees with surgery. Bella was an adorable, friendly, vivacious, cheeky seven-year-old boxer dog who came to see me in September 2016. She lived on a farm and from an early age it was her 'manor' and she roamed where she pleased. All of the local community knew and loved her. She visited their homes whenever she found the need for company and returned home only when it was raining or there was nobody around. Sadly, in a matter of seconds she went from being a gregarious rambler to being in extreme pain crushed under a tractor trailer. She was rushed to her primary care vet who promptly sent her to their local referral centre. Her abdomen was ripped open, with her urinary bladder hanging out, her pelvis was badly fractured, one hip joint was dislocated and the femur of the other back leg was shattered in many pieces. She had also fractured some bones in one of her back feet. The family were given the option of a long and arduous recovery or euthanasia, knowing that the outcome would likely be suboptimal because of the complexity of her injuries. The clinician made it clear that she may lose one of her back legs and that the function of the other would likely not be great. Bella's mum, Julie, stayed up all night and the entire family had an agonising time trying to decide whether it was the right thing to operate or to allow her to be put to sleep.

Julie and her family, especially her daughter Lorna, were all very close to Bella, so all they could think to do was the best they could in that particular moment and they had elected for surgery. Nobody could know for sure what would happen, as is the way for all surgery, but the surgeon did a fantastic job of piecing Bella back together. However, she was left with no femoral head on the dislocated hip side and the piecing together of the femoral fracture on the opposite side was challenging. This was all on top of fixing her pelvic and foot fractures. Bella's surgeries had gone as well as could be expected and most people were encouraging to Julie and her family, supportive of their efforts to give her a chance. However, some had not been and were quite disparaging, saying that she was suffering too much and should be put to sleep, and why were they spending so much money because she was 'just a dog'.

Bella was part of Julie and Lorna's family, she loved them and trusted them to watch over her and they loved her back. Obviously, if one of Julie's children had had a similar accident, trying to save life and limb wouldn't even have been questioned – the implications for recovery or the cost of the procedures wouldn't even be discussed. However, in some people's view, it's different with animals – they are disposable. We all understand the difference between a child and a dog – this isn't anthropomorphism – but Bella didn't need to die. If she could be saved, why should they not try? Julie, her husband Peter, and her children Lorna and Louis were by her side throughout the recovery and indeed it strengthened their resolve and love for each other as a family.

Julie and the family had then brought Daisy into their brood, a gorgeous white boxer puppy. She and Bella quickly became inseparable and finally Bella started to become more active. Unfortunately, because she had lost her hip joint on one side and her femur had been so badly damaged on the other, her mobility remained poor. And then tragedy struck for a second time. Her femur had never healed because the multiple fragments of bone (multi-comminuted) had become stripped of their blood supply (devascularised) by the trauma. The top and bottom of the bone had been held together by a large pin and two bone plates, but now the entire central part of the femur (diaphysis) had wasted away (atrophic defect non-union), the screws had broken and the leg had imploded. Only the uppermost (proximal) and lowermost (distal) couple of inches of femur remained with loose implants spanning a huge gap of dead tissue in the middle. Added to this, the quadriceps, which is the powerful muscle on the front of the leg that extends the knee, had become congealed onto the devitalised fragments in a large clump of scar tissue, such that the leg couldn't move much.

Full amputation of this right hind limb was the obvious first choice, as it had been from the outset. But sadly the top of the femur on the left side had congealed with scar tissue (fibrosis) around what had been the hip socket, had poor mobility and was tugging on the nerves in that area. As such it was painful, with a dramatically reduced range of motion, and Bella could barely get around now that the right femur had collapsed. Function after full amputation of the right limb was likely going to be poor. Bella was by now crawling, hopping and in significant pain. The right hind leg from the knee down was twisting and hanging on scar tissue alone now that the implants had failed. The original surgeon had done a very good job, but when bone doesn't properly heal, ultimately the majority of implants will fail.

It was love at first sight for Bella and me. It was as if we'd known each other forever. We had a big cuddle and I sat with her on the floor in my consulting room while Julie and Lorna told me the entire story. We discussed the ethics of doing anything at all, but clearly the options were limited. We could amputate the right leg but she would remain in pain with poor function on the left. We could possibly try to cut out the scar tissue on the left hip and put a hip replacement in, but there was significant risk of nerve trauma and unpredictable function, especially on three legs. We could put her to sleep. Or we could innovate a solution. Bella looked up at us, we all looked at Bella. It was heartbreaking and clearly deeply emotional. But, as always, all I could do was present the options, discuss the ethics and the risks, and ultimately the decision would rest with them.

That's the thing about innovation in clinical veterinary practice. As I've said before, one only considers it when one absolutely has to, to save a limb or life. If conventional solutions were adequate then there would be no need to innovate. There are many who would say just put Bella to sleep, but I would encourage all of them to sit in that room with us at that moment and feel what we felt. It's not that the technology didn't exist, it's whether it would work and whether deploying it was the right thing to do. Nobody knew that. We took 3D CT scans with a protocol that allows metal artefact removal (as for Millie's elbow replacement), meaning that we could see what was left of the bone to attach implants to. Julie had friends with all kinds of opinions as she had the first time, and there is no doubt that many vets and non-vets would have advised putting Bella to sleep right there and then.

Although to some extent I love all of my patients, some feel it's wrong for the clinician to be emotionally invested, but I'm not prepared to change my stance in that regard. At the same time, I am a surgeon, so I present the facts as we know them and cannot be swayed by my emotions or the emotions of the family with regard to the indication or con- traindication for surgery. The family knew that if any plan to save the right hind leg failed, then Bella would most certainly be lost. I met with my trusted engineering and surgical col- leagues to look at ethics and achievability. A technique had already been performed in experimental animals involving taking a honeycomb mesh of titanium to fill bone defects and spraying it with cells from the bone marrow of that same animal to fill the gap. The technique had worked in animals and had just begun to be used in human patients. It couldn't, therefore, be argued that the technique had not been tested before; however, an ethical question of 'innovation' remained because the technique had not been 'tried and tested' on a clinical animal with naturally occurring disease.

In the next decade, we are going to have to engage in challenging conversations about how we value the lives of animals, and whether it is possible to build a framework for medical innovation that incorporates lessons learned from naturally occurring diseases in animals. We will need to decide whether research dogs have less intrinsic sentient value than dogs like Bella, and we are going to need our professional and regulatory authorities to make clear and transparent decisions regarding where to draw the line between RVP and experimentation. We need to consider whether lessons learned from studies in research animals are only to benefit human patients, or whether it is possible to translate this information back to animals without additional, potentially superfluous, animal testing. Does Bella's family not have the right to consent to a relatively new technology being used to save her life, or does the veterinary profession have the right to deny access to innovation simply because there is no prior Patient Number One for a given implant or treatment? Innovation is inexorable and inevitable, and I believe that the veterinary profession has a moral responsibility to drive change for the better if an existing implant or technique is found to be suboptimal and a potentially better option is available.

We designed a long cylinder of titanium mesh with custom-made plates. We carefully cut out all of the dead bone and scar tissue, freeing up the muscle which was severely congealed to the scar, taking care to keep the blood and nerve supply intact, and we removed the loose implants. We placed the mesh spacer, which then accounted for more than half of the full length of the femur, and we secured it with screws to the remaining top and bottom parts of the bone. Then, during surgery, we spun down some of Bella's bone marrow into a concentrate that was sprayed onto the trabecular titanium to encourage the bone to grow into it. This is called 'bedside' treatment because it happens alongside the primary surgery. The postoperative CT scans looked good.

Then the real work began. We all knew that it would be very difficult to rehabilitate Bella. The muscle envelope around the previous collapsed congealed scar had been significantly traumatised and it would be essential to mobilise the limb several times daily to prevent the raw muscle sticking down to the metal. The perimysium is the smooth connective tissue coating on a muscle that allows it to glide easily around bones and joints and until that had healed to a new smoother coating again, Bella wasn't safe. Plus, the muscle was contracted, so that it would need stretching. All of this would be painful for a few weeks as it would be in a human, but with numerous painkillers we set about the rehabilitation at the practice. Bella returned home and was walking on the right pelvic limb better than she had been since the original injury.

Then the family did their very best at home, again with all of their friends and neighbours joining in. It is common after severe trauma for muscles to need to be mobilised, which is always very challenging. It was traumatic for both Bella and the family, but as with a human patient, we knew that if we could just get through these first few weeks, then hopefully all would be well. Everyone involved with this journey understood that innovation comes at a price. The question for veterinary medicine going forward is whether this price is worth it. Clearly if everything worked out and Bella was running happily around a field, most would say yes; if the opposite happened then perhaps many would feel that the decision had been wrong. Hindsight is 20/20, and biology will always play a driving role in determining whether medical or surgical innovations lead to positive impact for a patient.

Sadly, in spite of all our best efforts, the muscle again re-attached to the underlying bone and metal and even with one final intervention, we failed. Bella was becoming weaker and developed problems with her blood cells, platelets, immune system and had cardiac issues. On my birthday, 13 December 2016, Julie, Lorna and I cried our eyes out, held Bella's paw, told her we loved her very much and gave her the final injection in the knowledge that together we had done our absolute best. Bella will be remembered forever by me on my birthday and by Julie, Lorna and all who knew her. She was a best friend, a constant ray of sunshine, an endless ocean of unconditional love and, most of all, an integral family member.

Julie and I stay in contact and we hope that part of Bella's legacy is that she was Patient Number One to receive this technology, and though it didn't work for her because of circumstances beyond our control, this technology will undoubtedly save limbs for many other dogs and humans in the future. We filmed this entire story and the nation shared this pain with us in an episode of *The Supervet*.

Your opinion matters, and ultimately only *you* yourself can decide if innovation in veterinary medicine is appropriate and 'worth it' and whether it is important to try advanced technology if all routine options are not viable. Innovation in medicine should only come from a place of love, and Bella will live in that place of love forever. Innovation in your life is also a choice, each and every day. It requires consistent tenacity of purpose and dedication to your dreams. Only you can make that choice too.

Just six months later in 2017, technological innovation would take another step forward when I treated a seven-year-old Maine Coon cat called Ivor. When Joanne and Mark travelled five hours to see me, they knew that the next hour with me would be the difference between life and death for Ivor. They had already tried everything else and nothing in the world mattered to them more in that moment. In fact, for many months their lives had revolved around poor Ivor as they desperately sought a solution for his horrendous plight. Joanne told me that this massive 7.5kg fluff-ball of silver tabbiness held their hearts in his furry paws. I totally understood. He was utterly gorgeous, inside and out, and as he looked up at me with his big, gentle, yellow eyes and clearly pained purr, he cast his spell – and I too fell in love instantly. In fact, meeting Ivor had made me yearn for my own Maine Coon companion and so he paved the way for Ricochet to enter my life.

When he was four years old Ivor had lost one of his back legs in an unknown trauma. He had dragged himself home pouring blood from his shredded limb and through the cat-flap into their living room before collapsing. He had lost a lot of blood and faced an uncertain future, but pulled through and remained a big, gentle, clumsy character who made them laugh every day and was best pals with their miniature schnauzer Bluebelle.

Three years later, his remaining back leg was collapsing at the ankle and he had great difficulty standing. The injury likely actually dated back to his original trauma, but had worsened over time. In humans, we stand on our ankle (tarsus) and the arch of our foot is the metatarsus. A cat has similarly named bones, but stands up on his or her toes such that the metatarsus is long and used for forward propulsion, while the tarsus is high off the ground and used almost like a 'clasp-knife' spring for explosive jumping. By the time I saw him, Ivor was in significant pain; he was barely able to get around, and his quality of life had become very poor. He had horrendous arthritis in his ankle, which was hugely swollen, as well as severe collapse and marked deformity of the bones. His foot was effectively dangling from the bottom of his shin bone (tibia), and, critically, on top of the degeneration and inflammation he had now developed an aggressive infection. We cultured three different species of highly virulent bacteria from his joint.

Joanne, Mark and I had a soul-searching consultation, where we discussed the ethics and morals of putting Ivor through possibly more than one surgery, all with a guarded prognosis. They were emotionally torn about surgery, but medical management wasn't working and the only other reasonable option was euthanasia. Ivor was otherwise a normal healthy cat and, as in nearly all such circumstances, it was not an issue of 'nothing can be done', since generally there are many things that *can* be done: it was more an issue of what was the *right* thing to do.

None of us knew if surgery would work, as it was a very challenging biological environment. Joanne asked me what I would do if Ivor were mine, and, as always, I had to say that I could only objectively give them the facts as I saw them, and not sway their decision in any way. I'll never forget what Joanne said to me afterwards: 'Well, he's alive now, so we need to decide what to do right now.' And how right she was.

I tried to get the infection under control with antibiotics before bridging the ankle with a plate and screws and implanting bone graft in what is known as a fusion or arthrodesis. It didn't work. The ankle bones had been destroyed by the infection and had lost their blood supply, with dead (necrotic) bone that appeared 'moth-eaten' on the X-ray pictures. He ended up with a large discharging infected hole in his ankle (an infected necrotic defect non-union) and no healthy back leg on the other side to carry his weight. A heartbreaking discussion followed. Now we were on thin ice. How much more should we put Ivor through – even if it were possible?

There are plenty of people both inside and outside my profession who would have advised euthanasia at that moment. Ivor was suffering and there wasn't an existing treatment for his condition. Full limb amputation was not an option – he didn't have another leg to stand on, literally. If we were to amputate his leg mid-tibia and fit a stump-socket prosthesis, akin to a human artificial limb which fits on the outside of a stump, his quality of life would likely be poor. We were the only centre in the UK that could offer a proven skeleton-anchored prosthesis, but the risk was too high with the infection, and the resultant function of the 'bionic' limb would be unpredictable. Euthanasia, therefore, would have been an entirely legitimate choice to end Ivor's suffering – indeed many could understandably argue it was his best option for 'treatment'.

There was, however, one other possibility – but to my knowledge, nobody had ever tried it before. With Bella we had used 'bedside' bone marrow cells, but with Ivor we proposed to go one step further – before the actual operation we would extract stem cells from his fat tissue, grow them in the lab to turn them into bone cells, and then seed them onto a curved trabecular titanium spacer, much like a honeycomb block. These cultured stem cells would, we hoped, encourage the bone to grow into the titanium mesh (bone 'ingrowth'), with the goal of maximising integration and preventing breakdown of the construct, i.e. 'rejection' of the implant. Therein lay the dilemma. Many would say, 'Well, if it's not tried and tested then we shouldn't do it, because the animal may suffer.' This is true, the animal may suffer, but we do have a cut-off point – which is that if the animal is suffering without reasonable hope of resolution, or for too prolonged a time relative to life expectancy, then we euthanise. As I've previously mentioned, human medicine forbids euthanasia – and yet experimental, and sometimes high-risk, treatments are carried out frequently in human patients, otherwise medicine would never advance at all.

There is a danger in any surgery that decisions could be made for emotional or anthropomorphic reasons: emotion can take over and someone may just not be prepared to say goodbye to an animal friend, even if it's no longer in their best interests to stay alive. My moral responsibility is to help the animal's guardian(s) to understand that if improvement with medicine or surgery is not likely in a reasonable time frame, then euthanasia may be kindest. It's about putting one's feelings in context and judging how much the patient will have to go through – and for how long – to get a quality of life. So, the question regarding Ivor was similar to that faced in the case of Hermes the tortoise: should we attempt this new surgery and I risk the charge of 'overtreatment' and of pushing medicine too far? This decision needed to be made as quickly as possible, because Ivor was suffering and his life depended upon it.

Joanne and Mark decided that they wanted to have one last try to save Ivor's life with the proviso that, if at any point we felt he was suffering, they would accept the recommendation for euthanasia, and that this was a condition of any treatment.

During surgery, I scooped out all of the dead bone and attached the foot (metatarsus and toes) to the shin bone (tibia) with a plate and screws internally and a scaffolding frame externally – an 'external skeletal fixator' which consisted of aluminium rings and arches with supporting wires driven through the upper shin bone and the foot, like bicycle spokes, with the rings then connected using bars and clamps. This part of the procedure had a long track record and was first proposed by the Russian scientist Ilizarov in Siberia after the Second World War. At that time it was used to treat soldiers with infected fractures that were not healing (defect

Credit: Barney James/Timeless Pictures

Onstage at The O2 Arena in London for the last date of the 'Supervet Live' tour, only hours after completely losing my voice and nearly cancelling the show. Little did I know that back at the surgery, a letter waited for me that would cause so much pain and heartache . . .

The real star of the show, Keira – in her triple A pass.

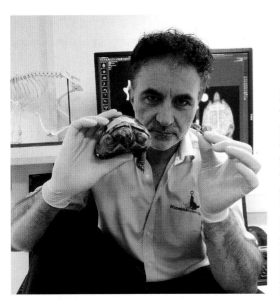

Hermes the Hermann's tortoise, who proved to be one of the greatest practical and ethical challenges of my entire career. Here I am, holding one of the three bionic limbs that I anchored to his remaining bone stumps, after rats had eaten off his feet. The decision to operate – a decision that in my heart I still feel was the right thing to do – resulted in many months of pain for me, as my professional integrity was called into question and my entire career hung in the balance.

With David and one-and-a-half-year-old Neapolitan mastiff Demon. He was 55kg of pure effervescent love, who would plop his massive paw into my hand every time I saw him.

Eight-and-a-half-year-old black Labrador Mac and his dad, Keith, had a profound and extraordinary bond, and I felt honoured to be able to give Keith a few more months with his best friend.

Spud, a beautiful Labrador cross German shepherd dog who gave his dad, Chris, a former addict, back his life. Time and again down through the years, I have seen how animals shine a light on darkness within us when sometimes no person can do that, no matter how hard they try. That's the enlightenment, sharing and companionship of unconditional love.

Credit: Chris Grewcock

Ivor, the seven-year-old Maine Coon who paved the way for Ricochet to enter my life. Ivor is, to my knowledge, the first cat in the world to have a titanium scaffold seeded with bone stem cells derived from fat to fill a defect in his leg.

Tongue-lolling, life-loving, joy-hugging spaniel Rocco, going to work in his dad's van.

It was love at first sight for cheeky seven-year-old boxer Bella and me. After being crushed under a tractor trailer, we innovated a solution to try to save her right hind leg but sadly it didn't work for her because of circumstances beyond our control. I hope that Bella's legacy is that, in having been Patient Number One to receive this technology, she will help to save limbs for many other dogs and humans in the future. Bella's treatment paved the way for Ivor's, and together they are the embodiment of a new paradigm of 'One Medicine'.

Olive, a beautiful eight-year-old dachshund who was like a little guardian angel sent from above – not just for me – but for many others too. Olive had a disc extrusion in the middle of her back that was squashing her spinal cord, and after recovering from her operation she was able to return to her career as a therapy dog.

Peanut the kitten, named because he was born with front leg deformities that meant he didn't have functional wrists or paws on his either of his front legs, and was therefore shaped like a peanut. This little black-and-white mischief machine had the heart of a lion, and was the first cat in the world to have double amputation prostheses for both front legs.

Credit: Denise Gregor

Suited and rather painfully booted at the wonderful wedding of Harry and Meghan. I haven't worn those shoes since!

Credit: Getty

Gorgeous nine-month-old black Labrador Tala with her new friend, a Maine Coon cat called Johnny Cash. Kirsty and Glenn sent me this picture of Tala after I'd operated on her bilateral hip dysplasia. It was the best Christmas present for all of us at the practice, and I'm so happy that her infectious joy continued to be an inspiration to us all for some time to come.

Credit: Kirsty & Glenn Pinnock

In a cage in the back of a van for *Animal Rescue Live*, in order to highlight the abominable way in which puppies from a puppy farm are transported. I hope there will be an end to this atrocious practice in my lifetime.

Odin and me with our neck braces on, after damage in exactly the same areas of our necks.

Mick, Anita, Odin and me. With his 'old-man-young-boy' bark, Odin was a ray of sunshine.

'There can never be enough hugs in the world.' Eight-year-old Cavapoo Ruben was Anne's soulmate, having been by her side during three years of cancer treatment. I'm blessed to have had both Anne and Ruben in my life.

Ten-year-old Staffordshire bull terrier cross Jen had been rescued from the life of a breeding dog confined to the corner of a cement yard. With a brindle and white coat, perky ears and big brown 'cuddle me' eyes, she was gorgeous and she and I had a special bond. She stayed at the practice for some time after her surgeries, and I would always try to say goodnight to her before I went to bed.

With Mike and Millie, the seven-year-old Labrador who was the first dog in the world to have a custom FitzElbow. Her success stands on the shoulders of failure with previous total elbow replacements like for poor Jen.

Dennis was a beautiful 80kg bull mastiff who loved the sound of his own voice. He suffered from very aggressive bone cancer, which you can see here in his left front leg. It was utterly heartbreaking for everyone involved that we couldn't save him. I sincerely hope that the echo of Dennis's surgery, just like his inimitable voice, will be heard across the divide between human and animal medicine and go on to help both.

I was so grateful to have Keira and Ricochet by my side to lift my spirits, and help me write this book! They put me back together again, and somehow I woke up each day a little bit healed by their glue of unconditional love.

My beloved Keira and Ricochet, who teach me something new every day. From morning nose nuzzles to calming night-time chin cuddles, Ricochet is a whirlwind of love, buoying me up in his vortex. Keira has been my trusty companion and comfort blanket for the past thirteen years.

Keira under Malcolm and Philip's trees – the three guiding lights of my life. She has been by my side through the most challenging years of my career, with the building of Fitzpatrick Referrals. She is the love of my life and my best friend in the whole world.

non-union), and since then it has been used in countless
human and veterinary patients. I packed the hole left behind
following removal of the dead bone with calcium carbonate
beads containing gentamicin – a potent antibiotic. The objective was resolution of infection before permanent fixation.

The titanium spacer had been manufactured by Jay and
his colleagues to fit between Ivor's tibia and the residual
metatarsus, and on the front of which was a plate that had
been custom-made to screw to the bone using the holes already drilled, distributing force from the toes to the upper
tibia. This was carefully implanted, preserving blood supply
to the foot.

I had extracted fat cells from Ivor's body at the same time
as I put in the antibiotic beads. Cells from adipose tissue can
be 'pluri-potential', meaning that they can be encouraged to
grow into different types of tissue such as tendon, bone or
cartilage. The fat was processed by my colleague Dr Anita
Sanghani-Kerai to obtain the useful cells (the stromal vascular fraction, SVF), which she then cultured in a special
medium that induces the cells to turn into osteoblasts – the
cells that make bone. When implanted back into the body on
the sterile mesh, these cells would hopefully form new bone
(osteogenesis), encourage new bone to grow from the ends
of the tibia and metatarsus into the metal (osteoinduction),
and provide a biological trellis in which bone could grow like
ivy up a wall (osteoconduction). We are all made up of pluri-
potential cells – over which we have a lot more control than
the harbingers of doom and disease would have you believe.
If we look after and nourish the cells well, don't expose them
to too many toxins, exercise them – that's both physical and
mental exercise – we too can begin to bridge defects in the
moment.

In Ivor's case it took six to twelve weeks for full integration of the implanted cells. He went from strength to strength and over time I grew to love him even more. I would often go down to the ward to say goodnight to him – apparently he used not to like new people much, but he loved seeing me and when I took him out of his cage he'd curl up on my knee and purr contentedly. The pure unbridled happiness in the eyes and hugs of Joanne and Mark when they picked him up from the practice was a joy to behold. They had trusted in me and had given him a chance when most would have put him to sleep.

Ivor went on to live a further very happy year and a half, before dying suddenly with a gut issue at Christmas in 2018 at his primary care practice. His family and I shall remember Ivor forever on Christmas Day. In fact, Ivor's story was recounted in a Christmas Special episode of *The Supervet* in December 2017. Joanne was happy that Ivor's story could be shown on TV and also for us to publish the science behind his operation – as his legacy for all of us. We purposely published in a human medical journal and the reviewers had no problems with our ethical approach. Ironically, some vets did, suggesting that this surgery was itself an 'experiment'. This is incredibly important because we have shown the technology works and this may save the life of an experimental research animal who might otherwise be killed to learn what was absolutely necessary to save Ivor's life. For me One Medicine is about saving a life to save a life, rather than taking a life to save a life, although clearly not everyone agrees.

The thing is, though, that I have written many scientific papers and I'll hazard a guess that very few of you have read any of them. In fact, when Ivor's story was broadcast I got way more queries about regenerative stem cell scaffolds than I ever did off the back of a scientific paper. Science is absolutely necessary – without education and evidence of efficacy, medicine can never move rationally forward. But without the will of the public to drive it forward, it won't advance on its own. There's no point in publishing medical science if it doesn't save more lives, and it can only save more lives if the public and professionals embrace positive change with a solid moral core. Scientists must do more to communicate truthfully in order to build trust that they will do the right thing, because unless we can tear down the knowledge barriers between ever-advancing science and the people and animals who are being treated by it, we shall struggle more and more with the ethical dilemmas. Ironically, therefore, perhaps this book may have more impact in raising awareness of animal welfare and advances in medical techniques than all the scientific papers I have ever written – and in terms of the perception of what is right and wrong in the moment of making the decision.

The time I spent with Ivor and his family and in telling his story here might make a real and tangible difference to animal welfare, innovation and understanding of how the framework needs to change in both veterinary and human medicine to make things better. Ivor's journey might even drive forward the ideal of One Medicine and help to make it a reality in my lifetime. He is to my knowledge the first cat in the world to have a fat cell-derived, stem cell-seeded scaffold – and again we had proven that it worked without killing him.

Millie, Bella and Ivor show us that innovation in veterinary or human medicine requires us to create better ways of doing things, not just from a technological perspective but also from that of looking after each other as colleagues with a common goal to seek evidence of efficacy in an ethical environment. Most importantly, we need to strive constantly to do the right thing for all of our patients – human or animal – and to give every one of them a fair deal. After all, what's the point in any innovation at all if it doesn't make things better?

CHAPTER EIGHT

Tenacity

'Genius is 1 per cent inspiration, 99 per cent perspiration.'

Thomas Edison

Tenacity is essential for success in relationships and business, and if you want to achieve anything at all in life in general. In fact, I would go so far as to argue that in all areas of life success is 75 per cent tenacity and 25 per cent talent.

It is no coincidence that 'doggedness' is synonymous with tenacity. Dogs are stubborn, persistent, resolute, steadfast, assiduous and relentless to the point of obstinacy. When they get something into their head, dogs simply refuse to let it go. Cats aren't far behind in their strength of will. When a dog wants that stick, and only *that* stick will do, they will tussle and tug at it ad infinitum to get it out of the hedgerow and then simply refuse to relinquish it. When a cat so desperately wants to sit on the windowsill and look outside – no matter what you put on there or what curtains you pull – that cat will find a way around your obstacles to reach that chosen spot.

Animals demonstrate that tenacity isn't just an earnest craving, but rather a deliberate act to focus one's attention in order to achieve the goal. How many times have you talked about wanting to run that marathon, play that guitar, pass that exam, write that book, or whatever goal you thought you had? Thinking you want something is one thing, but having the tenacity to truly pull it off is entirely another. If we could learn from Ricochet in his mission to find every bit of toilet roll in the house and tear it up so I'm left with only confetti; or Keira, the crumb hoover, who will not stop zigzagging around each nook and cranny of a room until every micro-morsel is consumed – we might just achieve our biggest dream. 'Like a dog with a bone' is a ubiquitous aphorism of tenacity for a good reason.

Ricochet especially is very much like me – when we get something in our heads and we want to do it, there is nothing in this world that will stop us. I've tried a hundred times to hide my earplugs from him, but he will find them out and he will eat them – and not only the cheap ones either. Oh no – Ricochet has expensive taste. He is so tenacious he sought out my second pair of top-dollar earplugs a fortnight after I thought he'd forgotten how good that ear rubber tasted. I had hidden them under a coat, two pillows and a rug. The converse is also true in that we're tenaciously obstinate and resolute in our determination *not* to do something if it doesn't suit us. If I need a quick nap to rest mind and body for a few minutes, and he doesn't, then he just repeatedly bops me on the head with his big paw until I acquiesce to playtime rather than naptime.

Many of us have big dreams, yet too few of us actually make them reality. The older we get, the harder it is to shake off the psychological baggage that stymies our efforts to be magnificent. All we see are the obstacles that hold us back. Children, provided they are in a supportive environment, are free from that burden. Children will get right back on that bicycle, skateboard or piano a million times – their tenacity knows no bounds. As adults, on the other hand, all it takes is the slightest setback, some negative feedback on social media or at work, or some kind of flippant remark from a partner, and we are right back in our box. We let everyone else's negativity dampen our resolve. Even after we have set sail with the best intentions, a fair wind and some talent behind us, we allow the least breeze to blow us off track.

We make all kinds of excuses for not succeeding at anything, but in the Western world where opportunities are endless, for most of us it comes down to three things: making a firm choice; having the self-belief and bravery to overcome any obstacle; and having the perseverance to just keep going, no matter what. The enemy of success and fulfilment isn't lack of talent, lack of opportunity or lack of resource; it's lack of willpower. Or, simply put, laziness. I know that lots of people will be appalled at my saying that, but we are often masters of self-deception. We invent all sorts of justifications, then delude ourselves that they are real. Conversely, we can create a new reality through the choices we make. We *can* achieve many things if we change our mindset and commit to devoting the necessary time and effort to make it happen.

If you want to be an Olympic champion, you can't simply claim that it's a bit too early or too late to get out and do your training. I have taken more exams than many, and for all professionals that in itself requires tenacity, but I can tell you that no examination will ever make you a good surgeon. Only being at the coalface with sweat rolling down your cheeks, the bright light bleeding your eyes dry and seeing things go wrong, will make you a good surgeon. It's the same with some diet or exercise-related challenges. I 100 per cent appreciate that there may be metabolic reasons or difficult circumstances for people, and I'm completely empathetic, but I hear people complain all the time about their diet or their body weight or their lack of time to exercise. For my own part, I readily admit that when I have been overweight, it was only me who consumed the calories and put the kilos on, and only me who can burn them off, and no amount of talking will replace my personal effort and exercise.

I have many delusions of my own and I make excuses all the time. Chris Evans has told me more than once that if I dedicated 'a small percentage of my professional tenacity to my personal life then I'd be married with several children by now'. I've too often made work-related choices at the cost of my relationships. Ouch – the truth hurts; it's stung for a long time. One night, I was inconsolable about a previous girlfriend who had left me for someone else, pouring my broken heart out in the dim light of a fancy nightclub bar to my wonderful friend Rick Lowe. He just looked at me, and quite matter-of-factly said, 'She has the right to choose what she does too, you know.' I didn't speak to him for a month. I didn't want to hear the truth. Of course she didn't want to be with someone who was a workaholic with poor work-life balance, and who was unable to fully commit. I had created my own reality – my dedication to the pursuit of romance was dwarfed by devotion to the animals and to my veterinary practice. I can use my practice as a defence all I like, but I could sell the practice, have enough money to live on and free my mind to put more effort into a different life, if I wanted to. That isn't the choice I made, but if one is lazy in love one loses, and I need to take responsibility for my life choices. The same is true for all of us.

I can count my close friends on two hands, and that's how I keep it, because I don't want bullshit in my life – I want the truth and I want it to my face. I don't need people blowing smoke up my arse! In 2013 when I was taking my specialist examinations, I confided in another close friend, my physiotherapist Stuart Gordon, that I didn't think I could get all the study done in time alongside my clinical work – and I was going to fail. He asked me to close my eyes and contemplate what I really wanted in my life, and whether paying the price in the short term was worth it. Then he helped me with mindfulness and breathing exercises so that I could access the tenacity that was needed to succeed.

The truth is that we self-sabotage all of the time, me included. We create an illusion of tolerance of our personal success or failure to avoid facing the fact that we simply lack tenacity. Instead, we think we're quite sane as we continue to pour the balm of self-pity onto the dull wounds of mediocrity and unfulfilled ambition. In fact, I'd go so far as to say that if we have a dream, the only way we'll ever achieve it is to go crazy – to get out of bed every day with the attitude of a seven-year-old child, a cat or a dog and say, 'Today I shall stop at nothing (bar hurting another creature) to do what I really want to do with my life. Today I shall make one tiny step to get me out of the hole that tells me I'm not good enough and I can't succeed.' It doesn't matter how inconsequential that first tiny step might feel – it could be writing a list, or making just a single phone call, or sending an email. The most important thing is actually the knowledge that you've started on the path of tenaciousness that will get you to where you want to be. First, though, and this is absolutely vital: you have to know what you *really* want to achieve.

I was fortunate because I knew from a very early age that I wanted to be the best surgeon that I was capable of being, and so I am doing what I want to do. In that respect, at least, my tenacity paid off. But I can't then complain that I don't have other things. Perhaps I might wish I could play guitar as well as The Edge from U2, sing as well as Bono, be as talented a performer as Dave Grohl or be as incredible an actor as Hugh Jackman – but I didn't practise guitar, singing, drums, dancing or acting enough. So how, therefore, could I compare myself with any of these great people, for example? (In fact, all of these men have been married for a collective ninety-seven years *and* can all play guitar. Actually, now that I think about it – I'm doomed!)

We all compare ourselves to other people all the time, but what we have to remember is that their success is usually the result of lots of determination, dedication and plain old hard work. Happiness comes from inside. We need to define what it is we really want in our hearts and go for it. We might fail, but, in my experience, truly targeted tenacity usually foils failure.

'Targeted tenacity' is vital for scientific and medical advance. If you're going to be tenacious, you had better make sure you're focused in the right direction. If you don't learn from your mistakes, then you're a tenacious idiot, which doesn't serve anything or anyone. There is no quick route to sustainable success. When they crossed the Antarctic unsupported, Colin O'Brady and Louis Rudd might have had good reason to moan about their hunger and tired legs, but they didn't just decide to set up camp and say, 'Oh well, I can't be arsed to go on today, because it's a bit chilly.' Nor did Richard Branson, Elon Musk, Jeff Bezos, Bill Gates or Steve

Jobs throw in the towel after their first failed venture. It doesn't matter how big or small your endeavour – our goals and sense of achievement are deeply personal to each of us – if it brings you fulfilment and you pursue it with tenacity, it is as valid as any other. If you want a promotion or a change of career you have to put in extra time, actively volunteer for learning experience, maybe take night classes. Clock-watching isn't acceptable. Whatever it is you want to do, if you don't have tenacity of purpose and effort, then, simply put, you probably don't deserve to succeed.

Of course tenacity isn't all about accomplishing 'greatness' or material success, it's about aiming to achieve a state of equilibrium within yourself, a contentedness about who and what you are. Motivation is a perennial and ubiquitous challenge for all of us, but I know from experience that nothing brings a greater sense of well-being than taking those first steps to achieving your goal. And once you've taken those steps, and keep on taking more, steady, meaningful and tenacious steps, the better and better you feel. To reiterate the lesson of a previous chapter, if you truly want 'the right thing' to happen, then you need to do that right thing, over and over again.

At a very literal level, take exercise, or eating healthily, for example. Fortunately, I have another friend, John Field, who kicks my arse and motivates me. When I sit on the floor of the gym, stiff everywhere from hours of surgery, not wanting to do anything at all, John just gently and firmly tells me to stop feeling sorry for myself and stop lying on the floor 'saying nice things to myself'. He gets me moving and before long I feel better. I think it's the same for everyone. I get nutritional advice from another friend, Peter White, and once you make the effort to eat sustaining and wholesome meals, you feel better, and with tenacity comes motivation and a yet more positive sense of achievement. It's a virtuous cycle of effort and reward.

You have to take care of the vehicle you're travelling in on any long journey. Life is hopefully a long journey, and you have to look after your body and mind. Tenacity begins with willpower, but to see anything through you need to surround yourself with supportive people on your journey. Whatever that journey might entail, you need people who see your sincere and earnest effort, who believe in you and pick you up with words of encouragement when you fall down. And you will fall down. I am very grateful to Michaela for believing in me even when I didn't believe in myself. I have also been very lucky to have two other very loyal and strong women in my life – my manager Ciara O'Flanagan and my financial director Dineke Abbing. Without these two amazing people, I would never have achieved what has been possible over the past few years, no matter how tenacious I have been. They have picked up my broken pieces, put me back together again and helped give me the will to carry on. Any life is full of highs and lows, and Ricochet and Keira have saved me from sadness many times. Keira lies beside me with her little paws on my leg and she raises me up from my gloom; and when Ricochet jumps on the bed and lies on my chest, I can feel his heartbeat next to mine as he reaches up his paws and pushes his nose tightly against my chin. It's as though he shares my burdens.

We all need some degree of tenacity to cope with the 'slings and arrows of outrageous fortune', and for many of the families who come to see me, their animal friends have picked them up and helped them find new resolve to fight on. When I met June and Scrumpy in early 2011, they rapidly became the very embodiment of this tremendous tenacity for me.

In early January 2009, June had driven with some trepidation to Devon on a freezing cold frosty morning, with her dear friend Sheila by her side for moral support. She was going to pick up a little bundle of white Clumber spaniel fluff whom she would call Scrumpy, after the well-known West Country cider. June knew she was about to have a big change in her life with the moral responsibility of a new family member, but she couldn't have known that Scrumpy would become the epicentre of her world for the next decade and would truly teach her the meaning of tenacity. In due course he would teach me and many others too.

Scrumpy, or Scrumptious Scrumps as he usually was known, was a troubled but golden nugget of unconditional love and one of the most tenacious dogs that I had ever met, or am ever likely to meet. He rapidly became the boss and June, her husband and friends all had to fall into his way of life, but June didn't yet realise that her life would soon be entirely dominated by Scrumpy's well-being.

One day at puppy class when he was little more than a year of age, the trainer asked why Scrumpy was always limping, and so his medical saga began. He was diagnosed with developmental elbow disease (DED). This used to be called elbow dysplasia, and often still is, but I first used the acronym DED in 1996 and it didn't make it into the textbooks properly until nearly twenty years of persistent tenaciousness later. I had been convinced that the main cause of the disease was a poor fit (incongruity) between the three bones that make up the elbow – the humerus, radius and ulna – and in motion, part of the ulna underneath the humerus (the medial coronoid process, MCP) was overloaded and cracked off like in an earthquake or an avalanche. When I had first presented this theory in the mid-nineties during a conference, I was laughed at. It would take no little tenacity to pick myself up and continue to find evidence to prove the theory.

It had been known for some time that one component of the disease was a condition called osteochondritis dissecans (OCD) whereby poorly vascularised cartilage fails to convert into bone and flakes off inside the joint, but a decade later, in 2006, we finally proved that a greater component of the disease in most dogs, and certainly for Scrumpy, was indeed overload between the humerus and ulna. Tenacity is essential for the discovery of new revelations and new evidence may refute even the most staunchly held old 'truths'. This is true in any endeavour.

We demonstrated that cracks occurred in the MCP underneath an intact cartilage surface and that this kind of overload wasn't a primary cartilage problem but rather like a bottom sitting in a saddle that didn't fit. The base of the humerus bone is shaped like a pair of buttocks which rests in the saddle formed from the ulna and radius side by side. In flexion, extension and rotation as a dog moves, the inside 'buttock' of the humerus bears down on the MCP, causing it to crack and then the cartilage wears away (humero-ulnar conflict due to supraphysiologic overload). It hurts – a lot – and poor Scrumpy was affected on both elbows.

We performed two keyhole (arthroscopic) procedures on each elbow, which some years ago I named subtotal coronoid ostectomy (SCO) and biceps ulnar release procedure (BURP). Again, when I first lectured on these procedures in the mid-nineties, many were cynical, and many still are – but both are now textbook techniques. SCO is a procedure that removes the cracked tip of the MCP. BURP is a procedure where we cut one of the tendons that pulls the ulna against the humerus. It's as if the bottom is being held by straps in the saddle – like a large foot in a smaller shoe – and the straps are then cut, again like snipping the laces on that too-tight, ill-fitting shoe. It still doesn't fit, but it's a tad more comfortable and chafes less. I then thought it would be fun to find an acronym for removing fragments produced from broken-off cracks and so I half-jokingly called this procedure FART – fragment arthroscopic removal technique. More than anything else, this was to help folks remember that, in fact, removing the fragment alone doesn't stop the progression of humero-ulnar conflict and therefore FARTing doesn't stop the build-up of a fairly unpleasant condition. I lectured in America once with the title 'BURP versus FART: whichever way the wind blows'. My sense of 'surgical humour' was lost on the audience and there was total silence as I died on the podium and carried on as if nothing had happened – and I hadn't FARTed or BURPed at all!

Scrumpy was a great patient. He recovered well and was so gentle with everyone that June decided to have him assessed as a 'Pets as Therapy' dog. June's mother had suffered from dementia and when she had visited her in the nursing home, she had often wished that there was more to stimulate her mother's mind. She therefore decided to investigate whether the joy and light of Scrumptious Scrumps could be brought into nursing homes for the elderly. He passed all of the necessary criteria with alacrity and together they went to work. Tenacity was Scrumpy's middle name. He never tired of being petted or making people smile and always remembered which folks kept him a bit of digestive biscuit and on each visit would expectantly seek them out. He also seemed to have a sixth sense about some of the patients – he would always go straight to a blind lady in one of the care homes and place his chin on her knee; she would put her hand on his head and say, 'Oh, *my* dog is here.'

Sadly when he was about two and a half, lightning struck suddenly again. He was doing his normal 'out and about' in the garden and June suddenly heard a horrendous howl, and then total and absolute silence. She went out to find him lying on his side with one front leg crumpled under him. He could not get up. With the help of a neighbour she got him into the car and to her local vet, who sent her straight to me. What happened is, in fact, commonly referred to as a 'lightning fracture' of the humerus bone, which breaks very suddenly with a jagged serrated fissure that extends from the elbow joint up into the shaft of the bone.

Scrumpy had also developed another condition called humeral intercondylar fissure (HIF). In HIF, a gradually emerging break occurs in the bottom part of the humerus, which, as I've said, is shaped like two butt cheeks, and so in essence the 'butt crack' cracks. One butt cheek sits on the radius and the other on the ulna bone of the forearm. The ulna forms a circular socket around the back of the 'butt crack' and I theorise that poor fit causes this socket to wedge open the butt like an axe in a block of wood. I call it my 'lumberjack butt-crack theory', but I haven't proved it yet and I suspect that my comedic analogy will be lost again on the uber-serious scientific world, though clients understand this much better than any scientific explanation I've ever used. As with all theories, research will prove or disprove this – and progress is made either way – so 'the book' is rewritten, one tenacious step at a time.

Normally we repair fractures like Scrumpy's by driving a large screw across the 'butt-crack' fracture and putting a plate up the humerus along the lightning-strike fracture. HIF is a chronic problem, however – the bone on either side of the chronic fissure has become sclerotic and inactive, and so the butt-crack fracture never actually heals. All one can do is hope that the screw that supports it is strong enough to stand the test of time. Historically, though, the failure rate is uncomfortably high.

For this reason, we had invented a new screw that was strong and could also have bone graft placed alongside it to try to provide a metal buttress and also some biological bridging. Over the past decade, I've redesigned this screw several times, trying to get closer to zero complications. I placed the new improved screw in Scrumpy's elbow and again he was confined to rest for a while. Again, he was patient, and again he healed quickly and was soon back sniffing around for digestive biscuits and pats on the head.

Nine months later, the opposite elbow fractured. Having not been in evidence on previous assessment, the HIF condition had unfortunately been rapidly progressive on that side too. I was in America lecturing at the time, and in my absence a standard screw and plate were used to repair the fracture. However, it loosened so I later replaced it with the newly invented screw. It was back to rest for Scrumpy. By this point four operations had been performed, and June said that he was 'used to it' by now. She just had to say, 'Bedtime,' and he would trot off to his den for the night. He was soon running around again, but I explained that, due to the severity of the problems affecting both elbows, he would have bad osteoarthritis even at this young age, and in spite of nutritional supplements and everything else she could do, sadly this could only get worse throughout his lifetime.

Around this time Scrumptious Scrumpy got a new job.

He had excelled in visiting nursing homes and soon began to visit colleges and universities during mental health and well-being weeks and in the run-up to examinations to help calm students' stress and anxiety. One of the first to bene-fit was Surrey University's veterinary school in Guildford, where I'm a professor of orthopaedics. It was amazing the difference that a Scrumpy cuddle could make. One vet stu-dent in particular, who was autistic, covered the walls of her room with pictures of Scrumpy to remind her why she was working so hard to become a vet. When she passed her exams she gave June a thank-you card of a painting of Scrumpy. He inspired tenacity, resilience and some kind of calm coping mechanism in everyone he met.

Among vet students Scrumpy also prompted lots of questions about his particular anatomical foibles which, unfortunately for Scrumptious Scrumpy, were about to get a whole lot worse. In the face of yet more adversity, both Scrumpy and I would need to muster all our tenacity.

There's no question that the first step on the road to tenacity is to try to choose something that you have a flair for. Scrumpy had a flair for being an emotional guidance counsellor, and I have a flair for surgery. Talent plus tenacity yields success, I would say, but to reiterate, given the choice I'd take ambition over talent any day. I've seen plenty of people who aren't gifted surgeons become quite good because of belligerent tenacity. If the first step on the road to tenacity is internal drive and focus towards something that you think you have a flair for – targeted tenacity – the second step is not to let anyone or anything dissuade you from your goal. For me, the single biggest obstacle is allowing our limiting beliefs to be dictated by others. I had to use every ounce of willpower to silence the voices that told me that I'd never be good enough, clever enough, talented enough and strong enough. If I had listened to the bullies – or to the voices in my own head – I wouldn't have tried at all and would never have become a vet. Even today, I still have to try to ignore all criticism and praise equally on social media and elsewhere, because to pay any heed is a futile distraction.

I had to study hard in secondary school and in college because I'm by no means the brightest spanner in the box. On more than one occasion, I turned up exhausted for an interview for an internship or a residency, went to sleep on a toilet floor, then freshened up with a deodorant bath and went into the interview. One fairly frank Scottish interviewer told me much later that I had 'smelled of piss' – but what can a fellow do? Nobody would train me to be a surgeon. I had to attend as many courses as I could all over the world and I hand-picked my mentors in Europe and the USA. I would go up to them at the end of lectures and ask or beg to come to see them at work. As I have said many times, being a good vet is a vocation of apprenticeship, rather than pure learning. I was very fortunate to have been trained by several clinicians in general practice, small animal practice and specialist practice. But I was never going to be a follower. I couldn't fall in line with a doctrine that said that veterinary medicine was always going to be the poor cousin of human medicine when in fact it was animal experiments that allowed human medicine to advance. I have been single-mindedly tenacious in my pursuit of the goal of One Medicine, and I'm nowhere near yet – there are many who say it can't be done but I shall continue to try, one small step at a time.

I have learned that in life there are generally two types of people who try to steal our dreams and hamper our progress: I call them the 'dumpers' and the 'drainers'. The 'dumpers' are usually like the bullies who were perhaps acting out their own shortcomings and insecurities. I actually don't think that they had thought it through. I think they just got some kind of pleasure and peer acknowledgement from picking on 'Nollaig' for being a 'stupid swot' who deserved a beating. Even today there are 'dumpers' all around – they dump all their crap on me with their moaning and complaining, and yet they are 'yes people' who tell me everything they think I want to hear in the hope that I'll keep them around me and absorb their problems along the way. Sycophants try to make you feel great as long as they're getting what they want, but when you fall they're nowhere to be seen. I cannot bear to be around the 'dumpers'.

The 'drainers' are just as bad. These are the negative, attention-seeking energy vampires who will bleed you dry of creative energy. They feed off your enthusiasm and generosity and give only negativity in return. They specialise in voicing all the reasons why something isn't possible, constantly pooh-poohing everyone else's ideas – all the while sucking up what they can for themselves like voracious vacuums when your back is turned. These 'no people' are even worse than the 'yes people'. Ever since I've become well known from television, the 'drainers' in my life seem to have grown in number; I can see them crawling out of the woodwork, vying for attention and ready to do their worst.

Dogs and cats quickly figure out time-wasters, 'dumpers' and 'drainers', and they avoid them like the plague. They don't want to be around incessant moaners or needy people who just want love without ever giving back. They are happy in their own skin, so they don't dump their emotional baggage on you or suck energy from you – rather they are always there for you no matter what and they give you endless energy.

I'm sure that you have recognised 'dumpers' and 'drainers' in your life. I strongly believe that if you want to be tenacious in your pursuit of your dreams then you need to dump these people and fill your life with positive, altruistic people instead. If you are true to yourself and tenacious about your passion, you will attract the people into your life who you want and deserve, who accept you for who you are, people who just 'are', and don't need or want anything from you to fill some gaping hole inside themselves. I call these people the 'pumpers' and 'remainers' – they will rekindle your resolve when you feel deflated, pick you up when you fall down, and bring you joy in your saddest hour. For me, the animals in my life have often played this role, and of course Ricochet and Keira are my resident 'pumpers' and 'remainers', filling my life with joy every day.

I am fortunate to have many positive, altruistic people in Fitzpatrick Referrals and I hope they'll be there long after I am gone. Senior orthopaedic surgeon Sarah Girling has been by my side for nearly fifteen years and deserves a tenacity medal. Clare Rusbridge leads the neurology team, while Nick Bacon and Laurent Findji lead our endeavours in oncology and soft tissue. I'm most proud of the junior members of the orthopaedic team who joined the practice on internships or residencies and have all now become boarded specialist surgeons: Padraig Egan, Susan Murphy, James Guthrie and Miguel Solano. Joana Tabanez and Carina Rotter are now neurology residents and well on their way too. All of these talented and compassionate people have manifested sustained tenacity for many years to get to where they are today, and they are the legacy of Fitzpatrick Referrals. Without the team spirit, collegiality, kindness and dedication of all of these people and the other great clinicians at Fitzpatrick

Referrals, through turbulent times of change in the entire financial structure of the veterinary profession, there would be no *Supervet,* and no anything really. I truly believe that the three keys to business success are:

1. Choose and believe in good people
2. Allow good people to achieve their dreams
3. Keep good people happy

The 'pumpers' and 'remainers' rapidly become apparent in any organisation and you must keep them above all else. The 'dumpers' and the 'drainers' can leave whenever they want.

My dear friend Philip Gilbert was my drama teacher and the very first person who genuinely believed that I could truly be anything I wanted to be. I was twenty-five in 1993 when I met Philip. Everybody had told me that I couldn't go to drama school and get proper work as an actor. They were wrong. Philip didn't see age or circumstance as a barrier to dreams, but rather emphasised the ambition and the tenacity to put in the necessary time and effort coupled with some modicum of talent for the endeavour. Philip encouraged me that I could do anything I wanted to if I could 'find a reason big enough' and he was right. The very fact that this book exists at all is born of Philip's belief in me that, if I put in the effort, everything is possible. I recognise that the older we get, the more difficult it is to reprogramme the neural pathways, but if we tenaciously pursue a new dream, we can achieve it, whatever our age. The tenacity of many late nights of writing comes from a deep belief that if I share how animals have saved my life and what they have taught me, it might help you and them in return. That's a reason big enough.

Scrumpy had proved time and again that he was a 'pumper' and a 'remainer', but two years after his last elbow surgery, he began to limp on his left hind leg and X-ray pictures identified that, due to hip dysplasia, he had severe osteoarthritis affecting both joints. Hip dysplasia is where the heads of the femur bones are not held properly in the developing hip sockets by the soft tissues and, as they get looser, they stretch the tissues further and rub on the rims of the sockets. Inflammation, rubbing away of cartilage, infilling of the sockets and production of new bone around the joints ensues, which results in worsening pain. Unfortunately, dogs that are affected on both sides and who are particularly tenacious in wanting to exercise, like Scrumpy, don't show lameness straight away. In fact, by the time Scrumpy did show lameness, his osteoarthritis was such that drug treatment was ineffective to control his pain. June and I needed to dig deep. We were never going to put him through a fifth surgery just because we could, but equally we were not going to give up on him without a well-thought-out and ethically sound plan, and so, after much discussion, we carried out a total hip replacement on the left side. Sometimes it's enough to operate just on one side to give relief, and we hoped hip replacement on the right side wouldn't be needed. Two days later he was so much better that he sauntered to the end of June's garden and headed straight for the park in wilful disregard of my instructions for confinement.

June got him a friend called Jack, also from Devon, and also named after the cider, and so Scrumpy and Jack became best friends. Unfortunately, about a year and a half later,

Scrumpy started lifting his left hind leg again and operation number six was performed to correct a slipping kneecap. Again Scrumpy patiently recovered, this time with Jack by his side, and was soon back in the game visiting nursing homes and schools. By now, his fan club had grown such that his den was covered with get-well-soon cards and soft toys.

During all of Scrumpy's recovery periods, his most regular visitor was June's dear friend Sheila. Sheila had been diagnosed in her fifties with early onset dementia, which had progressed rapidly. When June and her friends took her out for lunch, the only way they could calm her down to eat was to take Scrumpy so he could sit beside her. There were many things she could not remember, but she clearly never forgot Scrumpy. Sheila deteriorated very quickly and when accidentally she nearly set fire to her house, her daughter had no choice but to place her in a residential facility. She had a lot of difficulty settling in and spent days crying and shouting that she wanted to go home.

Finally, June got to visit with Scrumpy and when she arrived, Sheila was sitting on the edge of her bed, head in her hands, coat on, handbag at the ready, wailing. June let Scrumpy walk into her room first and he sat in front of Sheila, who lifted her head, looked at him, stopped crying and slipped slowly down onto the floor beside him and cuddled him. Some nurses came running down the corridor – they thought something was wrong because it was the first time in days that Sheila had been silent. The nurses also jokingly asked if Scrumpy could move in, because he had such a calming effect on many of the other patients. Scrumpy was a warm blanket of comfort for all.

Shortly after Scrumpy's visit to Sheila, she was diagnosed with terminal cancer. Just a few weeks later, she was nearing the end, barely conscious and couldn't speak or move, so the nurses had moved her mattress onto the floor so she wouldn't risk a fall. When June arrived with Scrumpy, he lay down and rested next to her. June gently placed Sheila's hand on Scrumpy's back, and soon noticed that she was weakly stroking his fur. Sheila might not have known that June was there, but she knew that her loyal friend Scrumpy was right beside her, and hopefully he brought her some comfort and peace. She passed away that night.

Just before Scrumpy's eighth birthday, he began to drag both back feet and was getting much slower on his walks. June wondered if he was getting prematurely old, but he had been asked to attend as a helper dog for a course on rehabilitation at the vet school, so along he and June went. The physiotherapist professionals took one look at Scrumpy, drew June aside and told her that he had a serious problem.

I was away lecturing and my phone lit up with text messages asking what they should do to help Scrumpy. He had deteriorated quickly, his tail was limp, he was reluctant to exercise, having difficulty standing up and was sitting down when he was trying to urinate. I examined him as soon as I got back, and when I applied any pressure to his sciatic nerves, he yelped loudly. We had become good pals down the years, and this was the first time I'd ever heard him yelp. He looked around at me as if to say, 'Help me, Noel, this time I'm really in trouble.' He was.

The fear and panic in June's eyes were palpable. Scrumpy just lay on the floor looking up at us. We performed an MRI scan of his spine and I called June into my consulting room to discuss the situation. She was a mess, eyes wide, heart visibly pounding. Every intervertebral disc in his spine was dried out, impacting his movement, and some had bulged.

241

The disc in the base of this spine, the lumbosacral junction, was causing the greatest problems, because he had a condition called degenerative lumbosacral stenosis (DLSS). In this condition, the nucleus of the disc between the vertebrae dries out, the annulus of the disc bulges upwards and sidewards, the adjacent vertebrae produce new bone called spondylosis and the facet joints which link the vertebrae on top can also become inflamed and enlarged. Scrumpy had aggressive manifestation of all features of the disease and had almost no room left for the nerve roots that lead to the sciatic nerves, the urinary bladder and the tail. It was no wonder that he was so weak and in so much pain – in fact, it was remarkable he had remained so steadfast in the face of such terrible disease. Scrumpy's circumstances were awful and nobody would argue with allowing him to pass away peacefully.

Poor Scrumpy faced the biggest challenge of his life. Sometimes we all face seemingly insurmountable adversity, when it's difficult to even have a dream at all. Perhaps you have no money, maybe even no home, no family or support system of any kind; perhaps you're in prison having really messed up. However, time and again we hear of people who have endured the greatest hardships, who somehow persevere and not only survive, but thrive. The biggest test of tenacity is to keep on believing in your goal and your dream, in spite of the unfavourable circumstances you may face and regardless of your own moments of weakness, no matter what the voices of naysayers in your head may tell you. Perhaps this is the biggest test of all – the test of resilience.

In this respect, to my mind, love is often a spur to tenacity. You must love and respect life and you must strive to live it well. My love and respect for animals has been the impetus and guiding light for all my endeavour. June loved Scrumpy and was devastated to watch his decline. Medical management with tablets and injections had failed and continued to fail. Extreme circumstances in life often require extreme measures, but Scrumpy was approaching the later stages of life, and given his history of chronic elbow arthritis, progressive arthritis in both knees and an arthritic hip plus a hip replacement, it was a genuine ethical dilemma for everyone whether it was in Scrumpy's best interests to perform his seventh operation. Of course, for human patients of equivalent age in human years, say sixty-five or so, in a similar situation, if surgery were necessary it would be performed without hesitation. In veterinary medicine it may be considered overtreatment.

The Supervet featured Scrumpy's appearance in a lecture theatre full of students, where I was giving a talk on the ethics of advanced surgery. I told the students that every situation is different, we must always act in the patient's best interests, and at the same time we must ethically do the right thing. I discussed how it's essential to examine ethics, evidence and efficacy, and that there had been great advances since I graduated, so that treatments were now possible for conditions for which back then I'd have said, 'I'm sorry, there's nothing I can do.' But of course, being able to do something, and it being *the right thing to do*, remained the dilemma, and students were torn. They wanted Scrumpy to live, but weren't sure if, in fact, the 'best treatment' would be to euthanise him. Some remained concerned that we had already put him through too much, and they felt that they would not put their own dog through so many operations. When his thought-provoking story was shown on *The Supervet*, there was mixed social media commentary too on whether it was right or not for Scrumpy, June and me to be tenacious and to try, or whether it was best to give up and put him to sleep.

And so the challenge for veterinary medicine remains: how do you provide evidence of efficacy and ethically well-founded decision-making if we don't think it through or continue to try? Scrumpy wasn't Patient Number One for any of his surgeries, so the moral question was not one of innovative treatment, rather that of 'how many surgeries is too many?' By the time I spoke to the students, Scrumpy's situation had already been through a rigorous discussion with colleagues and, of course, June. Scrumpy was not responding to painkillers and he was miserable. I have only ever operated for the reasons of my patient, and never the emotional reasons of their guardian. I shook my head as I explained to June that even if I did operate, the adhesions to the nerves were likely so chronic that they might be stretched during surgery, there were likely to be at least temporary side effects such as weakness and possible incontinence, and those deficits might be permanent, and in spite of this surgery he might still end up being put to sleep. No surgery, and especially not this one, comes with guarantees.

For the first time in Scrumpy's life, June felt despair. Scrumpy had deteriorated quickly in just the previous few days alone, and would only get worse. Poor June could barely think, let alone speak, so she went out for a walk while we woke Scrumpy up after his MRI. He was up to his eyeballs on painkillers, but even as I held his head and gave him a little kiss, I could see the pain in his eyes. Three weeks later, with medicine still not working, June brought Scrumpy back for surgery. She has told me since that she felt physically sick. She knew that I would operate with the proviso that if, for any reason, things were not going according to plan or were worse than I had expected, I would call her to ask permission for euthanasia. She had a quick cuddle with Scrumpy. I gave her a hug and she left with only his collar and lead in her hands. I have seen that walk thousands of times, and I always have a little prayer in my head as I go from my consulting room into the preparation area that today won't be the day of THE phone call. I have had to make the intra-operative euthanasia phone call on quite a few occasions in my career and it's absolutely horrendous.

I have seen hundreds of cases of DLSS, written papers and lectured dozens of times on the disease. It has been an intense personal passion of mine since the mid-nineties when I operated using a conventional technique on a German shepherd dog affected by this disease. The dog did not improve and ended up being put to sleep. Both the family and I were crushed and I was determined to do better. I had been seeking a better method of pushing neck vertebrae apart and alleviating pressure on the spinal cord when they have overgrown bone or a disc bulges squashing nerves (a condition called wobbler syndrome or cervical spondylomyelopathy) when by chance one day I had watched a man in the snow pushing Christmas trees, tip first, into the open end of a horsebox trailer. And so the Christmas tree spacer screw was born. Initially I considered placing this implant in the lumbosacral spine (the lower back where Scrumpy had his disease) by operating through the abdomen from underneath the spine. One would have to pull all the intestines, bladder and other organs out of the way, and then dissect into inflamed new bone formation on the underside of the vertebrae – it was a nightmare.

People had said it was impossible to place the Christmas tree spacer from the top in between the vertebrae because one would probably cause irreparable damage to the nerve roots, but I was convinced that it could be done. It was down to technique – how to drill the roof off the vertebrae, how to move the nerve roots out of the way, how to cut out the bulge in the disc and how to guide the spacer in to push the vertebrae apart, thereby relieving pressure on the nerve roots. I was determined that there must be a way, so I did intensive research and, after a few years of examining anatomy and operating on dogs that were voluntarily donated after death, I finally cracked it. (The donation of bodies for veterinary surgical and anatomy training is, of course, a challenging subject, but I know for sure that people can have every bit of my body to help students to learn when I die. You're welcome to this leprechaun shell when the spirit has left him.)

I had figured out how to place the spacer, but there was still the problem of how to keep the vertebrae spaced apart and stable without collapsing. Then one day I was lifting weights in the gym and it occurred to me to manufacture rods with a spherical ball on each end like a dumb-bell. Each ball could go into a C-shaped clamp mounted on screws in the vertebral bodies, and then the clamps could be tightened in any direction, depending on the position of the screws, giving permanent locking of the vertebrae once they had been pushed apart by the Christmas tree spacer. I called the spacer a FITS (Fitz Intervertebral Traction Screw) and the clamp-rod system a Lumbosacral Fitzateur. It was this system that I proposed for Scrumpy. This technique of lumbosacral distraction fusion is still considered a 'new' technique, as yet not accepted by the mainstream. It will take the next ten years or so, and considerable tenacity on my part, to make time to publish the necessary science on the many dozens of cases I have operated on over the past decades and to teach surgeons how to perform this operation. As with every technique that I have invented to circumvent a major problem for which we don't have a satisfactory solution, it will be for the next generation of vets to look at the evidence and efficacy before the technique might be 'accepted' wisdom.

Scrumpy was the king of resilience and when I chose to battle with his unfortunate biology, I was forced to be resilient too, because it was the only way forward. During the operation, the compression and adhesions around Scrumpy's nerve roots were horrendous, and the bleeding was horrendous too. This was one spinal surgery where all I could do was stay focused, work as fast as I could, apply suction and get the spacer in as quickly as possible so that the bleeding could be stopped. Fortunately, I managed to dissect all of the nerves from the compression, place the spacer, screws, clamps and rods, and close. Then I made the phone call to June – happily, from my consulting room and not the operating theatre.

I told June that I was hopeful, but I wasn't sure if Scrumpy would ever wag his tail again, a small price to pay if he was out of pain. The following day Scrumptious Scrumps was walking, and his tail slowly began to regain some mobility. But when I was also able to treat the pain of his joints, that's when his tail really started to wag. During the procedure, I had harvested fat from the surgery site from which my colleague Anita was able to extract stem cells with anti-inflammatory properties. Three weeks later, I injected these cells in a cocktail with blood platelets containing anti-inflammatory molecules into both elbows, both knees and his unoperated hip joint. Soon, Scrumpy was trying to play with Jack in the garden and enjoying his underwater treadmill and swimming exercise sessions back at the practice too. In fact, he loved being in the water so much, it was hard to get him out of the pool. It seemed as though he was back to his puppy days that had been cut short. After the final surgery, Scrumpy enjoyed an excellent further twenty months, free from pain, happy, playful and back visiting the nursing home.

Just after his tenth birthday he stopped wanting to play with Jack, frequently took to his bed and gradually couldn't stand up any more. Finally, old age had caught up with him. One morning he no longer had any sparkle left in his eyes, and June did what was right and kind for her tenacious friend. He had given her and everyone he met so much, and so she gave him the final gift of a gentle exit from this world. June told me that she would do it all over again, even knowing everything she now knows, because he was a happy soul and her best friend. Scrumpy wasn't an experiment – he was a dearly loved family member who brought joy and hope to hundreds of people in his lifetime.

When we examined the bone growing into his spinal spacer and the screws in his elbows using new types of metal artefact reduction CT while he was still alive (just as for Millie and Ivor before), we saw the evidence of efficacy that used to only be possible through trials using experimental research animals. As I've said, and it's worth saying a second time, a new era is upon us, where we don't need to take an animal life to see the effect of implants like these for human benefit, but at the moment the regulators of human medicine do not listen to this evidence at all, nor to our clinical evidence for stem cells. Scrumpy is a beacon of hope for a new way forward for medicine, studying animals and humans side by side: One Medicine. One day, I hope people will listen.

He was tenacious through all of his challenges and he lived every minute of life to the max. How tenacious will you be in pursuing your passion? Will you be honest with yourself when you look in the mirror? Will you hand on heart be able to say that you gave it your very best shot and lived every minute to the max? One day that minute will be the last one. It won't always be easy for any of us. We need to light an unquenchable fire of internal willpower to fuel our efforts. We must grow a thick skin to fend off the voices of dissension who will deflect us from our goal if we let them. We must overcome the intrinsic limitations of our circumstances, and finally we must keep going and be resilient.

As I write these words, this book has already been advertised for pre-order. I can use every excuse in the book not to write this book, but there's a publisher and there is 'you' waiting for it. Following my potentially life-changing accident, I'm a very lucky man to be alive. As I have been writing, I've had various issues with coping mentally, deadlines for scientific publications with moral responsibility to my colleagues who need these papers for their examination credentials, and commitments at the practice with patients, management or financial concerns that all go with the territory of owning your own business, which have multiplied during the coronavirus crisis. The point is that all of this is my choice, as is writing this book. We can all use excuses for not achieving anything at all, and targeted tenacity would be essential for me to finish this book – and is essential if you or I want to make an important difference in anything at all. I am very grateful that you have taken the time to read my words. Thank you for allowing me to try.

CHAPTER NINE

Youness

'I can be a better me than anyone can.'

Diana Ross

In all of the infinite complexity of the galaxy, you may forget that the molecular structure that makes up 'you' will never be created again – and the chances of you existing, a sperm and an egg coming together to make you, are about one in four hundred trillion. There is only one you, there will never be another you, and you are all you ever need. And yet, hardly any of us recognise our own true worth.

Of course, it's the ultimate cliché that there is 'only one you'. It trips off the page in every self-help and wellness book ever written. But do you *really* know who *YOU* even *is*?

We live in a society where there is so much pressure to be a certain way – you should look like this, act like that, do this, earn that, think this, feel like the other – that sometimes you're so busy worrying about who you *should* be, that you can lose sight of who you truly are. What motivates you? What makes you do or want one thing and not another? Are you happy in your own skin? Are you at peace with your own mind, body and soul?

Many of us never question the purpose of our existence, why we are here at all; instead we lurch from crisis to crisis and often make reactive rather than proactive decisions that determine who we 'think' we are. If we could only step back for a moment and look at dogs and cats, who are constantly intrigued by their worlds, we would discover that we can re-invent ourselves every single day by changing who we 'think' we are – and very importantly not just with our minds, but at a deeper level in our souls too.

I have wondered often about where I sit in the world. Since early childhood, as I've said before, I have always felt like an alien, like I don't fit in, and never more so than now. Sometimes I think I'm going crazy. I expect you do too. If you think, feel and act differently from the rest of your peer group, you are often seen as weird or strange or egotistical or self-centred or aloof, or whatever other word they choose to brand such people with. I think that's why the companion-ship of animals is so central to my well-being – little do they care about peer comparison; they're going to march to their own tune anyway.

Through animals I have understood that it is only by connecting with, appreciating and ultimately respecting the uniqueness of me that I might save myself from discour-agement or despondency. Every cat and every dog I have ever met knows their own mind; they are happy to be themselves. Sure, they have hang-ups about the past; they may have abandonment issues, separation anxiety, fears and phobias about this and that based on a past trauma – but they know they are unique and just get on with it. It's an invaluable lesson that we can all internalise. In a world that would homogenise us in the giant blender of society, given half a chance, it's only by embracing our 'weirdness' and how we are 'wired' – our 'wiredness'! – that we realise our whole potential.

If everyone acknowledged their own uniqueness, then perhaps they would also accept that all people have a right to be themselves – whatever their religion, their politics, their personal dreams or the football team they support! We might be more tolerant of the immutable truth that while we are born a certain colour, in a certain country and a certain family, we are *all* part of the magnificence of creation. I have little doubt that our biological family extends far beyond our mother, father, brothers and sisters. For all our individual wonder, it's worth remembering that we are made of the same stuff as the rest of all nature. We are linked at a molecular level to everything in the universe and we are all made of the same atoms that have existed for billions of years: carbon, hydrogen, oxygen and other elements make protein and water molecules which make DNA and cells. Cells make organs which make up each of our infinitely diverse bodies. Looked at in isolation, the proteins and even the cells of many organs of dogs and cats are the same or very similar to those of humans. We're all land mammals after all. The skeletal system of a dog or cat, which I spend my life as a surgeon navigating, is remarkably similar to that of a human; the bones even mostly have the same names – only the shape and size differ.

And yet, we pride ourselves as being uniquely sentient – our capacity to perceive our environments and external stimuli and experience subjective unique emotion, such as pain and suffering or pleasure and comfort. We can think or reason, rather than just *feel* in isolation, and this requires a level of awareness and cognitive capability. But almost all animals have brains and can think; and they have feelings too – they are sentient – yet we arrogant humans consider their thoughts and feelings of lesser consequence than our own. Still I'd argue that any dog or cat has a better sense of his or herself – and of being totally unique and not caring what others think of them – than you or I. So, who is the more intelligent, I wonder?

My father was a farmer, I became a vet. Others go into politics and finance, others become teachers, postal workers, mechanics, hairdressers, or whatever. In my view, none of these paths is better or worse than any other, just different variations of our 'youness', in the same way as a Border terrier is no better or worse than a Great Dane, or a Maine Coon is no better or worse than a Sphynx. We have a lot to learn from dogs and cats about how to treat ourselves and how to treat others. Sadly, some of us choose to hurt and inflict pain on our fellow humans simply out of rage, greed or revenge. Of course, in the wild, it's the survival of the fittest and eat or be eaten, but in my experience, it's very rare to see hurt or pain purposefully inflicted by a companion animal who has been responsibly bred and taken care of with kindness. Provided we have treated them already with dignity and respect, dogs and cats generally behave in the same way towards us.

I am one of my own worst critics and I compare myself to other people all of the time. I constantly underestimate my *me*-ness', and I expect you also often underestimate your *you*-ness'. It takes my patients in all their wondrous individuality to remind me that I am unique too. I have to constantly remind myself that even though I battle with feelings of inadequacy, everyone does; even though I want to have all the answers (and I don't), nobody does. I think that people who are capable of deeply feeling the emotional burden of others, animal or human, have a more difficult time because we constantly question our very existence and whether any of it matters. Sometimes we allow what we have been, where we have come from, or what people say about us to define who we are.

We have an estimated eighty-five billion neurons between our ears that make us *us* – and we have shaped our sense of identity since childhood. There are as many brain cells as there are stars in the Milky Way galaxy and the brain uses about one-fifth of all of our blood oxygen and of our daily calories. The brain is a very busy organ. Other organs – like the lungs, liver and kidneys – just spontaneously carry on doing what they do, seemingly without effort. These organs are powered by our autonomic nervous system which has two main parts, sympathetic and parasympathetic, both of which originate in the brainstem or spinal cord and ensure that the body responds appropriately to different situations. For example, the sympathetic system increases blood pressure and the parasympathetic decreases blood pressure. Generally all of this happens without us making a conscious decision or having conscious control – it works autonomously, i.e. without us having to think about it.

By contrast, the somatic nervous system communicates input and output between the central nervous system and our body, perceiving sight, smell, hearing and touch, and powering movement, speech and voluntary action. The first time I held a human brain in my hands, I was assisting with a human postmortem examination. As the brain was dissected free of the skull and just 'plopped' into my hands, I was overwhelmed by the thought that it is with this three pounds of 'meat' that I worry, fear, like, dislike and fall in love. When I hold a brain of any animal in my hands I always find it amazing to consider that the big lobes that constitute the cerebrum are entirely responsible for memory, emotion and the conscious thought process – in short, what makes me *myself*, and you *yourself* in a cognitive sense. Likewise, I would argue the cerebrum is primarily what makes Keira herself and Ricochet himself. And this leads me to the central reason behind why I became a vet in the first place and why I have striven for One Medicine and fairness for animals all of my life: if animals with a brain also have most of the same somatic and autonomic nerves as humans, why do we assume that their brain function is any less complex than our own? Why would a dog or a cat *think* less than we do? They have different types of thoughts, sure – but do they have less 'youness' than you or me?

This is not an attempt at anthropomorphism; our perception of our world is our own, but what if our perception of the dog or cat's world is not actually true? What if we're the crazy species and they have it all figured out? Cats and dogs teach us to let go of the delusion that we are in control, because, in fact, the more we try to control our lives, the more we deceive ourselves. The very concept of 'control' of our destiny is an egotistical fallacy. We have control only over our ability to respond to every emotional and psychological cue the universe deals us, and possibly to cue up a few ideas for ourselves and respond to the rebound. However, it is only in letting go and accepting our innate human fallibility and vulnerability that we can ever achieve the potential of 'youness' that animals show us all the time. Dogs and cats embody the sentiment of 'I am enough'. We poor humans, on the other hand, often feel 'not enough', and so we overcompensate by puffing out the peacock plumage of our egos to display how 'enough' we are – in romantic relationships, in our friendship groups, in our workplace and on social media.

The essence of 'you' actually has little to do with 'ego', nor does investment in your 'youness' constitute narcissism or egotism. In modern culture the word 'ego' has taken on a negative connotation, in that having a big ego somehow makes you a person to be wary of at best, and avoided at worst. Yet 'ego' just means 'I' in Latin, and without some form of ego it's hard to be anything at all in the conscious sense of 'being'. In a general sense, most of us associate our ego with a sense of self, self-esteem, self-worth, self-respect and what we offer to the world. Of course, as we shall soon discover, enlightened minds can rise above the ego to a more 'real' sense of self but, nevertheless, our perceptions of ourselves in our ego for most of us is integral to who we are and how we and others perceive us. Dogs and cats are pure ego. 'Look at me,' they scream (well, bark and meow), playing with this ribbon or ball or stick, running around your house, creating mayhem in the park, clawing at your leg, slobbering all over your face, or sitting on your head. We would never think to say that 'My cat/dog has a huge ego and I really hate it'; we'd say he was 'spirited' or 'characterful', or 'sweet, loving, adorable, always ready for giving and receiving joy'.

From my perspective, ego is a good thing since a surgeon needs a healthy sense of self – it's the emotion around ego that becomes potentially problematic. As I've said, biology can humble any surgeon, so when I put on my scrubs and prepare for theatre, I have to hang any 'arrogance' or 'cockiness' on the peg with my trousers. Arrogance has no place in an operating theatre and is generally an unpleasant trait in any path in life. I've met people in all walks of life who seem to care more about themselves, their professional credentials, their fame in men's mouths and what others think of them than about their fellow man – their sense of 'youness' is defined by slaps on the back rather than the slaps in the face of the failures they may not like to admit to. Dogs and cats don't adhere to any of this self-imposed nonsense that counterintuitively stifles our ability to truly be ourselves. The source of all happiness comes from inside – a special sacred place that has been called many things by spiritual leaders down the ages – the yin, the core, the all-seeing eye. I like to call it 'getting over yourself'.

Generally, an individual's self-esteem is intrinsically linked to success of some kind – simply being good at something. This too is a fallacy. You will never find either the source of your happiness or unhappiness outside yourself. You certainly won't find a sense of self-worth in social media, drugs, alcohol, sex, addictions or relationships as pursuits in and of themselves – though I recognise of course that there are people who have jobs for all the right reasons in social media, drug rehabilitation, making alcohol, or being a sex, addiction or relationship counsellor. Certainly, you can seek well-being and fulfilment in worthwhile goals, becoming skilled at, or achieving something – but deep, inner contented 'youness' is much more complex and requires tapping into what really makes you 'tick'. Sometimes, though, we're not honest with ourselves about what we really want. Instead we're busy ticking boxes for everyone else and not satisfying our own true incentives at all. We somehow acquiesce to the expectations of family, peer group, friends or work colleagues who want or expect us to be something we're not. Or perhaps we let our own feelings of not being ready, worthy, confident or able enough to get in the way of expressing our inner selves. It could be our taste in music or some quirky hobby, for example, or something more complex such as our sexuality, our religion, or a yearning to express some other deepest unspoken desire. You may be in a dead-end job, a restrictive relationship or with a loved one who is dependent on you, or perhaps you have a disability of some kind – so you never get the chance to express real 'youness'.

So many of us rarely dwell on what we really want at a deeper level – what makes our soul peaceful, what makes our heart flutter, what makes our spirit soar. It's as if we're afraid to allow ourselves to even think of it, perhaps because we don't want to hear the yearning beneath our rational mind, or someone else telling us, 'It'll never happen for you!' Therein lies the biggest lie that we and others tell ourselves.

I think that most dogs and cats have this figured out. They're not really bothered about doing what people expect of them but, in my experience, they know intuitively exactly what they want and they won't be told otherwise. Keira and Ricochet have their own behaviour quirks and things they like to do at a certain time in a certain way, and I just fall in line really. Keira will never ever give up on trying to find where I have hidden my midnight snack – because I wake up most nights and can't get back to sleep without eating something, but frequently Keira's got there first. Consequently, I started stashing my protein bar in the bath. Unfortunately, however, Ricochet and Keira were clearly in cahoots on the subject because one night recently I went into the bathroom to find them both there, looking all innocent – Ricochet reclining in the bath and Keira sitting on a protein-bar wrapper.

Similarly, I've tried a dozen times to stop Ricochet pulling down the blinds in my office – but he's so tall now when up on his back legs that he can reach the cord even when I wrap it up high. I came into my office the other day to find him standing with one back foot on Keira's bottom and one on a ledge while trying to snag the cord. He can stretch up about three feet already and will probably grow for another couple of years! The pair of them are always unapologetically just 'themselves' and they will do what they want to do. The thing is, though, I realise that I am exactly the same, and I will not be told otherwise by anyone, which is why I have loads of business associates but have never been good at having a boss. I suppose some element of my intransigent 'me-ness' has also meant I have found it difficult to commit to the permanence of marriage, for example. So, maybe there are both good and not so good things about this fervently independent 'youness' – and I should add, therefore, that I have now realised that at some point compromise needs to come into the equation, otherwise 'youness' just becomes 'get-lost-ness'!

Most well-adjusted dogs and cats are fine by themselves and you are an added bonus. They're just along for the ride and in it for the moment. It's a common aphorism that dogs adopt the characteristics of their guardians, and recent studies in both the USA and UK corroborate this. It has been shown that extroverted humans tend to have more excitable and active dogs, and agreeable folks have less fearful, less aggressive dogs, while those who were disagreeable (unconcerned with the needs of others, suspicious, unfriendly, hostile) have more fearful, less active dogs who were more unresponsive to training. I can confirm this from my own experience: I have hardly ever seen 'opposites attract' in my consulting room. Indeed, many of the less well-adjusted dogs tend to have assimilated the unfortunate traits of their guardians. Hypochondriacs often have super-sensitive animals, stoical folks often have 'well-hard' pets, and angry and confrontational guardians tend to have aggressive and hostile canine companions. It's hard to have a conversation with a timid person about how to coax their nervous dog to do physiotherapy, to explain to an obese person how to put a dog on a strict diet, or to find out what's wrong with a stoical pet who won't tell you anything no matter where you poke or prod, and nor will their guardian. Meanwhile, an aggressive dog may react no matter where you touch it, just as their guardian may react badly no matter what you say.

Similarly, research has shown that copycats *do* exist. Like children, cats can adopt the character traits of their human parents. Guardians who scored higher on the scale of neuroticism, for example, were more likely to have nutty cats, who displayed anxious, fearful and aggressive behaviours, and had more stress-related sickness and even obesity.

There is no question in my mind that the worst version of you is the enemy of being the best version of you, and it's all reflected in your relationship with your animal companion. A good person can do bad things sometimes; likewise for our canine and feline friends. Ricochet is very independent and sometimes naughty, except when he wants cuddles, when he's unbelievably affectionate and attentive, while Keira likes her own space and is a creature of habit. She can get cranky if disturbed prematurely from slumber – and she snores. I am well aware that I describe myself exactly!

For both dogs and cats, attachment to humans likely represents an adaptation of the 'offspring–caretaker bond'. Their attachment to us and vice versa has been shown to be an evolutionary and biologically relevant behaviour trait. Many dogs and cats, like children, have a 'source of comfort' relationship with humans. Your cat or dog depends on you when they are stressed, just like your children might do, and in turn it's scientifically proven that their companionship makes us healthier both mentally and physically, releasing the hormones of calm, optimism and self-esteem, like oxytocin and serotonin, and reducing stress hormones such as cortisol. Dr David Hamilton has called oxytocin the 'kindness' or 'cuddle' hormone. When we cuddle our cat or dog, oxytocin causes the release of a chemical called nitric oxide, which dilates the blood vessels and can reduce blood pressure. I often think of dogs and cats as a love stent unblocking our emotional arteries every single day. When I come into my office after a stressful operation, Keira waggles her bottom waiting for cuddles and Ricochet immediately jumps up on my desk and, like a graceful ballerina, pirouettes his muzzle up under my nose and strokes my face with his whiskers.

Their grounding effect is instantaneous – it's very difficult to be stressed or downtrodden with that much love in the air – and it seems for them the wonderment of the exchange is of equal magnitude. Keira and Ricochet have tapped into the very essence of who I am and everything I could become through accepting me as I am in unconditional love. This is a complex amalgam of moral responsibility, honest transparency and some kind of elated release epiphany which exposes a raw and bleeding part of us rarely accessed by humans, and yet we willingly share it with our companion animals and in the safe space we inhabit together we rejoice in its vulnerability. I can honestly say that if I didn't have that special place to go to when I am going out of my mind with the human stressors around me, I'm really not sure how my life would have turned out – but I do know for sure that I would have been a whole lot worse off. Wouldn't it be great if all of our relationships were equally mutually supportive?

Most of the pet parents who come to see me have exactly this close bond of trust and emotional support with their dog or cat, which is nigh-on impossible to explain to anyone who hasn't experienced it. I'd go so far as to say that if you haven't experienced it, you really are missing out on one of life's magnificent miracles of 'youness'. I think many of us don't tap into even half of our potential or the spectrum of feelings we could have if we allowed them – and in that sacred space of trust with a dog or cat, you really can be 'you'.

When I first met Kirsty and Glenn in July 2019, they absolutely embraced this munificent love with their gorgeous nine-month-old black Labrador Tala. Their primary care vet had diagnosed her with the worst hip dysplasia she had ever seen. Kirsty and Glenn were in bits. They didn't have children, but it was evident that they loved Tala (a Native American girl's name meaning 'wolf') unconditionally and felt exactly the same degree of moral responsibility for her as parents do for a child. People can be dismissive of this kind of language, but I understood exactly how they felt about her: she was the most adorable, beautiful, kind, friendly soul and they were beautiful, friendly and kind human beings – sensitive, loving, open and vulnerable in their frailty. Tala's hip dysplasia wasn't by any means the worst I'd ever seen, since I see the worst of the worst cases from all over Europe and beyond, but it was certainly up there, and just like in poor Scrumpy's case, this condition, which can produce significant painful osteoarthritis, usually self-perpetuates and worsens.

No matter how many dogs I treat with this same biological problem, I never cease to wonder at their individual personalities and unique 'youness' in coping with it. Much the same is true in human patients of course – some complain of the least twinge while others can be in excruciating chronic pain and just get on with their lives. Our anatomy may be similar, but as beings we are totally unique. Some dogs manage reasonably well with hip dysplasia; others, like Tala, don't. Not every case warrants surgery – but all medical management had failed for poor Tala at a very young age.

Both Tala's hips were completely dislocated, and the sockets had already filled in. She had become very stiff, not wanting to get up after lying down, wasn't putting any weight on one of her back legs and was certainly in significant pain on both sides, such that she was reluctant to exercise. In spite of every effort with painkillers, physio- and hydrotherapy, Tala wasn't coping at all and badly needed help. I discussed the options with Kirsty and Glenn. We could put her to sleep and that must always be considered, but there were surgical options. We could consider femoral head and neck excision (FHNE), leaving the top of the femur on both sides to move without a solid ball-and-socket joint. This, however, wasn't the optimal option for Tala bilaterally as she might still have some pain from bone rubbing or tethering of soft tissues – and it would be very challenging to build up her muscle mass with no solid joints. FHNE is used all over the world and has been for decades, but it has been scientifically proven that it does not result in the level of pain alleviation and function that total hip replacement (THR) does. This is true even with small dogs and cats. In 1990 when I graduated, FHNE was my first option, but that's no longer the case and in 2020, in my opinion, it is to be considered when THR isn't the right thing to do for whatever reason or is cost-prohibitive. Then there was a so-called pelvic osteotomy: in some young dogs, we can cut the hip socket off the pelvis and rotate it so that it better captures the head of the femur, but again this wouldn't work for Tala since she had no hip sockets and her femoral heads were misshapen.

When I first graduated, I had learned that THR was contraindicated in patients under a year of age. Since then, however, I have operated many hundreds of THRs, and

I have published academic papers in scientific journals on performing the procedure in dogs between six months and a year old, with no higher complication rate than with older dogs. After a long discussion about the practical confinement and the ethical, rehabilitation and financial implications, as 'parents' Kirsty and Glenn felt that Tala wasn't ready to give up and they decided to proceed with a THR. We operated on one hip using standard implants, as I had done myriad times before, and, once I was happy that everything seemed fine with the first side, on the second hip six weeks later. Initially Tala recovered well – but then on Friday 13 September 2019 her muscles got more and more loose and her hip joints dislocated on both sides. Kirsty and Glenn sat ashen-faced and close to tears in my consulting room, torn apart by the enormity of the decision they had to make. Tala was in considerable pain and they were inconsolable. One may only guess at Tala's emotional distress, but for Kirsty and Glenn this was as important as her physical well-being.

If we were to operate on Tala again, this time she would need bilateral simultaneous surgery, since there was no time to wait for one side to heal as both were badly dislocated, and she would again need a twelve-week recovery period. Under normal circumstances, I never perform bilateral simultaneous THR because of the incrementally increased risk. Should they put such a young dog through such a traumatic procedure again? What was ethically the 'right thing to do'? They couldn't really afford a second surgery, because they had planned to buy a new home in the United States, having spent many wonderful times there on road trips. Would they regret trying and failing again, since there were no guarantees, or would they regret not trying at all? Glenn was particularly concerned that it would put Tala through more perceived suffering with no certainty of a successful outcome.

They sat on the floor with Tala looking up at them, dozy with sedation and oblivious to the crisis, not knowing if life was about to be snatched away or if she would wake up the next day. I said to Kirsty and Glenn that I didn't want to cause a marital crisis on top of their sense of moral responsibility, but stressed that they both needed to agree on a route forward, and then sent them for a walk to make up their minds about what they wanted to do.

My team were on standby, knowing we'd all work late into the evening if they decided to proceed that day, or we would all finish on time with very heavy hearts if the decision was euthanasia. It was truly heartbreaking all round, but all I can do in any such situation is to give people the options. Many times in my career, I've known absolutely that I had a good chance of saving a life, but I couldn't because of other circumstances. In my heart I didn't feel that euthanasia was the best option for Tala. All I could think about was how Tala must have been feeling – and I was quite sure that she was actually *feeling* way more than we understand, not just in the sense of physical pain, but profoundly in the sense of emotional pain too.

Gregory Berns is a neuroscientist in Atlanta, Georgia, who has trained dogs to lie perfectly still inside an MRI scanner so that he can study their brains. I wish all dogs could do that every day in my practice, but the noise of the scanner and general kerfuffle means that all dogs are anaesthetised since even a small twitching motion disrupts the scan. Training the dogs to do this is a major feat, but an even greater feat has been to discover what they might be thinking. For example, in both man and dog the caudate nucleus of the brain, sitting between the cerebral cortex and the brainstem, plays a key role in anticipation of things we enjoy, like food, love, aesthetic beauty, music and money. This region 'lights up' on functional MRI studies in humans. Berns discovered the same response in a dog's brain in reaction to food and to the people that dog loves. This is hardly surprising as a reflection of what Charles Darwin called 'evolutionary continuity', in which he recognised that the differences among species in anatomical, physiological and psychological traits are differences 'in degree rather than in kind'. The finding of so-called 'functional homology' with a human brain doesn't categorically prove that dogs can love us, but it does infer that dogs have a level of sentience comparable to a human child and this forces all of us to rethink the phrase 'it's only a dog'. Or as Gregory Berns said, 'My one inescapable conclusion is this: dogs are people too.' His studies also found overwhelmingly that dogs are motivated by praise; aren't we all!

There are now thousands of studies showing that animals can experience emotions ranging from joy and happiness to deep sadness, grief, empathy, jealousy and resentment and even post-traumatic stress disorder – and that vertebrates have exactly the same areas of the brain that are important for consciousness and processing emotions as do humans. There is no doubt that dogs and cats can form predictions of how the world behaves around them, so that if they alter their actions, they will get a different reaction. In fact, they are quite good at this. Of course, we as simple human beings can be good at this too, but we also tend to make the same mistakes over and over and never seem to learn. We do the same thing and expect a different outcome. If you cheat and are found out, it doesn't necessarily stop some from cheating again; if someone gets drunk and says or does really stupid things, it doesn't stop that person getting inebriated again. A dog or a cat is unlikely to do that; after a few knock-backs, most quickly learn to take a different approach. Which species is most sensible, I wonder?

The environmental philosopher Kai Chan argues that recognising sentience in other life forms involves reaching beyond scientific evidence alone, because it is never certain: 'To assume no sentience in the face of some (inconclusive) evidence is to fail to imagine. [. . .] We cannot justify excluding any (living) entity from the possibility of sentience in some form.' The 'Golden Rule' in Chan's argument is, to quote the Holy Bible, that we should 'do unto others as we would have them do unto us'.

The animal studies theorist Anat Pick goes further, arguing that 'the neural or mental fact of sentience is hardly the point'. She focuses instead on 'vulnerability' as this is shared by all living creatures. In fact, I would go a step further, and argue that vulnerability applies to *all* of creation. We can see the effects of climate change across the planet – fire that has destroyed entire habitats in Brazil, Australia and California. Trees, insects and wild animals all gone, and likely as a direct result of our actions as arrogant, selfish, greedy human beings. In his book *The Hidden Life of Trees*, German forester Peter Wohlleben explains how trees have the capacity to communicate with, and heal, other trees. Trees' root systems, which spread out like the tendrils of neuronal structures, can detect the roots of their own versus another species and, using radioactive-marked sugar molecules, Wohlleben and his team have discovered that there is a flow of food and energy from healthy to sick trees. Four-hundred-year-old stumps of felled trees have been kept alive by neighbouring trees though they have no leaves to create sugars for themselves, while older trees also supply young trees with just enough sugar until they mature and begin to photosynthesise. Do we really believe that we are 'alone' in our unique human 'intelligence'? Rather, it would seem, our capacity to understand the world we live in is still in its infancy.

For most of history we have deemed that we alone are sentient, and that animals are without feeling or reason. In the early 1600s, Descartes famously asserted, 'I think, therefore I am.' As I've said before, I don't entirely agree with this. Sure, we mentally form a picture of who we are, how we behave, and how we choose to respond – and we are not our bodies, colour, sexuality, religion or nationality. But I believe we have a soul, which to my mind is that ethereal part of ourselves, fed by the moral conscience of the brain but quite distinct from our cognitive capabilities. Our soul guides the emotional state of our existence and constitutes our true legacy when we are gone. Those who believe in reincarnation feel that this soul lives on after us. I think that the soul, God and oneness with creation – that is, the entire universe at a molecular level – are all one and the same, and that there is a common thread by which all 'beings' are connected.

The concept of string theory aims to unify particle physics and quantum gravity, i.e. Einstein's general theory of relativity and quantum mechanics, to explain our multi-dimensional universe as well as the space-time continuum. It is irrefutable in my view that all life is linked by commonality of molecular structure and that our knowledge of the dimensions of space and time will not be the same in a hundred years from now. It is not too far a step, therefore, to conceive that all life could also be linked by another dimension, which, in our current language, we could call 'pure consciousness'. I'd like to go into this again in more detail later, but in other words, perhaps in some way, all 'souls' are innately linked and all inexorably return to one. What we as individuals do with that 'soul' is down to us. Then the question arises whether animals have the capacity for self-determination and can have as much 'youness' as you or me. If we accept this, then we can begin to divest our ego from the 'real selves' of our soul and truly begin to open ourselves to our full and unique potential. And that might just possibly include listening, both consciously and intuitively, to what our animal companions can teach us.

And that's where I personally vehemently refute Descartes' philosophy. He said that an animal's actions are merely 'expressions of their fear, their hope, or their joy; and consequently, they can do these things without any thought'. He proposed that if an animal shows signs of distress, for example, this isn't an actual conscious emotion; rather, they mechanistically respond as 'automata', i.e. they are devoid of feeling or a soul. This allowed the maltreatment of animals to be sanctioned in law and in society until the middle of the nineteenth century. This is anathema to me.

A few hundred years ago any public expression of my belief that dogs and cats have feelings, needs and wants would undoubtedly have ostracised me from my peers. But, by the Renaissance, the work of, among others, Leonardo da Vinci, Erasmus, Thomas More, Montaigne, Shakespeare and Francis Bacon intimated that animal sentience was accepted as part of secular knowledge. Leonardo da Vinci was also one of the first to explore the physical commonalities of man and animals side by side. His detailed anatomical drawings were not bettered for hundreds of years. At first his motivation was to learn about bodies through dissection in order to make his paintings more realistic, but soon he was intrigued by the riddle of creation itself and how incredibly similar the essence of man and animal actually are.

By the eighteenth century Scottish philosopher David Hume wrote that 'no truth appears to me more evident, than that beasts are endow'd with thought and reason as well as men'. In the early 1800s, pertaining to animals the English social reformer Jeremy Bentham asserted that: 'The question is not, Can they reason? nor Can they talk?, but Can they suffer?' Bentham maintained that animals' happiness and well-being were relevant and the capacity for suffering gives all sentient beings the right to equal consideration. It was this, rather than the ability to reason, that should provide what he called the 'insuperable line' regarding how we treat other animals. However, Hume and Bentham's utilitarianism – in other words, a philosophy which argues that the most ethical choice is the one that will produce the greatest good for the greatest number – wasn't widely accepted. Even though in 1839 English veterinarian William Youatt wrote that 'animals have senses, emotions and consciousness' and 'also have imagination and the moral qualities of courage, friendship and loyalty', as if it were accepted wisdom, little changed in societal recognition of animal sentience until relatively recently.

In 1997, with the Treaty of Amsterdam, the European Union agreed to recognise animals as 'sentient beings' under European law. And in 2006, in a review of 'The Changing Concept of Animal Sentience', the author Ian Duncan makes the very important point that animal welfare should be more than just the absence of suffering but also that, just like for humans, the presence of pleasure can add much to quality of life. All of us who love a dog or a cat automatically assume that we want them to be happy and we do all we can to bring enjoyment to their lives, but sadly for much of society and its treatment of animals, this vital understanding remains lacking.

Finally, on 7 July 2012, the Cambridge Declaration on Consciousness proclaimed that 'non-human animals have the neuroanatomical, neurochemical, and neurophysiological substrates of conscious states along with the capacity to exhibit intentional behaviours'. However, in my opinion the declaration needs to go further and not just recognise animals as sentient but enshrine it in international law. I really hope that this will happen in the next generation, because I think the children of today absolutely know what a mess we have made of our planet's natural habitats and the welfare of animals to date. My deepest wish is that we shall become more enlightened and accept our moral responsibility in this regard – if we don't, then all of humanity will pay the price for forgetting that animals have feelings too.

It's now scientifically established that animals who do not have a centralised nervous system, or have no nervous system at all, such as echinoderms (like starfish) or porifera (like sponges) aren't sentient by any measure we currently have. What's to say, however, that they don't 'feel' in different ways? It may be that we discover sentience, in more species as science evolves to measure it. For now, species with spines and brains have been proven sentient, as well as octopus and squid, and even crabs and lobsters. Most of the world recognises that chimpanzees, apes, dolphins, whales, elephants and other animals with large brains communicate and interact with each other and with us in complex ways. We've heard stories such as the two herds of wild South African elephants that made a twelve-hour trek to the home of the conservationist Lawrence Anthony when he died. They came ostensibly to mourn, but how could they have known that he had died? A few years previously, these formerly violent rogue elephants had been destined for extermination as pests to crops and villages, but had been rescued and rehabilitated by Lawrence. It is safe to say that many animals want to live in safety and free from fear, pain and suffering, just as we do, and there is also ample evidence that they worry and lose sleep over their well-being. I have spent many nights by the sides of dogs and cats in our hospital, and have witnessed this with my own eyes. I have also seen many dogs and cats pine endlessly following the death of their guardians and visit their bed, chair or grave.

I have looked in the eyes of many patients down the years and sensed that they were as vulnerable and as worried as I was, as lonely as I was, as scared as I was. I have also been acutely aware of my responsibility to make the right decision for them. It rests heavily on my shoulders, and on the shoulders of veterinary and human surgeons everywhere. Most of us do not want to play God; most of us just want to alleviate pain and suffering; and most of us feel like anything but God when we are making those difficult decisions on the part of our team.

While I waited for Kirsty and Glenn to return from their walk, I held Tala's head in my lap and looked into her eyes as she lay there. I couldn't simply go back in and put on a longer neck on the hip stem to tighten the lax muscles since I'd already done that during the first operation and it wasn't working. The X-ray pictures had suggested that standard implants should work, but sadly biology and specifically loose tissue around the joint (peri-articular tissue) had other ideas. The loose tissue had got looser, and I had failed. And so, the only surgical option that I could ethically justify was a new kind of hip socket called an 'AceFitz' which I invented several years ago.

A few years before I met Tala, I had had a near-identical case in a Labrador that I ended up putting to sleep. The conventional implants had also failed, and there were at that time only two viable revision options, FHNE and RADAR. I had previously developed a technique for cementing plastic acetabular cups under a plate screwed to the side of the pelvis which I have published in a veterinary journal as RADAR – Reinforced Augmentation of the Dorsal Acetabular Rim. Neither technique was by any means certain to provide satisfactory quality of life and so sadly the family elected for euthanasia. I was quite devastated that I wasn't able to save his hip joints and his life. For quite a few days afterwards, I remained profoundly sad. But there were better ideas to come.

It was a hot summer afternoon, the air hazy with heat over the crisp dry grass in the field outside my office window. Even the eddies of warm air weaving through the open window didn't bring me any joy but felt oppressive. Then, as I sat there writing clinical reports, something else wafted in through the window on the summer breeze – the familiar jingle jangle tune of an ice-cream van wending its way through the streets of the nearby housing estate. The sound waxed and waned and finally came to a halt. I stopped what I was doing too and I listened, but there was silence. Suddenly I was transported back to the seaside of my childhood vacations in Tramore on the south coast of Ireland, handing over my pennies for a 99 – a magnificent creamy, whipped ice cream with a giant chocolate flake.

I got up, grabbed my car keys and drove off in search of the ice-cream van. I made it just as the last child was gleefully cupping a giant ice-cream cone in her hands at the window of the van and walked up with cash at the ready to buy some joy for myself and my team at the practice. Standing there waiting to be served it was as if I had been cast back in time. The ice-cream man hovered over me, larger than life, at a window that is always taller than I imagine myself to be, because outside an ice-cream van, I'm eternally six years old. I peered up with my wide eyes, transfixed as he not only put the whipped ice cream onto a cone, but also scooped up ice cream of various colours into tubs for my colleagues from big containers that were laid out before me behind the glass. He scooped and scooped until all of the small tubs were filled to the brim with strawberry, chocolate, mint, coffee and raspberry ripple ice cream. My eyes followed the scoop like the wand of a magician crafting some marvellous spell, and my mind roamed free from the pain of failure that had ensnared me for the past few days. It was just like I was that little boy on holiday at the seaside again, my thoughts free to wander in the childhood playground of my imagination. And there it was, in my mind's eye – an 'ice-cream scoop' acetabular augmentation unit that could be bolted to the ilium to lateralise the acetabulum and enhance the dorsal rim to prevent coxo-femoral luxation! Or, in other words, a big cup with a handle which could attach to the pelvis to keep the head of a hip replacement in place, even when it wanted to slip out.

I rushed back to the practice, dished out the delicious frozen confections and scurried to my office where I drew the very first AceFitz device. I contacted the ever-trusty Jay Meswania, and within days we had drawn a prototype. The AceFitz looks like an ice-cream scoop, with a 'handle' plate and a large metal scoop-like shell which does five things:

1. Even where there isn't enough bone cover for a metal

socket of appropriate size, it allows a much bigger shell than would otherwise be possible, and with firm anchorage to bone using the integrated plate fixed firmly to the side of the pelvis (ilium) with multiple screws that lock into the plate.

2. A big plastic liner (acetabular component) can then be cemented in the shell, allowing the biggest femoral head possible. The bigger the head, the less chance of dislocation (luxation), all else being equal.

3. The plastic liner can be cemented in at a variable angle which isn't dependent on bone architecture to provide more cover for the head and decrease the chances of luxation, and to suit the position of any stem and head in the femur.

4. The titanium metal shell is covered in honeycombed mesh coated with hydroxyapatite which encourages the metal to become part of the body forever by 'osteointegration'. This is achieved by bone in-growth into the porous surface of the metal and bone on-growth onto the rough surface of the implant.

5. It allows the shell and therefore the plastic liner to be positioned a little further away from the side of the pelvis, and therefore increases the 'offset distance' of the femur from the pelvis, putting more tension on the muscles and therefore holding in the head better. I have since implanted the AceFitz many times to save limb and life.

For Tala it was crucial to minimise the chance of her luxating again in spite of the loose muscle around her hip joints. The proposed procedure, therefore, was to insert two of these acetabular augmentation ice-cream scoops, to push the cups slightly outwards from the pelvis and provide an appropriate cup position on both sides, while leaving the existing stems which I had already placed in the femur bones.

After what seemed like forever for all concerned, Kirsty

and Glenn came back into my room. In spite of the financial and practical implications, they didn't feel in their hearts that euthanasia was the best option and had decided to give Tala a chance. We had another discussion about ethics and risk and we collectively agreed that if the revision surgery did not go well, we would have done everything we could and we would let Tala pass away peacefully.

We finished the operation at about midnight and I called Glenn and Kirsty. We weren't home free yet, but the operation had gone as well as could be hoped for. Everyone except the night team went to bed, knowing in our hearts that we had done our absolute best.

I shall never forget the morning after the surgery, when the interns and I got Tala out of her ward and walked her with support to the garden behind the practice, where we all sat around her. The interns had never seen AceFitz in action before, and were amazed at the result. I had gone way beyond all of the intrigue that one feels as a young clinician developing solutions to problems and marvelling at the scientific achievement as some kind of epiphany. Instead, for me the experience was one of marvelling at the magnificence of life and the fragility of our hold on it – a rather more spiritual epiphany. Had a different decision been made less than twenty-four hours previously, Tala wouldn't be sitting with us wide-eyed and waggy-tailed at all. As the morning sun slipped free of the clouds and blessed a new day with serenity, I cradled Tala's paw in my hand and felt a profound sense of peace in our decision and in our beautiful vocation – the ability to give life. She was interested in absolutely everything, eyes darting at every new distraction and nose sniffing the air excitedly – rejoicing in just being alive, as if nothing at all had happened and still totally unaware how close she had come to death. She was yearning to play, but of course we couldn't let her. It was early days, but the signs were positive.

As Tala gulped down every golden drop of sunshine, tears welled up inside me. I was suddenly overwhelmed by the dichotomy of success and failure as a surgeon and the catharsis of succeeding on this particular day. I do the same operation the same way and I succeed or I fail; I'm a hero or a villain. I held the life of this vibrant, hairy Vesuvius of love in my hands, and it could so easily have been snuffed out. The millstone of responsibility that comes with decisions of life and death and how knife-edge it is for all of us overwhelmed me and I had to wander off and have a moment to myself to collect my thoughts. I am a surgeon who pushes the boundaries of possibility because I want to make a tangible difference to our animal friends and make veterinary medicine better, but I'm also a vulnerable and sensitive human being who takes failure deeply personally. Tala was an effervescent, effusive, ebullient soul and, thank God, her infectious joy would continue to be an inspiration to us all for some time to come.

We were both unique in our 'youness' – and all of that was to be celebrated. That morning and many other mornings, animals have saved my life. Glenn and Kirsty had made a momentous decision, and a huge personal and financial sacrifice to save Tala's life. They spent the next few weeks under house arrest looking after her, Kirsty always sleeping by her side, and were both frequently in floods of tears. They faced all kinds of opinions from all kinds of people. Some made ignorant comments like, 'I've got a shotgun if you want to borrow it', 'Really, it's just a dog', or 'Oh well, I guess just dumping her in a field and running away isn't an option.' Some pitied and criticised them for being so foolish spending thousands of pounds on 'just a dog'. Clearly if this was a brother, sister, mother, father or child, people would react differently and wouldn't question such commitment to another soul, but, when many would have given up on her, to Kirsty and Glenn, Tala *was* their family. Tala was part of their lives and she was their responsibility – and now she runs around as if nothing had ever ailed her.

Kirsty and Glenn sent me a wonderful picture of Tala next to their lighted Christmas tree with her new friend, a Maine Coon cat called Johnny Cash. It was the best Christmas present for all of us at the practice, and of course cemented my determination to get a Maine Coon cat myself one day, just like Ivor and Johnny C. Within a few months, Ricochet would become part of Tala's inheritance. It was as if I had in some way beckoned him into my life without even knowing it. Well, miraculously, somehow, he had reached out to Michaela through the magic of the internet and caught her attention. Given his proclivity for tapping my keyboard with his big mitts, I suspect he 'had a paw in it' somehow.

Ricochet is uniquely himself and came with all of his own quirks and challenges, as I most certainly come with mine. He rejoices in my own weirdly wired 'me-ness' and I rejoice in his individuality too. I love him desperately and I will do whatever it takes to take care of him, as I will for Keira too – till the end of time.

Thus it was also for Kirsty, Glenn and Tala. I have seen some couples split up following the distress of decision-making about a dog or cat in similar circumstances, but the crisis drew Glenn and Kirsty closer together. They both had a very clear sense of self, who they really were, what mattered and what didn't matter, and for them Tala mattered very much. They had given her the chance to live for more than a decade to come, regardless of what anyone else thought. In my experience, the couple who support each other through such traumas are very likely to stay together. They respect and appreciate the 'youness' of the other and of the animal they love.

Kirsty told me once that she thought that the love of an animal is somehow different from any other love, that she couldn't describe it, but she felt it in her heart. In their uncomplicated companionship and dependency on us, animals can teach us more about our 'youness' than a therapist or human partner ever could. In their infinite uniqueness, they teach us about who we really are and about who we could become. When you experience it, that unconditional love is the best emotion in the world, and I feel sad for those who have never felt it, and even sadder if they choose to denigrate it. Such commentary says far more about the lack of empathy and compassion in that individual than it ever could about the person feeling and doing the loving. If people say you're crazy for loving an animal, or for believing that they have feelings, for me the simultaneously beautiful and tragic irony is that in every single case, *they* are the crazy ones.

CHAPTER TEN

Compassion

'Compassion is the wish to see others free from suffering.'

Dalai Lama

Compassion is being selfless enough to treat others, man and animal, how you would wish to be treated yourself . . . with empathy, kindness and respect.

'Compassion' and 'care' have almost become platitudes: buzzwords for the latest wave of 'wellness' which permeates today's culture, but sadly the reality is that it can sometimes feel that human kindness is in short supply. You only have to turn on the television, open a newspaper or look at social media to see evidence of violence, prejudice, greed, deceit and exploitation of all kinds, and especially a basic lack of consideration. The challenge for all of us, I think, is to conquer hatred, bigotry, aggression and fear by internalising and enacting the true meaning of compassion in our everyday lives. Through empathy we gain insight and appreciation of the emotions of another, but it is only through compassion that we act on these feelings to help another.

I worry that in our thirst for meaning, the very concepts of compassion, sensitivity and kindness, in themselves the embodiment of enlightened social values, have too easily been co-opted by big brands who commodify them to sell their concepts or products. Compassion and kindness, and all the invested emotion these words should encompass, then become some kind of desirable but optional character traits homogenised into soundbite sales pitches for ourselves and the products we covet. We trot out these hollow aphorisms, especially on social media, to make us feel good about ourselves, all the while doing little to manifest these qualities in daily life. Pause for a moment, look inside yourself and ask, 'Do I show kindness and compassion in my routine interactions?' I think we're all guilty of a little hypocrisy here.

Over the past couple of years, I've had a masterclass in real and tangible compassion from being involved with animal rescue centres through making the TV show *Animal Rescue Live*. There's no superficial compassion when it comes to finding forever homes for as many animals as possible. Everyone involved oozes compassion from every pore.

I met many who have dedicated their lives to rescuing, fostering and rehoming animals. Some do so as volunteers and told me that they get far more reward from caring for animals than any other work they might undertake. I witnessed time and again how compassionate care can give a human or an animal a second chance in life. Through my interaction with animal shelters and trying to help rehome animals in different areas of the country, I met Danny who had been a heroin addict, endured homelessness and been in and out of jail for theft and other offences. By volunteering at the animal shelter and having the opportunity to show compassion for animals, he had somehow turned his life around and now had a part-time job and sheltered accommodation. I met Dave, a teenage boy who grew up on an estate surrounded by drugs, knife crime and gang culture. His mother was a crack addict and his father had left him and his two sisters to fend for themselves. It had seemed inevitable that he too would fall into crime, but through volunteering at a shelter he had then been taken on in another animal rescue centre in a salaried role that gave him a new start and paid his rent in a shared house with other young people who also worked with animal shelters in the area. I met a young girl who had been trafficked as a sex worker from Eastern Europe. She had been imprisoned in a house, beaten and horrifically abused. In her own words she was 'an animal' at the mercy of her traffickers. When she was finally rescued she found work at an animal shelter. After the unimaginable trauma she had suffered, she unsurprisingly felt deep empathy for the rescue animals with whom she shared a bond of compassion that had been so lacking in her earlier life. In each of these cases compassion shared with animals has enhanced human lives as much as those of the animals.

Also, when I was making *Animal Rescue Live* I suggested to producers that they film me travelling in a cage strapped in the back of a van, just as puppies from a puppy farm are transported. I wanted to highlight this abominable practice, but due to legal issues it proved harder to orchestrate than one might imagine. It turns out that it is against the law for a human being to travel in a cage in a vehicle on a public highway without being strapped into that cage for health and safety reasons, and for those same reasons I most certainly could not be placed in the hold of a ferry or a cargo plane – yet these are the very journeys inflicted upon these young animals. Laws have been passed in England to outlaw the sale of a puppy by a middle-person: licensed dog breeders are required to show puppies interacting with their mothers in their place of birth, and buyers should have sight of the parent dogs and be able to check the lineage. Consequently, there are now significant concerns that Ireland, Wales and Scotland will become even greater hubs for puppy-farming operations.

People get around the law: they heavily advertise these intensively bred pups in print or on the internet, trading on our emotions with pictures of 'cute puppies' and absurd fictitious stories of kindness – and people are trusting enough to fall for it. They turn up at fake homes or at meeting points in motorway service stations, and once they see a puppy, they just want to 'rescue' the poor animal in spite of their suspicions – and all the while we fuel this horrible trade. We are so very stupid. In doing so, we allow organised criminal gangs who also trade in drugs, firearms and prostitution, among other unscrupulous dealers of various kinds, to make money from the suffering of animals. In my practice we frequently see the results of bad breeding and poor environments for puppies born in such places including harmful genetic mutations. I think that anyone who has ever shared life-enriching love with any puppy should want to show care in return by trying to ensure the ethical provenance of all puppies and to uproot this cynical corruption of our compassion. This abomination on our own doorstep has to stop.

While I was travelling about in my cage, we stopped in a lay-by on a country road to meet Eileen, who runs a dog charity. Eileen and her team arrange similar regular pickups from the breeders of the females who can no longer be bred, rescuing them from being shot or disposed of in some other way. They sometimes take in more than a dozen females in one rendezvous. The dogs are then cared for by her charity's nurse to get them back into as good a physical shape as possible, but their psychological damage is profound. For Eileen, the hardest part of this work is knowing that no matter how many dogs they rescue, there are thousands more breeding bitches with litters living in squalid situations while their puppies are shipped off to unsuspecting families.

I subsequently travelled to Wales to meet the Wiley family. They had found a pug puppy on an online selling site and duly went to an address, which was clearly just a 'pretend' home from which she allegedly originated. They couldn't bear to leave the puppy there and so they paid the money, took her home and called her Coco. A few weeks later she was becoming progressively paralysed and having breathing difficulties, and a visit to a vet confirmed that Coco was affected by horrific spinal deformities and brachycephalic airway syndrome, conditions that are endemic in poorly bred members of this breed. Devastated, the Wileys had to put Coco to sleep. This was especially difficult for their young boy Casper, who had really fallen in love with Coco. It was heartbreaking to hear them talk about their experience – this was the loveliest, kind and sensible family, who would never have thought they could be in the least bit gullible. Sadly their compassion was their downfall. They fed me and all of the film crew at their kitchen table with no fuss and no asking for thanks – they must have taken one look at the dishevelled leprechaun in the cage at the end of his journey and thought, 'That fella could do with a bite to eat!' I loved meeting them, but felt so sorry that their innocent compassion had been so criminally abused.

I think the reason that kind people get taken advantage of is that they seek out the currency of compassion in their lives, which is of course a wonderful pursuit – and that's also why they love to have animals in their lives brimming with unconditional love. I could write hundreds of heart-warming stories about all the compassion that countless beautiful animals and their amazing guardians have shared with my colleagues and me down the years, and it would all be true. I have witnessed infinite shared compassion between animals and people of all ages and from all walks of life: people who have literally given up all their worldly possessions to take care of poorly animals. I have seen magnificent people raising money to rescue animals from appalling cruelty, such as the dog-meat trade. I have witnessed the enormous sacrifice of people who love all kinds of animals from donkeys to elephants, rhinoceroses to vultures, manatees to koala bears, coral reef fish to sharks, wolves to wild horses, voles to bats and everything in between, in doing all they can to save those animals in their natural habitats. In fact, that's why I started my podcast 'Animal People' – to celebrate the compassionate animal people out there, because they're the best kinds of people.

I am extraordinarily fortunate in that I see compassion between animal people and the animals they care about in my work every single day. I am also blessed that for the past thirteen years I have had the love of my life in Keira, who has been my little fuzzy furball of love through the entire journey of Fitzpatrick Referrals. I share her with my friend Amy and her son Kyle. Amy worked with me as a veterinary nurse at the time we got her and Keira has seen Kyle grow from boy to man, and me from someone emotionally stunted, I would say, into someone who is trying desperately to take in the enormity of human emotion and deed, and to change the world for the better through love and medicine. This may sound indulgent or even prosaic, but from way back when I was crying by the side of our farm dog Pirate in a cattle shed in the middle of Ireland, I have had a keen sense that we humans are not almighty, and the earth isn't just ours to abuse; people and animals aren't ours to abuse either.

In 2007 when Keira came into my life, I was often sleeping on the floor of my practice, which was a small wooden building in the woods, because we had no official night nurses and I needed to be there to look after some animals or to plug in the MRI truck when it arrived in the middle of the night. Back then I operated four or five cases per day, Monday to Friday, and on many Saturdays we'd perform scans on ten to twenty animals and operate on whichever needed urgent surgery that same weekend. We had very limited kennel space, so we'd get many of the cases home by Sunday night in order to start all over again on Monday morning. It was during these days and nights with a small team of wonderful nurses, support colleagues and my loyal companion, and brilliant surgeon, Sarah Girling that we raised enough money to leverage further bank loans to build the first of the three hospitals that exist today. In times of success and failure, elation and depression, anxiety and laughter, fear and courage, bewilderment and understanding, Keira was by my side throughout – a constant anchor of love every day, however choppy the seas of life may have seemed. I do not exaggerate when I say that Keira's friendship and our shared compassion for each other were sometimes the difference between my coping and slipping into depression.

As the years have gone by, and especially recently, I've realised the personal price one pays for this. Compassion is expected as a daily currency in every veterinary practice all over the world and is integral to one's very existence as a veterinarian. I've recently been mindful of the need to sustain that compassion for the longer term in looking at the length of my working day and making a little space for life alongside, since work has been my life for such a long time. I have long left behind the halcyon days of driving through the countryside looking after farm animals, and back then the hours were insanely long, such that during calving and lambing season we only slept when we had to. Over the last twenty years as I concentrated on my specialisms in companion animal practice and was building Fitzpatrick Referrals, the hours were very long too, but I don't regret a single second helping an animal in need or giving a hug to the person who loved that animal.

I'm grateful that I had the opportunity to work hard, though, because had I not then there would have been many thousands fewer animals treated by the team we've built; we wouldn't have state-of-the-art theatres; most techniques I use would not have been invented; Fitzbionics wouldn't exist to make the custom implants; and I would never have had the opportunity to make *The Supervet*, or write this book. I used to think I was invincible, that I could work until after midnight, sleep anywhere for a few hours and get up and do it all over again, seven days a week. I now realise this just isn't true as I get older. I have come to realise that compassion isn't an endless spring unless one finds a way to replenish the source. Compassion fatigue is, unsurprisingly, a common affliction in the medical professions, because much of our work involves managing the expectations and the emotional, mental and physical distress of our patients and their family members. Failure also eats away at the soul and can of course occur with standard treatment options, but dealing with the more difficult cases as my career has progressed does contribute to greater mental stress because, if failure happens, it may be more complex and emotionally demanding. One has to find some kind of mechanism for coping with that.

In devoting all my time to caring for animals, quite recently I've recognised that the trajectory won't end happily for me unless I make some time for self-compassion, and more love and time for the people and animals I care about in my life outside of work. I'm sure that Keira has been trying to tell me that for many years, but Ricochet has really made me sit up and listen. As I write this paragraph, Ricochet has jumped up on my knee and pulled my face away from the computer screen with his huge bear-like paws, literally forcing me to pay him attention. I get the message, Buddy – there's other things I'm supposed to do with my life too.

Writing this book with Keira at my feet and Ricochet on my knee has given me pause to reflect on how many days, hours and minutes might be left for me. All they want is fun and love, and meanwhile I'm busy writing, consulting, operating or doing other work of one kind or another.

I have always wanted to broadcast compassion in society and in medicine for the greater good of all creatures who live here, but it has taken me a long time to comprehend that I have shown very little compassion to myself. I only appreciated recently that while I give so much of myself emotionally on a daily basis, in many ways I have been running away from confronting the fact that I need to care about myself more. It might sound simplistic, but the truth is that if I don't look after myself, in other words practise self-care and compassion, I'm of no use to man or beast. I think the same is true for all of us – that's why they say at the start of every flight to put on your own oxygen-mask first and only then attend to those around you.

Most of us, from time to time, get overwhelmed by a profound feeling of 'there is nothing I can do about my own problems, or the problems of the world and those around me; I am only one person'. We are all only one person, but if we allow self-pity and helplessness to overwhelm us, and we each throw up our hands, then despair wins out and compassion doesn't stand a chance. I frequently remind myself that many people are so much worse off than me – but then compassion is a relative currency.

I've had to look in the mirror and take personal responsibility for my actions towards myself and others, because lack of self-care and understanding can lead to destruction of one kind or another – I hadn't grasped until lately that all kinds of challenges in my life have their root in my lack of self-compassion. I have learned the hard way about compassion in relationships from both sides of the fence. I have learned that if I never find true peace or happiness within myself, I can't ever share that with someone else. It may be that because I didn't respect myself enough to feel worthy of love and because I felt vulnerable and incapable of properly receiving affection, when people got close I self-sabotaged. Yet the irony was that day in, day out, I gave every molecule of my compassion to each and every one of my patients and to those who loved them to try to heal their ailments, when all the while I had no idea how to heal myself.

I guess I could have turned to alcohol or drug addiction to silence my anxious thoughts, but instead part of becoming a workaholic was perhaps an element of running away from all the things I feared and running towards all the things I thought I wanted – always running. Most of us are perhaps. Some of the things I'm running away from are buried in my childhood, such as the bullying and alienation, as I've said.

Others, I very much want to just leave where they are. I feel almost a fraud for writing this since there are kids in war zones, dealing with cancer, living with abusive adults, existing in isolation and fear – but we alone can take responsibility for our own past as we get older. It has taken me decades to reach this understanding.

As the RCVS complaints procedure was ongoing, the sleepless nights, long days, business, clinical and emotional stress became unbearable. As I've observed before, my whole identity was tied up in my vocation: I was trying to do something good with my life and had made many sacrifices to do just that, so when that sense of identity was, in my view, unjustly challenged, it proved to be the last straw. This, coming on top of a legacy of never feeling good enough, strong enough or brave enough, drove me into a profound darkness, in which I could see no light at all. I felt awful. It's not good when you find yourself sitting on the side of your bed, hugging your knees and yearning desperately for all of the pain in your head to go away – especially if that bed is six feet away from your office desk, and you're still at work at 4 a.m. I couldn't talk to anyone at all about it. I didn't even want to admit it to myself. I'd come through crises before and, anyway, farmers' sons don't ask for help – they put a brave face on it, and they get back up and go out to look after the sheep.

Until not long ago, I wasn't actually willing to speak to anyone about deep emotional and almost physical pain buried in my mind and my body. I began to talk to the animals when I went to check in on the wards before I went to bed, much as I would to a human being, if I'd been brave enough to do so. At first I thought maybe I was going a little mad, but I came to realise that, actually, it helped me to see my problems and mental crisis in a different light. As I have reflected before, ever since I was a young child on the farm in Ireland, I've always shared my problems with animals much more readily than with humans. My mother and father were great, humble, loving people who always did their very best for me and my siblings. I was very lucky in that regard, but even they couldn't protect me from the harm inflicted by misguided people; none of that anxiety and fear that I've carried with me to this day was their fault. It just was what it was, but sadly the pain still affects me. Only Pirate heard my secrets then, and I've continued to seek refuge with all of the animals, and especially Keira and Ricochet, ever since.

I have referred before to the emotional imprints, *samskaras* and childhood scars I have carried for all my life, like many do, but, of course, your past wounds don't define you if you don't let them. You can only take responsibility for the present, and so I've realised that it's how you heal yourself and move on that truly defines you. In my case, I thought that a clearly defined sense of purpose could in fact sustain and heal me. I do still have absolute conviction that working to achieve fair and compassionate treatment of all animals is the most important thing that I can do with my life. I also believe that if we are more compassionate to animals we become more compassionate to each other. However, I have also realised that no matter how I dress up my core mission in my head, it won't heal my own wounds and ultimately won't sustain me on its own.

Forgiveness of others and myself is something that I've only recently come to recognise as essential for my journey of compassion going forward. If I'm totally honest with myself, I was afraid of self-compassion and I have seen this in other people too. On the one hand I was afraid of being 'weak', because that's not what a farmer's son does, and on the other, in some weird subconscious way, I was reluctant to let go of my demons because, counterintuitively, I felt that if I let the pain go I might burn out – in some ways these demons had become the fuel that drove me and urged me on. Maybe on reflection, I was afraid to quench the spark of pain lest the fire in my belly be lost.

There's a cliché that you don't have a breakdown, you have a breakthrough. That's true to some extent, but when you are in the middle of it, it doesn't feel like any kind of breakthrough. Eventually the internal pain in such a storm will go one of two ways – towards destruction, including self-harm and suicide, or towards salvation, and all gradations in between which include self-sabotage, irascible moods and addictive behaviours antithetical to my core beliefs. In a survey of vets, one in five have thought about suicide at some point in their career, and the overall rate is four times that of the general population and twice that of other healthcare professionals. Many feel emotionally under-supported to deal with the daily stress of practice with high client expectations, the job not turning out to be what they thought it would be, the financial burden of student debt, difficult working hours and poor work-life balance – and, possibly most importantly, they have ready access to and knowledge of the means to commit suicide. To me, it's profoundly sad that in a profession defined by compassion, I have heard it voiced that taking one's own life might be viewed by some vets as a gentle release, just like euthanasia might be seen as a positive solution to the intractable problems of the patients we treat. Vets are trained to perceive that they can help an animal by ending its suffering, and consequently there is a school of thought that purports that, for a vet, death could become 'normalised' as a solution to problems – even, perhaps, their own mental health issues.

I have suffered from bouts of profound sadness all of my life and I know it's the same for many people, just because of the stresses of everyday life. The year or so after the RCVS complaint was particularly bleak for me from the point of view of mental well-being. However, as well as Keira and Ricochet, I'm very lucky to be surrounded by unconditional love in the patients I treat and the people I meet every day, and this especially saved me during this time. I am indebted to my friends, my family, my wonderful and very patient girlfriend and my many caring colleagues. I owe massive gratitude to the Fitz-Family at our practice; they look after me each and every day, even after a night of broken sleep or when I have been an irritable, impatient noise-phobic who turned off the music in the operating theatre and was sad in silence.

I sought professional help with my sadness this past year because I finally had to. Therapy and counselling have helped me to acknowledge that I have been short on self-compassion all of my life and to recognise the deep-seated feeling of unworthiness at the core of it all. Apparently this is common and I'm in good company with many people who are also intensely focused on their passion. I can now understand that ever since I lay muddied and humiliated in that quarry, I have suffered with 'imposter syndrome', the feeling that I don't deserve any of my successes and that nothing I could do would ever be good enough. The imposter pigeon on my shoulder is always there, and sadly when one chooses to be in the public eye, as I have done, that voice is ever-present on social media and in thinly veiled whispers. The best way that I have found to cope is to have an internal prayer of compassion wishing only well to all my detractors and to myself. Yet still, I battle daily to quell the pigeon.

As I said earlier, in the chapter on rightness, there is always a fear when one talks openly about mental health that people may not trust you in a relationship or in your profession. There is a stigma attached to any admission that you might be sad with the stresses of life or that one's brain might be wired slightly differently, and that one may be more likely to take to heart the things that others allow to roll off their shoulders. My mentors and advisers have offered me sage advice down the years and for that I am eternally grateful, yet I'll never forget that one once said to me, 'There is a fine line between one person's poor mental state and another person's unfitness to practise as a medical professional.' I think this perception is unfortunate. For the society we live in today – where there are more mental health issues than ever before – to be able to function coherently at all we need to be able to talk, and so that's what I'm doing right now, in the hope that it may help you too. I guarantee you this: there are way more vets and doctors with mental health challenges because of their vocations than are able to talk about it openly. The stigma doesn't help in this regard – and if I can help only one person to not feel alone in the darkness of their own mind, then it's worth sharing my thoughts and experiences, I think.

Like many people who become consumed with great detail, whether surgeons, painters, musicians or entrepreneurs, I have always been very passionate and highly sensitive. I think this is probably 'normal' for people with highly focused interests. I am a curious mixture of under- and oversensitive to sound, for example. I'm completely at home right up at the front of a Metallica, Iron Maiden or AC/DC concert and yet anxious when subjected to the repeated crinkling of a crisp packet or munching of an apple when I'm trying to concentrate. The dichotomy doesn't escape me. I clam up and I'm unable to speak when I get very emotional and I find change and unpredictability in my life outside of work deeply uncomfortable, to the extent that I sometimes run away deep inside myself when faced with such stress. Yet I enjoy giving lectures and teaching students, and I invite change into my working life on a daily basis, seeking innovative solutions to surgical dilemmas that other people haven't thought of before.

I think that we need to have more compassion for each other, respect diversity more, and grow out of any outmoded stigma attached to thinking in a 'weird' way. I'm happiest in the camp of the 'nerds and weird people' who still believe in comic books and superheroes, and who still refuse to believe there's a box that we need to either tick or live in to be accepted in the world. Wolverine is my favourite and he's a mutant. I stand with the mutants any day. If we all thought the same way and if we all followed the same path, medicine would never advance at all, for example. But disease forces change, and the cures that will be found for a deadly viral infection like coronavirus and diseases like cancer will require the human brain to think in different ways. Most of the things we do every day were once considered impossible, in all walks of life, and it was generally people who thought differently who made them possible. Throughout history the change-makers have always been the norm-breakers.

I spoke to a wonderful clinical psychologist called Tony recently and in my quest from now on to only surround myself with compassionate, passionate people, I struck gold with him because he's extraordinarily funny, profoundly caring and ruthlessly honest. He explained that there's no need to label any particular mental health issue unless it's helpful for the affected person and that we all need to figure out the best way to deal with our 'stuff' whoever we are, or however we are wired. Apparently, it's common for highly driven people to have a highly functional prefrontal cortex of the brain that is able to create a script for a scenario where others may not, to dream paths which others consider non-existent or not passable, and to mostly override any pain and ghosts that get in the way. Unfortunately, however, sometimes the pain and the ghosts come out to play, especially when you're at your most vulnerable and not thinking in straight lines. Tony also explained to me that uniquely sensitive people also empathise with the pain of others – especially of animals – with intense acuity of compassion, and that's OK; one just has to look after oneself too.

Alas, I recognised this only too well. It's sometimes as if I carry all the pain of the world on my shoulders and suddenly a single word or action by someone else, an upsetting event or a bad memory will send me tumbling downwards, and before I know it I'm very sad. Then with extreme pressure I might say or do things that are not coherent with my core values. Mentors like Tony have helped me to understand that if you are striving for something great or innovative in any field and dream bigger than the confines of your own rational thought, then it's quite normal to take things personally and to get sad from time to time, and it's important to cut yourself some slack and not be so hard on yourself.

Another such mentor for me has been Russell Brand, who has excelled as a comedian, actor and radio presenter, and has more recently been on his own voyage of self-discovery. In the past few years he has become a champion of compassion as he meets and chats to extraordinary 'big thinkers' through his acclaimed podcast 'Under the Skin'. He delves into the issues that really make us who we are. He also holds workshops and seminars on recovery where he shares his own personal insights into self-compassion and compassion for those around him during his recovery from drug, alcohol and sex addiction.

I got to know Russell when he came to see me in early February 2017 with his beautifully boisterous white German shepherd dog, Bear, whom I subsequently operated on with a total hip replacement for hip dysplasia and treated medically for degenerative lumbosacral stenosis. Almost exactly three years later, in February 2020, I was in theatre operating when Russell texted me from Los Angeles where he was working, asking for an urgent call if I could, because his cat Morrissey (or Mossy, after 'This Charming Man' himself) had been diagnosed with chronic kidney failure by his primary care vet. Kidneys are not my area of expertise, but certainly are for my colleagues at our Oncology and Soft Tissue centre. I called him back as soon as I could and the following day Mossy arrived at the practice. My colleague Gerard (interventional radiologist and internal medicine specialist) soon saw him and sadly it wasn't good news. I left a message with Russell in LA to give me a call to discuss Ger's findings and Mossy's prognosis.

I was walking in the pouring rain to an appointment with my trainer, who was helping me to keep up my running in spite of an ankle injury, late as usual, and the river in Guildford had flooded, so the footbridge I would normally cross was closed. I stood angry and frustrated for a moment, looking at the raging torrent, when my phone rang – it was Russell. My exasperation immediately evaporated because his and Mossy's needs were far greater than mine. It's amazing how compassion dissipates frustration. I sought shelter in the arch of an old church to take the call.

Russell was distraught. His dear friend Mossy was in big trouble, and he didn't know what to do for the best. As I stood with the rain dripping down around me, in that moment it seemed as if nature was empathising with Russell's sadness and the sky was crying for Mossy too. We talked about his worries and fears. On the one hand he wanted to do all he could for his friend, and on the other he didn't want to put him through too much if it was unfair, and he was looking to me for guidance. We discussed the ethics of putting a seventeen-year-old cat through any further treatment, by no means knowing whether it could give him a good quality of life – or for how much longer. All I could do was explain the situation and hold his hand in the decision-making process from afar.

Gerard and his colleagues had performed diagnostic ultrasound which had identified a stricture (narrowing) in one of Mossy's ureters – the pipe running from each kidney to the urinary bladder. He was indeed suffering chronic kidney failure, and when the kidneys don't filter the blood properly, toxins build up and ultimately kill. That's why human patients in similar situations have dialysis or a kidney transplant. Kidney transplants from donor cats then adopted by the same family have been performed in the USA, but with suboptimal results and so are controversial, and not currently available in the UK. Even if Gerard could unblock the ureteral stricture, it was unclear whether the filtration of urine would improve and allow Mossy to recover for a period of time with a good life, or whether he had a primary kidney disease that was untreatable. Russell needed to decide whether Mossy should have an operation to bypass the stricture or not – an incredibly difficult dilemma. Euthanasia would have been a reasonable option for Mossy and nobody would have argued with that decision.

As advocates for the animal, my fellow specialists at the practice and I always have to weigh up how much the patient will go through, whether they will suffer and how long they might live. In any field of medicine and surgery this is a challenge. Russell knew that Morrissey would need a blood transfusion and intricate complicated surgery with an unpredictable recovery, but felt that, like him, he was a fighter. Gerard also felt that Mossy had a reasonable chance of a quality of life; he would never be 'normally' healthy, and at best he would be a longer-term survivor of renal impairment, but with careful management, he could hopefully live out a happy life, *if* his kidneys weren't irreversibly damaged. This was the 'if' that nobody knew how to answer – for that was down to biology.

As Russell and I continued to talk it through, I finally noticed that the door of the church was ajar, so I ducked inside and sat in a pew. I had often pondered the line between life and death in a church, the importance of faith in our lives, and the peace it can bring, and so our conversation took on a kind of heightened meaning for me as I sat there looking up at the altar. Though I now have a universal appreciation of 'oneness' with religions of any denomination, I do not believe that what we call 'God' is a myth; I believe that this pure consciousness is inside every living creature. Looking up at the cross of Jesus, as I had done as a child serving Mass, I knew in my heart that faith is the essence of hope and that is all we have at the end of the day. These thoughts were foremost in my mind as I sat there in the quiet sanctuary of some kind of eternal presence and listened to Russell. My ankle problem had miraculously disappeared.

After a long discussion, Russell wanted us to try to do our best with surgery, as long as Mossy wasn't suffering. Some people complain about travelling an hour down the road to seek help for their animal friend, but not Russell. He was thinking about coming back from LA for the operation, but was worried that it was for selfish reasons; that it was for the satisfaction of his own 'myth' about their emotional journey together, and he asked me if I thought that his being there maybe didn't actually matter so much to Mossy. I answered that as we grow older, perhaps we realise that ultimately the spiritual and emotional connection with all those we love, man or animal, is in fact the most precious thing of all, and so who was to say that the 'myth', as he called it, *wasn't* the most important thing of all? I said that the key was having faith that he was doing the right thing, that I strongly believed that compassion and love transcended the physical world, and even death, and that if he felt in his heart that the right thing to do was to come home, then I felt sure that Mossy's time would be enriched by his being at his side. I have always believed that hope and holding a paw or a hand is half of healing, and so we agreed that it would be best if Russell was there on the day after surgery. He made the decision then and there, cancelled some of his live shows and booked his flight.

After Mossy was stabilised with drugs and a blood transfusion, surgery was performed by Ger and highly skilled soft tissue surgery specialist Jonathan Bray. Jonathan opened the abdomen and, under fluoroscopic guidance, Ger first confirmed the diagnosis of a ureteral stricture and then he placed a wire into the reservoir through which urine would ordinarily flow out of that blocked kidney. Along this wire he threaded the end of a silicone tube, the other end of which was fed in a similar fashion first under the skin outside the abdomen and then into the urinary bladder. Between the two ends a small flushing reservoir called a port was placed under the skin. The procedure is called a subcutaneous ureteral bypass (SUB) because it circumvents the stricture. This would hopefully mean that Mossy could pee again and clear toxins from his blood using that kidney.

The following afternoon, less than forty-eight hours after our phone call in the church, Russell and I were sitting on the floor of one of the consulting rooms, cuddling Mossy. Russell had flown through the night from LA, to stay for exactly twenty hours, and had come straight to the practice. He was delighted to see him gaining strength and walking around, and Mossy was delighted to see his daddy. I left Russell meditating with his recovering friend and returned to the Orthopaedics and Neurology hospital to operate on one of my own patients.

By his own admission, Russell's journey to recovery has been one of profound pain and awakening. Now more than seventeen years dry, he is happily married to an amazing lady, Laura, has two beautiful children and he is doing his best for his family, himself and the world. For Russell, Morrissey had been a witness, a confidant, a brother and a totem spiritual guide through all his struggles, the friend who had first come into his life when he had nothing, and stood by his side, or rather curled up on his knee, through it all.

When I had finished operating and before Russell flew back to America, I joined him again at our Oncology and Soft Tissue surgery centre. Morrissey was sleeping in the recovery ward and, at around midnight, Russell and I went for a walk with Bear. Russell took Bear off his lead, and he trotted along happily by our side while we talked about this and that. Russell reckons that Morrissey and Bear are his yin and yang spirit animals and that after he quit substance addiction he gave all of his madness to Bear and imbibed the Zen of Morrissey instead. I believe this, because just as we were talking, Bear promptly spurted off like a gazelle and disappeared around a nearby hedge. We called after him in vain, then watched a frantic cat dart across the road, Bear in hot pursuit. The irony wasn't lost on either of us as Russell, visibly crestfallen, put the lead back onto his maniacal alter ego.

I told Russell a little of what had been going on in my personal and professional life and how stress had taken a considerable toll. I told him about the RCVS case with Hermes and how we went through the same ethical dilemma with Mossy – to operate or not; would he suffer; what did Russell, Ger, Jon and myself think was the right thing to do, and was it kinder to put him to sleep? There was no question that others might have a different point of view about Mossy and definitely did about Hermes, when it comes to life and death. It was a difference of opinion, but sadly one in which my licence to practise was on the line.

Russell empathised with everything that I was telling him, both personally and professionally. Finally, I asked him where I should park all of the anxiety, sadness and pain. He reinforced what I'd already been trying to do with 'acceptance' and he said that I should wish blessings upon the complainants for doing what they felt was right, and meanwhile I should continue to do what I felt was right. I already knew this, but it was helpful to have someone with Russell's

COMPASSION

life experience say it to me anyway. I did that and continue
to do just that.

As Russell went to give Morrissey one final cuddle before
he flew back to LA, he was purring happily and eating well.
Nobody knew what the future would hold, but we both looked
at each other as Russell said a prayer and we knew we'd done
the right thing. It was a beautiful moment, as Russell leaned
in to give him a kiss goodbye, and one I shall remember forever – peaceful, calm, all-knowing and all-acquiescing to the
will of the universe.

In the car park outside, I quipped to Russell that he was
the sanest insane person I had ever met. Who was I kidding?
I looked in the mirror every morning at another candidate
for that position. I knew him well, or perhaps I barely knew
him at all. Maybe, I thought, it was time for me to make the
physical and mental effort to embark on a similar journey of
enlightenment, compassion for others and myself as Russell
had made. Looking back, it was an incredible serendipity
that Russell should have come back into my life at this
particular juncture, and very soon I would have yet more
reason to be grateful for the life lessons he would again share
with me.

On the evening after Russell's visit, I was curled up on
my bed in quite a lot of physical pain, because my old lumbar
spinal problem had flared, but mainly because my adrenal
glands were on fire with the cortisol of endless stress, all
of which I had invited into my life. I had hoped my body
would last longer, but I had aches everywhere and I knew
as I lay there in the bed next to my office at work that I
probably wasn't supposed to operate until I dropped dead,
like I'd thought before then. The thing was, I had never actually done anything different – all I knew was work. I had

wonderful friends and role models in my life, all of whom were pointing me in the same direction. A brief summary of all such advice would more or less say: 'Get over yourself and your hang-ups, stop making excuses and *GET A LIFE.*'

As I lay there I thought how pointless it was to keep agonising over what I felt was the injustice of the RCVS case, or any criticism of my belief structure and efforts generally. I could finally now acknowledge that the complainants completely had a right to travel their path and have their opinions too, and in the words of my friend, Chris Evans, all I could do was 'decide how I responded'. That was the only power I had, and it was down to me to use it. Until this point in my life I thought my power was to keep my head down, much like my father had, and also like him I always believed that hard work would win through – I'd help loads of animals and I'd change the world through One Medicine. But everything was conspiring to tell me that there would be no tomorrow if I didn't listen to the pain in my mind and body – and soon I would be compelled to listen.

Whether I liked it or not, I was about to be forced to re-evaluate everything in a new light, and conclude more than ever before that the only way I could continue to give compassion to others, animal or human, would be to give myself some compassion too. I think that's probably true for all of us. I'd need to go further, though, and take Russell's lead to try to heal myself from the addiction of not facing head-on the emotional challenges in my personal and professional life, when I know in my own heart that I am doing the right thing. To shine the light I wanted for the world of animals, I would have to become 'lighter', to see beyond my critics and let go of all of the darkness that was dragging me down – mainly my lack of self-esteem, self-worth and self-compassion. To continue to give light to other beings (man or animal) I'd have to embody that light in my own being.

I got out of bed and went down to look in on some of the patients from my week. The night staff were all doing the rounds on another ward. Because we have glass-fronted ward compartments rather than bars, and music is often playing, generally the dogs are quiet. But as I sat there I realised that the radio was off and there wasn't a sound. The practice is in the countryside so there was no traffic outside. There was no whimpering or barking, but if you listened very closely you could just hear the breathing of twenty or so dogs resting peacefully. For about five minutes I sat there, shrouded in the blanket of silence that I had made happen. All of these dogs, in one way or another, were in the wards seeking hope and recovery because of me, and in that moment there was absolute faith, hope, love and peace. This was indeed all I needed at the end of the day. I already had the compassion that I had been seeking all along.

CHAPTER ELEVEN

Appreciation

'No one has ever become poor by giving.'

Anne Frank

Most of us have so much to be grateful for, but we rarely stop long enough to be thankful for our blessings, or for even the simple fact of 'being'. Yet, none of us is above the laws of fate and, as a surgeon, I am only too aware that each of us might be a heartbeat away from a life-changing accident or disease. Almost every day I witness how a destiny can change in an instant. I too am guilty of complacency – taking my health, my friends, my relationships and my home for granted, barely giving a second thought to the fact that I have food on the table, a warm bed to lie in and a roof over my head. Soon all that would change when an accident would alter my perspective forever.

I recently spent some time with a number of homeless people and talked to them about their friendships with their dogs. I heard how day after day they face the uncertainty of surviving another night on the street. They don't know where the next meal is coming from or where they will find shelter – they can only dream of the comfort and peace of mind that the rest of us take as a given. It struck me, too, that but for a quirk of circumstance and fate, any one of us could find ourselves in their position, and never more so than today as millions face the prospect of unemployment in the wake of the current global pandemic.

Indeed, until coronavirus struck we took it for granted that we had a certain level of job security. Not only that but, on a more basic level, that we could go for a walk, pop into the pub, hug our sibling, go to the cinema, see a concert or take a flight abroad at the drop of a hat. In an instant, all that possibility vanished and suddenly our world felt very small – and all of it beyond our control. With no vaccine yet and no end to the global crisis in sight, it's tempting to give up hope, since loved ones have been lost and lives have been shattered. Life has changed beyond recognition across the world, and especially for those in countries afflicted by poverty, endemic disease and political corruption. However, throughout these months I have come to appreciate that even this period of loss, grieving and uncertainty has helped me at a deeply personal level to put my priorities in perspective.

For the first time in about twenty years, I've had some time away from work, to write this book, and to think a little, which has been both challenging and cathartic. All of this has led me to one ineffable truth: the only way forward is to be thankful for every day I have left on the planet; to graciously acquiesce to what life throws at me; and to learn the woefully underestimated art of appreciation. In this regard, Ricochet and Keira have again been my teachers. For me, simply watching them seize each and every day with both paws, unquestioningly appreciating every moment and careering excitedly towards the next, serves as a daily reminder of how utterly lucky I am to have this companionship and unconditional love in my life to allay the stresses of my day.

Long before coronavirus came along, the 'Big C' that I was most afraid of, and made me appreciate what I had possibly more than anything else, was a cancer scare. A few weeks before Easter in 2013, I discovered a lump in my nostril. I was on a flying visit to Italy to implant a custom-designed total knee replacement in a dog, a procedure previously considered impossible, because the dog's knee was totally collapsed following a previous infection, with almost no cartilage nor any of the normal ligaments left. Just before going into surgery I had gone to the toilet, as one does, and was sitting there idly picking my nose, as one does. (I know, 'TMI!' I hear you cry. And yes, it is obviously an utterly deplorable habit, for which I can only apologise.) Anyway, it was then that I felt an unfamiliar lump inside the base of my nostril. Once I had noticed it, I couldn't help but probe further, so I gingerly put my finger inside my nose, as deep in as I dared, and could feel a big hard mass that shouldn't have been there. I wasn't showing any symptoms, but putting my finger in blind orifices to feel for deviations from normal, or nefarious lumps and bumps that shouldn't be there, is what I do for a living. For once I could forgive my bad habit because right then a giant gong went off in my head. This wasn't my nasal turbinates, my cartilaginous septum, an outpouching of my cribriform plate. 'Fuck,' I thought: this was a tumour. I said nothing to anyone, and did what had to be done with the knee replacement, and thankfully my patient lived to a ripe old age, running around happily until the end.

I am a surgeon, but contrary to common assumption, I don't think picking up a scalpel is necessarily the solution to all problems. However, when a surgeon finds a lump, if the signs are ominous he or she doesn't just wait for things to happen. As soon as I got back to the UK, I had the diagnosis confirmed – I hadn't imagined the lump. It was real and soon I would be going back for surgery. I left the hospital imagining the worst and started to cry almost as soon as I got into my car. I drove straight over to see my friends Chris Evans and his wife Natasha. They were simply magnificent, as they always are, and gave me all the love and hugs I needed right then. I knew I was probably overreacting, but they didn't fill me with platitudes of 'Everything will be fine', but instead they simply and rather wonderfully said, 'We appreciate you,' and, 'We will be here no matter what.' I am so very grateful to Chris and Tash, a couple who profoundly appreciate the really important things in life – not fame, money or material possessions, but love, family and friends.

My specialist ENT surgeon, San Sunkaraneni, had offered me a biopsy or an excision. The lump was in a tough spot right up inside my nose, and no matter how little vanity you may think you possess, when you consider that someone might chop into your nose, your concerns regarding your appearance change somewhat. However, I like to try to fix things if I think they're going to go wrong anyway, and so without hesitation I said, 'Let's cut it out.' San did a fantastic job – he went up into my skull beside my nose and, with a mixture of cutting and pulling, shelled out the offending mass, much like Laurent would later do for Ricochet.

It turned out that it was a rare form of soft tissue tumour with a big fancy name that grows from blood vessels. I'm one of only a tiny number of cases of this tumour per year and there's not a lot written about it – but the good news was that it was not malignant. It may grow back and need cutting out again, but it's unlikely to spread elsewhere. After the operation, I was profoundly grateful to the universe and over the following weeks I was full of newly discovered joy. I treasured my friendships like never before and it was as if I was seeing the world and nature for the first time. Literally everything seemed new and fascinating. Every breath of air was sweet with the scent of being able to smell anything at all. I'd find myself gazing in awe at the bark of a tree, a leaf, a flower, a building or someone I hadn't seen for a while as a gift from heaven. In consultations with my patients I ran my fingers through their fur like I was walking through a golden field of barley on a hazy summer's day, tickling the long ears and whiskers of the grain. I was so incredibly grateful to be alive. For the first time in a long time, I was open to life; all was good; all was magnificent.

Looking back now, it's surprising how quickly such appreciation was dulled by the daily grind of routine, and how rapidly I came to take my health for granted again. Back then, I was working all day and studying much of the night for the impending specialist examinations and also doing battle to get a further bank loan in order to build the second of the three hospitals I had planned for the practice. I was soon locked in my own mind once more, mired in the mundane thoughts of bank applications and our precarious finances. One afternoon, I was sitting in the lecture theatre at our Orthopaedics and Neurology hospital, a space the bank didn't approve of because it wasn't directly profit-generating, but that I had built anyway in the top corner of one of the three converted farm buildings – a derelict hay barn – in memory of my father Sean. I knew that the legacy of the practice would profit from the knowledge imparted there, just as I had from the wise words spoken by my father as we stood together sheltering from the rain in our near-identical barn on the farm where I grew up.

I had just made my best pitch to the bank in an attempt to borrow the money needed to complete the next stage of the practice, but they hadn't appreciated any of it. The new stand-alone building I envisaged was to be customised to deal with cancer (oncology) and other soft tissue surgery treatments, and would ultimately include radiation therapy using a linear accelerator, or so-called cyber-scalpel, to treat cancers. One of the bankers remarked that he didn't think cancer 'would make money'. I asked him whether he knew that half of all dogs get cancer of some kind and that he had a one in two chance of getting cancer himself. He replied that it didn't matter 'whether I was baking bread or curing cancer and saving lives', the only thing he needed to know was 'how many loaves I sold with how many slices, and what the dough, the oven and the baker cost'.

I know that from a monetary point of view, this is completely understandable, but I wasn't selling bread, I was selling recovery, love and hope, none of which appears, needless to say, on any balance sheets. Soon after that meeting I had a new (and fourth) bank, but not before I made several presentations in the City of London to get the backing we so desperately required. I hated those train journeys, going off to financial institutions, cap in hand, but needs must and in late 2015 the second hospital opened. We still can't afford the linear accelerator, but I trust that it will come in due course. You can buy bricks with a bank loan, but you cannot buy hearts and so I am profoundly fortunate that each and every one of the people working alongside me in these buildings cares passionately for each and every one of the animals they treat. The appreciation in those buildings will far outweigh any depreciation over time.

On that February afternoon when Russell Brand had

visited Morrissey, I had left the two of them meditating in a consultation room in the Oncology and Soft Tissue centre and gone back to the Orthopaedics and Neurology centre where I am based, to take care of a really sweet eight-and-a-half-year-old black Labrador called Mac.

Mac's situation was critical and life-threatening. He had degenerative lumbosacral stenosis as severe as Scrumpy's, but with the added complication that the disc was infected with bacteria that had seeded to the inflammation in and around his disc through his bloodstream, a condition called discospondylitis. Even worse, he also had disc disease in his lower neck (cervical intervertebral disc protrusion) which was also likely infected. As with Scrumpy, the degeneration in Mac's discs was genetically predetermined: the discs break down, then the vertebrae on either side collapse against each other, causing damage in the bone (sclerosis), and then new bone (spondylosis) gets laid down at the junction of the vertebrae. The bulgy disc, new bone, inflammation with infection and consequent destruction of the surrounding bone lead to painful squashing (impingement) of the adjacent nerve roots in the hole between the vertebrae (neuroforamen). These L7 nerve roots travel out from the end of the spinal cord to form the peripheral nerve, which in this case is the sciatic nerve. Those of us with lower back issues may recognise this radiating pain as sciatica and in Mac's case the sciatica, along with compression of the spinal cord in his neck, was making first his back legs, and more recently his front legs, increasingly unsteady. Mac was now at a point where he was having great difficulty getting up at all. He was becoming progressively paralysed, medicine would not work and a decision had to be made.

Although we had never met, I had spoken to Mac's dad

Keith on the phone the night before the operation. He had recently retired after a long life of hard manual work and as we spoke he was choking back the tears as he tried to convey to me how much he appreciated Mac being there for him through thick and thin. In staccato bursts of ruptured thought and speech, he told me that he was so grateful for all the love that Mac had shared with him. He wanted to show that same appreciation for Mac who was in a very bad state, but didn't know whether he should put him through significant surgery with an unpredictable outcome, or allow him to pass away peacefully and no longer feel pain.

As I listened, I had an overwhelming sense of how much we all take things for granted and how it was usually only in moments of crisis that our true gratitude for the gifts of health and love become apparent. Keith and Mac clearly had a profound bond that transcended the ordinary. Keith begged me to do what I would do if Mac were my dog, so, as I always do, I simply explained that I couldn't influence his decision in any way, that we were racing against the ticking time bomb of infection and ongoing neurological impairment, and, of course, that we had a collective moral responsibility because Mac was in so much pain. I further explained that the infection could already be spreading to other sites of disc degeneration in the spine, which could scupper our efforts, that any surgery would be very challenging and that, although it was very unusual, because we couldn't get Mac out of pain without operating on both sites, we could operate on both sites in the spine at the same time. I also emphasised that, as with all surgery, I couldn't guarantee a positive outcome.

Keith was not a rich man by any means, but at the age of seventy-five, he said he couldn't bear to put his friend to sleep without trying. He was prepared to spend every penny he had because he loved Mac, and was grateful beyond words or monetary value for that love. Of course, in terms of surgery costs, we always do the best we can and I encourage everyone to compare like for like with other surgical centres where possible. He asked me to operate. I said I would do my best.

My team prepared Mac for two-site surgery and I carried out my regular pre-theatre routine – I had a pee, put on scrubs and theatre shoes, took off my glasses (I'm short-sighted, but my near sight is fine), smoothed down my spiky Mohican eyebrows, then on with my hat and mask, hands and nails washed and dried, hands rubbed with Sterillium® for ninety seconds, and said, 'Hit me' to a theatre auxiliary, who handed me a sterile gown. Then I slid sleeve cuff into left glove one, right glove two, left glove three, kicked door open while applying right glove four, handed end of waist-tie to intern, twirled on the spot, tied bow by my side, checked trays in a single glance, checked drapes on patient in an-other, asked 'OK?' to intern and anaesthetic nurse, incised primary drape, applied antibacterial secondary sticky drape, nodded to anaesthetic nurse to acknowledge it was fine to proceed, checked patient was stable, confirmed the site of surgery as C7-T1, looked up at my hand-drawn diagram of the site stuck beside the CT scan (I have never operated on a spine without it), incised sticky drape and skin in one sweep, stapled drape to skin, said 'incision' to nurse, handed retractor to intern – and we had begun. All this meticulously orchestrated preparation was simply 'routine', and I rarely truly appreciated that it was all ready for me on entry to theatre. But that day was different.

I was still inwardly glowing with happiness at the sight of Russell and Mossy meditating together and the words of

Russell's prayer rang in my head: 'Thank you, God, for allow-ing Morrissey to be here today,' so that particular day every minute detail was surrounded with a halo of gratitude. I was now a far cry from my origins in rural Ireland and long gone were the days as a newly qualified vet. Back then I would have been on some farm, perhaps operating at night with the lights of a tractor illuminating the prone animal, a ripped bedsheet boiled up on the stove and serving as a surgical drape slung over a cow lying in a byre. Now I had everything at my fingertips and I sometimes took it for granted. I say 'sometimes' because the reality is that in the hubbub of the day, one gets on with the job, but I never really take anything for granted, because I do realise how very lucky I am to have such a wonderful team and recognise the immense effort it took to get to this point for all involved.

I felt honoured to be able to bring some hope to Keith and to be given a chance to save Mac's life. I was operating with two fantastic interns and a brilliant nurse on anaesthesia, working in what was probably at that time the most advanced veterinary operating theatre built in the UK, equipped with all of the tools I could ever dream of to do my job. I said my own little thank-you prayer as I pulled the haloed lights into my operating field over Mr Mac, who was laid out on his back before me. I reached out my hands as if I was willing some kind of magic to emanate from the tips of my fingers. My hands were no different from what they had been on any other day, except again everything felt different that day.

I made an incision underneath Mac's neck just in front of the lungs at the tip of the breastbone, then separated the muscles, and isolated the windpipe, food pipe, blood vessels and nerves by gentle blunt dissection with my fingers, as I commonly did. Sternocephalicus, sternohyoideus, trachea, oesophagus, vagosympathetic nerve trunk, internal jugular vein, common carotid artery – all were pushed to the right since I always stood on the left, and yet there was nothing actually common about them at all; instead all were part of the amazing miracle of anatomy. These structures that kept Mac, and indeed all of us, alive were all second nature to me, and nearly always exactly the same – and therefore tempting to take for granted – but I never did, and especially not that day. I was grateful that I could sense every nuance of vessel and sinew with my fingertips and that my fingers had been trained to move like the conductor of an orchestra through the arrangements of the anatomical symphony.

The job of a surgeon is to register the normal, and try to fix the abnormal. As I alluded to earlier, at this stage of my career, I now work in a big team and operate a selective caseload often involving orthopaedic and neurosurgical challenges that others can't fix, don't want to fix, choose not to fix or don't have the technology to fix. This is not said in boastful arrogance, but just as a statement of my 'normal' and, as I've said, I don't take any success for granted, because failure happens to all surgeons. It is what it is. I reached inside and touched the wings on the underside of cervical vertebra number six, then the first pair of ribs on either side. Then I knew exactly where I was – at the junction of the last cervical and first thoracic vertebra. I had been here hundreds of times before; I knew the road map like Braille; I didn't need to look. But rarely was I so grateful for these biological signposts as I was that afternoon. I looked down, incised the ventral spinal muscles over the disc, placed my Gelpi retractors to hold the tissues apart, cut into the disc and delved deeper towards the spinal cord.

I pushed the vertebrae apart, removed the compressing

tissue of the collapsed disc from beneath the spinal cord as quickly as possible, and put up with the inevitable bleeding as I plucked the offending material out from this very inflamed site. I packed the area with antibiotic-impregnated calcium sulphate beads in an effort to combat the infection, put screws into the vertebrae and stabilised them with orthopaedic cement called polymethylmethacrylate. I then stitched Mac up as quickly as I could, placed him in a normal sitting position and repeated the same process on his lower back. This time I made an incision from the top between his pelvic hip bones (iliac wings), took the roof off the spine at the lumbosacral junction, gently moved the tiny nerves over to one side, scooped out the infection in his diseased disc, packed in some antibiotic beads, popped lots of pins in the last lumbar vertebra and the sacrum, and fused it all together on the top with the special cement.

The procedure took about six hours from beginning to end and we finished late. I had aches and pains everywhere and clambered sluggishly up the stairs to my office, changed my sweaty scrubs, washed my face and went back down to my consulting room where I sat for a moment with my head in my hands. In the room next door, a couple called David and Joy were visiting their beautiful one-and-a-half-year-old Neapolitan mastiff called Demon. Demon was 55kg of pure effervescent love but he suffered from bad hip dysplasia with painful osteoarthritis in both joints. In addition, his main thigh muscle (quadriceps) wasn't tracking properly with his knee on either side, and his kneecap dislocated badly (patellar luxation) because the ridge on his thigh bone (femur) that is supposed to keep the kneecap in place had not formed properly – a condition known as trochlear ridge hypoplasia. We had treated both conditions on the worst leg. Hip replacement had gone well, but after the knee surgery he had developed an infection with a highly resistant bacteria, which we could not get rid of despite intravenous antibiotics, surgical flushing and clearing out (debridement).

I went straight through to talk to David and Joy. They had been waiting patiently as I finished surgery on Mac, and were sitting forlornly on the floor by Demon's side. I sat down beside them, and immediately Demon plopped his massive paw into my hand as he had done every time I saw him. He was always pleased to see me. Every time I visited him in the wards during his nights of hospitalisation with us, he would shake his head in joy, his big jowly lips flapping from side to side, sending dribble everywhere. But that day it was different – his big head flopped on the floor, the dribble oozing sadly from his jowls. In that moment, I knew he had had enough, and that David and Joy had finally come to that devastating realisation as well. We had tried our best but there was no way to get rid of the infection without further surgery, and even with that there was still only a small chance of success. Combined with that, the hip and knee conditions affecting his other back leg warranted imminent further major surgery and it was clear that it just wasn't ethically right to carry on. Nobody wanted to say goodbye, but we absolutely had to. As we all sat there hugging each other and hugging Demon, it was utterly heartbreaking. I tried to comfort them, but as my team of four interns all came in one by one to kneel by his side and kiss him goodnight for the final time, it was all I could do to hold myself together. I thanked David and Joy for believing in him and for doing the right thing always; they thanked me for trying my best for him. I was in a state of total anguish because I had failed.

I gave them a hug goodbye, I got in my car and drove under a sombre cloud back to our other hospital to see Morrissey and Russell before he flew back to LA. That was when Russell and I took a walk around the building with Bear and discussed the meaning of life. I was in a rather more fragile and vulnerable state than normal, and I hadn't spoken to anyone who wasn't dependent on me or working with me all day, and when Russell talked to me about his concerns and worries for Morrissey I couldn't help but tell him how I was feeling right at that moment too. We shared our worries and fears and I think it helped us both. Most doctors and vets by necessity have to keep their emotions inside, because we have to hold it together in front of colleagues and clients, but in private I think it's equally important to talk to a good listener and let it all pour out – or eventually anxiety can become corrosive. Russell and I were good listeners for each other and, that night especially, I was very grateful for his wisdom. It appeared as if the universe was conspiring to encourage me to see the good and the love in everything and to be grateful for what I had. Russell has learned to savour every moment, and to appreciate what is important and what surely is not. He has realised the hard way that in the long run the things we *think* we want to make us happy – money, fame, sex, drugs, alcohol – in and of themselves do not. What he prioritises now is peace of mind, companionship, solidarity of purpose, giving to others, rejoicing in health, family and friends; the clasped fingers of prayer and the coupled palms of 'I bow to you', as he did to Morrissey – Namaste.

As a surgeon, failure hits hard, really hard – and one never gets used to it. In the two weeks leading up to that evening

with Demon I'd had three patients for whom treatment had
failed and euthanasia had been necessary. And on top of this,
only a week earlier, I had come within a whisker of saying
a final goodbye to another patient, a gorgeous five-year-old
Dobermann called Odin. His mum and dad, Anita and Mick,
had brought him to see me for wobbler syndrome, which
happens often in Dobermanns, who have a breed disposi-
tion to disease of the discs in the lower neck. It's a specific
form of disc bulge or protrusion called disc-associated cervical spondylomyelopathy. The discs degenerate and bulge,
and the vertebrae can also be misshapen and potentially
move abnormally, putting pressure on the spinal cord and
impairing nerve conduction, causing the dog to be unstable
on its feet – literally to 'wobble'. When wobbler syndrome is
caused by discs compressing the spinal cord, the condition
is known as 'disc-associated wobbler syndrome' (DAWS).
There's another form too where bony proliferation or misshapen vertebrae compress the cord, so a few years ago when
I was writing a manuscript about this disease I thought it
would be appropriate to call this 'osseous-associated wobbler
syndrome' (OAWS). Dogs with either condition can become
wobbly at first due to paresis (muscular weakness or partial
paralysis caused by spinal cord damage or disease), where
there is loss of control of the back legs firstly (furthest away
from the neck compression) and then even the front legs as
well, progressing in the very worst cases to paralysis and even
inability to move any limb. When the nerve roots coming out
from the side of the cord to the front legs are also squished,
this can cause significant pain, called 'nerve root signature'.
Odin had front leg pain and wobbliness affecting all four legs.

I could empathise with Odin, because I developed a similar
condition a few years ago. I had a bulging disc between my

C6 and C7 vertebrae, which had caused deformity of the ends of the vertebrae and the formation of bone spurs (spondylosis) with nerve root compression in the neuroforamen. The junction between the vertebrae was semi-fused and more rigid than it should have been and the nerve root compression was painful and was causing weakness in my arm and muscle wastage of my triceps. This condition is sadly all too common in surgeons who can pay the price for many hours stooped over the operating table, and a surgeon is no good to anyone with a stiff neck and a painful weak arm. As I've said before, if one can manage a condition with medicine and physiotherapy then I wouldn't want surgery on myself or my animal friends. Though I fix problems surgically, I generally see surgery as an option that should be considered if quality of life can't be achieved any other way. I have therefore coped with periodic neck pain and permanent lower back pain for more than twenty years with help from my stalwart, Stuart the physio. Unfortunately for Odin, however, management with painkillers or physio alone hadn't worked and surgery was the only reasonable option.

I had performed surgery on Odin's lower neck for collapse of two of his discs, just like Mac, but without any evidence of infection at that time. I had used the 'Christmas tree spacer' FITS devices I had used in Scrumpy to push the vertebrae apart. The vertebrae C5, C6 and C7 were held apart using custom-made saddle-shaped plates (conceived when I had looked at the architecture of a horse's saddle) with Odin's exact measurements. These plates were screwed into the vertebrae and everything was linked with rods to form a Cervical Fitzateur. Finally, bone marrow from his humerus bones was packed beneath the vertebrae to encourage them to fuse into one single block. The surgery had gone according to plan and Anita said it was like 'switching on a light bulb'. Within a week Odin had improved greatly and by four weeks he'd been walking normally, even on slippery floors.

Then tragedy struck. At six weeks postoperatively, when most dogs would continue to improve, he again began to show signs of front leg pain and wobbliness. Whenever I try to fix bone using metal implants, it's always a race between biology and mechanics – in this case the bone needed to fuse solid with the biological gold dust of the marrow transplant in order to sustain the load through his spine. Sadly with Odin, it seemed that we had lost the race; he had been in the back of his mum Anita's car, as he often was, when another car had smashed into them. This sudden jolt to his spine had broken two screws before the vertebrae had had a chance to fuse, and subsequently his vertebrae had started to crumble. I'd actually never seen his complication before or since, and at that point our options had been limited – I either had to operate again or put Odin to sleep.

It would be absolutely absurd and lacking any appreciation for my profession to maintain that the implants I deploy, including the devices that I myself have invented, always work. They don't. They're designed to be better than anything else I've ever used to achieve the desired objective – which in this case was pushing the vertebrae apart and keeping them stable until they fused solid with the graft. Sadly, all implants, simple or complex, can fail. I do my best and I'm always trying to do better. My heart was broken for Odin, but also for Anita and Mick. Mick, especially, was acutely aware of Odin's distress. When Mick was just eighteen he had been to a concert by The Who, which he described as 'brilliant until the end' because on the way back the van being driven by his closest childhood friend was involved in a crash. Mick was in the back and was flung forward and trapped; his friend died. Life would never be the same.

Mick was paraplegic and spent six months in a spinal unit. Now in a wheelchair, he set up a tattoo studio since he could no longer do the manual work that he had before in his small mining village in the Midlands. Anita had joined him as an apprentice more than twenty years earlier, and she and Mick got married. Mick was an example to us all – a humble and intensely gracious man, who always seemed to me to be grateful to be alive each and every day in spite of his disability. Odin was Mick and Anita's second Dobermann and a real character of the tattoo studio, with many customers coming in to see him and sneak him a treat or two. He recognised Mick's disability, and was forever patient, pulling more gently on the lead when he was out with Mick in his wheelchair. Anita had also trained Odin as a tracking and searching dog, but just as he was about to enter the big time of missing people cases, his diagnosis of wobblers scuppered all plans.

Mick and Anita had sought out a referral to me because they instinctively knew that I would give it to them straight, and, as Anita said, I wouldn't 'take the piss' with prices. As owners of an independent tattoo shop, they knew only too well how hard it was to survive in a corporate world. They had done their research and they wanted all the options for Odin laid on the table before them and they made that clear on day one. Now, however, all their money was spent, the operation had failed, and Odin needed my help more than ever.

Mick, Anita and I were all in the dilemma together. Odin and I had become great friends during his time at the hospital, and, just like with Demon, I would go to see him at night to give him a big hug before I went off to bed. I'm pretty sure Odin could tell my Irish accent at twenty paces, because when I was within earshot he would always bark loudly, trying to wag his whole body in excitement. He had a very distinctive bark – the husky voice of an old dog delivered with the enthusiasm of a pup. I called it his 'old-man-young-boy' bark. I loved him, and I think he loved me – but I always had to rush towards him and hug him tightly so that he wouldn't shake more damage in his neck. Then he'd 'lick the face off me'. I was now part of his wider family and I cared deeply about him, but I needed to maintain professional impartiality and give Mick and Anita the options and the time to decide. They were hugely grateful for all that we had done for Odin and for helping them with his aftercare to this point as much as we possibly could from a financial perspective. Unfortunately in this situation, when the money runs out, euthanasia is very often the outcome for cats and dogs. People think I have free rein to perform operations for free, but sadly I do not, because bank loans, wages, drugs, disposables and implant manufacturers still need to be paid. That's just the way it is. After much soul-searching in the emotional, ethical and financial departments, Mick and Anita did what they could and I did what I could to help them, and we proceeded with Odin's operation in early February 2020. I fixed the problem as best I could and prayed that he would begin to heal and everything would be OK.

The following day, however, I sadly did have to perform a euthanasia. A gorgeous tongue-lolling, life-loving, joy-hugging spaniel called Rocco had developed a blood-borne infection of his total hip replacement a full year after I put it in, and with various other challenges also affecting him, myself and his mum and dad, Sean and Sophie, agreed that

it was kindest to let him pass peacefully away. We were all totally devastated. Rocco had sat up proudly on the passenger
seat of Sean's van every single day for more than a decade
'supervising' his work as a carpenter, while for Sophie he was
like a child, sharing cuddles as the most precious gifts in the
universe. They told me how there hadn't been a single day
in all his eleven years that he didn't make them smile – and
now he was gone. For weeks afterwards, Sean would reach
over to open the passenger window for his buddy to stick his
head out, but his buddy wasn't there. All he could do was
appreciate and treasure the love they had shared.

It was particularly poignant then when I visited Odin in
the wards the same day to find that he was much brighter.
He looked like he was going to make it. I was very grateful
for his infectious smile and his inimitable resonant bark of
happiness in my life because also that very day I had committed to castrate poor Ricochet. Although I hadn't castrated a
cat for more than fifteen years, I was determined to do the
procedure myself because I felt it was my personal responsibility. And even though we had then discovered the extent of
his ear problem, and I knew we'd have to put him through
further anaesthesia and a major surgery, that night as I sat
with Ricochet in the peaceful wards of my newest hospital,
stroking his head, cuddling him and helping him cope with
his 'cone of shame', I was struck with the most profound
appreciation for his existence and for his love in my life. I
told him about all of my fears, hopes and dreams in this new
building and his throaty purr soothed my troubled thoughts.
I know that surgery won't always have a happy ending – but
I also know that, surrounded by a team of specialists like
we have, we can always give it our best shot. I am so very
grateful for all of the animals who have been entrusted to my

care, who, in spite of the pain every now and then, bring me so much hope and love.

That evening the 100th episode of *The Supervet* aired. I have only very rarely seen an episode live, because I'm generally operating. I was operating that night, but it was a significant milestone, and in the light of Rocco's euthanasia, my near-miss with Odin and the discovery of the growth inside Ricochet's skull, it was a timely reminder and lesson in gratitude and appreciation. In that show, we had told the truly wondrous story of a dachshund called Ruby, who had suffered more than thirty fractures to her spine and pelvis. There was absolutely no question that, had I been confronted with Ruby's injuries fifteen years earlier, I would have had no choice but to say, 'I'm sorry, nothing can be done,' and put her to sleep. Back then I lacked both the ability and the knowledge to deal with her injuries, so I am very grateful for the skills that I have gained over time. After a seven-and-a-half-hour procedure to put her back together using a combination of internal and external frames that I'd conceived several years earlier, Ruby eventually was able to run around again and her mum Maria has since sent me videos of her many adventures in fields and on beaches. This would have seemed like an impossible miracle to me in 1990 when I qualified, or even 2000, before I was any good at orthopaedics.

We rebuilt Ruby and through the hard work and good grace of wonderful colleagues, we have now finally been able to build all three hospitals I originally dreamed of. The first hospital is called FRONT, Fitzpatrick Referrals Orthopaedics and Neurology Team; the second FROST, Fitzpatrick Referrals Oncology and Soft Tissue Team; and in 2019, with the last tranche of borrowing from the bank, we opened the third and final hospital called FIRST, Fitzpatrick Institute for the Restoration of Skeletal Tissues. On the day the building was finished and signed off, I gave the cornerstone a polish, stood back and read: 'This is the cornerstone of my childhood dream and the beginning of a revolution. For the FIRST time, animals will benefit from regenerative and implant technology at the same time as humans. This stone will support our ideals of a more compassionate world fuelled by One Medicine, One Love and One Hope.'

Within the FIRST building, my specially designed, state-of-the-art operating theatre has highly specialised airflow, integrated cameras for minimally invasive surgery and broadcasting for teaching. It is future-proofed to allow for fluoroscopic and robotically assisted surgery when virtual reality can be interfaced with CT and fluoroscopic enhancement for mapping of surgical accuracy – which will hopefully happen in my lifetime. This was what I had dreamed for Vetman in his Bionic Bunker as a child, reading comic books about Wolverine and other superheroes – and would be the closest to X-ray vision that I would get in my lifetime. I built a viewing gallery where people can sit high up and observe what was happening within, as in the *Theatrum Anatomicum* of the European Renaissance. With statues of the god Apollo and Hippocrates, the father of medicine, looking on, these theatres saw medicine break off from a thousand-year-old perception that medical healing was the only way, and the era of surgery was born.

My hope is that in this theatre at Fitzpatrick Referrals, human and animal surgeons can one day soon learn side by side, paving the way for a new era of One Medicine. Without a bank that believed in me enough to lend me the money, a theatre like this and the equipment within it wouldn't have become a reality, and dogs like Mac and Odin would never have had a second chance. I wouldn't have the chance to lay a cornerstone with *The Supervet* TV show for the understanding of One Medicine for animals and humans. I don't ever know how the universe will actually provide, but time and again I have found that it invariably does when I intensely visualise my goal as if it actually exists and if I show appreciation at all times. When I have focused on penury and 'cannot do', that's what I got – nothing. When, however, I have focused on plenty and 'can do', and followed my heart in doing the right thing – from a position of have rather than have not, possible rather than impossible, gratitude rather than grumble – things have always worked out. Somehow that's how the laws of appreciation work.

In their abundant love, Keira and Ricochet remind me every day of why I signed up to be a vet, no matter how hard it can get. True appreciation for me has meant letting go of feelings of isolation and instead letting in light wherever possible. For me they are shining beacons of light. They remind me also why One Medicine is so important to me, because I want to give them the same level of medical care that I get myself. I will be by their side no matter what and I'll never let them down, and I tell them that often. They appreciate me and I them. As anyone who truly loves an animal will understand, they have opened my heart, my ears, my eyes and my soul to feelings that are impossible to describe. It is an understanding that transcends our limited human language to express, but sometimes we have to listen beyond the language of words. The true appreciation I experience with Ricochet and Keira is also unspoken – a deep mutual sense of belonging and strong validation of intent that goes beyond being liked and affirming our self-worth with a rush of happy hormones. With an animal friend, no words are needed: appreciation just 'is' and it's magnificent.

Mac did great for almost three months. Both he and Keith were grateful for his new lease of life. He was really happy without pain every day and went back to his favourite walks with a spring in his step, but then he suddenly started to wobble on his back legs and show pain again. It was Easter Sunday, 12 April 2020, at about 6 p.m. when I got the call from Keith and I saw Mac straight away. A CT scan revealed that he had developed discospondylitis at another site. As Keith held Mac's paw for the very last time, he cried desperately and told me how much he appreciated the last months he had had with his best friend. It was unbearably sad. I injected the final goodnight into his vein and said a silent prayer of love for Mac and for Keith too.

Easter is a time for rebirth and new hope. It was seven years almost to the day when I had found the lump in my nose and had thought the worst might happen for me, and just a few weeks since I had come within a few millimetres of death (more of which later) when I'd fallen and broken my neck. That night I lay in my bed, with my still-aching neck on the pillow, and I thought about how precarious life is. I thought about Demon and Rocco and Mac, and about Odin and Mossy, with a little inward prayer that they'd be OK. I thought about Ricochet and what might have happened if we hadn't found each other. I was very grateful that his former guardian was looking for a loving veterinary home that could look after his needs and grateful that Michaela had sought him out, knowing he would shine light into my life. I thought about how our animal friends become family members and can chart many years of our lives – our sadness and happiness, our pain and our joy. Ricochet had only just come into my life and now I couldn't imagine being without him. He had reached inside my chest with his big black paws and clasped my heart tightly, just as Keira had done a dozen years earlier.

Sometimes when my world closes in around me and I don't think I can face a new day, I reach out and they're there. Constant. Immutable. Ricochet nuzzles me in the eye socket and says 'Buurrrph'. Keira licks my face, wags her tail and says 'Yawnearrgh'. They have saved my life, full of joy and appreciation, open to the endless potential of a brand new day.

CHAPTER TWELVE

Respect

'There is no respect for others without humility in one's self.'

Henri-Frédéric Amiel

It's a common aphorism that 'you can't love another until you love yourself', but I have a bit of an issue with this. I know that it infers 'love' in the purest sense of having compassion for the all-too-human 'child' within oneself, and lack of self-worth is one thing, but for me this emphasis on 'self-love' can become just a little bit self-serving. I prefer to think of it in terms of 'respect', because I vehemently believe that unless you have self-respect (along with a healthy dose of humility), rather than just self-love, you can't respect others, nor inspire respect in others, nor effectively lead a team, nor be in a loving, sharing relationship. Without self-respect, you cannot live with any kind of integrity. Respect parks your ego and drives your empathy.

To have self-respect requires a kind of forgiveness for your faults, for all the bad decisions you may have made, and for all the times you have behaved in ways that aren't compatible with the person you aspire to be, or feel you really are. As I've explained before, I find this kind of self-compassion really challenging. In a general sense, too, I feel very strongly that advertising and social media can fuel overly self-critical tendencies, preying on our insecurities and almost coaxing us into unfavourable comparisons with others so that we buy products in the hope of feeling better about ourselves or garnering the 'respect' of our peers. But respect and self-respect cannot be bought.

It can almost feel sometimes as if one's failings aren't normal. They are. It's called being human. Most of us have done things aren't compatible with our best selves. I know that I certainly have. I have been forced to look in the mirror and do battle with my demons – and I have failed often in my life outside of work. I have suffered from a lack of self-respect all my life since childhood and yet I have chosen a vocation that demands respect – respect for life, love, the right of the guardian to choose, and for the moral imperative to do the right thing.

In February 2020 when Ricochet came into my life needing help for his ailments, I too was at an all-time low. I'd lost all self-respect. I was crying behind closed doors while putting on a smile to face the world, or just being quiet, insular and uncommunicative with my work colleagues. They had seen this before and I suppose had got kind of used to my being withdrawn from time to time. Some days it would be OK and I'd be happy enough, going about my day with consultations and surgery; on other occasions, especially when I had yet more communications to deal with about the RCVS complaint, it was like I had woken up under a black blanket of despair that would cloud my vision all day. I'd been depressed like this throughout the complaint investigation process, and in spite of seeking professional help, the black cloud wouldn't budge. It hadn't been until my whole world had come quite literally crashing down around me that it truly hit home just how badly I needed to rescue myself.

I hadn't been sleeping much, and when I did sleep it was often interrupted, so I had grown accustomed to not waking myself up fully when I got up to go to the toilet, because then I wouldn't sleep when I went back to bed. On one such night, I got up and shuffled from the bed to the bathroom in a state of almost sleepwalking as I had done a million times before, but I must have been even drowsier than normal and I don't remember exactly how but I must have slightly missed the door and walked straight into the door jamb. Unluckily for me, there's a steep flight of stairs right next to my bathroom and again I don't remember the beginning of the fall, but halfway down I partially woke up as my ribs and then my arm crashed against the sharp step edges. I thought it was some horrible nightmare. I had survived these before – but this time it was really happening. I finally woke up as my head crashed into the wall at the base of thirteen steps, my crumpled, still-half-asleep body flung against it like a sack of potatoes. As I collided with the wall, I heard a crack which echoed through my ears, then the momentum carried through and rolled me up in a ball at the foot of the stairs; my head had folded under, with the rest of my flailing torso and limbs following after, and me screaming and writhing in anguish.

The moment I heard the crack, I knew exactly what that meant – I had broken my neck. All of my conscious mind was praying to God that it wasn't true. Amid the whirlwind of thought and excruciating pain in those two or three seconds, I just kept saying over and over, 'Please God, no.

Please God, no,' my entire life flashing in front of my eyes. My brain, hard-wired with the workings of a surgeon, was trying to wrest back control, battling to process what had just happened as I tried desperately to convince myself that it was just a bad fall. Everything would be fine, it would just be a muscular injury, I told myself, but then a pain blazed like barbed wire searing through my neck and shoulders, followed by a volcanic eruption of all-consuming fire which burned through my entire body. I screamed again and again as I sat clutching at my neck at the bottom of the stairs.

I realised where I was, that my neck was badly injured and that I was curled up against my knees. I moved one hand and then the other. I moved one leg and then the other. I could still move. I continued to scream out loudly over and over – I wasn't paralysed and for that I was immediately grateful, but I was wound tightly in a ball of intense agony, the likes of which I don't even want to try to remember. It was hideous. I was in shock and didn't know what I was doing, just moaning and bewildered. I recall little of the ensuing period; all I remember is extreme pain.

An ambulance came. I don't remember the journey. It would have been about ten minutes. There was a wheelchair at the other end. I was taken to a bed and laid flat, and then at some point I suppose I was given some morphine. That was the last time I moved for a long time. The next words I remember were from a doctor firmly instructing some nurses to 'get that man in blocks now', and these large bricks of red foam were taped to my forehead and to the bed, where I continued to lie, staring at the ceiling, quietly paying my respects to the universe and praying that I could still feel my legs and arms. I knew I was in trouble. I knew it was really bad. It wasn't yet 6 a.m. and A&E was a hive of activity. Every half-hour or so a doctor or a nurse would come and pinch my toes and my fingers in turn and ask me if I could feel anything. I could see no one's face because I was strapped in, staring at the ceiling, but it seemed to be a different voice each time. I was very grateful that Michaela was sitting by my side with soothing words of reassurance.

I had never respected my body and its function as much as I did while lying there on that bed looking up at the bright strip lights directly above me. I stared intently at the damp stains in the ceiling tiles and, in my morphine haze, one minute this became an all-consuming black fog of despair and the next the rippling tide of a calm sea on a beautiful beach. Morphine is amazing. All problems seemed to float away towards some nebulous place of peace and serenity.

As soon as the wondrous opioid effects began to wear off, however, the searing pain tore through my upper body once more. My entire torso hurt everywhere so I couldn't even breathe without wincing. In my less lucid moments as I lay there, I wondered if some giant hand of fate had pushed me down the stairs to force me to deal with the growing horde of emotional demons in my head. I was strapped into my own body for the very first time in my life, unable to move, unable to escape any of the thoughts that crashed around in my head, unable to escape any action or inaction in my life that normally would have been sublimated into simply working harder. As a surgeon, it seems that I always had the perfect pretext to avoid dealing with my inner challenges, because there was always the next patient, or any of those from yesterday or the day before, that continued to need my attention. There was always an excuse to run away from myself – and I had been running for a very long time.

Truth was, I respected my patients way more than I had

respected myself and I'd lost my personal sense of self. I also had the underlying constant dull ache of attrition associated with just trying to survive in a rapidly changing veterinary business world. I worried about the family that surrounds me at the practice and I just wanted to do what I thought was the right thing for them and for the advancement of patient care. There was the constant pressure of delivering for the animals, the clients, my work colleagues, my fellow veterinary colleagues and the usual pressures of running one's own business. I lost myself in the midst of it all.

Then, on top of all that, the complaint concerning the alleged mistreatment of Hermes had also robbed me of respect for my profession and for how I felt about my role in it. I had lost perspective, and I'd inadvertently lost some respect for myself and my dream because of the pressure. Lying there in the hospital, I knew there would be a CT scan sometime that day, I just didn't know when, so I simply continued to stare at the ceiling, drifting in and out of pain, my mind troubled by various tortured thoughts as the different faceless people came and touched my fingertips and my toes, and now also asked me to raise a hand or a leg and to rate my pain on a scale of one to ten. I just answered eight, or sometimes nine, and asked for more morphine. As the drug worked its wondrous analgesic magic, I daydreamed that my trolley was being wheeled down the A3 to my own clinic, and then I was being scanned alongside Odin and Morrissey, who were also on my mind.

I also marvelled at how compassionate and attentive all of the NHS nurses and doctors were in spite of being pulled in a million directions and felt sad that, whereas I could have scanned myself within minutes of arrival at my own hospital seven miles down the road, such were the demands on a public healthcare system that here they had to wait for hours. And in my morphine bubble I didn't mind at all, I hasten to add. I understood completely. It struck me how easy it is to be indifferent to the immense cost of the wages, each of the beds, the monitoring equipment, the drugs and the scans, and, because we don't have to pay directly for receiving treatment, we forget to properly respect the NHS. In fact, most of the time I think we take it utterly for granted. That made me very sad indeed.

My mind drifted from half-asleep to half-awake wooziness. I was so angry with myself for falling down the stairs. How could I be so stupid? I was angry that I wouldn't be able to go to work that day. I *never* called in sick; I was *always* available. How could this have happened to me? As I lay there, immobilised in my foam and tape constraints, one by one my demons gnawed away at me. My brain slipped into panic for a while and it felt like their ghoulish fingers were coming to claw at my very reason for living at all. I was in turmoil and I couldn't escape my mind. I knew then that my emotional and psychological fractures would be much more difficult to heal than those I could feel in my neck.

Michaela wedged my mobile phone between my ear and the red Styrofoam block holding my head so I could call the practice and I was so grateful that my colleagues at work immediately stepped in to deal with my hastily reorganised diary. I was upset that many animals would inevitably need to wait on surgeries which at this time only I perform. I still didn't know if I had suffered significant neurological damage and if I would ever be able to work as a surgeon again. I wondered who would perform these operations then, because I hadn't yet been able to pass on all that I had learned.

Later on, one of the consultants told me that I had been

337

just a whisker away from permanent incapacitation or death. Had I twisted my neck another four or five millimetres, I could have irreparably damaged my spinal cord and been tetraplegic, and apparently the mortality rate associated with uncontrolled falls like mine is alarmingly high. I was a lucky man; I just didn't know it as I lay there waxing and waning between fear and anger.

People run away from confronting their problems in all kinds of different ways. As I've mentioned, I chose workaholism. It seemed like a good idea. I sacrificed quite a lot of my personal life but got to save as many animals as possible along the way, so it always somehow seemed like a price worth paying, and it was at least more socially acceptable than a drug or alcohol addiction. However, it was still addictive-avoidant behaviour, and as such I realised that I hadn't respected myself for quite some time. Workaholism isn't an addiction that should be praised.

Running away from emotional problems and dealing with issues of mental wellness is difficult within oneself and especially challenging to talk about openly. However, if mental health issues remain a dirty secret how can we as a society nurture respect for ourselves and for others? Unless we normalise open admission of mental illness, we can never prevent people imploding into depression and suicidal states. Bad things happen even to good people – and sometimes good people do bad things because they're in a bad place. I am only human. I make mistakes and can't always cope with life. I am very far from being superhuman and I'm only called 'the Supervet' because it would have been really tough to sell a show to the broadcasters entitled 'Fairly Good but Highly Driven, Hard-working but Occasionally Sad, and Coping as Best He Can Vet'. The genius that is Morrissey, after whom

Russell's cat was named, expresses it exactly – 'I am human and I need to be loved, just like everybody else does.'

As I lay in my cubicle in A&E, having a catheter inserted because I couldn't get up and nor could I roll over to urinate, I empathised with every patient who had ever had the same done by me. To my left a lady was screaming how much something was hurting while the nurses tried to calm her. In the bed opposite a nurse was softly talking to an old man called Charlie. She asked him his date of birth. He said 1926; that made him ninety-four years old. She told him that he might have a 'bit of fluid on his chest' or a 'bit of pneumonia'. I could hear him wheezing from across the corridor, louder than all of the passers-by and the sporadic wails of the lady to my left. The nurse asked Charlie if he'd like her to contact anyone in his family, but he said he had nobody. She asked if they should resuscitate should he have a heart attack. He said no, followed by a wheeze, a pause and, 'Thank you very much.' Poor Charlie. I moved the fingers on one hand and then the other, the toes on one foot and then the other. My situation wasn't too bad after all.

Then a nurse called Dennis came by. He did all the same tests wiggling my toes and fingers that his colleagues had performed assiduously every half-hour as I lay there. I chatted to him. He had worked all day Sunday and was now working Monday, more than a twelve-hour shift each day, seeing about 260 patients per shift. That was a normal day. He was a god among men, as were all of the men and women on that shift and every shift in the NHS healthcare system. I was so very thankful to have the NHS and the amazing caring people within it doing their very best for me on that fateful day.

At that point, the full realisation of the impact of

coronavirus was still a few weeks away and little did any of us know that, within a fortnight, a crisis of unprecedented proportions would hit emergency departments across the UK and the rest of the globe like a tsunami, dwarfing my personal medical challenges. Respect for ourselves and for our fellow man was about to take on a whole new meaning. And knowing what we now know, I can only hope with all of my heart that each and every one of us fully recognises and shows due and full respect for all that the NHS represents and for the personal sacrifices of each and every one of the deeply committed people who work within it. Nor should we continue to be impervious to the toll of the insane working hours endured by NHS staff whereby the goodwill of dedicated people can be taken for granted. I will gladly pay my taxes till the end of time to support this incredible institution and pray that, after the threat of the virus recedes, it won't simply be back to business as usual with public complacency and government cuts to funding. This cannot be allowed to happen.

Finally, I was wheeled down the corridor for my CT scan. I have seen the inside of a CT scanner many times in my practice, but from the perspective of a dog or cat rather than sticking my own head in it. As the X-ray generator started to spin in the gantry, an ominous sense of foreboding crept down my heavily sedated, rigidly corseted spine. I knew in my heart that I had broken my neck. I had heard the loud crack. I wondered what kind of fracture I had, what nerves it was squishing, and what kind of surgery I would need in order to fix it.

Back in my A&E bed, Charlie was gone, Dennis was nowhere to be seen and the lady next to me was still screaming. It got louder and louder and the woman was getting physical too, to the point where the nurse had to call a security person to come and help. He tried to calm her down, but louder and louder she got; from behind my curtain I could hear that she was clearly incoherent and to some extent 'out of her mind' and then I heard a couple of what sounded like smacks. The security guard urged her to show some respect and asked her not to hit him.

I think all of us have the potential to be 'out of our minds' from time to time. I don't believe that most people are born bad and I'm pretty sure that most animals aren't. I would imagine that some might be born with some kind of faulty wiring in their brains that predisposes them to doing bad things, but for the most part I think that humans and animals are influenced by their experiences and environment and their early responses to such conditions. Over time these responses and choices become neural pathways that make us who we are. I have met many badly behaved people and animals and it's a subjective opinion, I know, but it seems to me that I've seen the positive effects of behaviour modulation therapy in dogs and cats much more quickly and definitively in terms of respect and the resulting change than I have in humans. When I scold Keira for doing something she shouldn't, she knows it and generally doesn't do it again, at least not straight away. It may take a few times, but generally she gets the message and won't repeat that behaviour. Even Ricochet at only six months old was already fairly responsive to repeated prompting, and yet we humans think we always know best and it seems more difficult for us to break bad habits or show respect for well-meaning advice. The lady next door, meanwhile, continued to hit out at her would-be helpers.

Animals seem to have an intrinsic respect for the hierarchy

of creation, or, at the very least, they appear to have due deference for their place in the overall scheme of things. The signs of respect for a dog or cat might be different to ours, but they figure out the ground rules quickly and there is no disingenuousness or facade. They may sniff each other's bottoms, but to my mind this is much better than 'arse-licking' hypocrisy. I'm always conscious never to confuse sycophancy with respect, and I think we all need to be wary of people who purport to respect us, but only for their own gain. These are fundamental lessons in respect which are not to be sniffed at!

Generally, after initial growls or spits, the way of the world is apparent to a dog or a cat and they respect that. With humans, they can be all nice to your face and then later, behind your back, the claws come out. I have seen how Ricochet and Keira have navigated their relationship and grown to respect each other, and it's been fascinating. In the early days when they were in the same room and both vying for my attention or a spot on the sofa, Ricochet would hiss. He was just a scared baby and he didn't understand the company of a dog. A dog was 'different' and took a little getting used to. Keira didn't even notice because she's old and deaf now, but she is always more focused on having a nice life than squabbling. Ricochet rapidly learned this and before long cohabitation was mutually amicable. Now they happily sit side by side on the sofa or in their harness seatbelts in the car, and when I take them on walks together, each takes it in turn to lead the way. Perhaps we can all learn a lesson from Keira, ignoring occasional growls or snarls, and just going about our business, showing kindness, leading by example so that others may lead too when they are ready – and keeping going in spite of what others may say. Eventually we may find that we all want the same thing anyway – which is a kind of mutual respect, regardless of our differences.

Respect is paramount in relationships with friends, family, co-workers and especially partners. Yet we often let ourselves down – lack of self-respect leads to lack of respect and too often friendships, families, workplaces and relationships come crashing down when boundaries are not respected and the rights of others are not acknowledged. I have seen greater honesty, respect and faithfulness between animal and guardian in my consulting room than I have between the guardians themselves from time to time. When life-and-death decisions are to be made about the fate of a loved animal, all too often I've witnessed how quickly relationship tensions, lack of respect and trust all come to the fore. That's the thing about respect for love and for life – it can shine a light on the darkness where secrecy and lack of respect lives. There are none so blind as those who don't want to see.

I was pondering all this in the quagmire of my mind, doing battle with my own self-belief and self-respect – and if you fight in quicksand, you will sink quicker, so I began to sink. As I lay there motionless for hours and hours, it felt as if the film reel of my life was unwinding in my head. Trapped there, it felt like I was in some endless time warp of the years I'd spent alone studying night after night for exams or writing lectures for which I had no conclusion that particular day. It felt like I wasn't prepared for this particular exam or lecture at all – I wasn't mentally ready for isolation, or any kind of inner peace, because I'd had no practice or study whatsoever – and that was possibly going to cripple me way more than a broken neck.

I was forced to just lie there bombarded with these

343

memories, with nowhere to go and no ability to move even if I'd wanted to. My brain was on fire but then my thoughts were blunted by a gentle faceless male voice asking me to confirm my name and date of birth. He was holding my wrist to check my wristband, then gently placed it back onto the bed. I knew what was coming. He gave a gentle sigh and leaned in over my face. His name tag dangled down in my line of sight; 'Hello, my name is Dr Chang', I read. Dr Chang gently said to me, 'I have bad news for you.'

I had indeed broken my neck. However, the nature and extent were unclear and they were waiting for the opinion of a neurosurgeon at a different hospital, since they didn't have one on staff. I volunteered to have a look myself because I do this surgery in dogs, but Dr Chang just smiled and told me to relax and stay still. I did what I was told.

Still in the throes of morphine semi-consciousness, my thoughts turned to the steps that would be involved in my surgery as I imagined controlling a surgical robot to operate on myself with image guidance. Thankfully, as I became a little more lucid, slightly more constructive thoughts came to light. I went through in my head the list of specialist neuro-surgeons I knew. I reached down to move my catheter tube a bit and suddenly thought of Professor Stephen Langley, a urinary tract specialist. I had visited him in the previous year and I knew he worked in the same hospital. Stephen is an intensely talented clinician, a highly gifted surgeon and magnificent human being. I texted him and he was by my bedside within the hour. I asked his advice and he hooked me up with consultant neurosurgeon Matthew Crocker. From then on I knew everything was going to be OK. Whatever the outcome, I was in the best hands.

I would shortly learn that I had fractured my C7 vertebra,

right beside where I had previously suffered chronic disc collapse and compression. I had the same chronic problem in my lower back – also a common affliction of surgeons which is more than ironic, as while we are busy fixing our patients we create the same problems in ourselves. So it was with some trepidation that I looked at my own surgeon as he showed me my CT scan. It wasn't good.

When I had fallen down the stairs I had been half asleep, so had no control of any part of my body, and had not in any way attempted to break my fall. This may have been a good thing since I didn't break my arm or my wrist, which would also have been a serious problem for me as a surgeon. However, it also meant that my body had plummeted against my head, as it pummelled into the wall, and as my neck had curled beneath me I had propagated a torsional fracture of the vertebra, cracking through the arch that surrounds the spinal cord and breaking off one of the facets that make up the joint above the neuroforamen at the junction of C6 and C7. As I've observed, I have genetic, degenerative cervical disc disease like Odin and Mac, and in addition to my disc collapse at that site, the neuroforamen was narrowed further by displacement and by the presence of a bone fragment that had fractured off the facet joint. The left-sided nerve root was 'wound up' as a result of the inflammation around the site where it exited through the neuroforamen and I felt a persistent, stabbing, lightning strike going down my left arm. Meanwhile, the muscles around my neck and upper back had locked down in rigid spasm like a raging bonfire.

There was some good news, however – my injuries could have been much worse. It turned out that my existing chronic spine disease actually helped to save me from worse spinal cord and nerve root damage: two of my neck vertebrae had 'seized up' relative to each other due to collapse of the disc and associated spondylosis, producing a more rigid vertebral block. Because of this stability, it's likely that my fractured vertebra had displaced less than would have otherwise been the case. Nature had looked after me in a way. At that stage both Mac and Odin were doing well, so I tried to focus on the positive.

My spinal injury could be operated on, but as with all surgery, it wasn't without risks, and with a fracture through the lateral vertebral body and facet (that's the side of the arch and the joint above the spinal cord) on top of a chronic compression meant that it would be challenging. I needed to decide whether I should opt for an operation called an anterior cervical discectomy and fusion (ACDF) like Odin had, which could be performed straight away and which longer term I might end up needing anyway, or if I should wait and see whether the neuroforamen through which the nerve passes was able to remain wide enough. If it didn't, an operation could be performed to widen it at a later date – a procedure known as a foraminotomy. However, it wasn't wise to proceed with foraminotomy straight away since the site was unstable with the fracture and stabilising the fracture surgically would be very tricky indeed. I knew quite a few surgeons and of course sought loads of opinions on my situation but, much like in my field of surgery in animals, they were divided, some saying operate straight away if possible and others advising to stick with conservative management.

Mr Crocker and I agreed that there was a reasonable chance I could avoid surgery if I was very cautious, rested and remained as immobilised as possible. That would be challenging! So, for now, my neck was strapped into a rigid brace, where it would stay for several weeks and, even after all of that, I might still need surgery. I just hoped that the fracture would heal with the splint support and, if I was lucky, the neuroforamen would remain open enough to maintain nerve function without pain.

I went home, forced into self-confinement with my neck in its brace. Within a matter of three weeks the entire country was socially distancing as coronavirus continued its deadly march across the nation. 'Self-isolation' was about to become a societal norm. By 18 March, the NHS had started to cancel all non-critical surgery as hospitals prepared to train staff and began to reconfigure and set up makeshift intensive care wards, so the universe had made the decision for me. I would not be having surgery, for now anyway. Oh, how I suddenly empathised with all of the animal friends I had confined to similar enforced immobility with the 'cone of shame' post-surgery. There was to be no running, no jumping, no slipping, no sliding for me! The neck collar was very cumbersome and irritating, with daily changes needed to prevent pressure sores. I'm grateful to the lovely ladies from the NHS and to Michaela for helping me out. It was all a big pain in the neck!

For the first couple of weeks the pain running down the nerve into my left arm was horrendous – it's amazing how a nerve so small can cause pain so big. Fortunately, Ricochet was on my lap purring, playing with the Velcro straps on my collar and telling me to stop complaining because, of course, he had been in a collar as well and had no sympathy for my plight, since having his balls cut off had been much worse than me breaking my neck!

Meanwhile, throughout early March I was regularly communicating at three or four in the morning with Russell Brand, who was on tour in Australia – my body clock was so out of kilter by this point that time of day or night didn't matter to me, it was simply a continuum. After the surgery to save his life, Morrissey had initially rallied and had improved, but now, a few weeks later, in spite of all of our collective efforts with surgery and medication, he was getting thinner and quieter and was slowly wasting away due to chronic kidney failure which unfortunately had not stabilised.

In the third week of March, just before the UK government announced a nationwide lockdown, Russell and his family returned home from Australia. Everyone always hopes that death will be natural and peaceful for their animal companion, just as Russell did for Morrissey. We are all afraid of the turbulence of what Russell called the 'theatre' of death. We have a mental image of what it will look like and an even more vivid imagination of what euthanasia might look like. Sadly chronic renal disease like Mossy's is sometimes not that kind and, as the toxins build up in the bloodstream, seizures and respiratory distress can happen on top of ulceration of the mouth, constipation and other issues, and we both knew that there was no way we could allow Mossy to suffer. Morrissey had carried Russell when he could not carry himself and so we would carry him through to the end – we would not let him down. We agreed that when the time was right, he would call me.

Russell's loyal companion was close to the end of his life, and Ricochet had just come into mine. I had intense respect for the cycle of life, but I was profoundly sad when the phone call came. We both knew that it was time to let him go.

Until then I had remained in my neck collar and had been managing work matters from home. The pain had calmed somewhat, so, with the blessing of lovely Mr Crocker, I could take the collar off for short periods. I drove to the practice to pick up some things and get ready to drive over to Russell's house to facilitate poor Morrissey's peaceful passage from this world. I looked at the stethoscope in my hands which I'd used so many thousands of times – to diagnose, to deliberate, to reassure, to face desolation and to deliver compassion – and thought how strange it is that this tool is used both to detect the beginning of life and to confirm death. I picked up the bottle of pentobarbital euthanasia solution and held it in my hand a little longer than normal. I had picked up this red liquid countless times, I have put to sleep countless animals, but I have never done it without deference and respect for life and for the spirit of that animal.

Euthanasia comes with a huge moral responsibility. I know that there were animals that I euthanised early in my career because they were deemed 'unfixable' or of too little monetary value, and later in my career because there was no money to fix them. These are avoidable deaths and, as knowledge evolves, more is possible, but it still doesn't make any particular intervention always the right thing to do. It is patient- and circumstance-dependent and sometimes a very challenging ethical dilemma. Working within legal governance guidelines, vets have different personal and subjective opinions. Some see euthanasia as a 'treatment' for what they perceive as incurable conditions, some will exhaust all reasonable efforts and draw the line when suffering is perceived, but, even then, the line of suffering is drawn differently by different vets, all with good intent. As the advocates for the welfare of the animal, all vets see euthanasia as a necessary kindness.

All of this rushed through my mind, because Russell was one of very few people with whom I had discussed my anxiety about the complaints regarding Hermes' treatment. He had

NOEL FITZPATRICK

been a good friend to me during this crisis and had shared many vital insights about respect and self-respect that had helped me to cope. Now I was setting out to take the life of his special friend. I felt absolutely awful, but I absolutely knew it was the right thing to do.

I got the euthanasia consent form ready and collected the box with all the other bits and pieces that my nurse Lauren had prepared. Without her meticulous attention to detail and kindness to my patients, their families and me, every day would be a struggle. I was grateful for her help, but I felt like I was carrying a suitcase of death and, as I walked into the setting sun to my car across the yard, the entire scene of what was to follow played out vividly in my mind – the 'theatre' of death mooted by Russell himself. In my mind's eye I would turn up at the garden gate like the grim reaper, scythe in hand, silhouetted in the hazy glow of the smouldering embers of twilight. I would knock on the door, and Russell and his wife Laura would answer; I didn't know if his children would be in bed, but I hoped they would be. Russell and Laura would be in bits, I'd be in bits. We would go to where Morrissey lay on the bed. They would kiss him goodbye and hold each other tight as I sedated him and kissed him too, then gave him the final injection. It would be a swift passing, they would cry, I would cry, I would leave, they would bury him.

My phone buzzed just as I opened the car to put my kit in. Russell had texted: 'He's gone mate x.' Then the phone rang and we talked it through. Nature had gently claimed poor little Morrissey back into the infinite oneness. Russell's prayers had been answered and Morrissey had died naturally and peacefully after all. In many ways, through his companionship, Morrissey had saved Russell's life as a recovering

350

addict, and so it was almost as if, when Russell had made the decision to let him go, Morrissey had been able to stop fighting his inevitable fate and, as a final blessing for his daddy, saved him from the responsibility of taking his life. In the end there was no gasping, no struggle, no signs of pain, just gentle sleep.

I was comforted that Russell, Laura and the girls had been able to spend his final week with him, tell him how much they loved him, and make the decision when they deemed the time was right. The taking of life weighs heavily on me and I always want to be there to help resolve suffering – but the timing needs to be right for the family and the patient. Russell and his family had absolutely done their best, as we all had. It just wasn't to be. Morrissey himself decided to go when it was right for him, just as it should have been, and Morrissey and his family were now at peace.

As night closed in around the field at the back of the practice, I imagined that Russell and his family were likely in their garden too – digging a grave for Mossy. Lost in the shroud of sadness for Morrissey, Russell and his family, I was tearful as I shuffled along in the tufted grass, from time to time looking up at the silky white clouds floating in the deep cyan sky, as wispy yellow, orange and red fingers of twilight coaxed the evening into night. A beautiful sunset, a terrible evening. The air was fragrant with the early spring blossoms as I walked over towards the chestnut and cherry trees I had planted in the hedgerow in memory of my dear friends Philip Gilbert, who had been my wonderful teacher in drama school, and Malcolm Drury, who had graciously cast me in my first ever television show. I had shared an intense bond of respect with both of these great mentors many years earlier. Malcolm had loved snowdrops; they popped their heads out of the coldness to tell us there was hope: everything was going to be OK. I picked a few from a small clump growing in the hedgerow and laid them gently at the base of his cherry blossom tree. Philip had advised me to 'find a reason big enough' and Malcolm had guided me to 'chase your dream – as long as you're doing the right thing, even when nobody is watching'. Nobody was watching now, and I did absolutely feel that Russell and I had done the right thing for Morrissey. But that night I had a strange uneasiness in my soul and I didn't know why.

All of my career, I have seen time and again that people find it inordinately difficult to put their cherished animal friend to sleep. It's one of the most difficult decisions many will face in their life. You know you have to do it to prevent suffering, but you don't want to feel the guilt of doing it. You also don't want to feel the guilt of not doing it and potentially allowing suffering. It's a dagger through the heart and everyone always hopes that the universe will make the decision so they don't have to.

When the time comes for me to lose Keira, who is now thirteen years old, I honestly don't know how I'm going to cope. Her mum Amy and brother Kyle will also be utterly devastated. I can't think about it. As for Ricochet, although he's only been my pal for a relatively short time, because we have been in imposed isolation we have spent almost every waking moment together and some of the sleeping ones too. In fact, during my confinement – first with my broken neck and then with the coronavirus lockdown – I've experienced waves of love for my little animal friends quite like never before. During that difficult time the deep-glowing, all-consuming love I felt when I gave Keira or Ricochet a cuddle, and she gave me a face-lick or he a nose-rub, kept me from

going out of my mind. I felt the unbridled joy of that unconditional love every day, and still do. I never want them to die,
but of course, when the time comes that Keira and Ricochet
are no longer around, my love for them will never die. But
love doesn't sleep on your feet and poke your eye socket with
its muzzle. I can't bear to think how much I will miss them.

I perform euthanasia often and, for me, the emotional
fallout has got worse as I have got older. I seem to cry a
lot more. I'm not sure why. Maybe one treasures life more
when one's own life is on the countdown towards the end. As
Seamus, my best friend from university, said to me recently,
'Take a tape measure. Measure out seventy-five inches; cut
off fifty-two. That's the rest of your productive life in your
hand.' A sobering thought indeed. Who knows how long is
left for me? I am acutely aware that it could all end at any
time and that evening as I looked at the trees planted for my
dear friends, unable to move my neck, and turning my whole
body to look around at their beauty, I was cognisant more
than ever of my own mortality. Hundreds of thousands of
people globally had contracted coronavirus. Many were dying
and would continue to die, and many would die alone. In my
isolation, I guess a tangled web had clamped tightly around
my mind and I wondered whether it was the combination of
all of these thoughts that robbed me of any peace that night.

It was the first time I'd had an extended period away
from the practice and it had been wonderful to walk back
through the doors, immensely grateful that I could walk and
that I was alive at all. I guess I was just having difficulty
reconciling this and the sad irony that I'd come that night
to fetch the injection in order to euthanise Morrissey. I loved
and respected that place so very much. The practice wasn't
just a building: it was my home and that of the family I had

chosen to bring with me on the journey. I loved my office, my little bed, the wards, the theatres, the entire team and all of the animals we helped. That building had risen from a derelict farm and was buzzing with animals and their welfare; Vetman's bunker had become a reality. This place was my baby, and to a very large extent its cradle was my comfort and my protector too. I had missed it so much and I suppose it was that I had come back to take life rather than give life that troubled me so. I stared at the trees a while longer, then headed back towards my car.

My phone buzzed again. Another text. It was from a dear friend of Malcolm's from whom I hadn't heard since she sat looking up at me as I gave the eulogy at his funeral three and a half years earlier. Priscilla is a talented and much respected casting director, who shared a profound love of theatre with Malcolm and me. I had met her many years earlier when, like any aspiring actor, I was doing the rounds of casting directors and not being very good at anything at all. In fact, I had my very first audition in her house in Hammersmith, west London, in 1998, which Malcolm was looking after at the time. He sent me away with advice to be 'more comfortable with myself, more confident in myself, and less uneasy'. He told me that my 'anxiety was blocking my ability', and to come back another day. I did and I got the part. It was those formative experiences that taught me how to relate to a camera and how to interact with media, gave me respect for television and ultimately shaped *The Supervet*. It was wonderful to hear from Priscilla, especially at that exact moment. The chances of Malcolm's dear friend reaching out to me just when I had been thinking of him were a billion to one, especially as I hadn't kept in contact with her in any way. It was even more incredible in the midst of my anxiety that particular night how Malcolm's voice came back through the years to calm me down – to be 'less uneasy'. I got into my car, breathed deeply, rang Priscilla, told her how wonderful it was to hear her voice, and then listened to her as the light faded.

Priscilla was calling to ask my advice about Jojo, a friend's eleven-month-old puppy and playmate of her dog Caramel, whom Malcolm had been very fond of. Jojo was in trouble and in lots of pain. He was in Suffolk, where thankfully he had the support of their local vet, so I willingly gave her what information I could and I hoped that all would be well. I had a sense that at least I was helping to give hope for Jojo's young life. Priscilla and her friend thanked me so much for putting their minds at rest. Priscilla and I chatted about Malcolm and she said she'd love to come and sit by the cherry blossom with me as soon as she could. My heart was warmed and I absolutely knew deep down that Malcolm had reached out to tell me that I shouldn't worry and I should be 'more comfortable with myself', because I was doing my best, in death or in life.

I finally felt a sense of peace flow over me with respect for the miracles of nature that we can't explain. I got out of the car, took my box of sad tools with me and took one last look at the trees as I walked back inside. My phone buzzed again with a message about an operation I was performing the following day – my first day back at work in six weeks.

We were operating emergencies only and my emergency was Odin, the beautiful Dobermann that I had operated on twice already. He had been doing very well, walking better than he had done in many months, but then sadly had taken a turn for the worse again. My team had performed a CT scan and the screws were loosening in one of his vertebrae in spite of my best efforts. Eight weeks after his last surgery, the bone was collapsing before the bone marrow that I had transplanted had had a chance to fuse the adjacent vertebrae solid. As with Odin's broken screws after his accident, I had never seen such a situation with a cervical spinal surgery before and I now suspected that bacteria from ear and skin infections, which he had been prone to, might have seeded from his bloodstream to this site of injury, in spite of the antibiotic-impregnated cement – as had been the case with Mac and Rocco before him. The screws had loosened to the point that a big hole had formed in the bone, as if a scoop had gouged it from the inside out, munching up towards the base of the spinal canal. As a result, the bone was now eggshell thin and he was on a knife-edge of collapse: he could suffer a catastrophic vertebral fracture which could paralyse him, or the hole might erode into the venous sinus at the base of his spinal canal and he might bleed internally, with euthanasia inevitably following as an ethical prerogative.

I had never operated for a third time on a cervical spine in my entire career, and ironically it was at exactly the same region where I had fractured my own neck. My neck brace was finally, and hopefully permanently, coming off the following morning, because Odin again needed my help. This was an emergency and only I could attempt to fix it.

I walked back to the trees and looked at the snowdrops lying on the ground. We would at least have a chance to give Odin hope. As the very last ember of light faded from the sky, I looked up at the trees, their buds and blossoms heralding new life and hope after the passing of winter and the dawn of spring. I was very concerned about my friend Odin whom I had grown to love, but my memory of Malcolm's words, 'my anxiety was blocking my ability', calmed my unease and gave me a feeling of renewed hope, and now it seemed as if Philip was also whispering in my ear that I *had* found my reason big enough. I was standing in it: my home, my cocoon, my hope and my redemption. I was probably imagining things, but it seemed that the universe itself had conspired to offer me a chance for some peace and the self-respect of knowing I was doing my best. Tomorrow was another day.

I drove home to my own animal family, acutely aware that all of my physical and emotional pain would pass, as would my body someday – and that love would be all that remained – and that would be enough.

I subsequently learned that Russell and his family had indeed placed Morrissey's body in his final resting place under a tree in their garden. It was a cherry blossom tree, which meant the world to Russell too. A cherry blossom had stood outside the window of his childhood home and, as for Malcolm and me, its branches also lifted him and its flowers brought him rejuvenation and hope, even when he was broken and his own twigs were bare. He sent me a picture the following morning of candles flickering in the twilight beneath its fragile pink flowers. The fragility of life had been very real for Russell and me that night, but the precious gift of love and respect for Morrissey comforted Russell and his family as they stood around the candles, said their prayers and rejoiced in Morrissey and everything he brought into and left behind in their lives.

CHAPTER THIRTEEN

Eternalisation

'Your greatest awakening comes when you are aware about your infinite nature.'

Amit Ray

As I've slowly recovered from my neck fracture, thoughts of my own mortality, the legacy of anything I have striven for, the reasons for anything I do now, my purpose, hopes and dreams for what time remains in my life and the whole concept of 'eternalisation' have grown ever more prominent in my mind. In the immediate aftermath of the accident, I had found myself in the vortex of an unprecedented and 'perfect' storm. Time away from work for the first prolonged period since I set up my practice gave me pause to question why I had become a workaholic; massive challenges in my mental landscape along with coronavirus lockdown had compounded my inner solitude, and I had been torn apart by the first major crisis of confidence in my profession for my thirty years as a vet. Now circumstances had conspired to force my hand, and I had no choice but to let go of my ever-present need for control (which is I guess a ubiquitous trait of surgeons), to sit still while the inner maelstrom of my mind wreaked its havoc.

We all accept that thoughts, whether they be of crisis or of calm, originate in our brains and, indeed, we pride ourselves on our ability for rational and complex thinking. My personal experience, however, has been that feeling, emotion and even consciousness go far beyond the finite constraints of our nervous system. In that sense, other sentient creatures – in particular the cats and dogs that I look after – may, in fact, be more purely aware and in touch with their true nature than we are. These animals, either domesticated or wild, seem to be happy enough as they are as long as humans don't mess things up for them. We humans, on the other hand, tend to overcomplicate our lives. We overthink things; we yearn for stuff we don't need to survive or be happy; we look at what others have and envy them, then spend all our time striving to compete. In the process, we lose touch with who we actually are and then spend the rest of our lives trying to find our 'true self' when it's been right there, inside us all along.

Buddhists have always regarded animals as sentient beings that possess Buddha nature. In Buddhist morality, animal and human life is of equal value, all part of a single family – and all interconnected in oneness. Both animals and humans, therefore, have potential for what they call 'bodhi' or in Japanese Buddhism 'satori', i.e. awakening, understanding or 'enlightenment'. I am not a Buddhist, but I appreciate this view, since I grew up talking to the animals and have always found greater peace and serenity in their presence than with humans. Between February and September 2020, though, I think I did have a kind of awakening and understanding, which has changed my perspective on life forever. In Japanese Zen Buddhism, satori refers to the experience of 'kensho', which is 'seeing into one's true nature', and that's exactly what happened to me. I had always thought that 'enlightenment' was an unattainable goal – until through all of the pain I had finally looked inside me. I have referred to it earlier as 'getting over yourself', but to cut through any fancy 'wellness' jargon it was simply letting go of my ego, which was attached to things outside of my true nature.

No matter how I justified it to myself, all these years my ego was getting in the way of eternalisation. I realised that all of the battles I was fighting in my life – the troubles in my mind, my workaholism, the pain of the criticism of my peers – in one form or another, were all manifestations of my ego. I had been fighting *myself*. To end the war and to become enlightened, I had to let go of 'me' and my deeply buried scars.

The attainment of 'enlightenment' is the ultimate purpose of all sentience – it's a nirvana which releases us from *samskara*, the emotional scars of our pain, which as I've said have held me back all my life. Enlightenment sets us free from the mental prison of trying to rationalise the world and our existence, which we ourselves have designed in the likeness of our conscious desires. In other words, we have made ourselves who we *think* we are – which is to say, we are simply the product of our individual and collective conscience. I now realise how deceptively nihilistic this is, and that I have been fooling myself all this time. I thought I had it all figured out and instead I had been digging a big hole for myself, emotionally and psychologically.

Down the years, I have concluded that animals do not communicate through conscious thought alone, but rather they embody the essence of simply *being*, what we *are* when all conscious thought is stripped away, when we let go of our preoccupations about material things and renounce indulgence in the ego and petty cares about how we match up to others – for good or for bad. Animals seem to live in the eternal of the present, unencumbered by the transience of the past and future which preoccupies us humans so much. By their example, in this way animals give us direct access to eternalisation when we acquiesce to the oneness of nature and are 'present', just as an animal is present.

In truth, I have always known what it feels like to be 'awakened' or 'enlightened' in the presence of animals. I have glimpsed the peace of eternalisation in the silence of just being in the same space and thoughts with an animal; I had just never accepted that it could actually save my life – and it can save yours too. Throughout the writing of this book, I've had Ricochet and Keira as my little spiritual and philosophical guides. By their very existence, they 'eternalise' my day; although I can't quite put it into words, their presence in my life taps into the most important aspect of my being – why I exist at all. This 'eternalisation', or a profound sense of peace and oneness with creation, is really, I think, what we're all searching for, but we somehow lose sight of it amid the concerns of our daily lives. Many of us, including me, spend our lives chasing what we *think* is the key to happiness, only to meet with constant disappointment or lack of fulfilment, because that happiness can only be found within. Animals tap into this essence inside of us, and that's what I know as 'eternalisation'.

My mammy, Rita, is now ninety-one. After lockdown I managed to get to visit her in Ireland for just a few hours, with all the necessary precautions of course. It was at that time that I had also paid a short visit to poor Brother Maurice. Mammy's mind is as bright as it ever has been but her body is slowly failing. All my life my mammy is the one person who has always had a firm grasp on eternalisation in the sense I've described. She's always said 'what's gone is gone' and 'there may be no tomorrow'. She has never had attachment to past or future; rather, she's always been in the present, always giving everything she had to someone else – loving her children, looking after the neighbours, organising the relations, feeding the endless droves of cattle and sheep men, the silage cutters and hay-makers that Daddy would bring home, hungry at the end of a long day in the fields. She made the best of every situation, never had an ego and always showed her true nature. Even when she had nothing, she had eternal abundance and she had eternal enlightenment, bringing joy and hope even in the darkest hour. For Rita, every day was eternalisation.

She asked me 'why the rush?' and 'why couldn't I stay for a while?', and if I had come home because I thought she was dying and I wouldn't see her again. I've never lied to my mammy, so I said, 'Yes, Mammy.' My sisters had told me that she hadn't been well. Then she said, 'Sure, I'm grand in the here and now, Noel, and that's all we've got. I want for nothing and I've never wanted for anything, Noel, cause it just ties you down – and you can't take it with you anyway, in the end.' Then she paused, as if for dramatic effect, and added, 'Or is that the beginning? – as the man himself would say.' She smiled knowingly at me, referring to the all-seeing eye of God, for whom the end and beginning are one and the same. After another pause she told me she had 'her bags packed' and was 'ready to go whenever he makes the call for the next part of the journey'. Unshakable faith will be her travel blanket. She said this with peace, serenity and the perfect acquiescence of eternalisation.

My daddy Sean loved a piece of ancient bogland at home on our farm in County Laois, called The Glebe. There trees thousands of years old had rotted and given rise to new life, and so it is with us – we come from turf and to turf we shall return. Mammy told me that she's looking forward to a 'nice long rest' and 'eternal peace' with Daddy. Her grave will be next to his. As I said goodbye to her, Mammy's belief in one continuum of life and death without fear or apprehension, and my sense of her gratefully surrendering to the oneness of the universe, was a great comfort to me. Soon lockdown would be reimposed in her part of Ireland and I don't know when I might see her again – but as she says, it doesn't matter, because every end is just the beginning.

Nobody lives forever. I am only too aware that one day too, one breath will be my last. A human life amounts to approximately sixty-five thousand hours of existence, bounded by two eternities – before and after our physical presence on this planet. A human body amounts to thirty-seven trillion nucleated cells; it would take 1.2 million years, counting one cell per second, to count them all and each and every one of those cells carries two metres of DNA. Linked end to end, this string of nucleotides could stretch ten billion miles all the way to planet Pluto. This has always seemed to me a perilous puppet string by which we are all suspended – we should never forget that it could snap at any time.

Each day the average human adult routinely disposes of fifty to seventy billion unwanted cells due to preprogrammed cell death, or 'apoptosis', from the Greek meaning literally the 'falling off' of leaves from a tree or petals from a flower. Hippocrates used the term to relate to the 'falling off of the bones'. After a long day of operating, I can certainly relate to that feeling. Galen used the term for the 'dropping off of scabs'. In contrast with 'necrosis', which is traumatic cell death resulting from acute cellular injury, such as a leg becoming gangrenous, apoptosis is a highly regulated and systematic process occurring either as a result of an intrinsic pathway, in which the cell elects to self-destruct due to some inner turmoil, or an extrinsic pathway, where the death of the cell is triggered by signals from surrounding cells. Cells may commit suicide or signal others to do so when exposed to external stresses such as radiation, nutrient deprivation or viral infection. For all of our cells, however, the intrinsic pathway inevitably leads to death because our DNA itself contains apoptotic genes. If cells signal to others to die, they do so via mechanisms with great villainous names, like 'tumour-necrosis-factor (TNF)' and 'Fas-Fas ligand-mediated responses'. Activation of an enzyme called 'caspase' commits a cell to death and 'engulfment genes' prompt dead-cell removal. There is some toing and froing of biological molecules which promote (pro-apoptotic) or inhibit cell death (Inhibitor of Apoptosis Proteins, IAPs). My childhood imaginary hero Vetman was full of IAPs – and lots of other magic anti-apoptotic molecules so his cells were actually immortal, but that is the stuff of superheroes. We mere mortals have no such biological armour.

Cancer cells, on the other hand, don't die – apoptosis fails. The normal mechanisms of cell cycle regulation are dysfunctional, leading to overproduction of cells, decreased removal of cells, or a combination of the two. Cancer cells can don cunning disguises to evade the 'immune surveillance' processes that normally serve to eliminate faulty cells. Tumour cells can become immortal, for example, by expression of IAPs, which can be regulated by the 'p53 tumour suppressor gene'. P53 is mutated in over 50 per cent of all human cancers. Normally p53 rallies into action when cells suffer DNA damage and it churns out loads of p53 protein and either repairs the damage or, if it's too far gone, kills the cell before it can harm the organism. In addition, specialised white blood cells called 'T' cells and 'natural killer' (NK) cells can detect and destroy tumour cells via the 'death-receptor pathway'. But cancer is cunning and can also become immortal by tumour cells evading this terminal pathway.

Cancer doesn't care if you are human or animal, young or old – it can cause death before your due date. Humans and most mammals have only one copy of p53 in their genome, but elephants have twenty paired copies of p53 and only about 3 per cent of elephants get cancer. Elephants can churn out p53 proteins when their cells are damaged and their cells have evolved to kill themselves to stop would-be nascent tumours before they have the chance to grow. There are lots of other factors to consider too, of course, in that the metabolic rate of elephants' cells is also slower. Woolly mammoths apparently had more than a dozen copies of p53 but they became extinct nevertheless, likely from a combination of other genetic mutations, environmental changes and human hunting. Sadly, elephants are also an endangered species because human guns and cruelty are more potent than cancer. In fact, as a race, we are many times more deadly for the ecosystems of the planet than any disease. Furthermore, through our own actions, we are responsible too for our own cancer – by polluting the air we breathe, the water we drink and the food we eat and through the chemicals many of us use to do our jobs. In many ways, *we are our own cancer* and we are killing ourselves. Looking at the concept of eternalisation as it affects all of humanity in a physical sense – i.e. whether we'll be around on earth indefinitely – then I have to say that we're not doing a very good job of it.

Vetman, as I imagine him, has a hundred copies of p53 and another gene called vmONE which renders him immortal, and in fact it was his essence and his bond with animals that led me to explore the concept of eternalisation in the first place. In my childhood stories, Vetman's cloak was modelled on the colours of the red admiral butterfly. When I was a young boy, I thought that butterflies were the most beautiful creatures in the world and were sent by God to take us to heaven. I really believed that we were each made up of stardust and that when we died the butterflies carried us to heaven on their wings. I used to sit at the base of our chestnut tree and marvel over the wings of a red admiral for hours. Yet, these wondrous creatures are endangered too through the practice of intensive farming to feed our ever-growing appetite for meat and grain. Unless we change our ways and have a little more respect for the balance of our ecosystem, the red admiral and many other butterfly species won't be around to take us to heaven after all.

As I've recalled earlier, I have sent many animals to heaven with lethal injections, but two particular dogs that I have put to sleep because of bone cancer have charted the beginning and the end of my journey so far as 'the Supervet' – both Spud and Dennis broke my heart, but both also shared with me important lessons about eternalisation.

I met Spud, a beautiful Labrador cross German shepherd dog, and his dad Chris, in early 2015, soon after we had started filming *The Supervet*. Chris was a former heroin addict and had been homeless on the streets for years. By the time I met him, he was living in a charitable commune, which provided him with a roof over his head in return for restoring furniture and running a charity shop with his friends. A former veterinary nurse called Emma, who worked in mental health services, was involved with the charity and fell in love with Spud from seeing him at the shop sitting on a random sofa, sniffing a random leg or sprawled out near the till. One day Chris told her that there was something wrong with Spud. In fact, he was non-weight-bearing lame on his left hind leg. Emma reached out to lots of different vet organisations and a diagnosis of rupture of one of the cruciate ligaments in his knee was made. Corrective surgery or full limb amputation was suggested, but there were no finances and euthanasia seemed inevitable because he was in a lot of pain. All enquiries for help met a dead end and finally, in desperation, Emma wrote to me. As I have already explained, no vet can afford to perform surgery for free and that's an unfortunate reality of life in any business where wages and overheads have to be paid. I'm sure many veterinary practices, just like us, get requests like Emma's all the time and simply cannot help. Her email ended, 'Spud is an amazing dog and I know he can be helped if someone would give him a chance. Thank you so much for reading my plea.'

Chris had lost his dad when he was ten and then his brother had died in a young offenders' institution. By the time Chris was eleven he was drinking and smoking, and by the age of fifteen he was in foster care, hanging about with older lads who were into hard drugs and he began to smoke class A's. As a result, he had also started to get into trouble with the police. When we met, he described how smoking heroin was like being instantly 'wrapped in cotton wool', with no problems for a few hours and then the craving would set in for the next hit. Drinking vodka on a park bench was a slower-acting drug, but both dulled the senses and offered temporary respite against the pain of his world.

Chris's sister got Spud for him, thinking perhaps that Spud might be able to help him – and so it was. Soon Chris treated him like a brother or a son. He stopped using drugs because he needed to buy dog food and also because Spud gave him a sense of responsibility and respect for another life, even if he didn't have respect for his own. He suffered badly from anxiety, obsessive-compulsive disorder and depression. He recalled once sitting at the top of a cliff, feeling like he wanted to die, but he also knew that Spud would be clambering down after him if he jumped, and he couldn't do that. In a very real sense, Spud had saved his life and given him a glimpse of eternalisation that transcended the temporary escape from his thoughts which he had previously sought through drugs or alcohol.

Chris and Spud had a kind of telepathy. He shared many secrets that no human would ever know, and he gave Chris confidence he didn't have without him by his side. Chris was always self-conscious about his bad teeth and he told me that Spud was 'his smile' to the world. Because Chris respected and valued Spud so much, it had given him back some sense of self-respect and self-worth. With Spud's head on his lap, he felt comfort and hope that he had not known before – eternalisation without the need for words.

When Chris was offered accommodation, the community had a no-dogs policy and so Chris declined the offer unless Spud could come with him. Their love was unbreakable, and he'd rather stay on the streets than give him up. As a result, the commune changed the rules and Spud became a community dog and a friend to all the men living there, trying to forge a better life. Spud's positive influence in the house was extraordinary and care for his well-being brought all of the men together with a shared purpose, wanting to do their best for him. They were desolate because there was no money to help him.

Occasionally someone will leave us some money in a will or by donation to 'contribute towards the work of Fitzpatrick Referrals'. It is taxable income and needs to go through adjudication before we can pay any bills with it. Registered charities don't get taxed on donations, but understandably have to consider paying towards the good of one animal with a bigger bill versus the good of many with smaller bills, so their job is tough too. Nevertheless, the good news was that a benefactor helped us to cover the cost of an assessment for Spud and to give an opinion on what may be the right thing to do for him. The bad news came when I saw the X-ray picture.

It wasn't a ruptured cruciate ligament after all, but a tumour which was eating away at Spud's tibia and knee. It was an unmitigated disaster; almost certainly a primary bone tumour called an osteosarcoma. It was so aggressive that it had already burst through the bone and was invading the muscle. I couldn't cut this out even if it was the right thing to do, which it wasn't, and I couldn't have saved the leg even if I had wanted to. On top of this, it was unlikely that Spud would live more than a few months. This kind of aggressive osteosarcoma typically spreads rapidly, not just locally in the bone and surrounding tissue; the tumour cells leave the leg and may stay dormant for a while in locations such as other bones, undetectable, before awakening weeks or months later and travelling to the lung tissue where they start dividing. We performed a CT scan on Spud to check his lungs, abdomen and other bones, which is a more sensitive test than standard X-ray pictures for detecting small tumours, and at this stage he didn't have grossly evident metastatic spread. However, most dogs already have spread at a cellular level that we can't pick up with X-ray pictures or CT scans. Sometimes we are lucky and with current chemotherapy drugs given into the bloodstream we can extend life for up to a year or sometimes even longer. But sometimes we're not lucky at all and the tumour cells awaken and grow in spite of chemotherapy. We could have better drugs than the carboplatin we have been using for more than twenty years, but that would require some joined-up thinking between drug companies and human and animal care-givers.

As I have explained, at present animal models are used in experiments to provide potential drugs for human use, but it's very rare to see a concerted effort to study naturally occurring cancer in dogs alongside humans. I believe that this model of One Medicine will become more common and more acceptable over time provided that the profit margins remain the same for the companies, but at that time the reality for Spud was that we would amputate his leg and give him carboplatin four times, three weeks apart – and that was the best we could do. I really wish I could do better for all of my patients.

Sharing the diagnosis with Chris was one of the most difficult consultations I have ever had. Telling anyone that their friend and family member has cancer is always devastating, but this outcome was not expected in any way, and Chris relied emotionally on Spud so very much that I felt an enormous sense of responsibility. He cried bitterly on my shoulder as I hugged him and tried to comfort him. I told him he had to be brave for his friend, because now Spud needed him every bit as much as Chris had ever needed him. It was now Chris's turn to do his very best for Spud as he had done for him.

My respect for Chris continued to grow in the coming weeks and months. He was by Spud's side every step of the way as he went through the amputation and the chemotherapy. As soon as Spud went home on three legs, his tongue was lolling out to one side as it always did when he wanted to play. I had given strict instructions for 'no slipping, no sliding, no running, no jumping and no playing ball', as I always did. Chris took Spud for a pee in the park on their first night home and thought he'd let him have a sniff around in his 'cone of shame'. Spud scampered off into the undergrowth and came back a few minutes later as proud as punch, tongue lolling around in his mouth, and a dirty tennis ball wedged between his neck and his collar. In spite of my instructions Spud had found a ball to play with anyway.

Just six months later, in spite of our best efforts with surgery and chemotherapy, metastatic cancer spread to his lungs. He was on the shorter end of the survival curve and unfortunately nobody could predict that. Chris was sobbing his heart out again in my arms, as I gave him a hug and we held Spud's paw and kissed him goodbye. He told me subsequently that those six months with Spud had been most precious and amazing.

Spud had lent Chris's life meaning and given him the inner strength to change it for the better. Time and again down through the years, I have seen how animals shine a light on the darkness within us in a way that no person can, no matter how hard they try. That's the enlightenment, sharing and companionship of unconditional love. Spud saved Chris by communicating that life is important, for it is only love that is eternal, and only love that transcends space and time.

Chris carried Spud's ashes around with him in his rucksack for more than two months. His friend told him this had to stop because one day the cardboard tube was going to spill Spud all over him, and so he took a trip to their favourite spot by the sea and let him wander free through the waves. Chris still keeps pictures of Spud by his bedside – sitting on a cliff edge together, playing with a ball, or outside my practice on the day of the amputation, ready to make the most of what remained.

The goal of the charitable community of which Chris is now part is to help the less fortunate. Chris volunteers for trips to Srebrenica in Bosnia to prepare building sites and dig trenches where schools and houses can rise from the rubble of these once war-torn regions. He told me how humbling it was to see and touch the derelict walls of fallen buildings which had been peppered with bullets. Chris sometimes sits at the memorials to the tens of thousands of victims who died in the genocide in the mid-1990s and feels extraordinarily fortunate that he never had to experience the unthinkable extermination, rape, torture, plunder and destruction that took place in the name of ethnic cleansing. Through his journey with Spud and his community, Chris has made new friends who support each other, from Britain to Bosnia. This sense of our connection with others breeds respect for our common destiny, our 'oneness' – and, for Chris, that all began with respecting Spud.

Dennis, a beautiful bull mastiff, was another more recent cancer patient, suffering from a very aggressive osteosarcoma of the bottom part of his radius just above his wrist (carpus) on his left front leg, a common site for this tumour in large-breed dogs. He first came to see me with his mum Jacquie in late November 2019, two days after his sixth birthday. Dennis was a big dog in every sense of the word – he was all of 80kg and a huge character who loved the sound of his own voice and instantly owned every room he walked into. At night when he went out for a bedtime pee, and barked in response to some sound in the forested valley beyond his garden, he thought that the echo that returned was another dog barking back at him – and so in turn he answered this big brave friend in the distance, who clearly understood his unique language, and barked back at him. Each night he would converse with himself in the darkness across the valley and then return contentedly to 'the den of Dennis', because I was reliably informed that at home Dennis ruled the roost. He was everyone's friend – and an integral member of the family.

As a counsellor and support nurse for women diagnosed with breast cancer, caring for them through diagnosis to surgery and chemotherapy and out the other side, Jacquie knew all about the physical and psychological toll of the disease. Euthanasia isn't an option for her human patients. Jacquie, her husband John and their children couldn't bear to put Dennis to sleep without trying their best for him. Sadly, the tumour was too invasive, so it wasn't possible to remove it and put in a metal endoskeleton in order to save his foot. He would have really struggled without one of his front legs after a full limb amputation and so, having considered the ethical implications, the family elected to have the bottom part of the leg cut off above the tumour, and to have a limb amputation endoprosthesis PerFiTS fitted, as I had done for Peanut five years previously and have done for many others in the interim.

I cut the tumour off, placed the implant into the bone, anchored with a peg inside the radius of the forearm, and plates plus screws outside the radius and ulna. The bones rested on a platform and below that was the dermal integration module (DIM) for skin attachment. For the first few days after surgery, everything was going well but then a triangle of skin and muscle tissue on the back of the implant began to die from lack of blood supply. There's a lot of tension on the back of the forearm pulling on the tissue which may have contributed, but for whatever reason the dead (necrotic) area had left a hole.

Now it was a race against time to get a permanent seal around the metal rod (spigot) sticking out of the leg below the DIM, onto which the foot (exoprosthesis) attaches to form the bionic leg. We applied vacuum assisted closure (VAC) to try to suck tissue back into the void – foam covered in a thin plastic wrap onto which a limpet and tube is attached, and negative pressure applied in order to suck in granulation tissue, which forms the basis of a scar on which skin can subsequently grow either by encouragement from the periphery or by grafting. We encountered a further problem too with another big 'C' that surgeons dread – contamination. Up to a thousand species of bacteria live on a dog's skin (and ours) and they can take advantage of any exposed area, which indeed was the case in Dennis's wound. Thankfully we conquered the infection and four weeks after his surgery the skin had finally healed. By Christmas 2019, he was walking well and was happy.

Things were looking up for larger-than-life Dennis but then, just before the new year, he began to cough and became lethargic. Only six weeks earlier the CT scan of his lungs had been clear, but now new scans showed that tumours were present. This couldn't have been anticipated by anyone, and Jacquie and her family were abroad on holiday as all this unfolded. We had all fallen in love with Dennis at the practice and it was utterly heartbreaking for everyone involved when I had to make the call to Jacquie recommending euthanasia. Jacquie and I talked both then and for a long time subsequently and I hope it was a comfort to her as much as it was for me. She encouraged me not to see Dennis's surgery as a failure but rather as part of the journey of learning that she herself has seen in breast cancer treatment. She said that it is only by trying to progress that we learn to change our minds, adding that hope was essential, for without it we have nothing. We both smiled as we hoped that the echo of Dennis's surgery, just like his inimitable voice, would be heard across the divide between human and animal medicine and go on to help both. Then, as the sun set and dusk fell on New Year's Day 2020, my interns and I sat under chestnut and cherry blossom trees behind the practice and cuddled Dennis's beautiful big head and neck before we said goodbye for the last time. Philip and Malcolm would keep him safe.

It was a horrible start to what would rapidly become an *annus horribilis*. That same day the World Health Organization reported an outbreak of cases of an unexplained pneumonia affecting growing numbers in Wuhan in China and set up an incident management support team. On 11 January coronavirus would claim its first victim. It then rapidly began its deadly course across the world. The International Committee on Taxonomy of Viruses named the new virus 'Severe Acute Respiratory Syndrome Coronavirus 2' (SARS-CoV-2), because it was related to the virus that caused SARS in 2003. The WHO called it Covid-19 virus

– one of the smallest pathogens known to man but which would go on to cause the biggest global catastrophe of our generation.

As a general practitioner vet, and growing up in rural Ireland, I had seen highly virulent infections in animals with parvovirus, distemper and foot and mouth disease. The terms 'epidemiology' and 'herd immunity' were well known to me and to all vets. More recently, we all watched reports from far-flung lands of infections such as Ebola, SARS, MERS and Zika virus, and then in 2009 swine flu came closer to home, but somehow here in the UK these life-threatening infections didn't really affect public consciousness in any meaningful way. With Covid-19, suddenly everything changed. People everywhere had only one topic of conversation – coronavirus.

It seems strange looking back, but in 1990 I wrote a project on coronavirus in cats for my final year dissertation. Asymptomatic feline coronavirus (FCoV) can mutate to a form that causes a potentially fatal disease called feline infectious peritonitis (FIP). I remember asking if it could mutate and kill humans, only to be told I was silly. That may well have been true, but soon the world would know all about viral mutation in a strain of coronavirus that could kill humans. Viruses, unlike bacteria, don't reproduce on their own. They identify a possible host cell using surface receptors, inject their genetic material and hijack the cellular machinery to create more copies of their genes and proteins. The science is still unproven on the origins of SARS-CoV-2, but at the time of writing, gene sequencing suggests that it may have evolved in an animal like a bat or a pangolin and then jumped to a single person, and then spread by inter-human transmission. In any case, what we know is that it was somehow transmitted from animal to man, possibly from trade in wild animal meat, which is a cultural norm in Wuhan.

The genetic template of the virus causing Covid-19 had just a couple of very specific mutations that allowed it to rapidly infect and affect people, moving through populations exponentially. It's called *corona*virus because of the multiple spikes that appear like a crown on electron microscopy. A spike protein on the surface acts like a grabber, allowing the virus to stick like a limpet to the walls of human cells. One mutation allows the spike to bind via a 'docking portal' or receptor (the ACE2 protein whose function normally is to regulate blood pressure) on the surface of the cells which line the lungs and airways – and then a second mutation of the spike acts like a can opener to cleave open a doorway into the cell. The virus then cracks open the host cell wall, takes over the cells and then the organism, with sometimes deadly effect. That's how finely balanced our symbiosis with the natural world is.

Four months before the Covid-19 outbreak, I delivered a lecture at the Royal Society of Medicine in London in which I talked about how it's estimated that 75 per cent of all emergent infections in humans come from animals. In the 2014 Ebola outbreak in south-east Guinea, for instance, the virus likely transferred from a bat to a small boy. I cautioned that the Western world didn't take much notice because it didn't affect us, but that another pandemic could. I argued that we ignore this at our peril, and that One Medicine was the best way forward in tackling these global health challenges. Sadly, at the time, little did I realise how soon my dire warnings would become reality, and how rapidly SARS-CoV-2 would impact all of us.

For many the virus causes no more symptoms than a bad flu, but for some it is a tipping point into pneumonia, acute respiratory distress syndrome (ARDS), multiple organ failure and a horrible death. Along with the physical suffering, the wider societal consequences are harder to quantify, let alone remedy – other diseases including cancer going untreated or undiagnosed; untold psychological distress, anxiety and depression; domestic violence; unemployment, poverty and deprivation with economies facing financial meltdown – all of which will endanger lives too.

At the practice all veterinary care was restricted to emergency only. There were shortages of essential medical equipment which was understandably prioritised for human healthcare over veterinary care, and clients stayed outside the building while animals most in need were admitted. My colleagues across our two hospital locations were amazing. They pulled together like never before and did what needed to be done to save as many animals as possible. We had often referred to the spirit of the Fitz-Family before, but never was it more evident than now. I was intensely proud of all of them.

Privately, I worried about everything – the operations I couldn't perform, my work colleagues, the effect on the practice generally, and I still didn't know whether I would ever again operate without pain in my neck. In all of this I felt guilty, because there were people so very much worse off than me.

The pain in my neck and arm gnawed away at me, and, stuck at home following social distancing guidelines, the neck brace felt like a further cage within the prison of my house. I paid several visits to hospitals and then I got sick myself. I don't know for sure if it was coronavirus, since at that stage of the pandemic testing wasn't widely available, but the first symptom I noticed was that, all of a sudden, I realised that

Ricochet's poo didn't smell when I carried out the daily litter tray clean-up. Dizziness, headaches, cough and temperature followed. What started as a feeling of insects crawling all over my skin was followed by hot flushes and then a raging sweat trickling down my back and chest. Then I was cold, hot, cold and lying in a pool of sweat on the bed. My head felt like an industrial-metal concert in a dungeon – constant thumping and dizziness. My ears hurt. I woke up from a half-slumber with what felt like a spider crawling up from my trachea into my larynx, and then a dry cough started. The sneezing was explosive, but not as explosive as the diarrhoea, which lasted for three long days. Shortness of breath came next, but thankfully never to the point that I felt suffocated. Worryingly, my arm pain flared up even worse. Then muscular pain all over. I had aches where I didn't even know I had places. I was as weak as a dishcloth; I didn't want to eat much and I couldn't smell anyway. I was more lethargic than I can ever remember and all I could do was self-isolate and sweat it out.

I knew that I was getting physically better when Ricochet's litter tray began to stink again, but I remained in mental turmoil and in the cage of my collar. One day I spoke to Russell, who immediately knew that my emotional metabolism wasn't working properly. After the conversation, he sent me a text that simply read: 'I will organise TM for you, if you like.' Firstly, I didn't even know what TM stood for, so I had to google it; and, secondly, I knew absolutely nothing about transcendental meditation. In fact, truth be told, I thought it was all mumbo jumbo. I mean, how did it have any relevance whatsoever to an obsessive, fully switched-on, highly functioning, running 100 per cent of the time Type A personality?

Meditating had never entered my head as a possible solution to some of my problems. I always thought that it would be physically and mentally impossible for me, for a start. For twenty years I haven't taken a holiday for more than three or four days, and I find it hard to stay still for longer than two minutes, let alone twenty, so transcendental meditation probably wasn't going to work for me, or so I thought.

Full lockdown had not yet come into force, I no longer had any Covid-type symptoms, and so several days later a meditating guardian angel called Deirdre floated in on a magic breeze, knocked on my door, entered with a satchel over her shoulder, and brought with her the tantalising possibility of 'eternalisation'. Ricochet was creating mayhem and in no mood for meditation, so I set up two chairs in another room. On one of them, Deirdre created a little altar, with a picture of Guru Dev who was the teacher of Maharishi Mahesh Yogi, the founder of the transcendental meditation movement. She placed a candle, a small bowl with camphor, incense sticks, a golden tray with some grains of rice on, a small golden bowl with water and another bowl with what looked like yellow paste on top of a white cloth, then positioned a white handkerchief, some flowers and two apples on the gold tray. I was more scared than I had ever been of any woman or any altar, and I told her so. In fact, I was terrified and also profoundly cynical, but somehow at the same time strangely intrigued. I am a clinical scientist, where evidence trounces all argument, debate or opinion, after all, and not used to situations where argument, debate and opinion are rendered meaningless by what Deirdre called 'pure consciousness', a term I had often heard before as I've said, but didn't really understand. I had read up about the Maharishi in preparation for Deirdre's visit. A *Time* magazine article from 1967, the year I was born, reported that he had 'been sharply criticised by other Indian sages, who complain that his programme for spiritual peace without either penance or asceticism contravenes every traditional Hindu belief'. I thought that perhaps I could relate to this man after all!

I explained some of my struggles to Deirdre and that what I yearned for most was inner peace. She felt that she could help and began the puja ceremony, reciting the lineage of masters, which I learned was traditional at the start of any training. The burning incense filled my nostrils and I was flung back in time to all those years before, dressed in my cassock and surplice vestments and staring up at Father Meaney as we paced the Stations of the Cross, swinging the thurible around the church in Ballyfin in the middle of Ireland.

Deirdre chanted gently in Sanskrit. I didn't understand a word. Soon afterwards I didn't understand the word she gave me to recite in my mind either – and I never will – because it's not supposed to be understood. In fact, that's the whole point of a mantra. The chosen word should simply 'have a quality of vibration which corresponds to the vibrational quality of the individual', as Maharishi wrote in the 1963 book *The Science of Being and Art of Living*. Very sceptically, I started saying the mantra word over and over, loudly at first and then quieter and quieter until it became a soundless whisper inside my head. But still I just couldn't switch my mind off. It was racing at a million miles an hour, worrying about all of the problems that meditation was supposed to help me with. For me, sitting still for any purpose other than an essential power nap on a weekday afternoon was an abomination. Regardless of my neck collar or coronavirus, my head was telling me that I should be back at the helm of the ship, navigating the choppy seas in the practice during those uncertain days early in the pandemic. This all felt truly alien and very selfish. But, although I'd only just met her, Deirdre was kind and had an aura of serenity about her, so I persisted.

Deirdre instructed me not to try to say the mantra any louder than the noise in my head, to just keep saying it quietly. This state of transcendence, she explained, is to be found in the silence between thoughts, rather than in the thoughts themselves – in the same way that we don't hear music so much as the silences *between the notes*, and yet the notes cannot exist without the silence in between. Deirdre assured me that the mantra was a vehicle on which I may enter into the tranquillity of pure consciousness deep inside my mind, so that the crashing of the waves on the surface would seem distant. Still the cacophony persisted in my troubled head. After a while, I didn't know if the word was actually inside my head at all, because every now and again I had this fleeting sensation that in fact the thought of the word could be *outside* my head. 'Stupid,' I inwardly reasoned. 'Thoughts can't exist outside the head – I must be going out of my mind!' Of course, that was the problem: the perpetual whirring of my thinking was getting in the way, and *going out of my mind* – transcending conscious thought – was exactly what I needed to do, and exactly where I needed to go.

Then something very strange happened. I imagined that I was back on the beach in Tramore in the south of Ireland with my mammy. I was a small child trying to put on my inflatable armbands. One of them drifted away. Every time I tried to reach out and grab the armband in an irritated and almost panicked way, I nudged it with my fingers and it slipped away further on the tide. It floated back, I grabbed

for it again, and again it drifted away. I became quite distressed because I'm not a good swimmer at all, largely due to
the fact that work on the farm took priority over swimming
lessons, and so I felt like I was going to drown and started to
choke, then I panicked yet more. But Deirdre's voice came
back to me, coaxing me to say the word. I did, and I just let
it float out on the waves, and there it was, floating beside
the armband – and there I was, floating there too. Suddenly
a light, just a kind of glow, opened up my eyes and all inside
my mind, dim at first but then as if streaming through a
door. My body felt lighter, lifted up, hovering above the bed
on which I was sitting. It only lasted momentarily, because
as soon as I became aware of it, my rational mind decided
that it was all complete nonsense, and I promptly crashed
back to earth. Soon afterwards, Deirdre asked me to open
my eyes and she quietly and methodically packed away the
altar. She folded the little white cloth, then handed me the
handkerchief, the flowers and the two apples to keep – as
a gift. I wanted to give her a hug, but obviously I couldn't
because we were social distancing, and so she wafted out as
she had wafted in, leaving behind a mist of incense, some of
her gentle calm and a glimmer of that transient feeling of
peace, light and some kind of transcendence burning softly
in my mind.

Within an hour, I was again being bombarded by endless
phone calls and emails and my mind was a bubbling cauldron
of conscious thought once more. I had personal challenges,
the coronavirus crisis threatened my work colleagues at
the practice and our ability to do our jobs, and I was holed
up at home in a neck brace barely able to move about the
house. My neck pain seemed like it would never subside and
I still had shooting pain in my left arm. I was going crazy

with anxiety and it seemed impossible that any amount of meditation was ever actually going to alleviate any of this agony. The course with Deirdre was one hour each day for four consecutive days, however, and in my normal life before coronavirus, the chances of that happening would have been billions to one against, so I acquiesced to the flow of fate.

On day three, Deirdre drew a very simple diagram on a single sheet of white paper, and that was when the revolution began for me. Enlightenment and eternalisation beckoned. The top of the diagram was a wavy line representing the waves on an ocean, some big, some small. The bottom of the diagram was a straight line depicting the silence of the bottom of the seabed. From there, some tiny bubbles emanated, like in a bottle of fizzy pop, and some grew larger as they rose up towards the surface. These were my little random thoughts and worries growing bigger as I gave them life with my own energy of thought. Deirdre explained that her drawing was a picture of my mind on that actual day, and she was spot on. The surface of my mind was a turbulent storm of waves, crashing against each other, and the chances of me accessing any kind of peace at the lower levels seemed like zero. She then said that there is a mesh of knots spanning top to bottom in the nervous system. I imagined it like a giant fishing net hanging down from a boat, with the knots of stress fatigue tightly bound in the mesh. Deirdre told me that in order to float free from this mesh and to avoid engagement with the crashing waves, one has to somehow sink down below the turmoil of the bubbles and the stormy surface – and that's where the mantra word came in.

This process had nothing to do with willpower, tenacity and 'pushing through', which I had relied on for my entire life – it was all about surrender and acceptance of *what is*. The mantra word would be my guide and my oxygen reserve as I took the plunge. I had no other option. Everything I ever cared about was in jeopardy and all of my normal defences were expended. The relentless drive that had sustained me for more than thirty years was rapidly losing its momentum. I was a tightly coiled spring of self-loathing, self-destruction and flesh-crawling anxiety. Deirdre asked me to sit down and close my eyes. I wedged my neck brace against some pillows and sat there, rigid with tension and 'analysis paralysis'. Even though I recited the mantra over and over in silence, the oxygen wasn't working and the pain bubbles kept snagging on the knots of stress in my thoughts. I knew I needed to let go and allow myself to sink into the calm depth of my soul, but I just couldn't.

By the last day of my lessons with Deirdre I had done a little homework and tried to build a bridge between my rational scientific mind and what meditation can achieve. It felt like my brain was heavy with the weight of the world, but sceptical as I was, I'd give anything a shot that might lighten the load. I've mentioned before how string theory has tried to explain our physical world, and that Einstein spent his life chasing 'unified field theory' in which all of the principles of general relativity, quantum mechanics and the space-time continuum could be boiled down to one overarching Theory of Everything. Remarkably this hierarchy of the physical world made of 'space-time foam' is mirrored in the hierarchy of thoughts, from the choppy seas to the calm depths, as the mind transcends various levels of consciousness on a journey ultimately 'boiling down' towards transcendence, 'pure consciousness', pure 'oneness', or what I've described before as 'samadhi'. In basic language, all the 'stuff' of the physical world and all the 'stuff' of the mind ultimately 'boils down' to a unified field of everything.

At first I was as sceptical as anyone when I read the work of people like quantum physicist Dr John Hagelin – and indeed this unification of physical and metaphysical I've just described is rejected by most theoretical physicists. However, Dr Hagelin explains in lucid detail how the laws of physics are mirrored in the laws of consciousness and that all can be unified in 'oneness' if we can somehow access this 'inner peace'. I have now come to accept that this does make sense. To my mind it all 'boils down' to one simple unavoidable truth – both humans and animals are linked to the natural world by physical molecules and by some kind of shared universal consciousness, and for me that's eternalisation.

The perfect storm of circumstances which led me to this nadir had been a rude awakening for me physically, psychologically and spiritually. Something had to give after more than twenty years of intense workaholism – for a good cause, of course, but still not entirely conducive to emotional stability or sustainability. I realised for the first time in the midst of all of the churning of my mind that if I was to achieve my goal of leaving the world in a better state for animals, and giving them a fair deal, then I would have to change, and that I couldn't change the world without changing my attitude to myself; I couldn't reach any kind of eternalisation without internalisation of some kind of enlightenment first. It seemed that life had thrown up many roadblocks and signposts and it was now down to me to take notice.

At first the storm raged savagely within me, and then gradually the stillness grew *within*. All I could do was sit and watch, almost detached and intrigued, as it continued its path of destruction, to the point where I came to see the chaos *without* – without being caught up in it, but rather witnessed it as a kind of curious observer. This was a miraculous revelation for me, and I suppose the culmination of all my previous attempts to stay in 'nowness'. For the very first time in my life I had acquiesced to something much greater than myself or any of my efforts and in so doing I managed to escape the turbulence.

As ever I communicated with Keira and Ricochet every day, and this helped me to feel calmer and more stable, so I wondered if perhaps that transcendent sense of peace might exist in the depth of feeling I experienced by saying nothing at all to an animal? Perhaps simply being present in that pure consciousness was the closest I could come to the silence of the mind I was yearning for? I came to believe that this was the essence of what felt like 'telepathic' communication with animals and that the solution to my anxiety and mental turbulence was within my reach all along – in the very vocation I had chosen and my bond with animals.

Electroencephalography (EEG) has shown that in transcendence, referred to as a 'fourth state of consciousness', the alpha waves of the brain can be more calm, consistent and stable, surpassing the peace of mind afforded by sleeping or dreaming so that stress tension can be alleviated. I am a fan of scientific proof, so this helped me to understand. The cognitive brain that I live in all of the time is full of high-frequency gamma waves and sleep is full of delta waves. The goal of meditation is enlightened wakefulness, so one can tap into synchronous orderly alpha wave coherence across the big chunk of the brain which is our cerebrum. It's been shown that when the whole brain functions in concert in this way, learning, alertness, concentration, moral reasoning and happiness increase.

The more I read about it, the more I came to realise that being in this silent space of pure consciousness with animals could save me from myself. They were my path to eternalisation and oneness, but only if I was prepared to let go of my selfish worldly fixation. This was the ego in which all of my anxiety, sadness and confusion thrived. Finding peace and eternalisation was more about me coming to terms with *myself* than it was with my professional reputation, my interaction with other people, or any other external factor. All of my worry was ultimately the consequence of not being in touch with any sense of inner peace.

Through the process of acquiescing to a mantra, I came to realise that much of what I thought about myself was wrong: I wasn't what other people thought I was, or actually even what *I thought* I was; that my sense of self and self-respect could only be realised inside the very core of my being. I had read about the concept of the 'inner eye', which has been a cornerstone of Eastern medicine for centuries but is largely ignored in Western-world medicine. The inner eye represents the unified field of pure consciousness. I have often wondered where we store pain, respect, love or peace and after reading more, specifically about the chakras, I decided that pure consciousness probably doesn't reside in the brain at all. Obviously, dissection of chakras isn't taught in any anatomy book – but they are described as seven circular vortexes of energy at different points on the spinal column, all connected to the various organs, responsible for the ebb and flow qi or prana, meaning life energy and apparently forgiveness, which greatly improves the flow of healing energy within oneself and towards others. As soon as I began this process of forgiveness, not just for myself but for all of those who I felt had done me wrong, or who didn't see the world or my profession as I did, everything changed for the better for me. I have learned through the accusation of malpractice from my veterinary colleagues that they are not my enemy and they're just doing their best to make what awaits us all as peaceful as possible for animals.

What had started as an *annus horribilis* could still turn into an *annus mirabilis* after all. I even began to wonder if, when I had fallen down the stairs head-first into a wall, bashed my prefrontal cortex and broken my spine, perhaps this had opened some chakras that had been closed for all of my existence. Maybe the impact dampened the ever-dominant conscious thought in my cortex just enough to open my subconscious mind to some new possibilities? It felt as if the constant whirring of my mind that had fenced in my eternal potential was suddenly set free. Whether this is true or not, alongside Ricochet and Keira, who were like little conduits of calm, that period of lockdown while my spine healed had somehow brought me closer to enlightenment and a sense of eternalisation – which for me was a revolution of discovery.

Of course, at its most literal, eternalisation is perceived by most as the everlasting existence of matter and immortality, but more importantly for me, in the philosophical and spiritual sense, eternalisation is tapping into the universal, unified oneness of everything – all beings, man and animal, and the natural world. In a nutshell, eternalisation is my attempt to explain 'the meaning of life' for myself – and if others don't agree, I'm OK with that, because it helps me to find some sense of meaning amid the madness of it all.

I'd had to find all of this out the hard way, but now I understand what eternalisation actually means for me day-to-day. Firstly, it's acquiescence without resistance – the letting go of all arrogant attachments of the ego, my self-image and my descriptors in the minds and mouths of other people. Secondly, it's an immutable belief that an everlasting legacy can't be achieved through just *living*, but rather only through *giving*. And finally, it's recognising that I am simply passing through; we are each part of a universal pure consciousness which we must embrace without fear of death, because like all things in nature, we are part of an eternal cycle of oneness. This epiphany of eternalisation has turned my midlife *crisis* into a mid-life *calm*.

All of us have this eternalisation within us, but we need to let go of habitual ways of thinking to find it. Pain had opened my mind to meditation, and without all of the pain I would never have been motivated to look or to seek to change. So, through this process I have become grateful for everything – even the pain, both physical and emotional. Deirdre gave me the key, and Ricochet and Keira turned that key which opened the door to eternity for me.

I am very much a novice, but thus far even my baby steps to tap into the oneness of consciousness that pervades all things have resulted in less anxiety, less attachment to what other people think, less ego-indulgence, reduced blood pressure and less pain in my skeleton. If even I can overcome my intrinsic cynicism about what I thought of as airy-fairy mumbo jumbo then maybe anyone can re-evaluate the preconceptions that can bar us from eternalisation. Thankfully, life had also given me many blessings to help me on the way, and I could still move and operate after what could have been a life-ending accident and probable coronavirus infection. I am a very lucky man. Now I felt that life wanted to open me up to the possibility of the end of what had gone before and to the beginning of something more meaningful, fulfilling and better. Even death itself no longer holds the kind of sub-liminal fear that most of us, including me, try really hard not to think about.

At the time of writing, the coronavirus pandemic is a cruel daily reminder of life's fragility and has shown just how rap-idly the reality we cling to so tightly can be replaced with nerve-racking uncertainty. It has also shown us beyond doubt that we are all one in fighting this virus and in working to-gether towards what has been called a 'new normal' we could never have imagined. Actually, I think it's likely that our way of living and working might never be the same again – it's a new dawn for all of us. Perhaps the irony of isolation may be that through enforced social distancing, we might actually become closer to our fellow man than ever before. Perhaps it will teach us that, regardless of religion, colour, sexuality, nationality or politics, the virus doesn't care, even if we do, and that we have far more in common than ever drove us apart. We can only hope that once the fight against the virus is won, the lessons of togetherness, kindness and the public sense of collective moral responsibility we felt during corona-virus lockdown will become part of our new dawn.

I too have found my own new dawn by embracing the en-lightenment of being present in the silence with the animals. For forty years I've been so mired in my own little personal bubble of stress that I couldn't hear or see beyond the su-perficial maelstrom to grasp what really mattered. Whether or not I ever fully master transcendental meditation, what I absolutely do know is that I have discovered a form of medi-tation with the animals that I intuitively knew was there all along, but I never truly realised its importance or tapped into it as a cure for my troubled thoughts. It's a magnificent blessing that I have finally discovered what has been in plain sight all along – just spending a little time sitting quietly beside Keira, Ricochet and all the amazing patients I care for, seeking my own path to some kind of inner silence of pure consciousness. I think that's where eternalisation lies for me and that it's only there that I'll find any answers at all.

It is the pure consciousness of oneness that fuels what I do every day with every animal I treat, and also my belief that One Medicine is the best way forward for both veterinary and human medicine. I hope that some collaboration for the greater good can happen soon. It's the single biggest reason that I have for making *The Supervet*. Now, for the first time, people consistently see techniques and procedures performed on animals that historically have been considered the domain of human surgeons only. Importantly they also see the techniques that have innovated using stem cells and bionic implants to improve function and quality of life in the animals I treat. I think that people may begin to question, even at a subconscious level, whether human patients could have these treatments routinely too. This might just mark a turning point in respect and cooperation for the greater good between doctors and vets. I certainly hope so.

A few years ago I founded a charity called The Humanimal Trust which aims to educate, share ideas, change policy and fund projects investigating diseases that affect both humans and animals. The Humanimal Trust will not support any study that takes an animal's life and focuses on funding five related but distinct areas of research, which have formed the pillars of my endeavours from the beginning of my veterinary career – infection and antibiotic resistance, bone and joint disease, stem cell regeneration, brain and spinal disease, and cancer. I can only hope that this work will make a real and tangible difference to all of these areas in the coming years.

I am hugely grateful to the fantastic board of trustees, the staff, and all of the amazing volunteers of the Trust for doing their very best each and every day to make things better for animals and for medicine generally.

If there was ever a time we might recognise the commonality of infection in animals and humans it should be now after Covid-19. The same resistant bacteria that ultimately resulted in the euthanasia of Mac and Rocco, and could still prove to bring the demise of Odin, has also resulted in amputation and death for many humans. The same degenerative joint disease affecting Scrumpy, Tala, Jen and Millie makes life utterly miserable for millions of humans too. Ruben, Olive, Scrumpy, Mac, Odin and myself all had or have variants of spinal disc disease which could and should be studied side by side, if only the human and veterinary medical communities would listen. Most of us, at some time in our lives, will either suffer ourselves or have a family member who suffers from osteoarthritis, spinal disease or cancer. The Humanimal Trust has already funded studies seeking to identify circulating blood biomarkers that might detect prostate or bone cancer sooner, allowing earlier treatment and hopefully longer survival. The parallels between human and animal cancers are undeniable, and of course all of us could potentially benefit from regenerative stem cell medicine. One Medicine makes sense, but doesn't yet make money in the same way as the conventional pipeline for drugs and implants, so I have a real sense of urgency to show how the future of medicine within a more compassionate framework is viable and how the need for financial profit can also be satisfied.

Of course, even if studying disease in nature may be a more optimal, accurate and sustainable way forward, the only way to make One Medicine really happen is to show drug and implant companies that they can make the same or more money by treating naturally occurring disease rather than experimental disease. In a handful of projects, mainly in the United States, some types of naturally occurring osteosarcoma in dogs have been treated in a prospective clinical trial which has helped those dogs and will also help humans with the same disease. In this way, both species tackle cancer side by side. The reason that dogs are very helpful as a model for disease before human trials is that they have a metabolic rate and physiology more closely resembling humans than rats or mice. After removal of the primary tumour, companion dogs with natural cancer rather than dogs with experimentally induced cancer were treated using a genetically modified strain of bacteria that can penetrate cells and is programmed to upregulate immune cells that can kill metastatic tumour cells. This drug might have considerably prolonged Spud's or Dennis's life. I would like to see this model of cooperation become the norm rather than the exception.

On the day I fell down the stairs, operations had been scheduled for two human amputee patients to receive the most recent iteration of PerFiTS limb amputation prostheses to which skeleton-anchored bionic limbs could be attached to restore their independence and freedom. I had been scheduled to be in theatre alongside human surgical colleagues so that, as a team, we could share the lessons we have learned, both good and bad, from the past decade of use of the implant in animals, so that human patients may benefit too. This would have been a world-first example of One Medicine in action with these kinds of implants – animal and human doctors side by side sharing information for the greater good. Sadly, the surgeries had been cancelled several days earlier anyway for logistical reasons, and since then Covid-19 has interrupted the elective surgery schedule for most hospitals. I am really hopeful that one day soon this long-planned collaboration may finally happen.

For me both the literal and spiritual meanings of 'eternalisation' are reflected in my aspirations for One Medicine and for 'oneness' of our world when coronavirus is eventually conquered. In the literal sense, I will not achieve everlasting existence, nor do I want to, but I would dearly love if veterinary and human medicine re-converged on a common path that was everlasting. In the philosophical sense, I hope and pray that in a post-corona world we might continue to recognise our sense of universal oneness for man, animal and the natural world. My most profound desire is that the lessons we've learned about our connectedness with our fellow man through our enforced isolation might extend to all creatures on the planet. However, even as I write, it seems that the world is returning to its old ways and I worry that we'll instead continue on our insular and self-isolating path as a species. I fear that we may not have really listened to anything the universe has been telling us at all about eternalisation – but I really hope I'm wrong.

'Ar scáth a chéile a mhaireann na daoine' is an old Gaelic proverb which literally means 'people live in each other's shadows', but has come to reflect our mutual interdependence and how we are 'all in it together', a phrase that echoed in every clap for the NHS outside every home in the UK in recognition of our gratitude to those who care for us. We realised, I think, that we need to care for each other. I hope this sense of community lives on. During my isolation, I too learned that asking for help was the only way forward, and the bravest thing I could do, because I couldn't achieve any of my dreams on my own and I certainly couldn't seek any kind of inner peace. As one in togetherness, sharing, giving and caring, we humans can actually achieve greatness, if only we'd try. I hope we're not too late.

During lockdown, Ricochet, Keira and the enduring legacies of animals like Spud and Dennis have all paved the way for my journey of self-discovery. So too did the implosion of my emotions and body, the discovery of silent meditation with animals, and the realisation that working all the time wouldn't fulfil my dreams. Instead I now accept that working smarter while taking time out to look after myself and not crashing in the process just might give me enough years to make One Medicine a reality in my lifetime.

I've learned that eternalisation is not about the everlasting, because everything is transient except love – so for me it is letting go and embracing a peaceful oneness, which I find with my animal friends. This is the symphony of universal consciousness, as well as the Theory of Everything in physics – and I believe that it's reflected within each and every one of us. For my mammy Rita, eternalisation is also very much going back whence we came – dust. During my brief socially distanced visit to Ireland, I asked her if she believed in eternity. 'God is eternity and he is everywhere – especially in the dust,' she replied. I agree entirely and for me this is the stardust from which we all come and to which we all return – the eternal unified silence of all living things. Shining a light on this connectedness and looking after each other, man and animal, is how I'd like to spend the rest of my life.

As Mammy Rita sat in her chair in our sitting room, I read her the prologue of this book. I thought she was nodding off, dropping her chin lower and lower towards her chest, her breathing deepening as I read: '[. . .] *through the guidance of an animal's paw I travelled many journeys of enlightenment;*

a bit too late, I had the greatest awakening of my life.' I paused to see if she was listening and, all of a sudden, she lifted her head, turned towards me, looked right at me and said quite calmly, but urgently, as if she really needed me to hear the words: 'It's never too late, Noel. It's never too late.'

The Beginning

I woke up to the gentle bopping of Ricochet's paw on my forehead. As my arms reached out reflexively to embrace him, I thought of Morrissey, Russell and his family and said a little prayer for them in my head. I got up and raised the blackout drape that I need to sleep through the dawn when I've worked late into the night. I leaned forward and looked out. Through the curtains I could see the low morning cloud wrinkling the edges of the sky, frowning at the treetops and wondering whether to rain over Guildford. The sun briefly peeped through then slipped back again, tentative and unsure, as if it knew that the day could go either way – happy or sad, drizzle or brilliant blue skies. Ricochet jumped up onto the windowsill and said 'Buurrrph' to the day, then rose up on his back legs, thrust his nose up to meet mine and threw his furry mitts onto my chin.

During lockdown, with my broken neck in its brace, I spent more time at my house than I had done for twenty years, and had grown accustomed to the morning duel of cloud and sun over the thousand-year-old evergreen woods hugging the waking town. People just like me were getting up, minds consumed with transient everyday concerns which seem so big, and yet, in the enormity of time, are the blink of an eye. Keira looked up at me, her mind on breakfast, her backside shaking furiously and her hairy Border terrier tail tickling my feet.

That day in early April might indeed go either way, and not even Keira and Ricochet's habitually joyous wake-up greetings could lift my spirits. That day I didn't smile. I was still sad from Morrissey's passing and I was worried about Odin. It was my first day back operating after my accident and Odin was first on my list. That day, I prayed, could be the beginning of a great new chapter in his life and not the end of our beautiful friendship.

By the time I got the hairy twins in the car, I could feel a breeze on my face, which had resolved the temporary stand-off and blown the clouds away. The sun now radiated hazy rays of hope into the sky as I clipped Ricochet into his safety harness beside me in the front and Keira in the seat behind.

In Norse mythology, Odin was the wise 'Allfather', chief of the gods and father of Thor. Odin was believed to have many powers, including the ability to heal, shape-shift and to communicate with animals. Legend also had it that Odin never lost a battle. I was certainly hoping that, like his namesake, Odin the Doberman would have the power to heal after this next and final surgery and win the battle against his debilitating disease.

I parked the car where I always did – just twenty-five feet from the back door of the practice. I got out, stretched my neck backwards, winced a little, and took a deep breath of beautiful, fresh Fitzpatrick Referrals air. It was good to be back. This place was my sanctuary. I opened the back of the car and took out a large, heavy green bag, full of Ricochet poo from his litter tray for disposal. Master Ricochet always looked very self-satisfied as I went down on one knee to his tray and cleared up his daily offerings. Now he looked positively smug. I held the smelly sack at arm's length and headed over towards the poo-dumping destination, even managing a smile for the first time that day as I walked past Malcolm and Philip's trees. Then, as if out of nowhere, a ward auxiliary, Karen, was passing by and offered to dispose of it for me. She took the bag of poo like it was just the normal thing to do, with a flurry of efficiency that said, 'Good morning – good to have you back – I'll take that to make your load easier – thank you – and good day to you, sir!' Just this simple act of unsolicited kindness and help reminded me how wonderfully blessed I am to have such magnificent colleagues.

A short walk upstairs, Keira and Ricochet ensconced in 'their' office, and then to the preparation area where nurse Lauren and intern Nadine were waiting, ready for me to assess Odin before surgery. He was so happy to see his Uncle Noel and barked his head off, vigorously waggling his whole body as I examined him. I was terrified that the screws, which were loosening in his bone, might gouge out his damaged vertebra even more, so we had to hold him tightly since he was in pain and on the precipice of a disaster, as I too had been just weeks earlier. One shake too many and his vertebra could be fractured in exactly the same spot that mine had been.

Due to the social distancing requirements related to Covid-19, Anita and Mick couldn't come into the building to accompany Odin, but we had spoken regularly by phone and discussed the ethical implications of further surgery many times. Odin was otherwise fit, full of life and we all wanted to do the right thing for him, and our collective moral conscience would not have been at peace had we not tried. We all realised it could be the end for Odin, so Anita and Mick had been close to tears as they said goodbye and gave him one final cuddle outside in the car park.

I felt that Odin and I were kindred spirits, both with our respective neck problems. He was now a surgical emergency, so it was off with the neck brace and on with the scrubs for me. I needed to take prescription painkillers but Mr Crocker had authorised my return to work and I'd tried the previous week to build up my arm strength again at home, doing biceps and triceps exercises with shopping bags full of cans of beans. I would do whatever it took for my friend. Odin didn't have time to wait and there wasn't anyone else who could perform this surgery at that moment in time.

In the midst of the corona crisis, everyone was pulling together. One team on, one team off, alternating as we tried to get through those challenging early weeks of strict lockdown. We continued to look after and do our best for the animals in our care – animals who might die, become paralysed, or experience significant pain if we didn't take care of them. Some of our ventilators and patient monitors had been requisitioned for use in local hospitals and surgical disposables were in short supply. Disposable gowns were being rationed and we had reverted to reusable cloth gowns, which I hadn't seen since my days as a large animal vet. Every resource was being monitored, including the oxygen supplies we used during anaesthesia for our patients. The team moved like a well-oiled machine, with my stalwart colleague Brian managing the hospital, and my wonderful colleagues, surgeon Padraig and nurse Mhairi, coordinating the timetable and nursing arrangements. The sense of solidarity within the practice was tangible, with everyone doing their bit in every part of the organisation. I was very proud of them all.

Odin was anaesthetised. The CT scan showed we were just in time. The hole in the vertebra had worn through nearly to the spinal canal. I knew that the operation would be challenging. The team set to clipping hair and scrubbing skin. I lay on the bed beside my office, closed my eyes for a few minutes and repeated the mantra word. It was less like meditation and more like mediation with the god of biology; a kind of prayer for Odin to the universe. I got up and stretched, gingerly moving my head to the left and right, up and down, and then I was at the scrub sink.

As is always the case while I scrub, I ran through the surgical plan in my head; what could go wrong and how I might handle it. I suspected that the venous sinus in the base of the spinal canal would likely bleed as I cleared out the holes in the bone for grafting, but I still didn't know for sure if it was infection that was causing the ongoing loosening. I would need a bucketload of bone graft. I'd already taken bone marrow from the upper part of his humerus bones near the shoulders for use in the previous operations; this time I'd go for the pelvis and the knee. Graft had been taken from the wing of my pelvis (ilium) to fill cysts in my ankle bone, so Odin and I would have another thing in common. As shooting pain radiated down my arm, I wondered whether sometime soon a surgeon would operate on me in exactly the same way, cutting into my neck, pushing my trachea and oesophagus to one side and drilling into my vertebrae. If so, I hoped that my vertebrae would hold the implants better than Odin's had.

Odin was lying on his side as I cut down onto his ilium to harvest the graft. The ebb and flow of life, the endings and beginnings, are ever apparent to me when I perform surgery. Here the bone-forming (osteoprogenitor) stem cells which originated in the bone marrow would hopefully bring the hope of a new life for Odin by filling the holes in his neck vertebra. For us the process of life and death is shrouded in mystery – the elation of beginnings and the devastation of endings – but for biology, it's just business as usual. The graft would replace bone by osteoconduction facilitating ingrowth of bone, osteoinduction with growth factors forming new bone, and osteogenesis making new bone from the donor cells packed into the holes in Odin's vertebra – unless his greatest enemy, infection, stopped the healing process in its tracks.

Towards the end of the graft harvesting, the unthinkable happened for me. I could feel the urge to go to the toilet gradually becoming more urgent, bubbling and gurgling like a volcano in my belly and threatening to explode. I guess it was just the painkillers. Normally the autonomic nervous system of a surgeon kicks in as soon as we pick up a scalpel blade and the very thought of a bathroom visit is usually blocked out when I am in theatre. But for the first time in my career, my guts cramped – and my neck also cramped badly. Odin needed to be flipped from his side onto his back for the next stage of the operation, so thankfully I had a brief period of respite in which to leave the room, compose myself in the bathroom as necessary and scrub back in for the next stage as Nadine and the team prepared and draped his neck.

Revision surgeries aren't pleasant. The biological road map is disrupted by congealed scar tissue and anything can be stuck to anything. Dissection was challenging. Finally, I got in deep enough, removed the cement and the loose screws, then began the delicate task of pulling out any fibrous tissue that had formed a membrane around the holes in the bone. I couldn't see the edges or bottom of the cavities because the inside of the vertebra continuously oozed blood, so it was surgery by Braille – gently scooping and coaxing the fibrous tissue out of the hole while trying desperately not to perforate the eggshell-thin layer of bone which was all that separated my instruments from the blood-filled venous sinuses of the spinal canal.

Then it happened! A sudden geyser of bubbling blood erupted from the depths of the hole, gushing out what seemed like an ocean in the space of a few seconds. I could feel Nadine's hands tighten around the retracting devices and heard an audible gasp as the blood completely obliterated our view of the operating site. Fortunately, I knew this could happen and within a couple of seconds I had scooped the first big dollop of graft from the bowl and pushed it into the hole, my little finger delving deep into the pool of blood. I needed to pack it in tight enough to stop the bleeding and right down to the base of the hole so that it would heal properly, but just enough. If it went through the base of the hole and into the spinal canal, a mound of bone graft could compress the spinal cord and then Odin would be back to square one. Beneath the obscuring blood, it was a matter of blind judgement and stealth.

I had experienced the compliance of bone graft innumerable times before and therefore I know what it feels like as one presses it against solid bone, and so I packed it in until I could sense that I'd filled the hole with just the right amount of pressure. The blood stopped and we suctioned out the excess. Nadine and I could breathe again. I looked at Lauren who was running anaesthesia, cool as a cucumber as always. Everything was stable. The graft had saved the day – the beginning of new life snatched from the gaping jaws of death. I finished packing graft in and around the vertebral body, and did what else I needed to do to shore it up. As the levels of adrenaline and painkiller pumping through my body subsided, my neck pain kicked back in with a vengeance. As I stitched everything up, I whispered to Odin that this was the beginning and not the end, and then I shuffled, hunchbacked, upstairs to my office to wait for the CT scan. I stretched my neck slowly, wondering if I would ever operate without pain again, then held my breath as the first of the images came through; would the holes in the vertebra be filled and would the bone be thick enough to support the weight of Odin's neck? Thankfully, it all looked good. I called Anita and Mick, who were profoundly grateful. Sadly, soon afterwards we confirmed that he did indeed have a blood-borne infection with a multi-drug-resistant organism, methicillin-resistant *Staphylococcus pseudintermedius* (MRSP), which was Odin's greatest enemy (just as it had been for Mac). It was possible that this tiny bacterium could stay somewhere in his system forever, and that this could still spell the end, even for one of the gods among dogs.

That night I badly needed to get to my bed, but just before midnight when I finally finished work I went down to see Odin in the wards. He was sitting up. He was delighted to see me as he had been earlier that morning. His old-man-young-boy bark came out more like a squeak, however, because Uncle Noel had been pushing his windpipe around earlier in the day. I sat with him and gave him a cuddle for a few minutes, contemplating just how close we had both come to death and feeling very grateful for second chances. When I started out with *The Supervet* in the first place I just wanted to make veterinary medicine better than when I started and to give animals a fair deal. Sitting there with Odin I knew we had done just that – which in that moment was the only thing that mattered.

Doing my very best for every animal was always the goal, but looking back I recognise that in my early career I sought the respect of my peers in my lectures and publications – which is normal enough, as it is for any young surgeon starting out, but was for me possibly also fuelled by a perpetual lack of self-worth and imposter syndrome, partly because I wasn't deemed good enough for an internship or residency training, and partly because everyone wants to be 'accepted'. I also think that because my own father had never been one to hand out praise, all along there has been a certain yearning for a father figure in my profession; Daddy Sean had never said, 'Well done,' even if he had thought it. In hindsight I guess this turned out to be a good thing because it made me seek out teachers and mentors and to always be willing to learn with humility and without arrogance, knowing I was only as good as my next operation. I've since realised that what people inside or outside of my profession think of me won't actually fix an animal and that the ego of achievement is a comfortable trap, no more or less than my own craven indulgence. No amount of plumping up my ego will help any of my patients at all. Knowledge is essential – but self-importance does not a legacy build.

In recent years I have come to recognise that 'fame in men's mouths' is typically a futile goal in itself – a cup from which you can drink forever and never feel satisfied. I have realised that the only point of a scientific paper or lecture is if it has impact – by helping a colleague or the patients that they treat, human or veterinary – and that by giving rather than receiving, the gain is multiplied a million times.

I believe this is generally true in life for all of us too. I think we all struggle sometimes to be 'accepted', 'respected' and 'acknowledged', but the reality is that if I can inspire people like Lauren and Nadine, use my knowledge to help them in their careers, and help Odin live a better life, there is no greater reward. Nowadays, I'd rather someone gave me a hug of solidarity than any slap on the back or accolade. It is for future generations of vets and vet nurses that I question the status quo and tell the stories of Odin and Hermes – and for future patients that may benefit from the lessons I have learned along the way.

I'll continue to do my best to be a positive role model for people both inside and outside my profession. The complaints made against me in relation to Hermes had bruised me so deeply because they questioned my integrity and my judgement regarding his care in suggesting that I had 'engaged in a behaviour or activity that would be likely to bring the profession into disrepute or undermine public confidence in the profession'. That's why in this book I have focused on *integrity* and *care* above all else. I was even more hurt by some of the statements in the written complaints that, because *The Supervet* was on television, I had *more* responsibility than any other vet and that *someone* needed to be made *an example of* to counter what they saw as overtreatment of patients by the profession – and that person was me.

The large white envelope with the official RCVS lettering marked 'Private and Confidential' – mail that no veterinary surgeon ever wishes to receive – finally arrived on the morning that I called Jacquie, the mum of Dennis, the bull mastiff, to let her know his ashes were back for collection. Once I had read the letter, I called Helen, Hermes' mum, to let her know the adjudication. Both Jacquie and Helen's vocations were in caring for critically ill people, and I felt that they had an implicit understanding of the ethical implications of holding on to a patient too long for selfish reasons. Speaking to each of them that day, we again touched base with our consciences. We talked about knowing in our hearts that we had done our best to fashion a new beginning for Dennis and Hermes, even though our efforts had failed. In the same way, Anita, Mick and I knew that while challenges remained with Odin because of infection, or for other reasons outside our control, we knew that we were doing our very best for him. Like Hermes and Dennis, Odin had a zest for living. Each and every one of these families would do it all over again. However, the issue that arose for Hermes did not begin with my client, it began with members of my own profession.

The RCVS has a moral and legal responsibility to take disciplinary action against a veterinary surgeon if he or she is guilty of serious professional misconduct. If deemed not fit to practise, then that person's name is removed from the register of veterinary surgeons – they are 'struck off' or suspended for a period of time. If there is a realistic prospect of the allegations against the veterinary surgeon being deemed to amount to serious professional misconduct, and if it is in the public interest for the case to be ruled by a public hearing before the disciplinary committee, then the Preliminary Investigation Committee (PIC) are honour-bound to press for that hearing. The complaint against me was with the PIC for fourteen months.

With Hermes' best interests in all our hearts and minds, I had been tasked with providing him with three bionic limbs, because I was the only person who at that point in time had the knowledge and experience to do so. I did this to the best of my abilities, with the fully informed consent of his loving and knowledgeable guardian, and in cooperation with his exotics-exclusive primary care practice, a specialist colleague and my team of veterinary professionals. The committee felt that the previous experience, nursing background and desire of Helen to proceed with treatment were *not considered sufficient* justification. They felt that euthanasia for Hermes should not just have been discussed, as it was on many occasions, but it should, in fact, have been definitively recommended as the *best* option for Hermes, regardless of Helen's wishes. In the PIC's opinion the collective views of Helen, myself and the large team of veterinary clinicians involved in Hermes' procedure were likely erroneous and highly subjective.

The committee felt that I was *personally* responsible for all of his treatment, both before and after he was seen by me, even though I couldn't have seen him sooner and I had no control over how long it took for infection to resolve. The PIC asserted that the quality of life during his recovery should have been considered independently of his predicted longevity of forty-five years, and that this recovery time was 'too long'. They did not, however, specify how long was 'too long' or how much treatment was 'too much treatment' for a tortoise.

The PIC wrote that they recognised that there were disparate views in my profession with regard to my actions, with a body of opinion who felt that my conduct had fallen below the expected standard and others who honestly felt that my conduct was in fact appropriate. They commented that my care and attention were probably well intended, diligent and directed at relevant aspects and sound principles of analgesia, wound care, antibiosis and nutritional support, but despite this they felt that I had failed my patient and my profession. Their view, therefore, was that my conduct had been suboptimal in relation to making health and welfare my first consideration for Hermes, that I did not provide veterinary care that was adequate or appropriate, and that I had engaged in an activity that would be likely to bring the profession into disrepute or undermine public confidence in the profession. In conclusion, however, they acknowledged that there was no realistic possibility of proving that I had not communicated with other veterinary surgeons to ensure health and welfare in relation to ethical considerations, and they did not consider that my conduct fell so far below the standard as to constitute serious professional misconduct. They closed the case.

While I was relieved the case was over and I absolutely respected the authority of the RCVS, and indeed empathised with the views of the complainants from their perspective of ethics, I remain deeply concerned regarding this assessment of my actions. This is no longer from my own perspective, since, with much help, I've come to terms with the personal pain over the past twenty-two months, and in my heart I know I did what I felt was the right thing to do; it's rather a concern for the next generation of vets who need crystal-clear guidelines on what constitutes *overtreatment* and whether, in trying their best, their licence to practise could be revoked if a complaint was upheld against them, even in the absence of either a centralised ethics adjudication platform or clear, unequivocal written rules that are transparent for the profession and the public – equivalent for all vets and all animals, whether they are on TV or not, or whether in primary care or specialist referral practice. It is also of concern to me that if the views of the legal guardian are to be overridden, then a robust legal framework between the veterinary profession and the public needs to be figured out – to protect the vet against the reaction of the client, and to protect the client in the event of a judgement against their wishes. I wouldn't want vets like Nadine or guardians like Helen to be penalised just for loving too much. If the rules are clear then it's fair for all. That's what I hope is the legacy of Hermes.

The white envelope could have been consigned to a drawer somewhere, but I strongly believe that the *end* of this case is just the *beginning* of a dialogue, which in my opinion needs to happen in order to make veterinary medicine better for all animals, their guardians and vets. There need to be clear rules of engagement, with *integrity* and *care*, the central themes of this book, at the core of this endeavour. While I appreciate that it is difficult to provide hard and fast rules and that decisions on whether to attempt surgery or decide on euthanasia are, by necessity, patient and condition specific, I feel strongly that greater clarity must be found so that no vet need ever again go through the anxiety and sadness that a claim may bring. This discussion – and the actions that will be needed to bring about change – demand honesty, absolute transparency and total commitment. To create real and lasting change, one has to lay it all on the line and risk losing it all. I don't know what that might mean for you in your life, but for me it means a real change in our respect for the animal kingdom, real fairness for our animal friends, and real progress for veterinary medicine, including a mutual respect for human and animal medicine such that One Medicine may thrive. Change will happen anyway, but real progress is optional.

When the red admiral butterfly comes to collect my stardust, I would prefer to have left on good terms with my profession and in the knowledge that I have inspired others

411

to be their best. But unless we start this open and honest conversation right now, the big ethical questions at the heart of this book will remain unanswered long after I have stopped operating. As a symptom of this ongoing debate, during the recent broadcast of *The Supervet Revisited* on Channel 4, featuring some of my patients and the outcomes of their surgeries several years later, a vet on social media questioned whether it was ethical for a dog to have two custom knee replacements, even though the patient was running around happily with an excellent quality of life five years later, having been unable to walk previously for many months following multiple failed standard procedures. The more general social media response was one of joy for animal-loving families across the post-corona-lockdown land. My view is that the public and my profession need to engage in an honest and long-overdue dialogue about what we really want for the animals that we love and have entrusted to our care.

I have been emotionally raw throughout the months since November 2018 when I first received the letter from the RCVS – but through this journey I have healed. I hope I have become a stronger, more self-compassionate, less ego-invested and more empathetic human being. I know my truth and I am answerable only to my truth. You are too. I have learned that we can all build ourselves stronger with a little help from our friends. The Latin verb *recrudescere* means to 'become raw again', and I think we all need to experience this if we want to realise profound change and a new beginning. If the veterinary profession wants to retain the trust of the families of animals and to navigate the challenges and opportunities that come from medical innovation, we are going to need to have honest and difficult conversations – to be willing to 'become raw again' – and to open ourselves to the possibility of allowing the public to be more involved in making decisions regarding what is best for the welfare of the animals we all love. All veterinary professionals recognise the importance of listening when it comes to taking a clinical history and understanding the concerns of the families who bring their animals to us each and every day, and of course we remain the staunchest advocates of the animal. In this context, while we must never abdicate our responsibility to ensure the welfare of the animals in our care, I believe that as a profession we need to be better at listening to the perspectives of the people who live with and love those animals as integral family members. It's vital that we get the balance right with regard to the boundaries of what is and isn't acceptable as 'appropriate treatment' as opposed to 'overtreatment'. Ultimately, it's about doing the right thing for our animal friends and giving them a fair deal. We are all partners in this shared endeavour – let's help each other to be the best we can be and to answer to our truth together.

Sadly, not long after I received the RCVS adjudication, I faced many of the exact same dilemmas with Odin. After his third operation, his MRSP infection returned and caused all kinds of problems, including eating away another one of his vertebrae. Anita, Mick and I again considered whether we should put him through yet another surgery. Had Odin been a human patient, there would be no question we would operate again. The original objective had been achieved – stabilisation of his vertebrae and alleviation of pressure on his spinal cord – so we felt justified in operating one last time. We removed the hardware, placed more bone graft and antibiotic beads into the infected sites and administered intravenous antibiotics. Odin hasn't looked back since. His old-man-young-boy bark, announcing his new beginning to the world, is as loud as ever. The god Odin still hasn't lost a battle. His infection could possibly return, but now that the implants have done their job and have been removed, it's unlikely. He is as happy as the day is long and so are Mick and Anita. Though I did the very best I could for them financially, they sold their wedding rings to help pay for his treatment. They told me that a golden ring representing their love was superfluous because their boy Odin was all the love they could ever want in the world.

Keira and Ricochet have given me all the love in the world. There are times when I still feel like I'm that little boy in the cold night of a cattle shed on a farm in Ireland and I cannot talk to anybody because they would not understand. Back then I talked to Pirate the farm dog. Now I talk to my best friends, Keira and Ricochet. When the darkness of the world is closing in and I'm in bits, I lie on my bed with Ricochet or Keira, or both of them by my side. Their unconditional love glues me back together again so that I wake up the next day a little bit healed, ready once more to pick up the pieces for all the other animals and people I care for. They give me the strength to be 'enough' as I am, allowing others a path to wherever they need to get to without anyone noticing the cracks in my crazy paving. I am happy to try to point people and animals in the right direction – I just sometimes need to be careful not to let people walk all over me or to make a wrong turn. All the while I have been made whole again by the love of these two animals who have saved my life.

Keira was by my side as I fell into darkness and sadness after the professional complaint and both she and Ricochet sat close as I acquiesced to the consequences of breaking my neck in an accident that could easily have taken my life. For the first time in my life I was still and let their light in, and with it came an awakening and letting go of everything I had held on to as my identity for so long. I became free and open to a new beginning in the end.

Every time I drew close to the edge of the cliff in my mind, there was a giant Maine Coon paw to not only grab me by the collar and drag me back up again, but also to snap me out of my rumination and force me to get over myself. He unceremoniously roused me from huddled self-pity, made me stand tall and walk again in the right direction. But it was Keira with her wise old head who really steadied my feet and kept me on track. From the very beginning of Fitzpatrick Referrals she has been with me every single step of the way, through all the ups and downs, loyal, steadfast, a singular constant through the vagaries of my personal and professional life. Every day she's with me at work, we have the same routine. Now that she is deaf and a bit blind with cataracts, I get out of bed and I lay my hands on her gently to wake her. She opens her eyes, sees Daddy, rolls on her back and I rub her tummy. Then she yawns while doing that 'cute thing' with her paws over her eyes. When the eye-rubbing is done, she skips out of her little bed, waggles her bottom and tail, and greets the day with a smile and a skip in her step. She never ceases to make me happy. I love her more than I can describe – a deep connectedness that I can only feel and can't adequately express.

Keira was thirteen years old on 16 September 2020. We had a wonderful snuggle before lights out, with her snoring beside my bed. As I kissed her on the top of her head, she licked my chin and I felt a profound sense of calm and peace that she was my anchor, my rock and the love of my life. She kept me safe day and night. We slept soundly.

Two nights later I was holding her limp head in my arms not knowing if she would live another hour.

On the evening of 18 September 2020, it was the same routine as very many Friday nights when usually we would get to go home having slept at the practice during the week. I was leaving the building as I always did by the back door. I was carrying a box under my left arm, so I opened the door with my right hand, holding it open with my foot long enough for Keira to skip through after me, again as she always did. I never had her on a lead at that time because we had our routine – I would hold the door for her ladyship and she'd go through, across the driveway to have a pee by the bushes, and then would wait patiently for Dad to open the car, pop her on her blanket, strap her in and off we'd go home.

My car was no more than twenty-five feet away in the car park, and I was halfway across the driveway when lights came around the corner of the building to my left at great speed. It all happened so fast that I still find it hard to believe that it happened at all. I screamed and put my arms in the air, throwing the box to one side. 'Stop, stop!' Within a single second the van was upon me. I have no idea what speed he was doing, but it was too fast. The driver saw nothing at all – not me, not Keira. I lunged backwards and in that same split second saw Keira tootle in her usual way past me to my left. I lurched forwards again to try to grab her, but it was too late; I could not have been more than two feet away from the front-right wheel as she instinctively crouched down, me grabbing for her. She didn't see or hear anything until it was too late. I grasped frantically for any part of her, finally reaching her head. I heard the cracking and ripping of bones breaking and flesh tearing as she screamed. I screamed. She bit down hard on the thumb and fingers of my right hand. I screamed more – not because of my hand, but because she was motionless. I thought that the van's tyre had driven right over her back end and for sure she was dead.

I screamed and screamed. 'No, no, no, no, no, no . . . Aaaaaaaaaaaaaaaaa . . . no, no, no, no, please God, no!'

The delivery van screeched to a halt, and one of my colleagues, intern Cristina, ran across the yard to help me. I bundled her limp body in my arms and within seconds was in the preparation area of the practice, yelling for help. Within another few seconds there were at least ten people flocking around, pulling in the crash trolley, holding her, holding me, immediately swinging into action – one clipping for intravenous access, another listening for a heartbeat, another getting a heating blanket wrapped around her, and yet another drawing up drugs. My colleague Padraig Egan was on duty and immediately took control of the situation – everyone coordinated and each with a job to do. I was trembling and crying uncontrollably. Padraig gently put his hand on my shoulder and told me to step back from the table. Intern Lisa and resident Joana held me up as I sobbed in deep shock and looked on helplessly as resident Diogo and the intern and nurse did their best. I was a liability. I was no good to her, and no good to the team. I just stood there mumbling, crying, shaking – I thought that my baby Keira was dying and this was the end.

All kinds of things went through my head. The cracking sound was unmistakable, there would be broken bones, but would her spine be broken? Would she ever walk again? Would her insides be ruptured – bladder, guts, kidneys, liver or lungs? Would she be bleeding internally? Or would she die from shock immediately or soon? My entire life, and Keira's entire life, flashed in front of me. My first instinct was to try to squeeze her toes to see if she could move, just as I had checked for myself when I fell down the stairs, but Padraig quite rightly held me back. We needed to get painkillers and intravenous fluids on board and get her stabilised – diagnostic tests could follow. I was getting in the way and Padraig gently nudged me to one side. Looking back, I can only imagine how I would have felt, having a highly distressed and emotional 'client' getting in the way of me trying to do my job for their friend.

I was still shaking with fear as the team took her to X-ray and then to the CT scanner. If I hadn't stepped back from the path of the van I could have been killed – but could I have stopped it and prevented it from crushing her? I didn't know – probably not – too many ifs. If only I hadn't taken the emergency call from a worried client; if only I hadn't gone to kiss my surgical patient in the wards because I'd grown very fond of him; if only Keira hadn't for some unknown reason stopped on the stairs halfway down and then sat there in the stairwell for two seconds too long; if only my reactions had been quicker. I'd done the same little walk to the car with Keira thousands of times . . . If only, if only – if only I could save my baby now.

Finally, Keira was resting peacefully, stabilised on a cocktail of drugs, while we all huddled around the image viewer, scouring every nook and cranny of the scans. By then her mummy Amy and her brother Kyle had turned up and were just as distressed as I was. Her pelvis was crushed with multiple fractures and she had separated the ilium of her pelvis from her sacrum dramatically on the right and a bit on the left. There were possibly also fissures in the sacrum and she had dislocated her right hip joint. I was scared. Very scared. However, because any internal organ damage and haemorrhage was potentially life-threatening, now wasn't the time to focus on how many fractures – they could be dealt with later. Tears in her internal organs weren't visible on the initial scans, but we couldn't be sure at that stage. She had remained motionless throughout and was profoundly shocked, so anaesthetising her for further tests at that point was ill-advised. We'd need to stabilise her vital functions and monitor for any internal damage that might become apparent over the next few vital hours. I would need to leave her in the care of my team who would sit by her side all night long. I felt useless, helpless and like the ten-year-old child that wasn't strong enough or clever enough to save the lamb. I would lie down and try to sleep. I would let the team do what they are highly skilled at doing and I would trust them with my baby. I would acquiesce to circumstance and do my best, as Keira had taught me to do. That's what she would expect. We would take further scans and review her status as soon as it was safe to do so. My phone would be on standby at my pillow.

I went home to Ricochet, holding on to the only two good things – I had managed to grab her head away from the van and when she had bitten down on my hand that was a good sign, I hoped, since maybe at least her brain was spared. Secondly, she was at a fast-response trauma centre within one minute of her accident, so she could not have been treated more quickly.

Unfortunately, when I arrived back at the practice the following morning she was no better and remained critical. Padraig sent me to A&E to get a tetanus jab and some antibiotics for my hand. The last time I'd been there was the night I could have been killed by my fall down the stairs, and this time, but for a split second, I could have been killed by the van. None of us think about how quickly the lights can be switched off or it would drive us mad, and the driver didn't see a thing even though the driveway was fully lit like a city street. What shocked me most was how fast he was travelling so that there was no time to react. It was all over in the blink of an eye. And now my beautiful girl was critical and might die. I sat in A&E still mute with shock.

By the time I came out of the hospital, Padraig was on the phone telling me she was going downhill and I needed to get back to the practice. Although we couldn't see a tear in her soft tissues on the CT scan immediately after the trauma, Padraig and I suspected that she may have urine leaking into her abdomen from a tear in one of the ureters, the urinary bladder, the urethra, or even the kidneys themselves. Padraig slowly and delicately passed a needle into her abdominal cavity and confirmed our suspicions – there was urine leaking from somewhere. By the time I got back to the practice, it was clear to both of us that she was getting worse – rapidly. As I stroked her head, her breathing was becoming laboured and I was overwhelmed with fear. She seemed to be getting worse by the minute. Nobody could have seen this coming.

We responded immediately and I called our Oncology and Soft Tissue surgery hospital, which was fully equipped for all soft tissue surgery emergencies including internal organ damage. Within minutes they had mobilised a team and, in a few more minutes, Keira was on intern Mario's knee in my car. Fifteen minutes later she was on another examination table in their preparation area. Resident Andi and nurse Meg leapt into action straight away. Monitors on, samples taken, shock protocol initiated. Within a few more minutes, surgery specialist Jonathan Bray walked into the preparation area with his radiologist wife Sharyn, who is a radiologist and would operate the CT scanner. Keira's condition was now critical. Toxic shock was setting in and she would soon die if we didn't act fast. We tried to stabilise her with more drugs and intravenous fluids, then induced anaesthesia and within the hour she was in the scanner. Sharyn performed a special imaging sequence with contrast injected first into her bloodstream to check if her kidneys were working and then into her urethra to see where the leak might be. It was bad news.

The impact had ruptured her urinary bladder and had ripped the lining of her abdomen – her peritoneum – off the muscles on the underside of her spine. The differences between the two CT scans less than eighteen hours apart were like night and day. She was bleeding internally with hundreds of small severed blood capillaries in her peritoneum and her abdomen was full of toxic urine. She would die if Jon didn't operate immediately. I trust Jon implicitly, and like Laurent with Ricochet's surgery, though I have performed abdominal surgery frequently in my early career, I do not have Jon's skill set as a soft tissue surgeon and I was never more grateful for super-specialism and for our amazing team. Jon opened up her abdomen and, as her guts poured out into his hands and urine flowed out over the sides of her belly, I left the room. I was in bits and crying, and that was the last thing Jon needed. Seeing Keira splayed out on the table with all of her abdominal organs exposed was just too much for me. Jon did an amazing job, stitching the tear in her urinary bladder and reattaching her peritoneum back onto the muscles under her spine – and I was beyond thankful for his skill. On that day, at least, he saved Keira's life.

For the next three days she remained critical. We gave her blood and plasma transfusions to make up for the blood lost into her abdomen and to provide her with protein for clotting and to boost her energy reserves. She had a drain tube coming out of the side of her abdomen, still sucking out any further leaking blood or fluid, and another tube going through her nose into her stomach to give her liquid food for sustenance.

The transfusion worked wonders and soon afterwards when she woke up from her opioid dreams she licked my face. It was midnight and for the first time since the accident, my tears were of joy rather than pain. But she was by no means out of the woods and the team, guided by Jon and also Gerard McLauchlan (who as well as being an interventional radiologist is also a specialist in internal medicine), did their best with various combinations of drugs to get her strong enough for me to try to fix her pelvis. This was all complicated by her having Cushing's disease, where her adrenal glands overproduce cortisol. Now she needed steroids to deal with her shock and heparin to stop clots forming, since an embolus could kill her too. It was complicated and it was all hands on deck 24/7. She wouldn't eat much and though we tried to supplement her energy with fluid food down her nasogastric tube, she regurgitated due to the residual effects of her abdominal trauma and then got inflammation in her nose (rhinitis), so that, on top of being frustrated and in pain because she couldn't stand, she had bad snuffles too. Poor little girl.

Until then, even with Ricochet's operation, I hadn't fully taken on board the heart-rending pain and gut-churning fear of my clients waiting on news of their loved one's progress, desperate to visit, desperate for a phone call, desperate for anything and terrified of the worst. My empathy and compassion took on a whole new meaning on a deeply personal level. Life for me as a veterinary surgeon would never be the same again. Her life was entirely in my hands and I couldn't delegate her surgery – because this absolutely was my field – and the moment that I had been training for all my life.

It was a delicate balance with the timing of the surgery, but I had to get her out of pain so we could wean her off the heavy cocktail of painkillers and get her eating without regurgitation and breathing without snuffling, and get movement back in her legs to reduce her limb swelling, which was getting worse. The big fear I had was aspiration pneumonia – if she regurgitated and inhaled some fluid or food, it could spell the end for her. We needed to do everything possible to get her up and about. She could not survive and have any function or quality of life as she was, and already, eight days after the initial trauma, tissues would be contracting and scars forming around her smashed pelvis and sciatic nerve. She could ill afford to lose any blood and we had another transfusion on standby. She was finally stable enough for me to operate.

On Sunday 27 September, we mobilised a fantastic team with nurses Mhairi, Lauren and Meg on anaesthesia and preparation, interns Mario, Lisa and Johnny assisting with surgery, theatre auxiliary Rosie sorting all the kit, radiologist Felicity on the scanner and my loyal colleague Padraig managing the team. We meticulously prepared for battle. Over the preceding days my wonderful engineer colleague Jay had designed a custom plate with me based on her CT scans which would exactly fit her fracture, and machinist John had stayed as many hours as it took to get it delivered on time. Junior engineer Verity made drill guides for the repair and Jay personally drove them to the practice the day before with a simple text: 'We are one big family, and that's what family do.' He was right, and Keira was my family too.

I stood in theatre, gowned, gloved and ready to go, took a deep sigh, pulled the lights into the operative field and picked up the scalpel blade. Unfortunately, the tissues around the pelvis and the bones themselves were much more severely damaged and aggressively displaced and snared in non-compliant tissue than I had hoped. I would normally have expected to fix the configuration of injuries that she had in about three hours – but when I got in there, I found all kinds of challenges that we couldn't judge from the scans. She ended up under anaesthesia for eight hours and ten minutes. It was a nightmare. But I had done my very best for my baby girl – we all had. In spite of the difficulty putting everything back together, she had lost hardly any blood and the anaesthetic went smoothly thanks to the team. I sat with her for a while in recovery as she breathed oxygen and slept on her mixture of painkillers. I kissed her on the forehead, and told her that I loved her very much. I couldn't sleep.

As I write this it's twenty-four hours after her surgery. I have just lain beside her in her little compartment in the wards. She woke up enough to lick my face. She knew Daddy was there, but her breathing was heavy and the light was gone from her eyes. I am terrified that she will get pneumonia, or that her trauma will be too much for her. I tried to stand her up, but she was so weak she just flopped down again. I wish I could say that she was able to walk, but she couldn't. I injected some liquid food through the tube we had placed in the oesophagus, in the side of her neck. She lay there and looked up at me, motionless and helpless. It's early days and I truly remain full of hope that the right thing will happen for my little girl. I pray that soon she will turn the corner and take her first step. Writing this book has been my first step to the next part of my life, a little wiser, and a little more accepting with humility for what may come my way.

I really do have faith that she will pull through and the end will be 'happily ever after' for as long as we have together. No matter what I've talked about in this book as having been an irksome inconvenience or major issue for me, none of it comes close to the fear of losing my little companion. Amy and Kyle, who have shared her with me these past thirteen years, are also devastated and my heart aches for them too. Yet accidents happen to anyone, anytime, anyplace and I am so grateful for what I do have every day – the people and animals I care about and the blessing to be able to save their lives as a surgeon like they have saved mine by looking after me when I most needed someone to talk to.

It would be easy to wrap up this book with a tidy bow of platitudes and comforting lessons we have learned together, but that's not real. Real life is full of frayed ends and discontinued sentences, and so too is my journey with Keira and with you. Life is not composed of straight lines. It doesn't divide into distinct chapters without overlap. It's messy and unpredictable, and sometimes we find ourselves at the end of our tether, clinging on for dear life. While the puppet strings of fate had often left me flailing before now, Keira's accident has been next-level trauma for me. I can't sleep again – so tonight I'm writing to you, because we print this book tomorrow.

At the outset when I wrote that 'the raw core of ourselves' is only accessed by the unconditional love of an animal, I thought I knew what that meant. I really hadn't actually felt that until now, I had only observed it. Now I know the pain of that rawness.

Through my journey with Keira and all the other animals

I have been lucky enough to know, I have learned that caring with all my heart and with integrity of purpose is the only way we can save anything at all – the life of a person or an animal, and even the survival of our planet itself. I wrote this book about how the *care* and *integrity* of animals saved my life because I hoped that it might help you too – vets, doctors, and all those who care about medicine and the animals inside their own homes and in the wider home of our planet too. I wrote it for you in your own life, wherever you are, whatever your story is, whatever you hope for and whatever you dream of. I'm profoundly grateful to all of the animals and their families who have allowed me to tell their stories, their hopes and their dreams to inspire all of us.

Keira has made me the very best I can be and saved me from the worst. I am so grateful for the love and the light she has shared with me and I pray with all my heart tonight that the light won't fade from her eyes for long. We are the light we shine into the world – for we are all made of stardust. All beings – man and animal – are made of the same stuff; it's what we choose to do with this 'stuff' that defines us and the light we leave behind. Sometimes we need to be broken and see the darkness in order to appreciate the light, as I have tried to share with you as openly as I can, so that the path might be a little brighter for you.

As I said at the outset, one night as a boy I looked up at the millions of lights puncturing the heavens and I felt like a worthless speck of dust. I no longer feel worthless and I now know the value of my dust. I have grown and I know my truth. I don't want you to ever feel worthless either, and I hope you find your truth too.

The universe arose as a singularity of oneness 13.8 billion years ago. Most of it is composed of dark matter, about which we know nothing at all. I don't think the 'truth is out there', I think the 'truth is in here' – inside us – each and every one of us. This book has been about the 'light matter' inside every animal I have met along the way. We need to look for this truth inside of them and inside ourselves and reflect that truth out into the world, taking care of each other – man and animal – as 'one' on the one and only planet we still have at this point in time amid the infinite stars of the galaxy. There has never been a greater need for this truth than now.

We do not know how this story will end.

We do not know how any story will end.

What I absolutely know for sure, though, is that Keira and I are one, just as in pure consciousness we are all one with the stardust whence we came and to which we shall return. We will always be one, she and I, and death will not separate nor diminish the light of our love. As Bono says in what I consider to be the greatest song ever written – 'We're one, but we're not the same. We get to carry each other.'

CREDITS

Trapeze would like to thank everyone at Orion who worked on the publication of *How Animals Saved My Life* in the UK.

Editor
Anna Valentine
Rose Davidson

Copy-editor
Ian Greensill

Proofreader
Lorraine Jerram

Editorial Management
Jo Whitford
Charlie Panayiotou
Jane Hughes
Claire Boyle
Shyam Kumar

Contracts
Anne Goddard
Paul Bulos
Jake Alderson

Audio
Paul Stark
Amber Bates

Design
Lucie Stericker
Joanna Ridley
Nick May
Clare Sivell
Helen Ewing

Finance
Jennifer Muchan
Jasdip Nandra
Ibukun Ademefun
Rabale Mustafa
Sue Baker
Tom Costello

Marketing
Brittany Sankey

Production
Katie Horrocks
Nicole Abel
Fiona McIntosh

Publicity
Francesca Pearce
Elaine Egan

Sales
Jennifer Wilson
Victoria Laws
Esther Waters
Lucy Brem
Frances Doyle
Ben Goddard
Georgina Cutler
Jack Hallam
Ellie Kyrke-Smith
Inês Figuiera
Barbara Ronan
Andrew Hally
Dominic Smith
Deborah Deyong
Lauren Buck
Maggy Park

Linda McGregor
Sinead White
Jemimah James
Rachel Jones
Jack Dennison
Nigel Andrews
Ian Williamson
Julia Benson
Declan Kyle
Robert Mackenzie
Imogen Clarke
Megan Smith
Charlotte Clay
Rebecca Cobbold

Operations
Jo Jacobs
Sharon Willis
Lisa Pryde

Rights
Susan Howe
Richard King
Krystyna Kujawinska
Jessica Purdue
Louise Henderson

Listening to the Animals
Becoming the Supervet

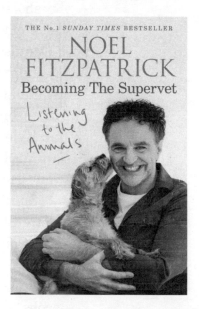

THE NO.1 *SUNDAY TIMES* BESTSELLER

World-renowned veterinary surgeon Professor Noel Fitzpatrick recounts his often-surprising journey to becoming 'the Supervet' in this inspiring and uplifting memoir.

From growing up on the family farm in rural Ireland, tending to the cattle and sheep with his beloved sheepdog Pirate by his side, to setting up Fitzpatrick Referrals in Surrey, one of the most advanced small animal specialist centres in the world, Noel has always listened to the many lessons the animals in his care have taught him.

As heart-warming and life-affirming as the TV show on which he made his name, *Listening to the Animals* is a story of love, hope, compassion and about the bond between humans and animals that makes us the very best we can be.

Now available in paperback, eBook and audio editions.

Humanimal Trust

ONE Medicine for humans and animals

Sign the Humanimal Trust Pledge for One Medicine

Vets and doctors around the world focus on the needs of their individual patients, treating naturally occurring disease every day, yet there is no formal platform to collate the learning from those treatments.

In our vision of One Medicine, human and veterinary medicine collaborate, sharing knowledge and ideas so that sustainable medical progress can be achieved for people and animals alike, without the scientific or legal need for animals to be used in laboratory models.

Add your voice to the growing global community calling for sustainable and equal medical progress - but not at the expense of an animal's life:

One Team, One Dream, One Medicine

- I pledge to champion One Medicine.
- I want human and veterinary medicine to collaborate for all people and all animals.
- I want regulatory bodies to actively support One Medicine.
- I want to help make animal testing obsolete by supporting its reduction, refinement and replacement.
- I want reciprocity – both humans and animals should benefit from sustainable medical progress.

To sign please visit:
www.humanimaltrust.org.uk/sign-humanimal-pledge-today

Text ONEMEDICINE to 70085 to donate £5

Texts cost £5 plus one standard rate message.

www.humanimaltrust.org.uk
Registered Charity No.s 1156927 & SC048960

Help us make the next generation of readers

We – both author and publisher – hope you enjoyed this book. We believe that you can become a reader at any time in your life, but we'd love your help to give the next generation a head start.

Did you know that 9 per cent of children don't have a book of their own in their home, rising to 13 per cent in disadvantaged families*? We'd like to try to change that by asking you to consider the role you could play in helping to build readers of the future.

We'd love you to think of sharing, borrowing, reading, buying or talking about a book with a child in your life and spreading the love of reading. We want to make sure the next generation continue to have access to books, wherever they come from.

And if you would like to consider donating to charities that help fund literacy projects, find out more at **www.literacytrust.org.uk** and **www.booktrust.org.uk**.

THANK YOU

*As reported by the National Literacy Trust

Professor Noel Fitzpatrick is a world-renowned neuro-orthopaedic veterinary surgeon, the founder of Fitzpatrick Referrals in Surrey, the star of the hit Channel 4 television show *The Supervet* and author of the No.1 bestseller *Listening to the Animals*. Globally recognised for his innovative surgical solutions for animals, Noel has developed dozens of new techniques, including several world firsts, that have provided hope where none seemed possible. Noel lives in Surrey with his Border terrier, Keira, and Maine Coon, Ricochet.